THIRD WORLD WOME
THE POLITICS OF FEMINISM

THIRD WORLD WOMEN AND
THE POLITICS OF FEMINISM

EDITED BY

CHANDRA TALPADE
MOHANTY

ANN
RUSSO

LOURDES
TORRES

INDIANA UNIVERSITY PRESS
BLOOMINGTON AND INDIANAPOLIS

The paper used in this publication meets the minimum requirements of American
National Standard for Information Sciences—Permanence of Paper for Printed
Library Materials, ANSI Z39.48–1984.

♾ ™

Manufactured in the United States of America

Library of Congress Cataloging-in-Publication Data
Third World women and the politics of feminism / edited by Chandra
  Talpade Mohanty, Ann Russo, Lourdes Torres.
       p.   cm.
    Includes index.
    ISBN 0-253-33873-5 (alk. paper). — ISBN 0-253-20632-4 (pbk. :
  alk. paper)
      1. Feminism—Developing countries.   2. Women—Developing
  countries—Social conditions.   I. Mohanty, Chandra Talpade, date.
    II. Russo, Ann, date.   III. Torres, Lourdes, date.
  HQ1870.9.T49   1991
  305.42'09172'4—dc20   90-43510

6 7 8 9 99 98 97 96

CONTENTS

ACKNOWLEDGMENTS

First, we thank all the women involved in organizing the "Common Differences: Third World Women and Feminist Perspectives" conference held April 9–13, 1983, at the University of Illinois at Urbana-Champaign. This volume would not have been possible without the conference. And the conference, in turn, would not have happened without the dedication, generosity, and commitment of the women who worked with us. In particular, we want to acknowledge the invaluable contributions of the following members of the initial conference-organizing committee: Evelyne Accad, Navaz Bhavnagri, Becky Brown, Berenice Carroll, Pat Cramer, Cheris Kramerae, Roopa Desai, Zahra Dowlatabadi, Resa Dudovitz, Betty Gabehart, Gin Goines, Soraya Paknazar, Norma Ramirez, Jean Rice, Lena Roberson, Sharifa Sharif, and Beth Stafford. The Urbana-Champaign YWCA and the Office for Women's Resources and Services offered much-needed institutional support for the conference, while the Office of Women's Studies and the Office of International Agriculture at the University of Illinois provided resources for the initial work on this collection.

We would especially like to acknowledge Berenice Carroll's commitment to the conference and then to the publication of its proceedings. She provided institutional support as well as intellectual and political guidance in the early stages of this manuscript. Numerous other people provided encouragement and support through the years it took us to bring this project to fruition. It is impossible to name them all. Suffice it to say that without the presence of an engaged, critical, lively, often tired, but supportive international feminist community, we would not be here. We owe this community our deepest thanks.

Also, Ann would like to acknowledge Joni Seager and Barbara Schulman for personal and institutional support from the Program in Women's Studies at MIT. And Chandra would like to thank Satya Mohanty, Jacqui Alexander, Gloria Watkins, and Biddy Martin for transforming what could just as well have been dreary, relentless struggles into meaningful, collective praxis. Finally, we thank Thelma Kime of Oberlin College's Stenographic Services for her impeccable word processing and great patience with our seemingly endless editorial changes.

PREFACE

In 1982 Ann Russo and Chandra Talpade Mohanty initiated an international conference called "Common Differences: Third World Women and Feminist Perspectives," which was held at the University of Illinois at Urbana-Champaign in April 1983. Lourdes Torres was part of the central organizing committee, a multiracial, international group of women consisting primarily of graduate and undergraduate students at the University of Illinois. This conference was one of the very first occasions for women of color and white women in the United States and women from third world countries to come together around their/our "common differences" (a term borrowed from a pathbreaking book by Gloria Joseph and Jill Lewis—many thanks!). It involved more than 150 speakers and drew an audience of 2,000 people. The conference called into question the very terms of the definition of *feminism* and changed our lives in fundamental ways. This collection of essays originates from the "Common Differences" conference and attempts to maintain the spirit of dialogue, conflict, contradiction, and solidarity that April 1983 produced in our lives.

Seven years later, the collection is no longer principally tied to the conference. The "Common Differences" conference was organized around three broad themes: Colonization and Resistance, Images and Realities, and International Women's Movements. While these themes still inform the essays in this collection, time, historical developments in third world women's struggles, the production and consolidation of transnational corporations and cultures, the institutionalization of discourses of pluralism in the U.S. academy, and the Reagan-Bush years have all intervened to locate us at a very different historical juncture in 1990. The anthology represents our efforts to address these shifts and developments. It focuses on the recent debates over the development of feminist theory and politics by third world women.

While the term *third world* is a much maligned and contested one, we use it deliberately, preferring it to *postcolonial* or *developing countries. Third world* refers to the colonized, neocolonized or decolonized countries (of Asia, Africa, and Latin America) whose economic and political structures have been deformed within the colonial process, and to black, Asian, Latino, and indigenous peoples in North America, Europe, and Australia.

Thus, the term does not merely indicate a hierarchical cultural and economic relationship between "first" and "third" world countries; it intentionally foregrounds a history of colonization and contemporary relationships of structural dominance between first and third world peoples. In drawing on histories of antiracist, antiimperialist struggles around the world, the term *third world* is also a form of self-empowerment. However, the unproblematized use of a term such as *third world women* could suggest the equation of struggles and experiences of different groups of women, thus flattening and depoliticizing all internal hierarchies. The term could also suggest that "third world" cultures or "ethnicity" is the primary (or only) basis of the politics of third world women. We intend neither. In fact, a number of essays in the collection problematize the very terms of the definition of the "third world," thus clarifying the contests over the meaning of this term.

In this collection, we make no claim to representation of all racial and national communities of women, nor do we attempt to achieve any "balance" of perspectives or ideologies. As it was in April 1983, the spirit of our struggles at the present moment, as we approach the end of a (Christian) millennium, is still one of deep commitment, contradiction, and disagreement in the context of forging networks and coalitions across cultures. It is this spirit we have tried to encapsulate, not a numerical accounting of "third world" groups. It is in this spirit that we have worked together to produce this anthology, maintaining a consistent dialogue amid political and intellectual disagreements among ourselves. And finally, it is in this spirit that we include essays by each of us, specifically soliciting an essay by Ann Russo, which addresses the ways in which white U.S. feminists respond to the ongoing challenges of third world feminists concerning the race and class contradictions of feminist politics. Even so, readers may well identify the absence of particular voices and some important conceptual and political gaps in the collection. The absences and gaps do exist, and we can only hope that this anthology will be seen as a contribution to ongoing dialogue, rather than a definitive assessment of "third world women and the politics of feminism."

In 1983 a leading feminist publisher told us (with kindly condescension) that there was no such field as "third world feminisms." In 1990 feminists of color are transforming the contours of the academy and the polity. Questions of race, class, sexuality, colonialism, and imperialism are (and always have been) the ground for political struggles around the world, just as they are now constitutive of knowledge production in a number of disciplines (not merely ghettoized in marginal fields). In this context, we can aim only for provocative, challenging analyses rather than comprehensive coverage. This collection maps a political and intellectual field which has gained increasing significance in the last decade.

These are maps which will of necessity have to be redrawn as our analytic and conceptual skills and knowledge, as well as historical shifts (most recently in Eastern Europe), transform the way we understand questions of history, consciousness, and agency.

This text thus merely scratches the surface of a vital intellectual and political endeavor. It engages debates which have their origins in the sexual politics of slavery and territorial colonialism, contemporary configurations of Western political hegemony, multinational capital, and localized and cross-national modes of political resistance—debates and struggles which will carry us forward into envisioning a more just and equitable world in the twenty-first century.

The Editors

"I Ain't the Right Kind of Feminist"
Cheryl L. West

First off I'm too confused
Secondly you know my blackness envelops me
Thirdly my articulateness fails me
When the marching feminists come by
I walk with them for awhile
And then I trip over pebbles I didn't see
My sexist heels are probably too high
I'm stuck in the sidewalk cracks

Oh where Oh where has my feminism gone . . .
Don't you know it's chasing after my
   blackness
Somewhere in the white sea

I'm in the movement
No chile
I'm not talking about dancing
I'm in the liberation movement
Yeah I'm talking about the PLO
Yeah I'm talking about South Africa and
   apartheid
No I didn't say you were fit to be tied

I am a woman
You are a lady
We are sisters in the movement
It's about neapolitan ice cream
Mixed and oh so sweet
It's not about white and sterility

Girl what are you talking about
I can have kids
My people have always had kids
No it's about oppression of all oppressees
But they never come in peace
They just got some different labels
Tell me
Is sisterhood the same as the 60's
   brotherhood

Oh where Oh where has my blackness
   gone

Don't you know its chasing after *Ms.*
  feminism
Somewhere in the white sea

I belong to a consciousness raising group
I have rhetoric
I am a sociologist
I study race, pride, sex, class, humanity
I also make mention of all the "isms"
I am a feminist

Well I am a sister
I am fluid in the dozens
I study us
I study urban renewal

Which includes my bathroom roaches
And my kitchen mice
And the animals down at Public Aid
Tell me about the man that has filled my
  belly
and ten others with babies

Come share with me sister feminist
Let us dance in the movement
Let my blackness catch your feminism
Let your oppression peek at mine
After all
I ain't the right kind of feminist
I'm just woman

© 1983

INTRODUCTION

Cartographies of Struggle
Third World Women and the Politics of
Feminism

Chandra Talpade Mohanty

The US and the USSR are the most
powerful countries
in the world
but only 1/8 of the world's population.
African people are also 1/8 of the world's
population.
of that, 1/4 is Nigerian.
1/2 of the world's population is Asian.
1/2 of that is Chinese.

There are 22 nations in the middle east.

Most people in the world
are Yellow, Black, Brown, Poor, Female
Non-Christian
and do not speak english.

By the year 2000
the 20 largest cities in the world
will have one thing in common
none of them will be in Europe
none in the United States.

> —Audre Lorde, January 1, 1989[1]

I begin this essay with Audre Lorde's words as a tribute to her courage in consistently engaging the very institutional power structures which define and circumscribe the lives of third world women. The poem also has deep personal significance for me: Lorde read it as part of her commencement remarks at Oberlin College, where I teach, in May 1989. Her words provide a poetic cartography of the historical and political location of third world peoples and document the urgency of our predicament in a Eurocentric world. Lorde's language suggests with a precise force and poignancy the contours of the world we occupy in the 1990s: a world which is definable only in *relational* terms, a world traversed with intersecting lines of power and resistance, a world which can be understood only in terms of its destructive divisions of gender, color, class, sexuality, and nation, a world which must be transformed through a necessary process of pivoting the center (in Bettina Aptheker's terms), for the assumed center (Europe and the United States) will no longer hold. But it is also a world with powerful histories of resistance and revolution in daily life and as organized liberation movements. And it is these contours which define the complex ground for the emergence and consolidation of third world women's feminist politics. (*Third world* is defined through geographical location as well as particular sociohistorical conjunctures. It thus incorporates so-called minority peoples or people of color in the U.S.A.)

In fact, one of the distinctive features of contemporary societies is the internationalization of economies and labor forces. In industrial societies, the international division of economic production consisted in the geographical separation of raw-material extraction (in primarily the third world) from factory production (in the colonial capitals). With the rise of transnational corporations which dominate and organize the contemporary economic system, however, factories have migrated in search of cheap labor, and the nation-state is no longer an appropriate socioeconomic unit for analysis. In addition, the massive migration of ex-colonial populations to the industrial metropolises of Europe to fill the need for cheap labor has created new kinds of multiethnic and multiracial social formations similar to those in the U.S. Contemporary postindustrial societies, thus, invite cross-national and cross-cultural analyses for explanation of their own internal features and socioeconomic constitution. Moreover, contemporary definitions of the "third world" can no longer have the same geographical contours and boundaries they had for industrial societies. In the postindustrial world, systemic socioeconomic and ideological processes position the peoples of Africa, Asia, Latin America, and the Middle East, as well as "minority" populations (people of color) in the United States and Europe, in similar relationships to the state.

Thus, charting the ground for a series of essays on third world women and the politics of feminism is no easy task. First, there are the questions of definition: Who/what is the third world? Do third world women make up any kind of a constituency? On what basis? Can we assume that third world women's political struggles are necessarily "feminist"? How do we/they define feminism? And second, there are the questions about context: Which/whose history do we draw on to chart this map of third world women's engagement with feminism? How do questions of gender, race, and nation intersect in determining feminisms in the third world? Who produces knowledge about colonized peoples and from what space/location? What are the politics of the production of this particular knowledge? What are the disciplinary parameters of this knowledge? What are the methods used to locate and chart third world women's self and agency? Clearly questions of definition and context overlap; in fact, as we develop more complex, nuanced modes of asking questions and as scholarship in a number of relevant fields begins to address histories of colonialism, capitalism, race, and gender as inextricably interrelated, our very conceptual maps are redrawn and transformed. How we conceive of definitions and contexts, on what basis we foreground certain contexts over others, and how we understand the ongoing shifts in our conceptual cartographies—these are all questions of great importance in this particular cartography of third world feminisms.

The essays in this collection engage with the above questions on different levels. I write this introduction as a companion piece to these essays. I also write from my own particular political, historical, and intellectual location, as a third world feminist trained in the U.S., interested in questions of culture, knowledge production, and activism in an international context. The maps I draw are necessarily anchored in my own discontinuous locations. In this essay, then, I attempt to formulate an initial and necessarily noncomprehensive response to the above questions. Thus, this introduction offers a very partial conceptual map: it touches upon certain contexts and foregrounds particular definitions and strategies. I see this as a map which will of necessity have to be redrawn as our analytic and conceptual skills and knowledge develop and transform the way we understand questions of history, consciousness, and agency. This essay will also suggest significant questions and directions for feminist analysis in the 1990s—an analysis which is made possible by the precise challenges posed by "race" and postcolonial studies to the second wave of white Western feminisms. I believe that these challenges suggest new questions for feminist historiography and epistemology, as well as point toward necessary reconceptualizations of ideas of resistance, community, and agency in daily life.

Definitions: Third World Women and Feminism

Unlike the history of Western (white, middle-class) feminisms, which has been explored in great detail over the last few decades, histories of third world women's engagement with feminism are in short supply. There is a large body of work on "women in developing countries," but this does not necessarily engage feminist questions. There is now a substantial amount of scholarship on women in liberation movements, or on the role and status of women in individual cultures. However, this scholarship also does not necessarily engage questions of feminist historiography. Constructing such histories often requires reading against the grain of a number of intersecting progressive discourses (e.g., white feminist, third world nationalist, and socialist), as well as the politically regressive racist, imperialist, sexist discourses of slavery, colonialism, and contemporary capitalism. The very notion of addressing what are often internally con- flictual histories of third world women's feminisms under a single rubric, in one (admittedly introductory) essay, may seem ludicrous—especially since the very meaning of the term *feminism* is continually contested. For, it can be argued, there are no simple ways of representing these diverse struggles and histories. Just as it is difficult to speak of a singular entity called "Western feminism," it is difficult to generalize about "third world feminisms." But just as we have chosen to foreground "third world women" as an analytical and political category in the title of this collec- tion, I want to recognize and analytically explore the links among the histories and struggles of third world women against racism, sexism, co- lonialism, imperialism, and monopoly capital. I am suggesting, then, an "imagined community" of third world oppositional struggles. "Imagined" not because it is not "real" but because it suggests potential alliances and collaborations across divisive boundaries, and "community" because in spite of internal hierarchies within third world contexts, it nevertheless suggests a significant, deep commitment to what Benedict Anderson, in referring to the idea of the nation, calls "horizontal comradeship.[2]

The idea of imagined community is useful because it leads us away from essentialist notions of third world feminist struggles, suggesting po- litical rather than biological or cultural bases for alliance. Thus, it is not color or sex which constructs the ground for these struggles. Rather, it is the *way* we think about race, class, and gender—the political links we choose to make among and between struggles. Thus, potentially, women of all colors (including white women) can align themselves with and participate in these imagined communities. However, clearly our relation to and centrality in particular struggles depend on our different, often conflictual, locations and histories. This, then, is what provisionally holds the essays in this text on "third world women and the politics of fem- inism" together: imagined communities of women with divergent his- tories and social locations, woven together by the *political* threads of opposition to forms of domination that are not only pervasive but also systemic. An example of a similar construct is the notion of "communities of resistance," which refers to the broad-based opposition of refugee, migrant, and black groups in Britain to the idea of a common nation—Europe 1992. "Communities of Resistance," like "imagined communities," is a political definition, not an essentialist one. It is not based on any ahistorical notion of the inherent resistance and resilience of third world peoples. It is, however, based on a historical, material analysis of the concrete disenfranchising effects of Europe 1992 on third world communities in Britain, and the necessity of forming "resistant/oppositional" communities which fight this.

In this collection, while some of the essays call into question notions of "third world" and of "universal sisterhood," a number of writers strongly assert their belief in international coalitions among third world women in contemporary capitalist societies, particularly on the basis of a socialist-feminist vision (see especially the essays by Mohanty, Harrison, Gilliam, and Wong). Others posit the empowerment of third world women based on the demystification of ideologies of gender and sexuality that affect women's daily lives, whether it be in Brazil (Barroso and Bruschini), Lebanon (Accad), Iran (Tohidi), China (Chow), Trinidad and Tobago (Alexander), or the U.S. (Russo, Torres, and Smith). However, while such imagined communities are historically and geographically concrete, their boundaries are necessarily fluid. They have to be, since the operation of power is always fluid and changing. Thus, neither the authors in this collection nor I posit any homogeneous configuration of third world women who form communities because they share a "gender" or a "race" or a "nation." As history (and recent feminist scholarship) teaches us, "races" and "nations" haven't been defined on the basis of inherent, natural characteristics; nor can we define "gender" in any transhistorical, unitary way.[3] So where does this leave us?

Geographically, the nation-states of Latin America, the Caribbean, Sub-Saharan Africa, South and Southeast Asia, China, South Africa, and Oceania constitute the parameters of the non-European third world. In addition, black, Latino, Asian, and indigenous peoples in the U.S., Europe, and Australia, some of whom have historic links with the geographically defined third world, also refer to themselves as third world peoples. With such a broad canvas, racial, sexual, national, economic, and cultural borders are difficult to demarcate, shaped politically as they are in individual and collective practice.

Third World Women as Social Category

As I argue in my essay ("Under Western Eyes") in this volume, scholars often locate "third world women" in terms of the underdevelopment, oppressive traditions, high illiteracy, rural and urban poverty, religious fanaticism, and "overpopulation" of particular Asian, African, Middle Eastern, and Latin American countries. Corresponding analyses of "matriarchal" black women on welfare, "illiterate" Chicana farmworkers, and "docile" Asian domestic workers also abound in the context of the U.S. Besides being normed on a white, Western (read progressive/modern)/ non-Western (read backward/traditional) hierarchy, these analyses freeze third world women in time, space, and history. For example, in analyzing indicators of third world women's status and roles, Momsen and Townsend (1987) designate the following categories of analysis: life expectancy, sex ratio, nutrition, fertility, income-generating activities, education, and the new international division of labor. Of these, fertility issues and third world women's incorporation into multinational factory employment are identified as two of the most significant aspects of "women's worlds" in third world countries.

While such descriptive information is useful and necessary, these presumably "objective" indicators by no means exhaust the meaning of women's day-to-day lives. The everyday, fluid, fundamentally historical and dynamic nature of the lives of third world women is here collapsed into a few frozen "indicators" of their well-being. Momsen and Townsend (1987) state that in fact fertility is the most studied aspect of women's lives in the third world. This particular fact speaks volumes about the predominant representations of third world women in social-scientific knowledge production. And our representations of third world women circumscribe our understanding and analysis of feminism as well as of the daily struggles women engage in in these circumstances.

For instance, compare the analysis of "fertility" offered by Momsen and Townsend (as a "social indicator" of women's status) with the analysis of population policy and discussions on sexuality among poor Brazilian women offered by Barroso and Bruschini in this volume. By analyzing the politics of family planning in the context of the Brazilian women's movement, and examining the way poor women build collective knowledge about sex education and sexuality, Barroso and Bruschini link state policy and social movements with the politics of everyday life, thus presenting us with a dynamic, historically specific view of the struggles of Brazilian women in the barrios. I address some of these methodological questions in more detail later on. For the present, however, suffice it to say that our definitions, descriptions, and interpretations of third world women's engagement with feminism must necessarily be simultaneously historically specific and dynamic, not frozen in time in the form of a spectacle.

Thus, if the above "social indicators" are inadequate descriptions/ interpretations of women's lives, on what basis do third world women form any constituency? First, just as "Western women" or "white women" cannot be defined as coherent interest groups, "third world women" also do not constitute any automatic unitary group. Alliances and divisions of class, religion, sexuality, and history, for instance, are necessarily internal to each of the above "groups." Second, ideological differences in understandings of the social mediate any assumption of a "natural" bond between women. After all, there is no logical and necessary connection between being "female" and becoming "feminist."[4] Finally, defining third world women in terms of their "problems" or their "achievements" in relation to an imagined free white liberal democracy effectively removes them (and the "liberal democracy") from history, freezing them in time and space.

A number of scholars in the U.S. have written about the inherently *political* definition of the term *women of color* (a term often used interchangeably with *third world women*, as I am doing here).[5] This is a term which designates a political constituency, not a biological or even sociological one. It is a sociopolitical designation for people of African, Caribbean, Asian, and Latin American descent, and native peoples of the U.S. It also refers to "new immigrants" to the U.S. in the last decade— Arab, Korean, Thai, Laotian, etc. What seems to constitute "women of color" or "third world women" as a viable oppositional alliance is a *common context of struggle* rather than color or racial identifications. Similarly, it is third world women's oppositional *political* relation to sexist, racist, and imperialist structures that constitutes our potential commonality. Thus, it is the common context of struggles against specific exploitative structures and systems that determines our potential political alliances. It is this "common context of struggle," both historical and contemporary, which the next section attempts to chart and define.

Why Feminism?

However, before proceeding to suggest the structural, historical parameters which lead to third world women's particular politics, it is important to understand how women in different sociocultural and historical locations formulate their relation to feminism. The term *feminism* is itself questioned by many third world women. Feminist movements have been challenged on the grounds of cultural imperialism, and of shortsightedness in defining the meaning of gender in terms of middle-class, white experiences, and in terms of internal racism, classism, and homophobia. All of these factors, as well as the falsely homogeneous representation of the movement by the media, have led to a very real suspicion of "feminism" as a productive ground for struggle. Nevertheless third world women have always engaged with feminism, even if the label has been rejected in a number of instances. Cheryl Johnson-Odim (in this volume) extends and develops this discussion of the contested nature of the definition of feminism and the problems involved in setting a common agenda for "first" and "third" world feminists. She, too, refuses to give up the term *feminism*, launching her critique of first world feminism by distinguishing between a limited, liberal "women's rights" focus and a more productive "feminism as philosophy" focus.

In the introduction to a collection of writings by black and third world women in Britain (*Charting the Journey*, 1988), the editors are careful to focus on the contradictions, conflicts, and differences among black women, while simultaneously emphasizing that the starting point for all contributors has been "the historical link between us of colonialism and imperialism" (Grewal et al. 1988, 6). The editors maintain that this book, the first publication of its kind, is about the "idea of Blackness" in contemporary Britain:

> An idea as yet unmatured and inadequately defined, but proceeding along its path in both "real" social life and in the collective awareness of many of its subjects. Both as an idea and a process it is, inevitably, contradictory. Contradictory in its conceptualization because its linguistic expression is defined in terms of colour, yet it is an idea transcendent of colour. Contradictory in its material movements because the unity of action, conscious or otherwise, of Asians, Latin Americans and Arabs, Caribbeans and Africans, gives political expression to a common "colour," even as the State-created fissures of ethnicity threaten to engulf and overwhelm us in islands of cultural exclusivity. (Grewal et al. 1988, 1)

This definition of the idea of "Blackness" in Britain, and of "the unity of action" as the basis for black and third world women's engagement with feminist politics, echoes the idea of a "common context of struggle." British colonialism and the migration of colonized populations to the "home country" form the common historical context for British third world women, as do, for instance, contemporary struggles against racist immigration and naturalization laws.[6]

The text which corresponds to *Charting the Journey* in the U.S. context was published a few years earlier, in 1981: *This Bridge Called My Back: Writings by Radical Women of Color*.[7] In the introduction to this groundbreaking book, Cherrie Moraga and Gloria Anzaldua delineate the major areas of concern for a broad-based political movement of U.S. third world women:

> 1) how visibility/invisibility as women of color forms our radicalism; 2) the ways in which Third World women derive a feminist political theory specifically from our racial/cultural background and experience; 3) the destructive and demoralizing effects of racism in the women's movement; 4) the

cultural, class, and sexuality differences that divide women of color; 5) Third World women's writing as a tool for self-preservation and revolution; and 6) the ways and means of a Third World feminist future. (Moraga and Anzaldua 1983, xxiv)

A number of ideas which are central to third world feminisms emerge from these two passages. Aida Hurtado in a recent essay (1989) adds a further layer. In discussing the significance of the idea "the personal is political" to communities of white women and women of color in the U.S., she distinguishes between the relevance of the public/private distinction for American white middle- and upper-class women, and working-class women and women of color who have always been subject to state intervention in their domestic lives:

> Women of Color have not had the benefit of the economic conditions that underlie the public/private distinction. Instead the political consciousness of women of Color stems from an awareness that the public is *personally* political. Welfare programs and policies have discouraged family life, sterilization programs have restricted reproduction rights, government has drafted and armed disproportionate numbers of people of Color to fight its wars overseas, and locally, police forces and the criminal justice system arrest and incarcerate disproportionate numbers of people of Color. There is no such thing as a private sphere for people of Color except that which they manage to create and protect in an otherwise hostile environment. (Hurtado 1989, 849)

Hurtado introduces the contemporary liberal, capitalist state as a major actor and focus of activity for women of color in the U.S. Her discussion suggests that in fact, the politics of "personal life" may be differently defined for middle-class whites and for people of color.[8]

Finally, Kumari Jayawardena, in writing about feminist movements in Asia in the late nineteenth and early twentieth centuries, defines feminism as "embracing movements for equality within the current system and significant struggles that have attempted to change the system" (Jayawardena 1986, 2). She goes on to assert that these movements arose in the context of (a) the formulation and consolidation of national identities which mobilized antiimperialist movements during independence struggles, and (b) the remaking of precapitalist religious and feudal structures in attempts to "modernize" third world societies. Here again, the common link between political struggles of women in India, Indonesia, and Korea, for instance, is the fight against racist, colonialist states and for national independence. Nayereh Tohidi's essay in this collection clarifies this link by analyzing the history of Iranian women's politicization in the 1979 national revolution, and the post-1979 domestication of feminist demands

through the ideologies of womanhood imposed by an Islamic fundamentalist state.

To sum up, third world women's writings on feminism have consistently focused on (1) the idea of the simultaneity of oppressions as fundamental to the experience of social and political marginality and the
grounding of feminist politics in the histories of racism and imperialism;
(2) the crucial role of a hegemonic state in circumscribing their/our daily
lives and survival struggles; (3) the significance of memory and writing
in the creation of oppositional agency; and (4) the differences, conflicts,
and contradictions internal to third world women's organizations and
communities. In addition, they have insisted on the complex interrelationships between feminist, antiracist, and nationalist struggles. In fact,
the challenge of third world feminisms to white, Western feminisms has
been precisely this inescapable link between feminist and political liberation movements. In fact, black, white, and other third world women
have very different histories with respect to the particular inheritance of
post-fifteenth-century Euro-American hegemony: the inheritance of slavery, enforced migration, plantation and indentured labor, colonialism,
imperial conquest, and genocide. Thus, third world feminists have argued
for the rewriting of history based on the *specific* locations and histories
of struggle of people of color and postcolonial peoples, and on the day-
to-day strategies of survival utilized by such peoples.

The urgency of rewriting and rethinking these histories and struggles
is suggested by A. Sivanandan in his searing critique of the identity politics
of the new social movements in Britain, which, he argues, leads to a flight
from class:

> For [the poor, the black, the unemployed] the distinction between the mailed
> fist and the velvet glove is a stylistic abstraction, the defining limit between
> consent and force a middle-class fabrication. Black youth in the inner cities
> know only the blunt force of the state, those on income support have it
> translated for them in a thousand not so subtle ways. If we are to extend the
> freedoms in civil society through a politics of hegemony, those who stand at
> the intersection of consent and coercion should surely be our first constituency
> and guide—a yardstick to measure our politics by. How do you extend a
> "politics of food" to the hungry, a "politics of the body" to the homeless, a
> "politics of the family" for those without an income? How do any of these
> politics connect up with the third world? . . . Class cannot just be a matter
> of identity, it has to be the focus of commitment. (Sivanandan 1990, 18–19)

In foregrounding the need to build our politics around the struggles of
the most exploited peoples of the world, and in drawing attention to the
importance of a materialist definition of class in opposition to identity-
based social movements and discourses, Sivanandan underscores both

the significance and the difficulty of rewriting counterhegemonic histories. His analysis questions the contemporary identity-based philosophy of social movements which define "discourse" as an adequate terrain of struggle. While discursive categories are clearly central sites of political contestation, they must be grounded in and informed by the material politics of everyday life, especially the daily life struggles for survival of poor people—those written out of history.

But how do we attempt such a history based on our limited knowledges? After all, it is primarily in the last two or three decades that third world historians have begun to reexamine and rewrite the history of slavery and colonialism from oppositional locations. The next section sketches preliminary contexts for feminist analysis within the framework of the intersecting histories of race, colonialism, and capitalism. It offers methodological suggestions for feminist analysis, without attempting definitive answers or even a comprehensive accounting of the emergence of third world women's struggles. It also addresses, very briefly, issues of experience, identity, and agency, focusing especially on the significance of writing for third world feminists—the significance of producing knowledge *for* ourselves.

Contexts: History, the State, and Relations of Rule

Do third world feminisms share *a* history? Surely the rise of the post-1947 women's movement in India is historically different from the emergence of black feminist politics in the U.K. or the U.S.? The major *analytic* difference in the writings on the emergence of white, Western, middle-class liberal feminism and the feminist politics of women of color in the U.S. is the contrast between a singular focus on gender as a basis for equal rights, and a focus on gender in relation to race and/or class as part of a broader liberation struggle. Often the singular focus of the former takes the form of definitions of femininity and sexuality in relation to men (specifically white privileged men).

Hurtado's (1989) analysis of the effects of the different relationships of white middle- and upper-class women and working-class women and women of color to privileged white men is relevant here in understanding the conditions of possibility of this singular focus on gender. Hurtado argues that it is the (familial) closeness of white (heterosexual) women to white men, and the corresponding social distance of women of color from white men, that leads to the particular historical focus of white women's feminist movements. Since the relationships of women of color to white men are usually mediated by state institutions, they can never define feminist politics without accounting for this mediation. For ex-

examples.
Colonialism

ample, in the arena of reproductive rights, because of the race- and class-based history of population control and sterilization abuse, women of color have a clearly ambivalent relation to the "abortion rights" platform. For poor women of color, the notion of a "woman's right to choose" to bear children has always been mediated by a coercive, racist state. Thus, abortion rights defined as a *woman's* right vs. men's familial control can never be the only basis of feminist coalitions across race and class lines. For many women of color, reproductive rights conceived in its broadest form, in terms of familial male/female relationships, but also, more significantly, in terms of institutional relationships and state policies, must be the basis for such coalitions. Thus, in this instance, gender defined as male/female domestic relations cannot be a singular focus for feminists of color. However, while Hurtado's suggestion may explain partially the exclusive focus on gender relationships in (heterosexual) white women's movements, this still does not mean that this unitary conceptualization of gender is an adequate ground for struggle for white middle- and upper-class feminists.

In fact, in terms of *context*, the history of white feminism is not very different from the history of the feminisms of third world women: all of these varied histories emerge *in relation to* other struggles. Rich, layered histories of the second wave of white feminism in the U.S. incorporate its origins in the civil rights and new left movements. However, often in discussing such origins, feminist historians focus on "gender" as the sole basis of struggle (the feminist part) and omit any discussion of the racial consolidation of the struggle (the white part). The best histories and analyses of the second wave of U.S. white feminism address the construction of whiteness in relation to the construction of a politicized gender consciousness.[9] Thus, it is not just third world women who are or should be concerned about race, just as feminism is not just the purview of women (but of women *and* men). Ann Russo argues just this point in her essay in this collection. Drawing on her own feminist trajectory as a white woman, she situates the urgency for white women to react to racism with *outrage* rather than the usual guilt or defensiveness. In other words, Russo suggests that racism is as much an issue for white people as for people of color, and in specifying outrage as the crucial response, she suggests how white people are implicated in racial formations, without losing sight of the hierarchies of power based on color and race.

Above all, gender and race are *relational* terms: they foreground a relationship (and often a hierarchy) between races and genders. To define feminism purely in gendered terms assumes that our consciousness of being "women" has nothing to do with race, class, nation, or sexuality, just with gender. But no one "becomes a woman" (in Simone de Beauvoir's sense) purely because she is female. Ideologies of womanhood have as much to do with class and race as they have to do with sex. Thus, during the period of American slavery, constructions of white womanhood as chaste, domesticated, and morally pure had everything to do with corresponding constructions of black slave women as promiscuous, available plantation workers. It is the intersections of the various systemic networks of class, race, (hetero)sexuality, and nation, then, that position us as "women." Herein lies a fundamental challenge for feminist analysis once it takes seriously the location and struggles of third world women, and this challenge has implications for the rewriting of all hegemonic history, not just the history of people of color.

The notion of an interdependent relationship between theory, history, and struggle is not new. What I want to emphasize, however, is the urgent need for us to appreciate and understand the complex *relationality* that shapes our social and political lives. First and foremost this suggests relations of power, which anchor the "common differences" between and among the feminist politics of different constituencies of women and men. The relations of power I am referring to are not reducible to binary oppositions or oppressor/oppressed relations. I want to suggest that it is possible to retain the idea of multiple, fluid structures of domination which intersect to locate women differently at particular historical conjunctures, while at the same time insisting on the dynamic oppositional agency of individuals and collectives and their engagement in "daily life." It is this focus on dynamic oppositional agency that clarifies the intricate connection between systemic relationships and the directionality of power. In other words, systems of racial, class, and gender domination do not have *identical* effects on women in third world contexts. However, systems of domination operate through the setting up of (in Dorothy Smith's terms) particular, historically specific "relations of ruling" (Smith 1987, 2). It is at the intersections of these relations of ruling that third world feminist struggles are positioned. It is also by understanding these intersections that we can attempt to explore questions of consciousness and agency without naturalizing either individuals or structures.

Dorothy Smith (1987) introduces the concept of relations of ruling while arguing for a feminist sociology which challenges the assumed coincidence of the standpoint of men and the standpoint of ruling by positing "the everyday world as problematic":

> "Relations of ruling" is a concept that grasps power, organization, direction, and regulation as more pervasively structured than can be expressed in traditional concepts provided by the discourses of power. I have come to see a specific interrelation between the dynamic advance of the distinctive forms of organizing and ruling contemporary capitalist society and the patriarchal forms of our contemporary experience.

> When I write of "ruling" in this context I am identifying a complex of
> organized practices, including government, law, business and financial man-
> agement, professional organization, and educational institutions as well as
> discourses in texts that interpenetrate the multiple sites of power. (Smith
> 1987, 3)

Although Smith's analysis pertains specifically to Western (white) capitalist patriarchies, I find her conceptualization of "relations of ruling" a
significant theoretical and methodological development which can be
used to advantage in specifying the relations between the organization
and experience of sexual politics and the concrete historical and political
forms of colonialism, imperialism, racism, and capitalism. Smith's concept
of relations of ruling foregrounds (1) forms of knowledge and (2) organized practices and institutions, as well as (3) questions of consciousness,
experience, and agency. Rather than posit any simple relation of colonizer
and colonized, or capitalist and worker, the concept "relations of ruling"
posits multiple intersections of structures of power and emphasizes the
process or *form* of ruling, not the frozen embodiment of it (as, for instance,
in the notion of "social indicators" of women's status), as a focus for
feminist analysis. In fact, I think this concept makes possible an analysis
which takes seriously the idea of simultaneous and historicized exploitation of third world women without suggesting an arithmetic or even a
geometric analysis of gender, race, sexuality, and class (which are inadequate in the long run). By emphasizing the *practices* of ruling (or domination), it makes possible an analysis which examines, for instance, the
very forms of colonialism and racism, rather than one which assumes or
posits unitary definitions of them. I think this concept could lead us out
of the binary, often ahistorical binds of gender, race, and class analyses.

Thus I use Dorothy Smith's definition of relations of rule to suggest
multiple contexts for the emergence of contemporary third world feminist
struggles. I discuss the following socioeconomic, political, and discursive
configurations: (1) colonialism, class, gender, (2) the state, citizenship,
and racial formation, (3) multinational production and social agency, (4)
anthropology and the third world woman as "native," and (5) consciousness, identity, writing. The first three configurations focus on state rule
at particular historical junctures, identifying historically specific political
and economic shifts such as decolonization and the rise of national liberation movements, the constitution of white, capitalist states through a
liberal gender regime and racialized immigration and naturalization laws,
and the consolidation of a multinational economy as both continuous and
discontinuous with territorial colonization. I want to suggest that these
shifts, in part, constitute the conditions of possibility for third world wom-
en's engagement with feminism. Section four identifies one hegemonic

mode of discursive colonization of third world women, anthropology, and outlines the contours of academic, disciplinary knowledge practices as a particular form of rule which scholarly third world feminist praxis attempts to understand and take apart. Finally, the last section/context briefly introduces the question of oppositional practice, memory, and writing as a crucial aspect of the creation of self-knowledges for third world feminists. The first two sections are developed in more detail than the last three, and all the sections are intentionally provisional.[10] My aim is to suggest ways of making connections and asking better questions rather than to provide a complete theory or history of third world women's engagement with feminisms.

Colonialism, Class, Gender

> The case might be argued that imperial culture exercised its power not so much through physical coercion, which was relatively minimal though always a threat, but through its cognitive dimension: its comprehensive symbolic order which constituted permissible thinking and action and prevented other worlds from emerging. (Callaway 1987, 57)

> The history of feminism in India . . . is inseparable from the history of anti-feminism. (Sangari and Vaid 1989, 19)

Colonial states and imperial cultures in the nineteenth century were consolidated through specific relations of ruling involving forms of knowledge, and institutions of sexual, racial, and caste/class regulation—institutions which, in turn, solicited their own modes of individual and collective resistance. Here, I briefly discuss the following symptomatic aspects of the operation of imperial rule: (1) the ideological construction and consolidation of white masculinity as normative and the corresponding racialization and sexualization of colonized peoples; (2) the effects of colonial institutions and policies in transforming indigenous patriarchies and consolidating hegemonic middle-class cultures in metropolitan and colonized areas; and (3) the rise of feminist politics and consciousness in this historical context within and against the framework of national liberation movements. I draw on British colonial rule partly because it is impossible to make generalizations about *all* colonial cultures, but mainly because I am interested in providing an example of a historically specific context for the emergence of feminist politics (in this case, to a large extent, I draw on material on India) rather than in claiming a singular history for the emergence of feminisms in third world contexts. However, I believe this analysis suggests methodological directions for feminist analysis which are not limited to the British-Indian context.

Dorothy Smith describes the ruling apparatus in this way:

> The ruling apparatus is that familiar complex of management, government administration, professions, and intelligentsia, as well as the textually mediated discourses that coordinate and interpenetrate it. Its special capacity is the organization of particular places, persons, and events into generalized and abstracted modes vested in categorial systems, rules, laws, and conceptual practices. The former thereby become subject to an abstracted and universalized system of ruling mediated by texts. (Smith 1987, 108)

Smith is referring to a capitalist ruling apparatus, but the idea of abstracting particular places, people, and events into generalized categories, laws, and policies is fundamental to any form of ruling. It is in this very process of abstraction that the colonial state legislates racial, sexual, and class/caste ideologies. For instance, in drawing racial, sexual, and class boundaries in terms of social, spatial, and symbolic distance, and actually formulating these as integral to the maintenance of colonial rule, the British defined authority and legitimacy through the difference rather than commonality of rulers and "natives." This, in turn, consolidated a particular, historically specific notion of the imperial ruler as a white, masculine, self-disciplined protector of women and morals.

In recent years, feminist scholars have examined the constitution of this imperial (white) masculine self in the project of Western colonialism. The institutions of direct control of colonial rule—the military, the judiciary, and, most important, the administrative service—have always been overwhelmingly masculine. White men in colonial service *embodied* rule by literally and symbolically representing the power of the Empire. There was no work/leisure distinction for colonial officers; they were uniformed and "on duty" at all times. As Helen Callaway (1987) states in her study of European women in colonial Nigeria, white women did not travel to the colonies until much later, and then too they were seen as "subordinate and unnecessary appendages," not as rulers. Thus, the British colonial state established a particular form of rule through the bureaucratization of gender and race specifically in terms of the institution of colonial service. This particular ruling apparatus made certain relations and behaviors visible, for instance, the boundaries of the relations between white men in the colonial bureaucracy and "native" men and women, and the behavior of imperial rulers who seemed to "rule without actually exerting power."[11] Thus, the embodiment of the power of Empire by officers in colonial service led to particular relations of rule and forms of knowledge. This was accomplished through the creation of the "English gentleman" as the natural and legitimate ruler—a creation based on a belief system which drew on social Darwinism, evolutionary anthropology, chivalry myths, Christianity, medical and "scientific" treatises, and the literary tradition of Empire.

Institutionally, colonial rule operated by setting up visible, rigid, and hierarchical distinctions between the colonizers and the colonized. The physical and symbolic separation of the races was deemed necessary to maintain social distance and authority over subject peoples. In effect, the physical details (e.g., racial and sexual separation) of colonial settings were transmuted to a moral plane: the ideal imperial agent embodied authority, discipline, fidelity, devotion, fortitude, and self-sacrifice. This definition of white men as "naturally" born to rule is grounded in a discourse of race and sexuality which necessarily defined colonized peoples, men and women, as incapable of self-government. The maintenance of strong sexual and racial boundaries was thus essential to the distinctions which were made between "legitimate rulers" and "childlike subjects." These boundaries were evident in the explicit and implicit regulation against the intermingling of the races in colonized countries as well as, for instance, in another, very different colonial context, in the miscegenation laws of American plantation slavery. As a matter of fact, South African apartheid is also founded on the delineation of these kinds of boundaries.

In 1909, a confidential circular was issued by Lord Crewe to colonial officers in Africa. This circular, which became known as the "Concubinage Circular," stated moral objections to officers' consorting with native women, claiming that this practice diminished the authority of colonial officers in the eyes of the natives, thus lowering their effectiveness as administrators (Callaway 1987). The last copy of this circular was destroyed in 1945, but its contents were nevertheless kept alive as folklore, and as unwritten rules of conduct. Here is an excellent example of the bureaucratization of gender and race through a particular form of colonial rule. The circular constructs and regulates a specific masculinity of rulers—a masculinity defined in relation to "native women" (forbidden sexuality) as well as to "native men" (the real object of British rule). Furthermore, it is a masculinity also defined in relation to white women, who, as the real consorts of colonial officers, supposedly legitimate and temper service officers' authority as administrators (rulers) capable of restraint, and also form the basis of the Victorian code of morality.

The effect of the consolidation of this bureaucratic masculinity was of course not necessarily restraint. Sexual encounters between white men and native women often took the form of rape. This racialized, violent masculinity was in fact the underside of the sanctioned mode of colonial rule. In fact, it is only in the last two decades that racialized sexual violence has emerged as an important paradigm or trope of colonial rule. Jacqui Alexander's essay in this collection argues this point in a different post-colonial context, Trinidad and Tobago. Her analysis of the racialized construction of masculinity, in part through state legislation in the form of the Sexual Offences Bill, substantiates the historical continuity between colonial and postcolonial tropes of (hetero)sexuality and conjugal relations. Similarly, Angela Gilliam's discussion in her essay of rape and the issue of sex/color lines in Latin America specifies the relation of racialized violent masculinity to the class/gender system.

Thus colonial states created racially and sexually differentiated classes conducive to a ruling process fundamentally grounded in economic surplus extraction. And they did this by institutionalizing ideologies and knowledges which legitimated these practices of ruling. Clearly one such form of knowledge fundamental to colonial rule in Asia, Africa, and Latin America was/is the discourse of race and racism.[12] Racism in the context of colonialism and imperialism takes the form of simultaneous naturalization and abstraction. It works by erasing the economic, political, and historical exigencies which necessitate the essentialist discourse of race as a way to legitimate imperialism in the first place. The effects of this discourse, specifically its enforcement through the coercive institutions of colonial rule (e.g., police and legal systems), has been documented by a number of third world intellectuals, including Franz Fanon, Albert Memmi, W. E. B. Du Bois, and Zora Neale Hurston. But colonial rule did not operate purely at the level of discourse. All forms of ruling operate by constructing, and consolidating as well as transforming, already existing social inequalities. In addition to the construction of hegemonic masculinities as a form of state rule, the colonial state also transformed existing patriarchies and caste/class hierarchies.

Historians and critics have examined the operation of colonial rule at the level of institutional practices, policies, and laws. There are numerous studies on the effect of colonial policies on existing sexual divisions of labor, or on sexually egalitarian relations.[13] One of the best analyses of the relation of caste/class hierarchies to patriarchies under British colonialism is offered by KumKum Sangari and Sudesh Vaid in their introduction to a book of essays on Indian colonial and postcolonial history.[14] Sangari and Vaid begin by stating that patriarchies are not systems which are added on to class and caste but are intrinsic to the very formation of and transformations within these categories. In other words, they establish a dynamic, necessary relation between understandings of class/caste and patriarchies under British rule. An example of this is a rich analysis of colonial regulation of agrarian relations.

Analysis of agrarian regulations usually focuses on the construction, transformation, and management of class/caste relations. However, by drawing on essays which analyze British intervention (rules and laws) in land settlements as well as in local patriarchal practices, Sangari and Vaid are able to point to the effect of agrarian regulation on the process of the restructuring and reconstitution of patriarchies *across* class/caste hierarchies. For instance, some of the effects of colonial policies and regulations are the reempowering of landholding groups, the granting of property rights to men, the exclusion of women from ownership, and the "freezing" of patriarchal practices of marriage, succession, and adoption into laws. The cumulative effect of these particular institutions of colonial rule is thus, at least partially, an aggravation of existing inequalities as well as the creation of "new" ones.

The complex relationship between the economic interests of the colonial state and gender relations in rural Indian society are examined by Prem Chowdhry (in Sangari and Vaid, 1989, 302–336). Writing about colonial Haryana (then in the province of Punjab), Chowdhry demonstrates how the "apparent contradiction in the coexistence of indices of high status and low status" for Haryanavi peasant women is explainable in terms of the agrarian political economy. Peasant women were much sought after as partners in agricultural labor, and physically strong women were much in demand as brides. Scriptural sanctions against widow remarriage were, understandably, generally disregarded; indeed, such remarriage was encouraged by custom and folk proverbs. But since widows could inherit their husband's property, there was considerable restriction placed on whom they could marry. The primary interest was in retaining the land in the family, and thus male elders circumvented the law by forcing them to remarry within the family (this practice was known as *karewa.*)

The colonial state, which had an economic interest in seeing land holdings stable (to ensure revenue collection), actively discouraged unmarried widows from partitioning land holdings. It even strengthened *karewa,* ostensibly in the name of the avowed policy of "preserv[ing the] village community" and the "cohering [of] tribes." Even when the patriarchal custom was challenged legally by the widows themselves, the colonial state sanctified the custom by depending on a "general code of tribal custom." The official British argument was that although this was a "system of polyandry[,] . . . probably the first stage in development of a savage people after they have emerged from a mere animal condition of promiscuity" (*Rohtak District Gazetteer*, cited in Chowdhry, p. 317), the rural population of Haryana itself did not follow either the Hindu or the Muslim law and should therefore be allowed to determine "its" own customs. But the catch was that these customs were complied with and codified (as Chowdhry points out) "in consultation with the village headmen of each landowning tribe in the district, these being acknowledgedly 'men of most influential families in the village' " (p. 317). Thus patriarchal practices were shaped to serve the economic interests of both the landowning classes and the colonial state; even the seemingly progressive customs such as widow remarriage had their limits determined within this gendered political economy.[15]

Another effect of British colonial rule in India was the consolidation of public and private spheres of the Indian middle class in the nineteenth century, a process which involved a definite project of *sexualization*. Sangari and Vaid (in their introduction, pp. 1–26) draw on the work of Partha Chatterjee and Sumanta Banerjee to discuss the creation of the middle-class "private" sphere of the Bhadralok. The Bhadralok notion of middle-class Indian womanhood draws on Victorian ideas of the purity and home-bound nature of women but is specifically constructed in opposition to both Western materialism and lower caste/class sexual norms. For instance, the process of the "purification" of the vernacular language in the early nineteenth century was seen as simultaneous sanskritization and anglicization. Similarly, nineteenth-century versions of female emancipation arose through the construction of middle-class Indian womanhood and were inextricably tied to national regeneration. Sangari and Vaid maintain that the formation of desired notions of spirituality (caste/class-related) and of womanhood (gender-related) is part of the formation of the middle class itself.

This, then, is the historical context in which middle-class Indian feminist struggles arise: nationalist struggles against an imperial state, religious reform and "modernization" of the Indian bourgeoisie, and the consolidation of an Indian middle class poised to take over as rulers. In fact, it is Indian middle-class men who are key players in the emergence of "the woman question" within Indian nationalist struggles. Male-led social-reform movements were thus preoccupied with legislating and regulating the sexuality of middle-class women, and selectively encouraging women's entry into the public sphere, by instituting modes of surveillance which in turn controlled women's entry into the labor force and into politics. This particular configuration also throws up the question of the collusion of colonialist and nationalist discourses in constructions of Indian middle-class womanhood. Again, Jacqui Alexander's essay (this collection) is instructive here. She provides a provocative reading of the Trinidad and Tobagan state engaged in "redrafting morality" through the regulation of sexuality within middle-class, conjugal, heterosexual bounds.

The above discussion suggests that the early history of the emergence of women's struggles in India encapsulates tensions between progressive and conservative ideas and actions. After all, histories of feminism also document histories of domination and oppression. No noncontradictory or "pure" feminism is possible. In India, the middle-class women's movement essentially attempted to modernize earlier patriarchal regulation of women and pave the way for middle-class women to enter the professions and participate in political movements. On the other hand, what Sangari and Vaid call "democratizing" women's movements focused on gender equality in the home and workplace and questioned both feudal and colonial structures, but were nevertheless partially tied to middle-class familial ideologies and agendas as well as to feudal patriarchal norms. This formulation is of course a partial one and illustrates one mode of examining the relations of colonialism, class, and gender as a significant context for the emergence of the *organized* struggles of, in this case, Indian women against a racist, paternal, imperial state (Britain) and a paternal, middle-class, national liberation movement.

In outlining the operation of relations of ruling at this historical moment, I am attempting to suggest a way of understanding and a mode of feminist inquiry which is grounded in the relations between gender, race, class, and sexuality at a particular historical moment. Feminist struggles are waged on at least two simultaneous, interconnected levels: an ideological, discursive level which addresses questions of representation (womanhood/femininity), and a material, experiential, daily-life level which focuses on the micropolitics of work, home, family, sexuality, etc. Colonial relations of rule form the backdrop for feminist critiques at both levels, and it is the notion of the *practice* of ruling which may allow for an understanding of the contradictory sex, race, class, and caste positioning of third world women in relation to the state, and thus may suggest a way of formulating historically the location of third world women's feminist struggles.

The State, Citizenship, and Racial Formation

Unlike the colonial state, the gender and racial regimes of contemporary liberal capitalist states operate through the ostensibly "unmarked" discourses of citizenship and individual rights. In contrast to the visible racialized masculinity of nineteenth- and early twentieth-century territorialist imperialism, white capitalist patriarchies institute relations of rule based on a liberal citizenship model with its own forms of knowledge and impersonal bureaucracies. According to R. W. Connell, the contemporary Euro-American state operates through the setting up of a "gender regime": a regime whereby the state is the primary organizer of the power relations of gender.[16] In other words, the state delimits the boundaries of personal/domestic violence, protects property, criminalizes "deviant" and "stigmatized" sexuality, embodies masculinized hierarchies (e.g., the gendered bureaucracy of state personnel), structures collective violence in the police force, prisons, and wars, and sometimes allows or even invites the countermobilization of power.

While imperial rule was constructed on the basis of a sharp sexual division of labor whereby (white) masculinity was inseparable from social authority and masculine adventure was followed by masculinized rule, the notion of citizenship created by bourgeois liberal capitalism is predicated on an impersonal bureaucracy and a hegemonic masculinity organized around the themes of rationality, calculation, and orderliness. Thus, Connell argues, contemporary liberal notions of citizenship are constitutively dependent on and supported by the idea of the patriarchal household, and formulated around the notion of a "rationalized" hegemonic masculinity (in contrast to the violent masculinity of colonial rule or of the military). This rationalized masculinity is evident in the bureaucratic sexual division of labor of people employed by the state: 80 to 90 percent of the political elite, civil-service bureaucracy (railways, maritime services, power, and construction), judiciary, and military are male, while women are overwhelmingly employed in the human services (education, nursing, social work, etc.) and secretarial arms of the state.

Besides instituting this particular gender regime, the state also regulates gender and sexual relations by instituting policies pertaining to the family, population, labor force and labor management, housing, sexual behavior and expression, provision of child care and education, taxation and income redistribution, and the creation and use of military forces. For instance, Juanita Diaz-Cotto's essay in this collection focuses on one particular coercive arm of the state: the construction of a race- and class-based "woman prisoner," and her treatment in the criminal justice system. Through a detailed analysis of the "typical" incarcerated woman in the U.S. penal system, Diaz-Cotto provides a way of understanding the inherently racialized and class-based discourse of the female criminal in feminist as well as patriarchal texts, and its articulation within a coercive state-controlled penal system.

However, to return to Connell, this complex analysis of the gender and sexualized regime of the state excludes any discussion of racial formation. Thus, Connell provides at best a partial analysis of citizenship. White liberal capitalist patriarchies have always been the focus of feminist resistance. But to fully appreciate and mobilize against the oppressive rule of this state, the relations of rule of the state must be understood and analyzed in terms of gender, class, and sexual as well as racial formation. In fact, this is essential if we are to explain why the state is a significant nexus for the mobilization of feminist constituencies in overwhelmingly racialized cultures.

A conceptualization of race and racism is thus essential to any contemporary discussion of feminist politics in, for instance, the U.S. and Britain. In the contemporary U.S. context, Elizabeth Higginbotham (1983) defines racism as an ideology within which people of color in the United States have to live. It is an ideology that legitimates the exclusion of nonwhite people from particular areas of social and economic life, simultaneously promoting a tolerance of these inequities on the part of the ruling class. In effect, at the economic level, the definition of labor ("free" vs. "slave"), the differential allocation of workers, the composition of the "underclass" and "welfare recipients," are all constitutively dependent on race as an organizing principle. In addition, race is a primary consideration in the definition of ideas of "citizenship" and the regulation of these through immigration and naturalization laws. Drawing on three specific contexts, the U.S., Britain, and South Africa, this discussion briefly delineates the relations of rule of the state and racial formation through immigration and nationality laws. An analysis of historicized ideologies of gendered and racialized citizenship in these countries illustrates a particular form of rule of contemporary (white) capitalist states and, taken in conjunction with Connell's discussion of the state as the arbiter of patriarchies, simultaneously defines an important context for contemporary third world feminist struggles. This discussion is thus an extension of the earlier discussion of Connell's argument regarding the gender regime of the state.

Historically, (white) feminist movements in the West have rarely engaged questions of immigration and nationality (one exception is Britain, which has a long history of black feminist organizing around such issues). In any event, I would like to suggest that analytically these issues are the contemporary metropolitan counterpart of women's struggles against colonial occupation in the geographical third world. In effect, the construction of immigration and nationality laws, and thus of appropriate racialized, gendered citizenship, illustrates the continuity between relationships of colonization and white, masculinist, capitalist state rule.

In an important study of U.S. racial trajectories, Michael Omi and Howard Winant[17] introduce the idea of "racial formation," which "refer[s] to the process by which social, economic and political forces determine the content and importance of racial categories, and by which they are in turn shaped by racial meanings" (Omi and Winant 1986, 61). Omi and Winant maintain that in the contemporary United States, race is one of the central axes of understanding the world. Particular racial myths and stereotypes change, but the underlying presence of a racial meaning system seems to be an anchoring point of American culture. While racial formation is a matter of the dynamic between individual identities and collective social structures, the racial parameters of the U.S. state include citizenship and naturalization laws, and social and welfare policies and practices which often arise as a response to oppositional movements. Historically, citizenship and immigration laws and social policies have always been connected to economic agendas, and to the search for cheap labor. These state practices are anchored in the institutions of slavery, capitalist neocolonialism, and, more recently, monopoly, multinational capitalism. Thus, racism is often the product of a colonial situation, although it is not limited to it. Blacks and Latinos in the U.S., Asians and West Indians in Britain, and North Africans in France, all share similarly oppressive conditions and the status of second-class citizens.

A comparison of the history of the immigration of white people and of the corresponding history of slavery and indentured labor of people of color in the U.S. indicates a clear pattern of racialization tied to the ideological and economic exigencies of the state. White men were considered "free labor" and could take a variety of jobs. At the same time, black men and women were used as slave labor to develop the agriculture of the South, and Mexican-Americans were paid much lower wages than whites for their work in the mines, railroads, lumber camps, oil extraction, and agriculture in the Southwest. These relations of inequality are the context for the entry of U.S. women of color into the labor force—usually in domestic or laundry work, or slave labor in the fields. In part it is this history of low-wage, exploitative occupations which have been the purview of U.S. third world women which contributes to the racist definitions they must endure vis-à-vis a dominant white, middle-class, professional culture.

In effect, then, citizenship and immigration laws are fundamentally about defining insiders and outsiders. The U.S. Naturalization Law of 1790, the state's original attempt to define citizenship, maintained that only free, "white" immigrants could qualify. It took the Walter-McCarran Act of 1952 to grant Japanese-Americans U.S. citizenship. Racial categorization has remained very fluid throughout the nineteenth and twentieth centuries, dependent on labor needs. For instance, in the nineteenth century there were three racial categories: white, Negro, and Indian. Mexicans were legally accorded the status of "free white persons" after the 1848 treaty of Guadalupe Hidalgo, while a California Supreme Court ruled in 1854 that the Chinese, who were a major source of cheap labor on the West Coast, were to be considered "Indian" (Omi and Winant 1986, 75).

The most extensive work on feminism and racial formation in the U.S. concerns black/white relations and history. In fact, the recent historiography on slavery and contemporary black feminist thought is one of the most exciting, insightful, and well-documented fields in feminist and antiracist scholarship. Historians such as Eugene Genovese (1979), Elizabeth Fox-Genovese (1988), John Blassingame (1979), Paula Giddings (1984), and Jacqueline Jones (1985) and critics such as bell hooks (1984, 1988), Hortense Spillers (1987), Judith Rollins (1987), and Audre Lorde (1984) have contributed invaluable analyses of the intersection of racial formations with sexual, class, and economic structures (see also Okihiro 1986). Instead of summarizing their work, I would like to look closely at a different context of racialization in the U.S.: the history of immigration and naturalization, which parallels the process of racialization that has occurred through the history of slavery and civil rights (black/white relations). Some of the history of slavery and contemporary racism in the U.S. is encapsulated in Barbara Smith's essay in this collection. In analyzing the representation of black lesbians in the work of Alice Walker, Gloria Naylor, and Audre Lorde, Smith reads against the grain of both racist, patriarchal texts and the texts of black feminists, discussing in some detail historical constructions of black womanhood, specifically the conjuncture of racist and heterosexist characterizations of black women.

A chronological listing of the U.S. Exclusion Acts illustrates the intersection of morality and race, class, gender, and sexuality in the construction of Asian peoples as the "yellow peril."[18] It was the 1870 hearings on Chinese prostitution that led to "An Act to Prevent the Kidnapping and Importation of Mongolian, Chinese, and Japanese Females for Criminal and Demoralizing Purposes." This act granted immigration officers the right to determine if women who chose to emigrate were "persons of correct habits and good character." It also assumed that all "Oriental women" wanting to emigrate would engage in "criminal and demoralizing acts." While the general purpose of the exclusion acts is clear—to keep Asians (and possibly other non-European "foreigners") out—the focus on defining the *morality* of Asian women as a basis for entry into the country indicates the (hetero)sexism and racism underlying U.S. immigration and naturalization laws. The purpose of the prostitution acts may well be different from that of the exclusion acts. However, both are fundamentally anchored in definitions of gender, race, and sexuality. The ideological definition of women's morality thus has significant material effects in this situation.

The first law explicitly based on nationality was the 1882 Chinese Exclusion Act. The 1907 Gentlemen's Agreement curtailed Japanese and Korean immigration, the 1917 Act restricted Asian Indian immigration, the 1924 Oriental Exclusion Act terminated all labor immigration from mainland Asia, while the 1934 Tydings-McDuffie Act restricted Filipino immigration to the U.S. Citizenship through naturalization was denied to all Asians from 1924 to 1943. Beginning in 1943, and until the mid-1960s, when immigration laws were liberalized, the state instituted a quota system for Asian immigrants. Quotas were available only for professionals with postsecondary education, technical training, and specialized experience. Thus, the replacement of the "yellow peril" stereotype by a "model minority" stereotype is linked to a particular history of immigration laws which are anchored in the economic exigencies of the state and systemic inequalities.

In the contemporary American context, the black/white line is rigidly enforced. This is evident even in the recent legal cases on affirmative action, where the very basis for affirmative action as a form of collective retribution is being challenged on grounds of "reverse discrimination," an argument based on individual rather than collective demands. These arguments are made and upheld in spite of the ostensibly liberal, pluralist claims of the American state.[19] On the other hand, racial categorization in Brazil varies along a black/white color continuum which signifies status and privilege differences. Similarly, in South Africa, Chinese people have the same status as Asians (or "coloreds"), while Japanese are referred to as "honorary whites." Omi and Winant's notion of racial formation allows us to account for the historical determinants of these ideological definitions of race.

The most developed discussion of the state's regulation of third world peoples through immigration and naturalization laws can be found in the U.K. Third world feminists in Britain position the racist state as a primary focus of struggle. British nationality and immigration laws define and construct "legitimate" citizenship—an idea which is constitutively racialized and gender-based. Beginning in the 1950s, British immigration laws were written to prevent black people (commonwealth citizens from Africa, Asia, the Far East, Cyprus, and the Caribbean) from entering Britain, thus making the idea of citizenship meaningless. These laws are entirely constructed around a racist, classist ideology of a patriarchal nuclear family, where women are never accorded subject status but are always assumed to be legal appendages of men.[20] For instance, the 1968 Commonwealth Immigrants Act, in which ancestry was decisive, permitted only black men with work permits to enter Britain and assumed that men who were the "heads of families" could send for their "wives," but not vice versa. The focus on familial configurations also indicates the implicit heterosexual assumptions written into these laws. Women can be defined only (a) in relation to men, and (b) through the heterosexual nuclear family model. Similarly, the 1981 British Nationality Act translated immigration legislation into nationality law whereby three new kinds of race- and gender-specific citizenships were created: British citizenship, dependent territories citizenship, and British overseas citizenship.

The effects of this act on women's citizenship were substantial: it took away the automatic right of women married to British men to register as citizens; it disenfranchised all children born in Britain who were originally entitled to automatic citizenship (children were entitled to citizenship only if one of their parents was born or settled in Britain); and it allowed British (white) women to pass on citizenship to children born abroad for the first time in history. Thus, as the Women, Immigration and Nationality Group (WING) argues, immigration and nationality laws in Britain are a feminist issue, as they explicitly reflect the ideology of (white) women as the reproducers of the nation. The construction of such legislation thus is a central form of state rule and clearly a crucial location for black women's struggles. The WING group describes the significance of the laws thus:

> The intermeshed racism and sexism of British immigration legislation affects black and immigrant women in all areas of their lives. As wives, they are assumed to live wherever their husbands reside and to be dependent on them. As mothers, particularly single mothers, they have difficulty in bringing their children to join them. As workers, they are forced to leave their families behind. . . . It is this system of immigration control which legitimizes institutionalized racism in Britain today. It has far-reaching effects not only for black and third world people seeking to enter Britain but also for those living here who are increasingly subject to internal immigration controls. (WING 1985, 148)

Finally, racial formation takes its most visibly violent and repressive form in Apartheid South Africa. Here, the very language of apartheid (and of course the denial of "citizenship" to black people)—"separate but equal development," "White areas vs. Bantustans (less than 13% of the land)," black women workers as "superfluous appendages"—encapsulates the material force of ideological definitions of race. Working-class solidarity across racial lines is impossible because of racialization:

> the racist ideology of South Africa is an explicit, systematic, holistic ideology of racial superiority—so explicit that it makes clear that the White working class can only maintain its standard of living on the basis of a Black underclass, so systematic as to guarantee that the White working class will continue to remain a race for itself, so holistic as to ensure that the color line is the power line is the poverty line. (Sivanandan 1981, 300)

This equation of the color line with the power line with the poverty line[21] encapsulates the contours of racial formation under apartheid, and it is this context that determines the particular emergence of the struggles of South African women: struggles around racial, political, and economic liberation, work, domestic life, housing, food, and land rights. Racist ideology has the hegemonic capacity to define the terms whereby people understand themselves and their world. The project of decolonization thus involves the specification of race in political, economic, and ideological terms, for the meanings of race are necessarily shaped as much in collective and personal practice (identity politics) as by the state (colonial or contemporary capitalist).

The above discussion of immigration, naturalization, and nationality laws suggests the relationships between the liberal capitalist state and gender and racial formations. By analyzing the discourse and concept of citizenship as constructed through immigration and nationality laws, I have attempted a specification of the gender and racial regime of the contemporary Euro-American liberal democratic state and its relations of rule. The fact that notions of sexuality (morality of women), gender (familial configurations), and race ("Oriental") are implicitly written into these laws (a) indicates the reason why this particular aspect of the contemporary state is a crucial context for third world women's feminist struggles, and (b) provides a method of feminist analysis which is located at the intersections of systemic gender, race, class, and sexual paradigms as they are regulated by the liberal state. This discussion suggests the relationships between the economic exigencies of the state (the original reason for migration/immigration) and its gender and racial regimes.

Multinational Production and Social Agency

Questions of gender and race take on a new significance in the late twentieth century, when, as a consequence of the massive incorporation of third world women into a multinational labor force and into domestic service, feminist theorists are having to rethink such fundamental concepts as the public/private distinction in explanations of women's oppression. Indeed, questions pertaining to the situation of "third world" women (both domestic and international), who are often the most exploited populations, are some of the most urgent *theoretical* challenges facing the social and political analysis of gender and race in postindustrial contexts. Of course, no discussion of the contemporary contexts of third world women's engagement with feminism could omit a sketch of the massive incorporation and proletarianization of these women in multinational factories. While this location is not just a "social indicator" of third world women's economic and social status (Momsen and Townsend 1987), it is a significant determinant of the micropolitics of daily life and self-constructions of massive numbers of third world women employed in these factories. In fact, the 1960s expansion of multinational export-processing labor-intensive industries to the third world and the U.S./Mexican border is the newest pernicious form of economic and ideological domination.

World market factories relocate in search of cheap labor, and find a home in countries with unstable (or dependent) political regimes, low levels of unionization, and high unemployment. What is significant about this particular situation is that it is young third world women who overwhelmingly constitute the labor force. And it is these women who embody and personify the intersection of sexual, class, and racial ideologies. Faye Harrison's essay in this volume clarifies some of these intersections of multinational capital, work, and third world women's location by analyzing women in the urban informal economy in Jamaica. Placing Jamaica within the paradigm of "development studies," Harrison suggests a model for understanding the sex- and class-based contradictions in the lives of poor working women in Kingston slums.

Numerous feminist scholars have written about the exploitation of third world women in multinationals.[22] While there are a number of studies which provide information on the mobilization of racist and (hetero)sexist stereotypes in recruiting third world women into this labor force, relatively few studies address questions of the social agency of women who are subjected to a number of levels of capitalist discipline. In other words, few studies have focused on women workers as *subjects*—as agents who make choices, have a critical perspective on their own situations, and think and organize collectively against their oppressors. Most studies of third world women in multinationals locate them as victims of multinational capital as well as of their own "traditional" sexist cultures. I discuss this "victim-oriented" analysis in some detail in my essay "Under Western Eyes," in this volume.

Aihwa Ong (1987) provides an analysis which goes against the grain of constructing third world women workers as pure victims. Ong's analysis illustrates (1) how the lives of factory women in Malaysia are determined in part by economic and ideological assumptions on an international scale, (2) the historical links of the colonial (British) and the postcolonial state in the construction of a social space for women workers, and (3) the construction of third world women's resistance and subjectivities in the context of deep material and structural transformations in their lives.

Tracing the introduction of new relations of production and exchange from the days of British colonial administration, Ong analyzes a corresponding construction of Malay identity in relation to subsistence agriculture, land, and other social structures. She goes on to delineate the role of the contemporary Malaysian state as the manager of different structures of power where multinational corporate investments were incorporated into ideological state apparatuses which policed the new Malay working-class women:

> [This study] discussed novel power configurations in domains such as the family, factory, *kampung*, and state institutions which reconstructed the meanings of Malay female gender and sexuality. In Japanese factories, the experiences of Malay women workers could be understood in terms of their use as "instruments of labor," as well as reconstitution by discursive practices as sexualized subjects. Discipline was exercised not only through work relations but also through surveillance and the cooperation of village elders in managing the maidens and their morality. Assailed by public doubts over their virtue, village-based factory women internalized these disparate disciplinary

schemes, engaging in self- and other-monitoring on the shopfloor, in *kampung* society and within the wider society. (Ong 1987, 220)

Ong's work illustrates the embodiment of sexist, racist stereotypes in the recruitment of young Malay village women into factory work, and delineates factors pertaining to their subjectivities. Thus, Malay women face economic exploitation, sexual harassment, and various levels of discipline and surveillance as workers. Ong's discussion of their sexuality and morality recall earlier discussions of the morality of immigrant women in the U.S. These particular constructions of morality to which third world women are subject inform their notions of self, their organizing, and their day-to-day resilience.

The counterparts to world market factories in third world countries are garment sweatshops in U.S. cities and electronics industries in the Silicon Valley in California. These sweatshops operate illegally to avoid unemployment insurance, and child labor laws, and regulations. For instance, 90 percent of the garment workers are women, the majority being immigrants from the Caribbean, Latin America, and Asia. They have few alternatives—as heads of households, mothers without daycare, women on welfare—in other words, they are poor third world women. Like the Malaysian factory workers, these women are subject to racist and sexist stereotypes such as "sewing is a women's job," and "third world women are more docile and obedient." Here again, a number of scholars have detailed the effects of this particular proletarianization of third world women in the U.S. Suffice it to say that constructions of self and agency in this context too are based on indigenous social and ideological transformations managed by the state in conjunction with multinational corporate capitalism. Within this framework of multinational employment, it is through an analysis of the ideological construction of the "third world women worker" (the stereotypical [ideal] worker employed by world market factories) that we can trace the links of sexist, racist, class-based structures internationally. It is also this particular context and juncture that suggest a possible coalition among third world women workers.[23]

Thus, an analysis of the employment of third world women workers by multinational capital in terms of ideological constructions of race, gender, and sexuality in the very definition of "women's work" has significant repercussions for feminist cross-cultural analysis. In fact, questions pertaining to the social agency of third world women workers may well be some of the most challenging questions facing feminist organizing today. By analyzing the sexualization and racialization of women's work in multinational factories, and relating this to women's own ideas of their work and daily life, we can attempt a definition of self and collective agency which takes apart the idea of "women's work" as a naturalized category.

Just as notions of "motherhood" and "domesticity" are historical and ideological rather than "natural" constructs, in this particular context, ideas of "third world women's work" have their basis in social hierarchies stratified by sex/gender, race, and class. Understanding these constructions in relation to the state and the international economy is crucial because of the overwhelming employment of third world women in world market factories, sweatshops, and home work. Thus, this forms another important context for understanding the systemic exploitation of poor third world women, and provides a potential space for cross-national feminist solidarity and organizing.

Anthropology and the Third World Woman as "Native"

One of the most crucial forms of knowledge produced by, indeed born of, colonial rule is the discipline of anthropology. While I do not intend to offer a comprehensive analysis of the origins of this discipline in the racialized and sexualized relations of colonial rule, a brief example of these links clarifies my point. I want to suggest that anthropology is an important discursive context in this cartography, and that it is an example of disciplinary knowledge which signifies the power of naming and the contests over meaning of definitions of the self and other. Trinh T. Minh-ha (1989) formulates the racial and sexual basis of the "object of anthropological study" thus:[24]

> It seems clear that the favorite object of anthropological study is not just *any* man but a specific kind of man: the Primitive, now elevated to the rank of the full yet needy man, the Native. Today, anthropology is said to be "conducted in two ways: in the pure state and in the diluted state." ... The "conversation of man with man" is, therefore, mainly a conversation of "us" with "us" about "them," of the white man with the white man about the primitive-native man. The specificity of these three "man" grammatically leads to "men"; a logic reinforced by the modern anthropologist who, while aiming at the generic "man" like all his colleagues, implies elsewhere that in this context, man's mentality should be read as men's mentalities. (Trinh 1989, 64–65)

The above quote illustrates both the fundamentally gendered and racial nature of the anthropological project during colonial rule, and the centrality of the white, Western masculinity of the anthropologist. A number of anthropologists have engaged the discursive and representational problems of classical anthropology in recent years. In fact, one of the major questions feminist anthropology has had to address is precisely the question of both *representing* third world women in anthropological texts (as a corrective to masculinist disciplinary practices) and simultaneously

speaking for third world women.[25] As Trinh states, we must be concerned
with the question of third world women:

> "Why do we have to be concerned with the question of Third World women?
> After all it is only one issue among others." Delete "Third World" and the
> sentence immediately unveils its value-loaded clichés. Generally speaking, a
> similar result is obtained through the substitution of words like *racist* for
> *sexist*, or vice versa, and the established image of the Third World Woman
> in the context of (pseudo-) feminism readily merges with that of the Native
> in the context of (neo-colonialist) anthropology. The problems are intercon-
> nected. (Trinh 1989, 85)

Here Trinh suggests that there is a continuity between definitions of
the "Native" (male) and the "Third World Woman." Both draw on sexist
and racist stereotypes to consolidate particular relations of rule. In both
cases, gender and race (white men and white women) are central to the
definition of superior/inferior. This, then, is an example of the interconnectedness of the processes of racialization and sexualization in the production of knowledge conducive to colonial rule. Anthropology and its
"nativization" of third world women thus forms a significant context for
understanding the production of knowledge "about" third world women.
Knowledge production in literary and social-scientific disciplines is clearly
an important discursive site for struggle. The practice of scholarship is
also a form of rule and of resistance, and constitutes an increasingly
important arena of third world feminisms. After all, the material effects
of this knowledge production have ramifications for institutions (e.g.,
laws, policies, educational systems) as well as the constitution of selves
and of subjectivities. For instance, Rey Chow, in her essay "Violence in
the Other Country," addresses such paradigms when she suggests that
Chinese women "disappear" in popular and academic discourses on
China, only to reappear in "case studies" or in the "culture garden."
Similarly, in my essay in this volume I discuss the discursive production
of the "third world woman" in the discourse of international development
studies. Questions of definition and self-definition inform the very core
of political consciousness in all contexts, and the examination of a discourse (anthropology) which has historically authorized the objectification
of third world women remains a crucial context to map third world women
as subjects of struggle.

Consciousness, Identity, Writing

Numerous texts on third world women's political struggles have focused on their participation in organized movements, whether it be in
nationalist or antiracist liberation struggles, organized peasant working-

class movements, middle-class movements pertaining to the legal, political, and economic rights of women, or struggles around domestic violence. In fact, the focus of the three earlier sections detailing historical and contextual issues (colonialism, class, gender; citizenship, the state, and racial formation; and multinational production and social agency) has also been on such macrostructural phenomena and organized movements. However, not all feminist struggles can be understood within the framework of "organized" movements. Questions of political consciousness and self-identity are a crucial aspect of defining third world women's engagement with feminism. And while these questions have to be addressed at the level of organized movements, they also have to be addressed at the level of everyday life in times of revolutionary upheaval as well as in times of "peace."

This section foregrounds the interconnections of consciousness, identity, and writing and suggests that questions of subjectivity are always multiply mediated through the axes of race, class/caste, sexuality, and gender. I do not provide a critique of identity politics here, but I do challenge the notion "I am, therefore I resist!" That is, I challenge the idea that simply being a woman, or being poor or black or Latino, is sufficient ground to assume a politicized oppositional identity. In other words, while questions of identity are crucially important, they can never be reduced to automatic self-referential, individualist ideas of the political (or feminist) subject. Three of the essays in this volume, Barbara Smith's essay on black lesbians in contemporary fiction, Lourdes Torres's essay on U.S. Latina autobiographies, and Nellie Wong's largely autobiographical essay on "coming to consciousness" in a classist, heterosexist, racist culture, address these questions at differing levels. Issues of self and consciousness are central to each of the three essays, and each writer subtly emphasizes the importance of *writing* in the production of self- and collective consciousness.

This section focuses on life story–oriented written narratives, but this is clearly only one, albeit important, context in which to examine the development of political consciousness. Writing is itself an activity which is marked by class and ethnic position. However, testimonials, life stories, and oral histories are a significant mode of remembering and recording experience and struggles. Written texts are not produced in a vacuum. In fact, texts which document third world women's life histories owe their existence as much to the exigencies of the political and commercial marketplace as to the knowledge, skills, motivation, and location of individual writers.

For example, critics have pointed to the recent proliferation of experientially oriented texts by third world women as evidence of "diversity" in U.S. feminist circles. Such texts now accompany "novels" by black and

third world women in Women's Studies curricula. However, in spite of
the fact that the growing demand among publishers for culturally diverse
life (hi)stories indicates a recognition of plural realities and experiences
as well as a diversification of inherited Eurocentric canons, often this
demand takes the form of the search for more "exotic" and "different"
stories in which individual women write as truth-tellers, and authenticate
"their own oppression," in the tradition of Euro-American women's autobiography. In other words, the mere proliferation of third world wom-
en's texts, in the West at least, owes as much to the relations of the
marketplace as to the conviction to "testify" or "bear witness." Thus, the
existence of third world women's narratives in itself is not evidence of
decentering hegemonic histories and subjectivities. It is the way in which
they are read, understood, and located institutionally which is of para-
mount importance. After all, the point is not just "to record" one's history
of struggle, or consciousness, but how they are recorded; the way we
read, receive, and disseminate such imaginative records is immensely
significant. It is this very question of reading, theorizing, and locating
these writings that I touch on in the examples below.

The consolidation and legitimation of testimonials as a form of Latin
American oral history (history from below) owes as much to the political
imperatives of the Cuban revolution as to the motivations and desires of
the intellectuals and revolutionaries who were/are the agents of these
testimonials. The significance of representing "the people" as subjects of
struggle is thus encapsulated in the genre of testimonials, a genre which,
unlike traditional autobiography, is constitutively public, and collective
(for and of the people).[26]

Similarly, in the last two decades, numerous publishing houses in
different countries have published autobiographical, or life story–
oriented, texts by third world feminists. This is a testament to the role of
publishing houses and university and trade presses in the production,
reception, and dissemination of feminist work, as well as to the creation
of a discursive space where (self-)knowledge is produced by and for third
world women. Feminist analysis has always recognized the centrality of
rewriting and remembering history. This is a process which is significant
not merely as a corrective to the gaps, erasures, and misunderstandings
of hegemonic masculinist history, but because the very practice of remembering and rewriting leads to the formation of politicized consciousness and self-identity. Writing often becomes the context through which
new political identities are forged. It becomes a space for struggle and
contestation about reality itself. If the everyday world is not transparent
and its relations of rule, its organizations and institutional frameworks,
work to obscure and make invisible inherent hierarchies of power (Smith
1987), it becomes imperative that we rethink, remember, and utilize our

lived relations as a basis of knowledge. Writing (discursive production) is one site for the production of this knowledge and this consciousness.

Written texts are also the basis of the exercise of power and domination. This is clear in Barbara Harlow's (1989) delineation of the importance of literary production (narratives of resistance) during the Palestinian Intifada. Harlow argues that the Israeli state has confiscated both the land and the *childhood* of Palestinians, since the word *child* has not been used for twenty years in the official discourse of the Israeli state. This language of the state disallows the notion of Palestinian "childhood," thus exercising immense military and legal power over Palestinian children. In this context, Palestinian narratives of childhood can be seen as narratives of resistance, which write childhood, and thus selfhood, consciousness, and identity, back into daily life. Harlow's analysis also indicates the significance of written or recorded history as the basis of the constitution of memory. In the case of Palestinians, the destruction of all archival history, the confiscation of land, and the rewriting of historical memory by the Israeli state mean that not only must narratives of resistance undo hegemonic recorded history, but they must also *invent* new forms of encoding resistance, of remembering.

Honor Ford-Smith,[27] in her introduction to a book on "life stories of Jamaican women," encapsulates the significance of this writing:

> The tale-telling tradition contains what is most poetically true about our struggles. The tales are one of the places where the most subversive elements of our history can be safely lodged, for over the years the tale tellers convert fact into images which are funny, vulgar, amazing or magically real. These tales encode what is overtly threatening to the powerful into covert images of resistance so that they can live on in times when overt struggles are impossible or build courage in moments when it is. To create such tales is a collective process accomplished within a community bound by a particular historical purpose. . . . They suggest an altering or re-defining of the parameters of political process and action. They bring to the surface factors which would otherwise disappear or at least go very far underground. (Sistren with Ford-Smith 1987, 3–4)

I have quoted this passage at length because it suggests a number of crucial elements of the relation of writing, memory, consciousness, and political resistance: (a) the codification of covert images of resistance during nonrevolutionary times; (b) the creation of a communal (feminist) political consciousness through the practice of storytelling; and (c) the redefinition of the very possibilities of political consciousness and action through the act of writing. One of the most significant aspects of writing against the grain in both the Palestinian and the Jamaican contexts is thus the invention of spaces, texts, and images for encoding the history of resistance. Therefore, one of the most significant challenges here is the question of decoding these subversive narratives. Thus, history and memory are woven through numerous genres: fictional texts, oral history, poetry, as well as testimonial narratives—not just what counts as scholarly or academic ("real?") historiography. An excellent example of the recuperation and rewriting of this history of struggle is the 1980s genre of U.S. black women's fiction which collectively rewrites and encodes the history of American slavery and the oppositional agency of African-American slave women. Toni Morrison's *Beloved* and Gayle Jones's *Corregidora* are two examples which come to mind.

Ford-Smith's discussion also suggests an implicit challenge to the feminist individualist subject of much of liberal feminist theory, what Norma Alarcon, in a different context, calls "the most popular subject of Anglo-American feminism. . . . an autonomous, self-making, self-determining subject who first proceeds according to the *logic of identification* with regard to the subject of consciousness, a notion usually viewed as the purview of man, but now claimed for women" (Alarcon 1989, 3). Alarcon goes on to define what she calls the "plurality of self" of women of color as subjects in the text *This Bridge Called My Back* (1981) in relation to the feminist subject of Anglo-American feminism. Both Ford-Smith and Alarcon suggest the possibility, indeed the *necessity*, of conceptualizing notions of collective selves and consciousness as the political practice of historical memory and writing by women of color and third world women. This writing/speaking of a multiple consciousness, one located at the juncture of contests over the meanings of racism, colonialism, sexualities, and class, is thus a crucial context for delineating third world women's engagement with feminisms. This is precisely what Gloria Anzaldúa refers to as a "mestiza consciousness" (Anzaldúa 1987).[28]

A mestiza consciousness is a consciousness of the borderlands, a consciousness born of the historical collusion of Anglo and Mexican cultures and frames of reference. It is a plural consciousness in that it requires understanding multiple, often opposing ideas and knowledges, and negotiating these knowledges, not just taking a simple counterstance:

> At some point, on our way to a new consciousness, we will have to leave the opposite bank, the split between the two mortal combatants somewhat healed so that we are on both shores at once, and at once see through the serpent and the eagle eyes. . . . The work of mestiza consciousness is to break down the subject-object duality that keeps her a prisoner and to show in the flesh and through the images in her work how duality is transcended. The answer to the problem between the white race and the colored, between males and females, lies in healing the split that originates in the very foundation of our lives, our culture, our languages, our thoughts. A massive uprooting of dualistic thinking in the individual and collective consciousness is

the beginning of a long struggle, but one that could, in our best hopes, bring us to the end of rape, of violence, of war. (Anzaldúa 1987, 78–80)

This notion of the uprooting of dualistic thinking suggests a conceptualization of consciousness, power, and authority which is fundamentally based on knowledges which are often contradictory. For Anzaldúa, a consciousness of the borderlands comes from a recentering of these knowledges—from the ability to see ambiguities and contradictions clearly, and to act collectively, with moral conviction. Consciousness is thus simultaneously singular and plural, located in a theorization of being "on the border." Not any border—but a historically specific one: the U.S./ Mexican border. Thus, unlike a Western, postmodernist notion of agency and consciousness which often announces the splintering of the subject, and privileges multiplicity in the abstract, this is a notion of agency born of history and geography. It is a theorization of the materiality and politics of the everyday struggles of Chicanas.

Some of these questions are also taken up by Lourdes Torres in her essay in this volume on the construction of the self in U.S. Latina autobiographies. Torres speaks of the multiple identities of Latinas and of the way particular autobiographical narratives create a space to theorize the intersection of language and sexuality, and to examine and define the historical and cultural roots of survival in Anglo society.

Finally, the idea of plural or collective consciousness is evident in some of the revolutionary testimonials of Latin American women, speaking *from within* rather than *for* their communities. Unlike the autobiographical subject of Anglo-American feminism characterized by Alarcon, testimonials are strikingly nonheroic and impersonal. Their primary purpose is to (a) document and record the history of popular struggles, (b) foreground experiential and historical "truth" which has been erased or rewritten in hegemonic, elite, or imperialist history, and (c) bear witness in order to change oppressive state rule. Thus, testimonials do not focus on the unfolding of a singular woman's consciousness (in the hegemonic tradition of European modernist autobiography); rather, their strategy is to speak *from within* a collective, as participants in revolutionary struggles, and to speak with the express purpose of bringing about social and political change. As Doris Sommer argues, testimonials are written so as to produce complicity in the reader. Thus, they are fundamentally about constructing relationships between the self and the reader, in order to invite and precipitate change (revolution). Sommer identifies the "plural" or "collective" self of Latin American women's testimonials as "the possibility to get beyond the gap between public and private spheres and beyond the often helpless solitude that has plagued Western women even more than men since the rise of capitalism" (Sommer 1988, 110).

Alarcon, Ford-Smith, Anzaldúa, and Sommer thus together pose a serious challenge to liberal humanist notions of subjectivity and agency. In different ways, their analyses foreground questions of memory, experience, knowledge, history, consciousness, and agency in the creation of narratives of the (collective) self. They suggest a conceptualization of agency which is multiple and often contradictory but always anchored in the history of specific struggles. It is a notion of agency which works not through the logic of identification but through the logic of opposition. This is a complex argument which I want to introduce rather than work through here.

At the furthest limit of the question of oppositional agency is a problem addressed by Rosalind O'Hanlon (1988) in her analysis of the work of the South Asian subaltern studies group which focuses on the histories of peasants, agricultural laborers, factory workers, and tribals. In her examination of the "history from below" project of *Subaltern Studies*, O'Hanlon suggests the crux of the difficulty in defining and understanding the subjectivity of the subaltern as outside the purview of liberal humanism.

> In speaking of the presence of the subaltern, we are, of course, referring primarily to a presence which is in some sense resistant: which eludes and refuses assimilation into the hegemonic, and so provides our grounds for rejecting elite historiography's insistence that the hegemonic itself is all that exists with the social order. Our question, therefore, must in part be what kind of presence, what kind of practice, we would be justified in calling a resistant one: what is the best figure for us to cast it in, which will both reflect its fundamental alienness, and yet present it in a form which shows some part of that presence at least to stand outside and momentarily to escape the constructions of dominant discourse. (O'Hanlon 1988, 219)

O'Hanlon suggests one aspect of the dilemma with which I began this section: how do we theorize and locate the links between history, consciousness, identity, and experience in the writings of third world women, writings and narratives which are constitutively about remembering and creating alternative spaces for survival which figure self and political consciousness? If, as I suggested earlier, certain narratives by third world women operate not through a logic of identification but through one of opposition, how is domination and resistance theorized? Firstly, resistance clearly accompanies all forms of domination. However, it is not always identifiable through organized movements; resistance inheres in the very gaps, fissures, and silences of hegemonic narratives. Resistance is encoded in the practices of remembering, and of writing. Agency is thus figured in the minute, day-to-day practices and struggles of third world women. Coherence of politics and of action comes from a sociality which itself perhaps needs to be rethought. The very practice of remembering against the grain of "public" or hegemonic history, of locating the silences and the struggle to assert knowledge which is outside the parameters of the dominant, suggests a rethinking of sociality itself.

Perhaps Dorothy Smith's concept of relations of rule can provide a way of linking institutions and structures with the politics of everyday life that is the basis of the above formulation of struggle and agency. For instance, the notion "the personal is political" must be rethought if we take seriously the challenge of collective agency posed by these narratives. Similarly, the definition of personal/public life as it has been formulated in feminist theoretical work has to undergo a radical reexamination. I introduce these questions here in an attempt to suggest that we need to renegotiate how we conceive of the relation of self- and collective consciousness and agency; and specifically the connections between this and historical and institutional questions. These narratives are thus an essential context in which to analyze third world women's engagement with feminism, especially since they help us understand the epistemological issues which arise through the politicization of consciousness, our daily practices of survival and resistance.

To summarize, this essay on "third world women and the politics of feminism" is divided into two parts: questions of definition, and questions of context. The first part delineates the urgency and necessity to rethink feminist praxis and theory within a cross-cultural, international framework, and discusses (a) the assumption of third world women as a social category in feminist work, and (b) definitions and contests over feminism among third world women. The second part suggests five provisional contexts for understanding third world women's engagement with feminism. The first three chart political and historical junctures: decolonization and national liberation movements in the third world, the consolidation of white, liberal capitalist patriarchies in Euro-America, and the operation of multinational capital within a global economy.

The last two sections focus on discursive contexts: first, on anthropology as an example of a discourse of dominance and self-reflexivity, and second, on storytelling or autobiography (the practice of writing) as a discourse of oppositional consciousness and agency. Again, these are necessarily partial contexts meant to be suggestive rather than comprehensive—this is, after all, one possible cartography of contemporary struggles. And it is admittedly a cartography which begs numerous questions and suggests its own gaps and fissures. However, I write it in an attempt to "pivot" the center of feminist analyses, to suggest new beginnings and middles, and to argue for more finely honed historical and context-specific feminist methods. I also write it out of the conviction that we must be able and willing to theorize and engage the feminist politics of third world women, for these are the very understandings we need to respond seriously to the challenges of race and our postcolonial condition.

Organization of the Book

Cheryl West's poem "I Ain't the Right Kind of Feminist" and this introductory essay frame this collection on *Third World Women and the Politics of Feminism*. The poem was written as a response to the "Common Differences" conference, and problematizes the idea of the "politically correct" feminist, or the normative white, liberal feminist for whom gender is the primary (and only) ground of struggle. The introduction was written as a companion to the essays in this collection. It charts definitional and contextual parameters for third world women's engagement with feminisms, and as such attempts to provide provisional frameworks for reading the particular essays in this text.

Section I, "Power, Representation, and Feminist Critique," includes essays by Chandra Talpade Mohanty, Rey Chow, and Barbara Smith which focus on questions of theory, culture, and the politics of representation in scholarly, popular culture/media, and literary texts respectively. This section delineates the specifically discursive parameters of the production of knowledge about and by third world women.

Section II, "Public Policy, the State, and Ideologies of Gender," addresses political, economic, and ideological constructions of racialized womanhood in the context of the relations of rule of the state. This section contains essays by Jacqui Alexander on the postcolonial state in Trinidad and Tobago, and its regulation of black women's sexuality; Carmen Barroso and Cristina Bruschini on the politics of family planning in Brazil, and feminist discussions on sexuality in relation to state policy; Faye Harrison on poor women's informal economic networks as a crucial aspect of the Jamaican urban economy; and Juanita Diaz-Cotto on "women and crime" in the U.S., an essay which discusses feminist as well as state regulation of the "woman of color as criminal."

Section III, "National Liberation and Sexual Politics," contains two essays which present more or less opposite positions on the relation of nationalism and sexuality: Angela Gilliam argues against what she refers to as the "sexualism" of certain Western feminist perspectives on women's liberation, while Evelyne Accad foregrounds the contradictions inherent in national liberation movements which are built on masculinist assumptions about war and sexuality. Accad goes on to argue in favor of the recognition of the deeply embedded sexual politics of nationalist struggles. Gilliam and Accad, in part, enact one of the major debates in the 1983 "Common Differences" conference—a debate around the relative importance of sexuality in third world women's revolutionary struggles. Nayereh Tohidi's essay on women in the 1979 Iranian revolution also addresses the relation of nationalism and sexuality, this time within the framework of Islamic fundamentalism. Tohidi provides a careful analysis of women's mass mobilization during the revolution, detailing issues of consciousness and identity in relation to class divisions. She goes on to address religious ideologies of womanhood, and the recuperation of women's revolutionary potential by the Islamic state. Section III is thus concerned with aspects of the relation of national liberation and sexual politics.

Finally, Section IV, "Race, Identity, and Feminist Struggles," focuses on questions of identity and feminist practice. Lourdes Torres, Nellie Wong, and Ann Russo address the constitution of race, class, and sexualized identities in the context of feminist struggles in the U.S., while Cheryl Johnson-Odim articulates the complex interrelationships among and between the feminisms of third world women from different geographical locations. This concluding essay picks up on the questions raised in the introduction, and extends them. While each section has a certain thematic and political coherence, the authors speak from very different, sometimes contradictory positions. But this is symptomatic of the issues and the territory of third world women's feminist praxis—a praxis which engenders more challenges than "solutions" to the world Audre Lorde characterizes so deftly and urgently in her poem at the beginning of this essay.

Notes

I thank Satya Mohanty and Jacqui Alexander for their thoughtful and incisive comments on this essay. I remain indebted to my students at Oberlin College, whose enthusiastic engagement with the politics of feminism continually challenges me to clarify and refine my own thinking about the issues in this introduction. Teaching about these issues has made it possible to write about them.

1. Audre Lorde, unpublished poem, quoted in her commencement address to Oberlin College, 29 May 1989.

2. Benedict Anderson, *Imagined Communities: Reflections on the Origin and Spread of Nationalism*, New York: Verso Books, 1983, especially pp. 11–16.

3. See Joan W. Scott, "Gender: A Useful Category of Historical Analysis," *American Historical Review* 91, no. 5 (1986), pp. 1053–75, and essays in *Signs* 14, no. 4 (1989), special issue entitled "Common Grounds and Crossroads: Race, Ethnicity and Class in Women's Lives."

4. I argue this point in detail in an earlier essay on the politics of experience entitled "Feminist Encounters: Locating the Politics of Experience," *Copyright* 1 (Fall 1987), pp. 30–44.

5. See, for instance, Chela Sandoval's work on the construction of the category "Women of Color" in the U.S., and her theorization of oppositional consciousness in "Women Respond to Racism: A Report on the National Women's Studies Association Conference, Storrs, Connecticut," Occasional Paper Series, Oakland: Center for Third World Organizing, 1983; and her "Towards a Theory of Oppositional Consciousness: U.S. Third World Feminism and the U.S. Women's Movement," unpublished manuscript, 1988. Norma Alarcon offers an important conceptualization of third world women as subjects in her essay "The Theoretical Subject(s) of *This Bridge Called My Back* and Anglo-American Feminism," in Gloria Anzaldúa, ed., *Making Face, Making Soul/Haciendo caras: Creative and Critical Perspectives by Women of Color*, San Francisco: Aunt Lute Books, 1990). See also essays in Moraga and Anzaldúa, 1983, Trinh T. Minh-Ha, 1989, hooks, 1984, and Anzaldúa, 1987, for similar conceptualizations.

6. Shabnam Grewal, Jackie Kay, Liliane Landor, Gail Lewis, and Pratibha Parmar, *Charting the Journey: Writings by Black and Third World Women*, London: Sheba Feminist Publishers, 1988, p. 1; see also B. Bryan et al., *The Heart of the Race*, London: Virago, 1985; J. Bhabha et al., *Worlds Apart: Women under Immigration and Nationality Law*, London: Pluto Press, 1985; and "Many Voices, One Chant: Black Feminist Perspectives," special issue of *Feminist Review* 17 (Autumn 1984).

7. Cherríe Moraga and Gloria Anzaldúa, eds., *This Bridge Called My Back: Writings by Radical Women of Color*, New York: Kitchen Table: Women of Color Press, 1983.

8. My use of Hurtado's analysis is not meant to suggest that the state does not intervene in the "private" sphere of the white middle and upper classes; merely that historically, people of color and white people have a differential (and hierarchical) relation to state rule.

9. A number of white feminists have provided valuable analyses of the construction of "whiteness" in relation to questions of gender, class, and sexuality within feminist scholarship. See especially Biddy Martin's work on lesbian autobiography (1988); Elizabeth Spelman's book *Inessential Woman: Problems of Exclusion in Feminist Theory*, Boston: Beacon, 1989; Katie King's "Producing Sex, Theory and Culture: Gay/Strait ReMappings in Contemporary Feminism," in M. Hirsch and E. Fox Keller, eds., *Conflicts in Feminism* (forthcoming); and Ruth Frankenberg's dissertation on the social construction of whiteness.

10. I develop the theoretical suggestions in these sections in my forthcoming book *Gender, Race and Cross-Cultural Analysis: Revising Feminist Theory*.

11. See S. P. Mohanty's discussion of this in his "Kipling's Children and the Colour Line," *Race and Class* 31, no. 1 (1989), pp. 21–40.

12. Perhaps a brief intellectual history of "race" as an organizing social construct would be useful here. Consciousness of race and racism is a specifically modern phenomenon, arising with post-fifteenth-century territorial colonialism. Interpretation and classification of racial differences was a precondition for European colonialism: human beings (Europeans) had to be differentiated from "natives" to allow for the colonizing practices of slavery and indentured labor, the denial of political rights, the expropriation of property, and, of course, the outright extermination of the colonized. For racism to be fully operational, "race" had to function as a naturalized concept, devoid of all social, economic, and political determinations. Race had to be formulated in terms of innate characteristics, skin color and physical attributes, and/or in terms of climatic or environmental variables.

Richard Popkin identifies the philosophical roots of modern racism in two theories developed to justify Christian European superiority over nonwhite and non-Christian groups during the Spanish and Portuguese conquest of America and colonization of Indians in the sixteenth century, and later during the British and British-American institution of slavery in North America (Popkin, 1974). The first theory explains the "naturally inferior" state of Indians and Africans as the result of a degenerative process caused by climate or environmental conditions, isolation from the "civilized" Christian world, or biblical "divine action." The second, the polygenetic theory, attributes the inferiority of nonwhite peoples to the fact that they were pre-Adamite peoples who were the result of a separate and unequal creation. Thus, while the degeneracy theory identifies "common origins" and posits that people of color can ostensibly "rise" to the level of Europeans by acquiring the "civilization" of white peoples (a version of contemporary cultural liberalism), pre-Adamite polygenetic theory is the precursor of the nineteenth-century "scientific" justification of racism and of slavery in America (now a version of South African apartheid).

13. See essays in R. Reiter, ed., *Toward an Anthropology of Women*, New York: Monthly Review Press, 1975; and in M. Etienne and E. Leacock, eds., *Women and Colonization*, New York: Praeger, 1980.

14. *Recasting Women*, 1989, pp. 1–26. See my review (with Satya Mohanty) of this book which develops an analysis of gender and colonizer-colonized relations, "Contradictions of Colonialism," *The Women's Review of Books*, March 1990, p. 19–21. For analyses of the emergence of women's struggles in the context of national liberation in India, see also Joanna Liddle and Rama Joshi, *Daughters of Independence: Gender, Caste and Class in India*, London: Zed Books, 1986; Gail Omvedt, *We Will Smash This Prison*, London: Zed Press, 1980; and Madhu Kishwar and Ruth Vanita, eds., *In Search of Answers: Indian Women's Voices from Manushi*, London: Zed Press, 1984. An excellent recent book by the members of Stree Shakti Sanghatana documents women's participation in "democratizing" movements, specifically the armed peasant struggle in Telangana. See *We Were Making History: Women and the Telangana Uprising*, London: Zed Press, 1990. For documentation of the emergence of women's organized resistance in other third world countries, see *Third World/Second Sex*, vols. 1 and 2, compiled by Miranda Davis for Zed Press, 1981 and 1987; Kumari Jayawardena, *Feminism and Nationalism in the Third World*, London: Zed Press, 1986, and *Slaves of Slaves*, by the Latin American and Caribbean Women's Collective, London: Zed Press, 1977. Essays by Gilliam, Tohidi, and Johnson-Odim in this collection also incorporate additional references to this aspect of feminist organization.

15. The two preceding paragraphs are adapted from our "Contradictions of Colonialism" (see note 14).

16. R. W. Connell, *Gender and Power*, Stanford: Stanford University Press, 1987, esp. pp. 125–32; and R. W. Connell, "The State in Sexual Politics: Theory and Appraisal," unpublished manuscript, 1989. For a radical feminist analysis of the state, see Catherine MacKinnon, *Towards a Feminist Theory of the State*, Cambridge: Harvard University Press, 1989; see also Sylvia Walby, *Patriarchy at Work*, Cambridge: Polity Press, 1986; C. Burton, *Subordination*, Sydney: Allen and Unwin, 1985; K. E. Ferguson, *The Feminist Case against Bureaucracy*, Philadelphia: Temple University Press, 1984; Sue Ellen M. Charlton et al., *Women, the State, and Development*, Albany: SUNY Press, 1989; F. Anthias and N. Yuval-Davis, *Women and the State*, London: Macmillan, 1990.

17. M. Omi and H. Winant, *Racial Formation in the United States: From the 1960s to the 1980s*, New York and London: Routledge and Kegan Paul, 1986. See

also Howard Winant's recent essay "Postmodern Racial Politics: Difference and Inequality," in *Socialist Review* 90, no. 1 (1990), pp. 121–47. For similar discussion of racial formation in the British context, see Paul Gilroy, *There Ain't No Black in the Union Jack*, Cambridge: Polity Press, 1987.

18. This discussion of Asian immigration to the U.S. is based in part on Asian Women United of California, ed., *Making Waves: An Anthology of Writings by and about Asian American Women*, Boston: Beacon Press, 1989.

19. See Z. Eisenstein, *The Female Body and the Law*, Berkeley: University of California Press, 1988, especially chap. 4 for a discussion of the pluralist nature of the U.S. state.

20. Women, Immigration and Nationality Group, *Worlds Apart: Women under Immigration and Nationality Law*, London and Sydney: Pluto Press, 1985.

21. A. Sivanandan, "Race, Class and Caste in South Africa: An Open Letter to No Sizwe," *Race and Class* 22, no. 3 (1981), pp. 293–301; see also his recent essay "All That Melts into Air Is Solid: The Hokum of the New Times," *Race and Class* 31, no. 3 (1990), pp. 1–30.

22. See especially essays in J. Nash and M. P. Fernandez-Kelly, eds., *Women, Men and the International Division of Labor*, Albany: State University of New York Press, 1983; see also M. Patricia Fernandez-Kelly, *For We Are Sold, I and My People: Women and Industry in Mexico's Frontier*, Albany: State University of New York Press, 1983; E. Leacock and H. Safa, eds., *Women's Work: Development and the Division of Labor by Gender*, South Hadley, Mass.: Bergin and Garvey, 1986; Saskia Sassen, *The Mobility of Labor and Capital*, New York: Cambridge University Press, 1988; and L. Beneria and C. Stimpson, eds., *Women, Households and the Economy*, New Brunswick: Rutgers University Press, 1987.

23. I have developed this argument in detail in a chapter, "Feminism and the Ideology of Women's Work," of my book in progress, *Gender, Race and Cross-Cultural Analysis: Revising Feminist Theory.*

24. Gayatri Chakravorty Spivak's work also addresses similar questions. See especially her book *In Other Worlds: Essays in Cultural Politics*, New York: Methuen, 1987.

25. For a comprehensive analysis of these questions, see Henrietta Moore's *Feminism and Anthropology*, Oxford: Basil Blackwell, 1988. Two particularly influential (self-critical) texts which develop the notion of the politics of interpretation and representation in the constitution of anthropology as a discipline are George Marcus and Michael Fischer's *Anthropology as Cultural Critique*, Chicago: University of Chicago Press, 1986, and James Clifford and George Marcus, eds., *Writing Culture: The Poetics and Politics of Ethnography*, Berkeley: University of California Press, 1986. For a feminist critique of these texts and their premises, see Frances E. Mascia-Less et al., "The Postmodernist Turn in Anthropology: Cautions from a Feminist Perspective," *Signs* 15, no. 1 (Autumn 1989), pp. 7–33.

26. Doris Sommer makes this point in her excellent essay "Not Just a Personal Story: Women's *Testimonios* and the Plural Self," in Bella Brodzki and Celeste Schenck, eds., *Life/Lines: Theorizing Women's Autobiography*, Ithaca: Cornell University Press, 1988, pp. 107–30. My discussion of testimonies draws on Sommer's analysis.

27. Sistren with Honor Ford-Smith, *Lionhart Gal: Life Stories of Jamaican Women*, Toronto: Sister Vision Press, 1987. Another text which raises similar questions of identity, consciousness, and history is *I, Rigoberta Menchu, an Indian Woman in Guatemala*, London: Verso Books, 1984.

28. For texts which document the trajectory of third world women's consciousness and politics, see also the recent publications of the following feminist

publishers: Firebrand Press, Crossing Press, Spinsters/Aunt Lute, Zed Press, South End Press, Women's Press, and Sheba Feminist Publishers.

REFERENCES

Alarcon, Norma. 1989. "The Theoretical Subject(s) of This Bridge Called My Back and Anglo-American Feminism." In H. Calderon and J. D. Saldivar, eds., *Chicana Criticism in a Social Context*. Durham: Duke University Press.

Anderson, Benedict. 1983. *Imagined Communities: Reflections on the Origin and Spread of Nationalism*. New York: Verso Books.

Anthias, F., and N. Yuval Davis. 1990. *Women and the State*. London: Macmillan.

Anzaldúa, Gloria. 1987. *Borderlands/La Frontera*. San Francisco: Spinsters/Aunt Lute.

———, ed. 1990. *Making Face, Making Soul/Haciendo caras: Creative and Critical Perspectives by Women of Color*. San Francisco: Aunt Lute Books.

Asian Women United of California, eds. 1989. *Making Waves: An Anthology of Writings by and about Asian American Women*. Boston: Beacon Press.

Beneria, L., and C. Stimpson, eds. 1987. *Women, Households and the Economy*. New Brunswick: Rutgers University Press.

Bhabha, J., et al. 1985. *Worlds Apart: Women under Immigration and Nationality Law*. London: Pluto Press.

Blassingame, John. 1979. *The Slave Community: Plantation Life in the Antebellum South*. New York: Oxford University Press.

Bryan, B., et al. 1985. *The Heart of the Race*. London: Virago.

Burton, C. 1985. *Subordination*. Sydney: Allen and Unwin.

Callaway, Helen. 1987. *Gender, Culture, and Empire: European Women in Colonial Nigeria*. Urbana: University of Illinois Press.

Charlton, Sue Ellen M., J. Everett, and Kathleen Staudt, eds. 1989. *Women, the State, and Development*. Albany: SUNY Press.

Chowdhry, Prem. 1989. "Customs in a Peasant Economy: Women in Colonial Haryana." In Sangari and Vaid, 302–36.

Clifford, J., and G. Marcus, eds. 1986. *Writing Culture: The Poetics and Politics of Ethnography*. Berkeley: University of California Press.

Connell, R. W. 1987. *Gender and Power*. Stanford: Stanford University Press.

Davis, Miranda. 1981. *Third World/Second Sex, Vol. 1*. London: Zed Press.

———. 1987. *Third World/Second Sex, Vol. 2*. London: Zed Press.

Eisenstein, Zillah. 1988. *The Female Body and the Law*. Berkeley: University of California Press.

Etienne, Mona, and Eleanor Leacock, eds. 1980. *Women and Colonization*. New York: Praeger.

Ferguson, K. E. 1984. *The Feminist Case against Bureaucracy*. Philadelphia: Temple University Press.

Fernandez-Kelly, M. P. 1983. *For We Are Sold, I and My People: Women and Industry in Mexico's Frontier*. Albany: SUNY Press.

Fox-Genovese, Elizabeth. 1988. *Within the Plantation Household: Black and White Women of the Old South*. Chapel Hill: University of North Carolina Press.

Genovese, Eugene. 1979. *From Rebellion to Revolution: Afro-American Slave Revolts in the Making of the Modern World*. Boston: Beacon Press.

Giddings, Paula. 1984. *When and Where I Enter: The Impact of Black Women on Race and Sex in America*. New York: William Morrow.

Gilroy, Paul. 1987. *There Ain't No Black in the Union Jack*. Cambridge: Polity Press.

Grewal, S., et al. 1988. *Charting the Journey: Writings by Black and Third World Women*. London: Sheba Feminist Publishers.

Harlow, B. 1989. "Narrative in Prison: Stories from the Palestinian Intifada." *Modern Fiction Studies* 35, no. 1:29–46.

Higginbotham, Elizabeth. 1983. "Laid Bare by the System: Work and Survival for Black and Hispanic Women." In A. Swerdlow and H. Lessinger, eds., *Class, Race and Sex: The Dynamics of Control*. Boston: G. K. Hall. 200–215.

hooks, bell. 1984. *Feminist Theory: From Margin to Center*. Boston: South End Press.

———. 1988. *Talking Back: Thinking Feminist, Thinking Black*. Boston: South End Press.

Hurtado, Aida. 1989. "Relating to Privilege: Seduction and Rejection in the Subordination of White Women and Women of Color." *Signs* 14, no. 4:833–55.

I, Rigoberta Menchu, an Indian Woman in Guatemala. 1984. London: Verso Books.

Jayawardena, Kumari. 1986. *Feminism and Nationalism in the Third World*. London: Zed Press.

Jones, Jacqueline. 1985. *Labor of Love, Labor of Sorrow: Black Women, Work, and the Family from Slavery to the Present*. New York: Random House.

King, Katie. 1990. "Producing Sex, Theory and Culture: Gay/Straight ReMappings in Contemporary Feminism." In M. Hirsch and E. Fox-Keller, eds., *Conflicts in Feminism*. New York: Methuen (forthcoming).

Kishwar, M., and R. Vanita, eds. 1984. *In Search of Answers: Indian Women's Voices from* Manushi. London: Zed Press.

Latin American and Caribbean Women's Collective. 1977. *Slaves of Slaves*. London: Zed Press.

Leacock, E., and H. Safa, eds. 1986. *Women's Work: Development and the Division of Labor by Gender*. South Hadley, Mass.: Bergin and Garvey.

Liddle, J., and R. Joshi. 1986. *Daughters of Independence: Gender, Caste and Class in India*. London: Zed Press.

Lorde, Audre. 1984. *Sister Outsider*. Freedom, Calif.: Crossing Press.

MacKinnon, Catherine. 1989. *Towards a Feminist Theory of the State*. Cambridge: Harvard University Press.

Marcus, G., and M. Fischer. 1986. *Anthropology as Cultural Critique*. Chicago: University of Chicago Press.

Martin, Biddy. 1988. "Lesbian Identity and Autobiographical Difference(s)." In. B. Brodzki and C. Schenck, eds., *Life/Lines: Theorizing Women's Autobiography*. Ithaca: Cornell University Press. 77–106.

Mascia-Lees, F.E., et al. 1989. "The Postmodernist Turn in Anthropology: Cautions from a Feminist Perspective." *Signs* 15, no. 1:7–33.

Mohanty, Chandra Talpade. 1987. "Feminist Encounters: Locating the Politics of Experience." *Copyright* 1:30–44.

——— and Satya P. Mohanty. 1990. "Contradictions of Colonialism." *The Women's Review of Books* 7, no. 6:19–21.

Mohanty, Satya P. 1989. "Kipling's Children and the Color Line." *Race and Class* 31, no. 1:21–40.

———. 1991. *Literary Theory and the Claims of History*. Oxford: Basil Blackwell

Momsen, J. H., and J. Townsend. 1987. *Geography of Gender in the Third World*. New York: SUNY Press.

Moore, H. 1988. *Feminism and Anthropology*. Oxford: Basil Blackwell.

Moraga, C., and G. Anzaldúa, eds. 1983. *This Bridge Called My Back: Writings by Radical Women of Color*. New York: Kitchen Table: Women of Color Press.

Nash, J., and M. P. Fernandez-Kelly, eds. 1983. *Women, Men and the International Division of Labor*. Albany: SUNY Press.

O'Hanlon, R. 1988. "Recovering the Subject: Subaltern Studies and Histories of Resistance in Colonial South Asia." *Modern Asian Studies* 22, no. 1:189–224.

Okohiro, G. Y., ed. 1986. *In Resistance: Studies in African, Caribbean and Afro-American History*. Amherst: University of Massachusetts Press.

Omi, M., and H. Winant. 1986. *Racial Formation in the United States, from the 1960s to the 1980s*. New York: Routledge and Kegan Paul.

Ong, Aihwa. 1987. *Spirits of Resistance and Capitalist Discipline: Factory Women in Malaysia*. Albany: SUNY Press.

Popkin, Richard. 1974. "The Philosophical Bases of Modern Racism." *Journal of Operational Psychiatry* 5, no. 2.

Reiter, Rayna, ed. 1975. *Toward an Anthropology of Women*. New York: Monthly Review Press.

Rollins, Judith. 1987. *Between Women: Domestics and Their Employers*. New Brunswick: Rutgers University Press.

Sandoval, Chela. 1983. "Women Respond to Racism: A Report on the National Women's Studies Association Conference, Storrs, Connecticut." Occasional Paper Series, Oakland, Center for Third World Organizing.

Sangari, KumKum, and Sudesh Vaid, eds. 1989. *Recasting Women: Essays in Colonial History*. New Delhi: Kali Press.

Scott, Joan W. 1986. "Gender: A Useful Category of Historical Analysis." *American Historical Review* 91, no. 5:1053–75.

Sistren with Honor Ford-Smith. 1987. *Lionhart Gal: Life Stories of Jamaican Women*. Toronto: Sister Vision Press.

Sivanandan, A. 1981. "Race, Class and Caste in South Africa: An Open Letter to No Sizwe." *Race and Class* 22, no. 3:293–301.

———. 1990. "All That Melts into Air Is Solid: The Hokum of the New Times." *Race and Class* 31, no. 3:1–30.

Smith, Dorothy. 1987. *The Everyday World as Problematic: A Feminist Sociology*. Boston: Northeastern University Press.

Sommer, Doris. 1988. "Not Just a Personal Story: Women's Testimonios and the Plural Self." In Brodzki and Schenke, 107–30.

Spelman, Elizabeth. 1989. *Inessential Woman: Problems of Exclusion in Feminist Theory*. Boston: Beacon Press.

Spillers, Hortense. 1987. "Mama's Baby, Papa's Maybe: An American Grammar Book." *Diacritics*, Summer 1987.

Spivak, G. C. 1987. *In Other Worlds: Essays in Cultural Politics*. New York: Methuen.

Stree Shakti Sangathana. 1990. *We Were Making History: Women and the Telengana Uprising*. London: Zed Press.

Trinh T. Minh-ha. 1989. *Women, Native Other*. Bloomington: Indiana University Press.

Walby, Sylvia. 1985. *Patriarchy at Work*. Cambridge: Polity Press.

Winant, Howard. 1990. "Postmodern Racial Politics: Difference and Inequality." *Socialist Review* 90, no. 1:121–47.

1 Power, Representation, and Feminist Critique

UNDER
WESTERN
EYES

Feminist Scholarship and Colonial Discourses*

Chandra Talpade Mohanty

Any discussion of the intellectual and political construction of "third world feminisms" must address itself to two simultaneous projects: the internal critique of hegemonic "Western" feminisms, and the formulation of autonomous, geographically, historically, and culturally grounded feminist concerns and strategies. The first project is one of deconstructing and dismantling; the second, one of building and constructing. While these projects appear to be contradictory, the one working negatively and the other positively, unless these two tasks are addressed simultaneously, "third world" feminisms run the risk of marginalization or ghettoization from both mainstream (right and left) and Western feminist discourses.

It is to the first project that I address myself. What I wish to analyze is specifically the production of the "third world woman" as a singular monolithic subject in some recent (Western) feminist texts. The definition of colonization I wish to invoke here is a predominantly *discursive* one, focusing on a certain mode of appropriation and codification of "scholarship" and "knowledge" about women in the third world by particular

*This is an updated and modified version of an essay published in *Boundary* 2 12, no. 3/13, no. 1 (Spring/Fall 1984), and reprinted in *Feminist Review*, no. 30 (Autumn 1988).

analytic categories employed in specific writings on the subject which take as their referent feminist interests as they have been articulated in the U.S. and Western Europe. If one of the tasks of formulating and understanding the locus of "third world feminisms" is delineating the way in which it resists and *works against* what I am referring to as "Western feminist discourse," an analysis of the discursive construction of "third world women" in Western feminism is an important first step.

Clearly Western feminist discourse and political practice is neither singular nor homogeneous in its goals, interests, or analyses. However, it is possible to trace a coherence of *effects* resulting from the implicit assumption of "the West" (in all its complexities and contradictions) as the primary referent in theory and praxis. My reference to "Western feminism" is by no means intended to imply that it is a monolith. Rather, I am attempting to draw attention to the similar effects of various textual strategies used by writers which codify Others as non-Western and hence themselves as (implicitly) Western. It is in this sense that I use the term *Western feminist*. Similar arguments can be made in terms of middle-class urban African or Asian scholars producing scholarship on or about their rural or working-class sisters which assumes their own middle-class cultures as the norm, and codifies working-class histories and cultures as Other. Thus, while this essay focuses specifically on what I refer to as "Western feminist" discourse on women in the third world, the critiques I offer also pertain to third world scholars writing about their own cultures, which employ identical analytic strategies.

It ought to be of some political significance, at least, that the term *colonization* has come to denote a variety of phenomena in recent feminist and left writings in general. From its analytic value as a category of exploitative economic exchange in both traditional and contemporary Marxisms (cf. particularly contemporary theorists such as Baran 1962, Amin 1977, and Gunder-Frank 1967) to its use by feminist women of color in the U.S. to describe the appropriation of their experiences and struggles by hegemonic white women's movements (cf. especially Moraga and Anzaldúa 1983, Smith 1983, Joseph and Lewis 1981, and Moraga 1984), colonization has been used to characterize everything from the most evident economic and political hierarchies to the production of a particular cultural discourse about what is called the "third world."[1] However sophisticated or problematical its use as an explanatory construct, colonization almost invariably implies a relation of structural domination, and a suppression—often violent—of the heterogeneity of the subject(s) in question.

My concern about such writings derives from my own implication and investment in contemporary debates in feminist theory, and the urgent political necessity (especially in the age of Reagan/Bush) of forming strategic coalitions across class, race, and national boundaries. The analytic principles discussed below serve to distort Western feminist political practices, and limit the possibility of coalitions among (usually white) Western feminists and working-class feminists and feminists of color around the world. These limitations are evident in the construction of the (implicitly consensual) priority of issues around which apparently *all* women are expected to organize. The necessary and integral connection between feminist scholarship and feminist political practice and organizing determines the significance and status of Western feminist writings on women in the third world, for feminist scholarship, like most other kinds of scholarship, is not the mere production of knowledge about a certain subject. It is a directly political and discursive *practice* in that it is purposeful and ideological. It is best seen as a mode of intervention into particular hegemonic discourses (for example, traditional anthropology, sociology, literary criticism, etc.); it is a political praxis which counters and resists the totalizing imperative of age-old "legitimate" and "scientific" bodies of knowledge. Thus, feminist scholarly practices (whether reading, writing, critical, or textual) are inscribed in relations of power—relations which they counter, resist, or even perhaps implicitly support. There can, of course, be no apolitical scholarship.

The relationship between "Woman"—a cultural and ideological composite Other constructed through diverse representational discourses (scientific, literary, juridical, linguistic, cinematic, etc.)—and "women"—real, material subjects of their collective histories—is one of the central questions the practice of feminist scholarship seeks to address. This connection between women as historical subjects and the re-presentation of Woman produced by hegemonic discourses is not a relation of direct identity, or a relation of correspondence or simple implication.[2] It is an arbitrary relation set up by particular cultures. I would like to suggest that the feminist writings I analyze here discursively colonize the material and historical heterogeneities of the lives of women in the third world, thereby producing/re-presenting a composite, singular "third world woman"—an image which appears arbitrarily constructed, but nevertheless carries with it the authorizing signature of Western humanist discourse.[3]

I argue that assumptions of privilege and ethnocentric universality, on the one hand, and inadequate self-consciousness about the effect of Western scholarship on the "third world" in the context of a world system dominated by the West, on the other, characterize a sizable extent of Western feminist work on women in the third world. An analysis of "sexual difference" in the form of a cross-culturally singular, monolithic notion of patriarchy or male dominance leads to the construction of a similarly reductive and homogeneous notion of what I call the "third world difference"—that stable, ahistorical something that apparently oppresses most if not all the women in these countries. And it is in the production of this "third world difference" that Western feminisms appropriate and "colonize" the constitutive complexities which characterize the lives of women in these countries. It is in this process of discursive homogenization and systematization of the oppression of women in the third world that power is exercised in much of recent Western feminist discourse, and this power needs to be defined and named.

In the context of the West's hegemonic position today, of what Anouar Abdel-Malek (1981) calls a struggle for "control over the orientation, regulation and decision of the process of world development on the basis of the advanced sector's monopoly of scientific knowledge and ideal creativity," Western feminist scholarship on the third world must be seen and examined precisely in terms of its inscription in these particular relations of power and struggle. There is, it should be evident, no universal patriarchal framework which this scholarship attempts to counter and resist—unless one posits an international male conspiracy or a monolithic, ahistorical power structure. There is, however, a particular world balance of power within which any analysis of culture, ideology, and socioeconomic conditions necessarily has to be situated. Abdel-Malek is useful here, again, in reminding us about the inherence of politics in the discourses of "culture":

> Contemporary imperialism is, in a real sense, a hegemonic imperialism, exercising to a maximum degree a rationalized violence taken to a higher level than ever before—through fire and sword, but also through the attempt to control hearts and minds. For its content is defined by the combined action of the military-industrial complex and the hegemonic cultural centers of the West, all of them founded on the advanced levels of development attained by monopoly and finance capital, and supported by the benefits of both the scientific and technological revolution and the second industrial revolution itself. (145–46)

Western feminist scholarship cannot avoid the challenge of situating itself and examining its role in such a global economic and political framework. To do any less would be to ignore the complex interconnections between first and third world economies and the profound effect of this on the lives of women in all countries. I do not question the descriptive and informative value of most Western feminist writings on women in the third world. I also do not question the existence of excellent work which does not fall into the analytic traps with which I am concerned. In fact I deal with an example of such work later on. In the context of an overwhelming silence about the experiences of women in these countries, as well as the need to forge international links between women's political struggles, such work is both pathbreaking and absolutely essen-

Western feminism needs to look @ political & economic diff. when writing

tial. However, it is both to the *explanatory potential* of particular analytic strategies employed by such writing, and to their *political effect* in the context of the hegemony of Western scholarship that I want to draw attention here. While feminist writing in the U.S. is still marginalized (except from the point of view of women of color addressing privileged white women), Western feminist writing on women in the third world must be considered in the context of the global hegemony of Western scholarship—i.e., the production, publication, distribution, and consumption of information and ideas. Marginal or not, this writing has political effects and implications beyond the immediate feminist or disciplinary audience. One such significant effect of the dominant "representations" of Western feminism is its conflation with imperialism in the eyes of particular third world women.[4] Hence the urgent need to examine the *political* implications of our *analytic* strategies and principles.

My critique is directed at three basic analytic principles which are present in (Western) feminist discourse on women in the third world. Since I focus primarily on the Zed Press Women in the Third World series, my comments on Western feminist discourse are circumscribed by my analysis of the texts in this series.[5] This is a way of focusing my critique. However, even though I am dealing with feminists who identify themselves as culturally or geographically from the "West," as mentioned earlier, what I say about these presuppositions or implicit principles holds for anyone who uses these methods, whether third world women in the West, or third world women in the third world writing on these issues and publishing in the West. Thus, I am not making a culturalist argument about ethnocentrism; rather, I am trying to uncover how ethnocentric universalism is produced in certain analyses. As a matter of fact, my argument holds for any discourse that sets up its own authorial subjects as the implicit referent, i.e., the yardstick by which to encode and represent cultural Others. It is in this move that power is exercised in discourse.

The first analytic presupposition I focus on is involved in the strategic location of the category "women" vis-à-vis the context of analysis. The assumption of women as an already constituted, coherent group with identical interests and desires, regardless of class, ethnic or racial location, or contradictions, implies a notion of gender or sexual difference or even patriarchy which can be applied universally and cross-culturally. (The context of analysis can be anything from kinship structures and the organization of labor to media representations.) The second analytical presupposition is evident on the methodological level, in the uncritical way "proof" of universality and cross-cultural validity are provided. The third is a more specifically political presupposition underlying the methodologies and the analytic strategies, i.e., the model of power and struggle

56   Power, Representation, and Feminist Critique

they imply and suggest. I argue that as a result of the two modes—or, rather, frames—of analysis described above, a homogeneous notion of the oppression of women as a group is assumed, which, in turn, produces the image of an "average third world woman." This average third world woman leads an essentially truncated life based on her feminine gender (read: sexually constrained) and her being "third world" (read: ignorant, poor, uneducated, tradition-bound, domestic, family-oriented, victimized, etc.). This, I suggest, is in contrast to the (implicit) self-representation of Western women as educated, as modern, as having control over their own bodies and sexualities, and the freedom to make their own decisions.

The distinction between Western feminist re-presentation of women in the third world and Western feminist self-presentation is a distinction of the same order as that made by some Marxists between the "maintenance" function of the housewife and the real "productive" role of wage labor, or the characterization by developmentalists of the third world as being engaged in the lesser production of "raw materials" in contrast to the "real" productive activity of the first world. These distinctions are made on the basis of the privileging of a particular group as the norm or referent. Men involved in wage labor, first world producers, and, I suggest, Western feminists who sometimes cast third world women in terms of "ourselves undressed" (Michelle Rosaldo's [1980] term), all construct themselves as the normative referent in such a binary analytic.

"Women" as Category of Analysis, or: We Are All Sisters in Struggle

By women as a category of analysis, I am referring to the crucial assumption that all of us of the same gender, across classes and cultures, are somehow socially constituted as a homogeneous group identified prior to the process of analysis. This is an assumption which characterizes much feminist discourse. The homogeneity of women as a group is produced not on the basis of biological essentials but rather on the basis of secondary sociological and anthropological universals. Thus, for instance, in any given piece of feminist analysis, women are characterized as a singular group on the basis of a shared oppression. What binds women together is a sociological notion of the "sameness" of their oppression. It is at this point that an elision takes place between "women" as a discursively constructed group and "women" as material subjects of their own history.[6] Thus, the discursively consensual homogeneity of "women" as a group is mistaken for the historically specific material reality of groups of women. This results in an assumption of women as an always already constituted group, one which has been labeled "powerless," "exploited," "sexually harassed," etc., by feminist scientific, economic, legal, and sociological discourses. (Notice that this is quite similar to sexist discourse

Women bound by sociological oppression - not merely biological sameness labeling women weak, emotional, having math anxiety, etc.) This focus is not on uncovering the material and ideological specificities that constitute a particular group of women as "powerless' in a particular context. It is, rather, on finding a variety of cases of "powerless" groups of women to prove the general point that women as a group are powerless.

In this section I focus on five specific ways in which "women" as a category of analysis is used in Western feminist discourse on women in the third world. Each of these examples illustrates the construction of "third world women" as a homogeneous "powerless" group often located as implicit *victims* of particular socioeconomic systems. I have chosen to deal with a variety of writers—from Fran Hosken, who writes primarily about female genital mutilation, to writers from the Women in International Development school, who write about the effect of development policies on third world women for both Western and third world audiences. The similarity of assumptions about "third world women" in all these texts forms the basis of my discussion. This is not to equate all the texts that I analyze, nor is it to equalize their strengths and weaknesses. The authors I deal with write with varying degrees of care and complexity; however, the *effect* of their representation of third world women is a coherent one. In these texts women are defined as victims of male violence (Fran Hosken); victims of the colonial process (Maria Cutrufelli); victims of the Arab familial system (Juliette Minces); victims of the economic development process (Beverley Lindsay and the [liberal] WID School); and finally, victims of *the* Islamic code (Patricia Jeffery). This mode of defining women primarily in terms of their *object status* (the way in which they are affected or not affected by certain institutions and systems) is what characterizes this particular form of the use of "women" as a category of analysis. In the context of Western women writing/studying women in the third world, such objectification (however benevolently motivated) needs to be both named and challenged. As Valerie Amos and Pratibha Parmar argue quite eloquently, "Feminist theories which examine our cultural practices as 'feudal residues' or label us 'traditional,' also portray us as politically immature women who need to be versed and schooled in the ethos of Western feminism. They need to be continually challenged . . ." (1984, 7).

Women as Victims of Male Violence

Fran Hosken, in writing about the relationship between human rights and female genital mutilation in Africa and the Middle East, bases her whole discussion/condemnation of genital mutilation on one privileged premise: that the goal of this practice is "to mutilate the sexual pleasure and satisfaction of woman" (1981, 11). This, in turn, leads her to claim that woman's sexuality is controlled, as is her reproductive potential. According to Hosken, "male sexual politics" in Africa and around the world "share the same political goal: to assure female dependence and subservience by any and all means" (14). Physical violence against women (rape, sexual assault, excision, infibulation, etc.) is thus carried out "with an astonishing consensus among men in the world" (14). Here, women are defined consistently as the *victims* of male control—the "sexually oppressed."[7] Although it is true that the potential of male violence against women circumscribes and elucidates their social position to a certain extent, defining women as archetypal victims freezes them into "objects-who-defend-themselves," men into "subjects-who-perpetrate-violence," and (every) society into powerless (read: women) and powerful (read: men) groups of people. Male violence must be theorized and interpreted *within* specific societies, in order both to understand it better and to effectively organize to change it.[8] Sisterhood cannot be assumed on the basis of gender; it must be forged in concrete historical and political practice and analysis.

Women as Universal Dependents

Beverly Lindsay's conclusion to the book *Comparative Perspectives of Third World Women: The Impact of Race, Sex and Class* (1983, 298, 306) states: "dependency relationships, based upon race, sex and class, are being perpetuated through social, educational, and economic institutions. These are the linkages among Third World Women." Here, as in other places, Lindsay implies that third world women constitute an identifiable group purely on the basis of shared dependencies. If shared dependencies were all that was needed to bind us together as a group, third world women would always be seen as an apolitical group with no subject status. Instead, if anything, it is the *common context* of political struggle against class, race, gender, and imperialist hierarchies that may constitute third world women as a strategic group at this historical juncture. Lindsay also states that linguistic and cultural differences exist between Vietnamese and black American women, but "both groups are victims of race, sex, and class." Again black and Vietnamese women are characterized by their victim status.

Similarly, examine statements such as "My analysis will start by stating that all African women are politically and economically dependent" (Cutrufelli 1983, 13), "Nevertheless, either overtly or covertly, prostitution is still the main if not the only source of work for African women" (Cutrufelli 1983, 33). *All* African women are dependent. Prostitution is the only work option for African women as a *group*. Both statements are illustrative of generalizations sprinkled liberally through a recent Zed

Press publication, *Women of Africa: Roots of Oppression,* by Maria Rosa Cutrufelli, who is described on the cover as an Italian writer, sociologist, Marxist, and feminist. In the 1980s, is it possible to imagine writing a book entitled *Women of Europe: Roots of Oppression*? I am not objecting to the use of universal groupings for descriptive purposes. Women from the continent of Africa can be descriptively characterized as "women of Africa." It is when "women of Africa" becomes a homogeneous socio-logical grouping characterized by common dependencies or powerless-ness (or even strengths) that problems arise—we say too little and too much at the same time.

This is because descriptive gender differences are transformed into the division between men and women. Women are constituted as a group via dependency relationships vis-à-vis men, who are implicitly held re-sponsible for these relationships. When "women of Africa" as a group (versus "men of Africa" as a group?) are seen as a group precisely because they are generally dependent and oppressed, the analysis of specific his-torical differences becomes impossible, because reality is always appar-ently structured by divisions—two mutually exclusive and jointly ex-haustive groups, the victims and the oppressors. Here the sociological is substituted for the biological, in order, however, to create the same—a unity of women. Thus, it is not the descriptive potential of gender dif-ference but the privileged positioning and explanatory potential of gender difference as the *origin* of oppression that I question. In using "women of Africa" (as an already constituted group of oppressed peoples) as a category of analysis, Cutrufelli denies any historical specificity to the location of women as subordinate, powerful, marginal, central, or other-wise, vis-à-vis particular social and power networks. Women are taken as a unified "powerless" group prior to the analysis in question Thus, it is then merely a matter of specifying the context *after the fact.* "Women" are now placed in the context of the family, or in the workplace, or within religious networks, almost as if these systems existed outside the relations of women with other women, and women with men.

The problem with this analytic strategy, let me repeat, is that it as-sumes men and women are already constituted as sexual-political subjects prior to their entry into the arena of social relations. Only if we subscribe to this assumption is it possible to undertake analysis which looks at the "effects" of kinship structures, colonialism, organization of labor, etc., on women, who are defined in advance as a group. The crucial point that is forgotten is that women are produced through these very relations as well as being implicated in forming these relations. As Michelle Rosaldo ar-gues, "woman's place in human social life is not in any direct sense a product of the things she does (or even less, a function of what, biolog-ically, she is) but the meaning her activities acquire through concrete social interactions" (1980, 400). That women mother in a variety of societies is not as significant as the value attached to mothering in these societies. The distinction between the act of mothering and the status attached to it is a very important one—one that needs to be stated and analyzed contextually.

Married Women as Victims of the Colonial Process

In Lévi-Strauss's theory of kinship structure as a system of the exchange of women, what is significant is that exchange itself is not constitutive of the subordination of women; women are not subordinate because of the *fact* of exchange, but because of the *modes* of exchange instituted, and the values attached to these modes. However, in discussing the marriage ritual of the Bemba, a Zambian matrilocal, matrilineal people, Cutrufelli in *Women of Africa* focuses on the fact of the marital exchange of women before and after Western colonization, rather than the value attached to this exchange in this particular context. This leads to her definition of Bemba women as a coherent group affected in a particular way by colonization. Here again, Bemba women are constituted rather unilaterally as victims of the effects of Western colonization.

Cutrufelli cites the marriage ritual of the Bemba as a multistage event "whereby a young man becomes incorporated into his wife's family group as he takes up residence with them and gives his services in return for food and maintenance" (43). This ritual extends over many years, and the sexual relationship varies according to the degree of the girl's physical maturity. It is only after she undergoes an initiation ceremony at puberty that intercourse is sanctioned, and the man acquires legal rights over her. This initiation ceremony is the more important act of the consecration of women's reproductive power, so that the abduction of an uninitiated girl is of no consequence, while heavy penalty is levied for the seduction of an initiated girl. Cutrufelli asserts that the effect of European colonization has changed the whole marriage system. Now the young man is entitled to take his wife away from her people in return for money. The implication is that Bemba women have now lost the protection of tribal laws. However, while it is possible to see how the structure of the traditional marriage contract (versus the postcolonial marriage contract) offered women a certain amount of control over their marital relations, only an analysis of the political significance of the actual practice which privileges an initiated girl over an uninitiated one, indicating a shift in female power relations as a result of this ceremony, can provide an accurate account of whether Bemba women were indeed protected by tribal laws *at all times*.

However, it is not possible to talk about Bemba women as a homogeneous group within the traditional marriage structure. Bemba women *before* the initiation are constituted within a different set of social relations compared to Bemba women *after* the initiation. To treat them as a unified group characterized by the fact of their "exchange" between male kin is to deny the sociohistorical and cultural specificities of their existence, and the differential *value* attached to their exchange before and after their initiation. It is to treat the initiation ceremony as a ritual with no political implications or effects. It is also to assume that in merely describing the *structure* of the marriage contract, the situation of women is exposed. Women as a group are positioned within a given structure, but there is no attempt made to trace the effect of the marriage practice in constituting women within an obviously changing network of power relations. Thus, women are assumed to be sexual-political subjects prior to entry into kinship structures.

Women and Familial Systems

Elizabeth Cowie (1978), in another context, points out the implications of this sort of analysis when she emphasizes the specifically political nature of kinship structures which must be analyzed as ideological practices which designate men and women as father, husband, wife, mother, sister, etc. Thus, Cowie suggests, women as women are not *located* within the family. Rather, it is *in* the family, as an effect of kinship structures, that women as women are *constructed*, defined within and by the group. Thus, for instance, when Juliette Minces (1980) cites *the* patriarchal family as the basis for "an almost identical vision of women" that Arab and Muslim societies have, she falls into this very trap (see especially p. 23). Not only is it problematical to speak of a vision of women shared by Arab and Muslim societies (i.e., over twenty different countries) without addressing the particular historical, material, and ideological power structures that construct such images, but to speak of the patriarchal family or the tribal kinship structure as the origin of the socioeconomic status of women is to again assume that women are sexual-political subjects prior to their entry into the family. So while on the one hand women attain value or status within the family, the assumption of a singular patriarchal kinship system (common to all Arab and Muslim societies) is what apparently structures women as an oppressed group in these societies! This singular, coherent kinship system presumably influences another separate and given entity, "women." Thus, all women, regardless of class and cultural differences, are affected by this system. Not only are *all* Arab and Muslim women seen to constitute a homogeneous oppressed group, but there is no discussion of the specific *practices* within the family which constitute women as mothers, wives, sisters, etc. Arabs and Muslims, it appears, don't change at all. Their patriarchal family is carried over from the times of the prophet Mohammed. They exist, as it were, outside history.

Women and Religious Ideologies

A further example of the use of "women" as a category of analysis is found in cross-cultural analyses which subscribe to a certain economic reductionism in describing the relationship between the economy and factors such as politics and ideology. Here, in reducing the level of comparison to the economic relations between "developed and developing" countries, any specificity to the question of women is denied. Mina Modares (1981), in a careful analysis of women and Shi'ism in Iran, focuses on this very problem when she criticizes feminist writings which treat Islam as an ideology separate from and outside social relations and practices, rather than a discourse which includes rules for economic, social, and power relations within society. Patricia Jeffery's (1979) otherwise informative work on Pirzada women in purdah considers Islamic ideology a partial explanation for the status of women in that it provides a justification for the purdah. Here, Islamic ideology is reduced to a set of ideas whose internalization by Pirzada women contributes to the stability of the system. However, the primary explanation for purdah is located in the control that Pirzada men have over economic resources, and the personal security purdah gives to Pirzada women.

By taking a specific version of Islam as *the* Islam, Jeffery attributes a singularity and coherence to it. Modares notes, " 'Islamic Theology' then becomes imposed on a separate and given entity called 'women.' A further unification is reached: Women (meaning *all women*), regardless of their differing positions within societies, come to be affected or not affected by Islam. These conceptions provide the right ingredients for an unproblematic possibility of a cross-cultural study of women" (63). Marnia Lazreg makes a similar argument when she addresses the reductionism inherent in scholarship on women in the Middle East and North Africa:

> A ritual is established whereby the writer appeals to religion as *the* cause of gender inequality just as it is made the source of underdevelopment in much of modernization theory. In an uncanny way, feminist discourse on women from the Middle East and North Africa mirrors that of theologians' own interpretation of women in Islam. . . .
>
> The overall effect of this paradigm is to deprive women of self-presence, of being. Because women are subsumed under religion presented in fundamental terms, they are inevitably seen as evolving in nonhistorical time. They virtually have no history. Any analysis of change is therefore foreclosed. (1988, 87)

While Jeffery's analysis does not quite succumb to this kind of unitary notion of religion (Islam), it does collapse all ideological specificities into economic relations, and universalizes on the basis of this comparison.

Women and the Development Process

The best examples of universalization on the basis of economic reductionism can be found in the liberal "Women in Development" literature. Proponents of this school seek to examine the effect of development on third world women, sometimes from self-designated feminist perspectives. At the very least, there is an evident interest in and commitment to improving the lives of women in "developing" countries. Scholars such as Irene Tinker and Michelle Bo Bramsen (1972), Ester Boserup (1970), and Perdita Huston (1979) have all written about the effect of development policies on women in the third world.[9] All three women assume "development" is synonymous with "economic development" or "economic progress." As in the case of Minces's patriarchal family, Hosken's male sexual control, and Cutrufelli's Western colonization, development here becomes the all-time equalizer. Women are affected positively or negatively by economic development policies, and this is the basis for cross-cultural comparison.

For instance, Perdita Huston (1979) states that the purpose of her study is to describe the effect of the development process on the "family unit and its individual members" in Egypt, Kenya, Sudan, Tunisia, Sri Lanka, and Mexico. She states that the "problems" and "needs" expressed by rural and urban women in these countries all center around education and training, work and wages, access to health and other services, political participation, and legal rights. Huston relates all these "needs" to the lack of sensitive development policies which exclude women as a group or category. For her, the solution is simple: implement improved development policies which emphasize training for women fieldworkers, use women trainees, and women rural development officers, encourage women's cooperatives, etc. Here again, women are assumed to be a coherent group or category prior to their entry into "the development process." Huston assumes that all third world women have similar problems and needs. Thus, they must have similar interests and goals. However, the interests of urban, middle-class, educated Egyptian housewives, to take only one instance, could surely not be seen as being the same as those of their uneducated, poor maids. Development policies do not affect both groups of women in the same way. Practices which characterize women's status and roles vary according to class. Women are constituted as women through the complex interaction between class, culture, religion, and other ideological institutions and frameworks. They are not "women"—a coherent group—solely on the basis of a particular economic system or policy. Such reductive cross-cultural comparisons result in the colonization of the specifics of daily existence and the complexities of political interests which women of different social classes and cultures represent and mobilize.

Thus, it is revealing that for Perdita Huston, women in the third world countries she writes about have "needs" and "problems," but few if any have "choices" or the freedom to act. This is an interesting representation of women in the third world, one which is significant in suggesting a latent self-presentation of Western women which bears looking at. She writes, "What surprised and moved me most as I listened to women in such very different cultural settings was the striking commonality— whether they were educated or illiterate, urban or rural—of their most basic values: the importance they assign to family, dignity, and service to others" (1979, 115). Would Huston consider such values unusual for women in the West?

What is problematical about this kind of use of "women" as a group, as a stable category of analysis, is that it assumes an ahistorical, universal unity between women based on a generalized notion of their subordination. Instead of analytically *demonstrating* the production of women as socioeconomic political groups within particular local contexts, this analytical move limits the definition of the female subject to gender identity, completely bypassing social class and ethnic identities. What characterizes women as a group is their gender (sociologically, not necessarily biologically, defined) over and above everything else, indicating a monolithic notion of sexual difference. Because women are thus constituted as a coherent group, sexual difference becomes coterminous with female subordination, and power is automatically defined in binary terms: people who have it (read: men), and people who do not (read: women). Men exploit, women are exploited. Such simplistic formulations are historically reductive; they are also ineffectual in designing strategies to combat oppressions. All they do is reinforce binary divisions between men and women.

What would an analysis which did not do this look like? Maria Mies's work illustrates the strength of Western feminist work on women in the third world which does not fall into the traps discussed above. Mies's study of the lace makers of Narsapur, India (1982), attempts to carefully analyze a substantial household industry in which "housewives" produce lace doilies for consumption in the world market. Through a detailed analysis of the structure of the lace industry, production and reproduction relations, the sexual division of labor, profits and exploitation, and the overall consequences of defining women as "non-working housewives" and their work as "leisure-time activity." Mies demonstrates the levels of exploitation in this industry and the impact of this production system on the work and living conditions of the women involved in it. In addition, she is able to analyze the "ideology of the housewife," the notion of a woman sitting in the house, as providing the necessary subjective and sociocultural element for the creation and maintenance of a production system that contributes to the increasing pauperization of women, and keeps them totally atomized and disorganized as workers. Mies's analysis shows the effect of a certain historically and culturally specific mode of patriarchal organization, an organization constructed on the basis of the definition of the lace makers as "non-working housewives" at familial, local, regional, statewide, and international levels. The intricacies and the effects of particular power networks not only are emphasized, but they form the basis of Mies's analysis of how this particular group of women is situated at the center of a hegemonic, exploitative world market.

This is a good example of what careful, politically focused, local analyses can accomplish. It illustrates how the category of women is constructed in a variety of political contexts that often exist simultaneously and overlaid on top of one another. There is no easy generalization in the direction of "women" in India, or "women in the third world"; nor is there a reduction of the political construction of the exploitation of the lace makers to cultural explanations about the passivity or obedience that might characterize these women and their situation. Finally, this mode of local, political analysis which generates theoretical categories from within the situation and context being analyzed, also suggests corresponding effective strategies for organizing against the exploitation faced by the lace makers. Narsapur women are not mere victims of the production process, because they resist, challenge, and subvert the process at various junctures. Here is one instance of how Mies delineates the connections between the housewife ideology, the self-consciousness of the lace makers, and their interrelationships as contributing to the latent resistances she perceives among the women:

> The persistence of the housewife ideology, the self-perception of the lace makers as petty commodity producers rather than as workers, is not only upheld by the structure of the industry as such but also by the deliberate propagation and reinforcement of reactionary patriarchal norms and institutions. Thus, most of the lace makers voiced the same opinion about the rules of *purdah* and seclusion in their communities which were also propagated by the lace exporters. In particular, the *Kapu* women said that they had never gone out of their houses, that women of their community could not do any other work than housework and lace work etc. but in spite of the fact that most of them still subscribed fully to the patriarchal norms of the *gosha* women, there were also contradictory elements in their consciousness. Thus, although they looked down with contempt upon women who were able to

These women were respected house wives & all workers

work outside the house—like the untouchable *Mala* and *Madiga* women or women of other lower castes, they could not ignore the fact that these women were earning more money precisely because they were *not* respectable house-wives but workers. At one discussion, they even admitted that it would be better if they could also go out and do coolie work. And when they were asked whether they would be ready to come out of their houses and work in one place in some sort of a factory, they said they would do that. This shows that the *purdah* and housewife ideology, although still fully internal-ized, already had some cracks, because it has been confronted with several contradictory realities. (157)

It is only by understanding the *contradictions* inherent in women's location within various structures that effective political action and chal-lenges can be devised. Mies's study goes a long way toward offering such analysis. While there are now an increasing number of Western feminist writings in this tradition,[10] there is also, unfortunately, a large block of writing which succumbs to the cultural reductionism discussed earlier.

Methodological Universalisms, or: Women's Oppression Is a Global Phenomenon

Western feminist writings on women in the third world subscribe to a variety of methodologies to demonstrate the universal cross-cultural operation of male dominance and female exploitation. I summarize and critique three such methods below, moving from the simplest to the most complex.

First, proof of universalism is provided through the use of an arithmetic method. The argument goes like this: the greater the number of women who wear the veil, the more universal is the sexual segregation and control of women (Deardon 1975, 4–5). Similarly, a large number of different, fragmented examples from a variety of countries also apparently add up to a universal fact. For instance, Muslim women in Saudi Arabia, Iran, Pakistan, India, and Egypt all wear some sort of a veil. Hence, this in-dicates that the sexual control of women is a universal fact in those coun-tries in which the women are veiled (Deardon 1975, 7, 10). Fran Hosken writes, "Rape, forced prostitution, polygamy, genital mutilation, pornog-raphy, the beating of girls and women, purdah (segregation of women) are all violations of basic human rights" (1981, 15). By equating purdah with rape, domestic violence, and forced prostitution, Hosken asserts its "sexual control" function as the primary explanation for purdah, whatever the context. Institutions of purdah are thus denied any cultural and his-torical specificity, and contradictions and potentially subversive aspects are totally ruled out.

In both these examples, the problem is not in asserting that the practice of wearing a veil is widespread. This assertion can be made on the basis

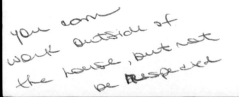

you can work outside of the house, but not be **Respected**

of numbers. It is a descriptive generalization. However, it is the analytic leap from the practice of veiling to an assertion of its general significance in controlling women that must be questioned. While there may be a physical similarity in the veils worn by women in Saudi Arabia and Iran, the specific meaning attached to this practice varies according to the cultural and ideological context. In addition, the symbolic space occupied by the practice of purdah may be similar in certain contexts, but this does not automatically indicate that the practices themselves have identical significance in the social realm. For example, as is well known, Iranian middle-class women veiled themselves during the 1979 revolution to indicate solidarity with their veiled working-class sisters, while in contemporary Iran, mandatory Islamic laws dictate that all Iranian women wear veils. While in both these instances, similar reasons might be offered for the veil (opposition to the Shah and Western cultural colonization in the first case, and the true Islamicization of Iran in the second), the concrete *meanings* attached to Iranian women wearing the veil are clearly different in both historical contexts. In the first case, wearing the veil is both an oppositional and a revolutionary gesture on the part of Iranian middle-class women; in the second case, it is a coercive, institutional mandate (see Tabari 1980 for detailed discussion). It is on the basis of such context-specific differentiated analysis that effective political strategies can be generated. To assume that the mere practice of veiling women in a number of Muslim countries indicates the universal oppression of women through sexual segregation not only is analytically reductive, but also proves quite useless when it comes to the elaboration of oppositional political strategy.

Second, concepts such as reproduction, the sexual division of labor, the family, marriage, household, patriarchy, etc., are often used without their specification in local cultural and historical contexts. Feminists use these concepts in providing explanations for women's subordination, apparently assuming their universal applicability. For instance, how is it possible to refer to "the" sexual division of labor when the *content* of this division changes radically from one environment to the next, and from one historical juncture to another? At its most abstract level, it is the fact of the differential assignation of tasks according to sex that is significant; however, this is quite different from the *meaning* or *value* that the content of this sexual division of labor assumes in different contexts. In most cases the assigning of tasks on the basis of sex has an ideological origin. There is no question that a claim such as "women are concentrated in service-oriented occupations in a large number of countries around the world" is descriptively valid. Descriptively, then, perhaps the existence of a similar sexual division of labor (where women work in service occupations such as nursing, social work, etc., and men in other kinds of occupations) in a variety of different countries can be asserted. However, the concept of the "sexual division of labor" is more than just a descriptive category. It indicates the differential *value* placed on "men's work" versus "women's work."

Often the mere existence of a sexual division of labor is taken to be proof of the oppression of women in various societies. This results from a confusion between and collapsing together of the descriptive and explanatory potential of the concept of the sexual division of labor. Superficially similar situations may have radically different, historically specific explanations, and cannot be treated as identical. For instance, the rise of female-headed households in middle-class America might be construed as a sign of great independence and feminist progress, whereby women are considered to have *chosen* to be single parents, there are increasing numbers of lesbian mothers, etc. However, the recent increase in female-headed households in Latin America,[11] where women might be seen to have more decision-making power, is concentrated among the poorest strata, where life choices are the most constrained economically. A similar argument can be made for the rise of female-headed families among black and Chicana women in the U.S. The positive correlation between this and the level of poverty among women of color and white working-class women in the U.S. has now even acquired a name: the feminization of poverty. Thus, while it is possible to state that there is a rise in female-headed households in the U.S. and in Latin America, this rise cannot be discussed as a universal indicator of women's independence, nor can it be discussed as a universal indicator of women's impoverishment. The *meaning* of and *explanation* for the rise obviously vary according to the sociohistorical context.

Similarly, the existence of a sexual division of labor in most contexts cannot be sufficient explanation for the universal subjugation of women in the work force. That the sexual division of labor does indicate a devaluation of women's work must be shown through analysis of particular local contexts. In addition, devaluation of *women* must also be shown through careful analysis. In other words, the "sexual division of labor" and "women" are not commensurate analytical categories. Concepts such as the sexual division of labor can be useful only if they are generated through local, contextual analyses (see Eldhom, Harris, and Young 1977). If such concepts are assumed to be universally applicable, the resultant homogenization of class, race, religious, and daily material practices of women in the third world can create a false sense of the commonality of oppressions, interests, and struggles between and among women globally. Beyond sisterhood there are still racism, colonialism, and imperialism!

Finally, some writers confuse the use of gender as a superordinate category of organizing analysis with the universalistic proof and instan-

tiation of this category. In other words, empirical studies of gender differences are confused with the analytical organization of cross-cultural
work. Beverly Brown's (1983) review of the book *Nature, Culture and
Gender* (Strathern and McCormack 1980) best illustrates this point. Brown
suggests that nature:culture and female:male are superordinate categories
which organize and locate lesser categories (such as wild/domestic and
biology/technology) within their logic. These categories are universal in
the sense that they organize the universe of a system of representations.
This relation is totally independent of the universal substantiation of any
particular category. Her critique hinges on the fact that rather than clarify
the generalizability of nature:culture :: female:male as subordinate organization categories, *Nature, Culture and Gender* construes the universality of this equation to lie at the level of empirical truth, which can be
investigated through fieldwork. Thus, the usefulness of the nature:culture
:: female:male paradigm as a universal mode of the organization of representation within any particular sociohistorical system is lost. Here,
methodological universalism is assumed on the basis of the reduction of
the nature:culture :: female:male analytic categories to a demand for empirical proof of its existence in different cultures. Discourses of representation are confused with material realities, and the distinction made earlier
between "Woman" and "women" is lost. Feminist work which blurs this
distinction (which is, interestingly enough, often present in certain Western feminists' self-representation) eventually ends up constructing monolithic images of "third world women" by ignoring the complex and
mobile relationships between their historical materiality on the level of
specific oppressions and political choices, on the one hand, and their
general discursive representations, on the other.

To summarize: I have discussed three methodological moves identifiable in feminist (and other academic) cross-cultural work which seeks
to uncover a universality in women's subordinate position in society. The
next and final section pulls together the previous sections, attempting to
outline the political effects of the analytical strategies in the context of
Western feminist writing on women in the third world. These arguments
are not against generalization as much as they are for careful, historically
specific generalizations responsive to complex realities. Nor do these arguments deny the necessity of forming strategic political identities and
affinities. Thus, while Indian women of different religions, castes, and
classes might forge a political unity on the basis of organizing against
police brutality toward women (see Kishwar and Vanita 1984), an *analysis*
of police brutality must be contextual. Strategic coalitions which construct
oppositional political identities for themselves are based on generalization
and provisional unities, but the analysis of these group identities cannot
be based on universalistic, ahistorical categories.

The Subject(s) of Power

This last section returns to an earlier point about the inherently political nature of feminist scholarship, and attempts to clarify my point about the possibility of detecting a colonialist move in the case of a hegemonic first-third world connection in scholarship. The nine texts in the Zed Press Women in the Third World series that I have discussed[12] focused on the following common areas in examining women's "status" within various societies: religion, family/kinship structures, the legal system, the sexual division of labor, education, and finally, political resistance. A large number of Western feminist writings on women in the third world focus on these themes. Of course the Zed texts have varying emphases. For instance, two of the studies, *Women of Palestine* (Downing 1982) and *Indian Women in Struggle* (Omvedt 1980), focus explicitly on female militance and political involvement, while *Women in Arab Society* (Minces 1980) deals with Arab women's legal, religious, and familial status. In addition, each text evidences a variety of methodologies and degrees of care in making generalizations. Interestingly enough, however, almost all the texts assume "women" as a category of analysis in the manner designated above.

Clearly this is an analytical strategy which is neither limited to these Zed Press publications nor symptomatic of Zed Press publications in general. However, each of the particular texts in question assumes "women" have a coherent group identity within the different cultures discussed, prior to their entry into social relations. Thus, Omvedt can talk about "Indian women" while referring to a particular group of women in the State of Maharashtra, Cutrufelli about "women of Africa," and Minces about "Arab women" as if these groups of women have some sort of obvious cultural coherence, distinct from men in these societies. The "status" or "position" of women is assumed to be self-evident, because women as an already constituted group are *placed* within religious, economic, familial, and legal structures. However, this focus whereby women are seen as a coherent group across contexts, regardless of class or ethnicity, structures the world in ultimately binary, dichotomous terms, where women are always seen in opposition to men, patriarchy is always necessarily male dominance, and the religious, legal, economic, and familial systems are implicitly assumed to be constructed by men. Thus, both men and women are always apparently constituted whole populations, and relations of dominance and exploitation are also posited in terms of whole peoples—wholes coming into exploitative relations. It is only when men and women are seen as different categories or groups possessing different *already constituted* categories of experience, cognition, and interests as *groups* that such a simplistic dichotomy is possible.

What does this imply about the structure and functioning of power relations? The setting up of the commonality of third world women's struggles across classes and cultures against a general notion of oppression (primarily the group in power—i.e., men) necessitates the assumption of what Michel Foucault (1980, 135–45) calls the "juridico-discursive" model of power, the principal features of which are "a negative relation" (limit and lack), an "insistence on the rule" (which forms a binary system), a "cycle of prohibition," the "logic of censorship," and a "uniformity" of the apparatus functioning at different levels. Feminist discourse on the third world which assumes a homogeneous category—or group—called women necessarily operates through the setting up of originary power divisions. Power relations are structured in terms of a unilateral and undifferentiated source of power and a cumulative reaction to power. Opposition is a generalized phenomenon created as a response to power—which, in turn, is possessed by certain groups of people.

The major problem with such a definition of power is that it locks all revolutionary struggles into binary structures—possessing power versus being powerless. Women are powerless, unified groups. If the struggle for a just society is seen in terms of the move from powerless to powerful for women as a *group*, and this is the implication in feminist discourse which structures sexual difference in terms of the division between the sexes, then the new society would be structurally identical to the existing organization of power relations, constituting itself as a simple *inversion* of what exists. If relations of domination and exploitation are defined in terms of binary divisions—groups which dominate and groups which are dominated—surely the implication is that the accession to power of women as a group is sufficient to dismantle the existing organization of relations? But women as a group are not in some sense essentially superior or infallible. The crux of the problem lies in that initial assumption of women as a homogeneous group or category ("the oppressed"), a familiar assumption in Western radical and liberal feminisms.[13]

What happens when this assumption of "women as an oppressed group" is situated in the context of Western feminist writing about third world women? It is here that I locate the colonialist move. By contrasting the representation of women in the third world with what I referred to earlier as Western feminisms' self-presentation in the same context, we see how Western feminists alone become the true "subjects" of this counterhistory. Third world women, on the other hand, never rise above the debilitating generality of their "object" status.

While radical and liberal feminist assumptions of women as a sex class might elucidate (however inadequately) the autonomy of particular women's struggles in the West, the application of the notion of women as a homogeneous category to women in the third world colonizes and appropriates the pluralities of the simultaneous location of different groups of women in social class and ethnic frameworks; in doing so it ultimately robs them of their historical and political *agency*. Similarly, many Zed Press authors who ground themselves in the basic analytic strategies of traditional Marxism also implicitly create a "unity" of women by substituting "women's activity" for "labor" as the primary theoretical determinant of women's situation. Here again, women are constituted as a coherent group not on the basis of "natural" qualities or needs but on the basis of the sociological "unity" of their role in domestic production and wage labor (see Haraway 1985, esp. p. 76). In other words, Western feminist discourse, by assuming women as a coherent, already constituted group which is placed in kinship, legal, and other structures, defines third world women as subjects *outside* social relations, instead of looking at the way women are constituted *through* these very structures.

Legal, economic, religious, and familial structures are treated as phenomena to be judged by Western standards. It is here that ethnocentric universality comes into play. When these structures are defined as "underdeveloped" or "developing" and women are placed within them, an implicit image of the "average third world woman" is produced. This is the transformation of the (implicitly Western) "oppressed woman" into the "oppressed third world woman." While the category of "oppressed woman" is generated through an exclusive focus on gender difference, "the oppressed third world woman" category has an additional attribute— the "third world difference!" The "third world difference" includes a paternalistic attitude toward women in the third world.[14] Since discussions of the various themes I identified earlier (kinship, education, religion, etc.) are conducted in the context of the relative "underdevelopment" of the third world (which is nothing less than unjustifiably confusing development with the separate path taken by the West in its development, as well as ignoring the directionality of the first-third world power relationship), third world women as a group or category are automatically and necessarily defined as religious (read "not progressive"), family-oriented (read "traditional"), legal minors (read "they-are-still-not-conscious-of-their-rights"), illiterate (read "ignorant"), domestic (read "backward"), and sometimes revolutionary (read "their-country-is-in-a-state-of-war; they-must-fight!") This is how the "third world difference" is produced.

When the category of "sexually oppressed women" is located within particular systems in the third world which are defined on a scale which is normed through Eurocentric assumptions, not only are third world women defined in a particular way prior to their entry into social relations, but since no connections are made between first and third world power shifts, the assumption is reinforced that the third world just has not evolved to the extent that the West has. This mode of feminist analysis, by homogenizing and systematizing the experiences of different groups of women in these countries, erases all marginal and resistant modes and experiences.[15] It is significant that none of the texts I reviewed in the Zed Press series focuses on lesbian politics or the politics of ethnic and religious marginal organizations in third world women's groups. Resistance can thus be defined only as cumulatively reactive, not as something inherent in the operation of power. If power, as Michel Foucault has argued recently, can really be understood only in the context of resistance,[16] this misconceptualization is both analytically and strategically problematical. It limits theoretical analysis as well as reinforces Western cultural imperialism. For in the context of a first/third world balance of power, feminist analyses which perpetrate and sustain the hegemony of the idea of the superiority of the West produce a corresponding set of universal images of the "third world woman," images such as the veiled woman, the powerful mother, the chaste virgin, the obedient wife, etc. These images exist in universal, ahistorical splendor, setting in motion a colonialist discourse which exercises a very specific power in defining, coding, and maintaining existing first/third world connections.

To conclude, then, let me suggest some disconcerting similarities between the typically authorizing signature of such Western feminist writings on women in the third world, and the authorizing signature of the project of humanism in general—humanism as a Western ideological and political project which involves the necessary recuperation of the "East" and "Woman" as Others. Many contemporary thinkers, including Foucault (1978, 1980), Derrida (1974), Kristeva (1980), Deleuze and Guattari (1977), and Said (1978), have written at length about the underlying anthropomorphism and ethnocentrism which constitute a hegemonic humanistic problematic that repeatedly confirms and legitimates (Western) Man's centrality. Feminist theorists such as Luce Irigaray (1981), Sarah Kofman (see Berg 1982), and Helene Cixous (1981) have also written about the recuperation and absence of woman/women within Western humanism. The focus of the work of all these thinkers can be stated simply as an uncovering of the political *interests* that underlie the binary logic of humanistic discourse and ideology whereby, as a valuable recent essay puts it, "the first (majority) term (Identity, Universality, Culture, Disinterestedness, Truth, Sanity, Justice, etc.), which is, in fact, secondary and derivative (a construction), is privileged over and colonizes the second (minority) term (difference, temporality, anarchy, error, interestedness, insanity, deviance, etc.), which is in fact, primary and originative" (Spanos 1984). In other words, it is only insofar as "Woman/Women" and "the East" are defined as *Others*, or as peripheral, that (Western) Man/Humanism can represent him/itself as the center. It is not the center that determines the periphery, but the periphery that, in its boundedness, determines the center. Just as feminists such as Kristeva and Cixous deconstruct the latent anthropomorphism in Western discourse, I have suggested a parallel strategy in this essay in uncovering a latent ethnocentrism in particular feminist writings on women in the third world.[17]

As discussed earlier, a comparison between Western feminist self-presentation and Western feminist re-presentation of women in the third world yields significant results. Universal images of "the third world woman" (the veiled woman, chaste virgin, etc.), images constructed from adding the "third world difference" to "sexual difference," are predicated upon (and hence obviously bring into sharper focus) assumptions about Western women as secular, liberated, and having control over their own lives. This is not to suggest that Western women *are* secular, liberated, and in control of their own lives. I am referring to a *discursive* self-presentation, not necessarily to material reality. If this were a material reality, there would be no need for political movements in the West. Similarly, only from the vantage point of the West is it possible to define the "third world" as underdeveloped and economically dependent. Without the overdetermined discourse that creates the *third* world, there would be no (singular and privileged) first world. Without the "third world woman," the particular self-presentation of Western women mentioned above would be problematical. I am suggesting, then, that the one enables and sustains the other. This is not to say that the signature of Western feminist writings on the third world has the same authority as the project of Western humanism. However, in the context of the hegemony of the Western scholarly establishment in the production and dissemination of texts, and in the context of the legitimating imperative of humanistic and scientific discourse, the definition of "the third world woman" as a monolith might well tie into the larger economic and ideological praxis of "disinterested" scientific inquiry and pluralism which are the surface manifestations of a latent economic and cultural colonization of the "non-Western" world. It is time to move beyond the Marx who found it possible to say: They cannot represent themselves; they must be represented.

NOTES

This essay would not have been possible without S. P. Mohanty's challenging and careful reading. I would also like to thank Biddy Martin for our numerous discussions about feminist theory and politics. They both helped me think through some of the arguments herein.

1. Terms such as *third* and *first world* are very problematical both in suggesting oversimplified similarities between and among countries labeled thus, and in implicitly reinforcing existing economic, cultural, and ideological hierarchies

which are conjured up in using such terminology. I use the term *"third world"* with full awareness of its problems, only because this is the terminology available to us at the moment. The use of quotation marks is meant to suggest a continuous questioning of the designation. Even when I do not use quotation marks, I mean to use the term critically.

2. I am indebted to Teresa de Lauretis for this particular formulation of the project of feminist theorizing. See especially her introduction in de Lauretis, *Alice Doesn't: Feminism, Semiotics, Cinema* (Bloomington: Indiana University Press, 1984); see also Sylvia Wynter, "The Politics of Domination," unpublished manuscript.

3. This argument is similar to Homi Bhabha's definition of colonial discourse as strategically creating a space for a subject people through the production of knowledges and the exercise of power. The full quote reads: "[colonial discourse is] an apparatus of power.... an apparatus that turns on the recognition and disavowal of racial/cultural/historical differences. Its predominant strategic function is the creation of a space for a subject people through the production of knowledges in terms of which surveillance is exercised and a complex form of pleasure/unpleasure is incited. It (i.e. colonial discourse) seeks authorization for its strategies by the production of knowledges by coloniser and colonised which are stereotypical but antithetically evaluated" (1983, 23).

4. A number of documents and reports on the UN International Conferences on Women, Mexico City, 1975, and Copenhagen, 1980, as well as the 1976 Wellesley Conference on Women and Development, attest to this. Nawal el Saadawi, Fatima Mernissi, and Mallica Vajarathon (1978) characterize this conference as "American-planned and organized," situating third world participants as passive audiences. They focus especially on the lack of self-consciousness of Western women's implication in the effects of imperialism and racism in their assumption of an "international sisterhood." A recent essay by Valerie Amos and Pratibha Parmar (1984) characterizes as "imperial" Euro-American feminism which seeks to establish itself as the only legitimate feminism.

5. The Zed Press Women in the Third World series is unique in its conception. I choose to focus on it because it is the only contemporary series I have found which assumes that "women in the third world" are a legitimate and separate subject of study and research. Since 1985, when this essay was first written, numerous new titles have appeared in the Women in the Third World series. Thus, I suspect that Zed has come to occupy a rather privileged position in the dissemination and construction of discourses by and about third world women. A number of the books in this series are excellent, especially those which deal directly with women's resistance struggles. In addition, Zed Press consistently publishes progressive feminist, antiracist, and antiimperialist texts. However, a number of the texts written by feminist sociologists, anthropologists, and journalists are symptomatic of the kind of Western feminist work on women in the third world that concerns me. Thus, an analysis of a few of these particular works in this series can serve as a representative point of entry into the discourse I am attempting to locate and define. My focus on these texts is therefore an attempt at an internal critique: I simply expect and demand more from this series. Needless to say, progressive publishing houses also carry their own authorizing signatures.

6. Elsewhere I have discussed this particular point in detail in a critique of Robin Morgan's construction of "women's herstory" in her introduction to *Sisterhood Is Global: The International Women's Movement Anthology* (New York: Anchor Press/Doubleday, 1984). See my "Feminist Encounters: Locating the Politics of Experience," *Copyright* 1, "Fin de Siecle 2000," 30–44, especially 35–37.

7. Another example of this kind of analysis is Mary Daly's (1978) *Gyn/ Ecology*. Daly's assumption in this text, that women as a group are sexually victimized, leads to her very problematic comparison between the attitudes toward women witches and healers in the West, Chinese footbinding, and the genital mutilation of women in Africa. According to Daly, women in Europe, China, and Africa constitute a homogeneous group as victims of male power. Not only does this label (sexual victims) eradicate the specific historical and material realities and contradictions which lead to and perpetuate practices such as witch hunting and genital mutilation, but it also obliterates the differences, complexities, and heterogeneities of the lives of, for example, women of different classes, religions, and nations in Africa. As Audre Lorde (1983) pointed out, women in Africa share a long tradition of healers and goddesses that perhaps binds them together more appropriately than their victim status. However, both Daly and Lorde fall prey to universalistic assumptions about "African women" (both negative and positive). What matters is the complex, historical range of power differences, commonalities, and resistances that exist among women in Africa which construct African women as "subjects" of their own politics.

8. See Eldhom, Harris, and Young (1977) for a good discussion of the necessity to theorize male violence within specific societal frameworks, rather than assume it as a universal fact.

9. These views can also be found in differing degrees in collections such as Wellesley Editorial Committee, ed., *Women and National Development: The Complexities of Change* (Chicago: University of Chicago Press, 1977), and *Signs*, Special Issue, "Development and the Sexual Division of Labor," 7, no. 2 (Winter 1981). For an excellent introduction of WID issues, see ISIS, *Women in Development: A Resource Guide for Organization and Action* (Philadelphia: New Society Publishers, 1984). For a politically focused discussion of feminism and development and the stakes for poor third world women, see Gita Sen and Caren Grown, *Development Crises and Alternative Visions: Third World Women's Perspectives* (New York: Monthly Review Press, 1987).

10. See essays by Vanessa Maher, Diane Elson and Ruth Pearson, and Maila Stevens in Kate Young, Carol Walkowitz, and Roslyn McCullagh, eds., *Of Marriage and the Market: Women's Subordination in International Perspective* (London: CSE Books, 1981); and essays by Vivian Mota and Michelle Mattelart in June Nash and Helen I. Safa, eds., *Sex and Class in Latin America: Women's Perspectives on Politics, Economics and the Family in the Third World* (South Hadley, Mass.: Bergin and Garvey, 1980). For examples of excellent, self-conscious work by feminists writing about women in their own historical and geographical locations, see Marnia Lazreg (1988) on Algerian women, Gayatri Chakravorty Spivak's "A Literary Representation of the Subaltern: A Woman's Text from the Third World," in her *In Other Worlds: Essays in Cultural Politics* (New York: Methuen, 1987), 241–68, and Lata Mani's essay "Contentious Traditions: The Debate on SATI in Colonial India," *Cultural Critique* 7 (Fall 1987), 119–56.

11. Olivia Harris, "Latin American Women—An Overview," in Harris, ed., *Latin American Women* (London: Minority Rights Group Report no. 57, 1983), 4–7. Other MRG Reports include Ann Deardon (1975) and Rounaq Jahan (1980).

12. List of Zed Press publications: Patricia Jeffery, *Frogs in a Well: Indian Women in Purdah* (1979); Latin American and Caribbean Women's Collective, *Slaves of Slaves: The Challenge of Latin American Women* (1980); Gail Omvedt, *We Shall Smash This Prison: Indian Women in Struggle* (1980); Juliette Minces, *The House*

of Obedience: Women in Arab Society (1980); Bobby Siu, *Women of China: Imperialism and Women's Resistance, 1900–1949* (1981); Ingela Bendt and James Downing, *We Shall Return: Women in Palestine* (1982); Maria Rosa Cutrufelli, *Women of Africa: Roots of Oppression* (1983); Maria Mies, *The Lace Makers of Narsapur: Indian House-wives Produce for the World Market* (1982); Miranda Davis, ed., *Third World/Second Sex: Women's Struggles and National Liberation* (1983).

13. For succinct discussions of Western radical and liberal feminisms, see Hester Eisenstein, *Contemporary Feminist Thought* (Boston: G. K. Hall & Co., 1983), and Zillah Eisenstein, *The Radical Future of Liberal Feminism* (New York: Longman, 1981).

14. Amos and Parmar describe the cultural stereotypes present in Euro-American feminist thought: "The image is of the passive Asian woman subject to oppressive practices within the Asian family with an emphasis on wanting to 'help' Asian women liberate themselves from their role. Or there is the strong, dominant Afro-Caribbean woman, who despite her 'strength' is exploited by the 'sexism' which is seen as being a strong feature in relationships between Afro-Caribbean men and women" (9). These images illustrate the extent to which *paternalism* is an essential element of feminist thinking which incorporates the above stereotypes, a paternalism which can lead to the definition of priorities for women of color by Euro-American feminists.

15. I discuss the question of theorizing experience in my "Feminist Encounters" (1987) and in an essay coauthored with Biddy Martin, "Feminist Politics: What's Home Got to Do with It?" in Teresa de Lauretis, ed., *Feminist Studies/ Critical Studies* (Bloomington: Indiana University Press, 1986), 191–212.

16. This is one of M. Foucault's (1978, 1980) central points in his reconceptualization of the strategies and workings of power networks.

17. For an argument which demands a *new* conception of humanism in work on third world women, see Marnia Lazreg (1988). While Lazreg's position might appear to be diametrically opposed to mine, I see it as a provocative and potentially positive extension of some of the implications that follow from my arguments. In criticizing the feminist rejection of humanism in the name of "essential Man," Lazreg points to what she calls an "essentialism of difference" within these very feminist projects. She asks: "To what extent can Western feminism dispense with an ethics of responsibility when writing about different women? The point is neither to subsume other women under one's own experience nor to uphold a separate truth for them. Rather, it is to allow them to *be* while recognizing that what they are is just as meaningful, valid, and comprehensible as what we are. . . . Indeed, when feminists essentially deny other women the humanity they claim for themselves, they dispense with any ethical constraint. They engage in the act of splitting the social universe into us and them, subject and objects" (99–100).

This essay by Lazreg and an essay by S. P. Mohanty (1989) entitled "Us and Them: On the Philosophical Bases of Political Criticism" suggest positive directions for self-conscious cross-cultural analyses, analyses which move beyond the deconstructive to a fundamentally productive mode in designating overlapping areas for cross-cultural comparison. The latter essay calls not for a "humanism" but for a reconsideration of the question of the "human" in a posthumanist context. It argues that (1) there is no necessary "incompatibility between the deconstruction of Western humanism" and such "a positive elaboration" of the human, and moreover that (2) such an elaboration is essential if contemporary political-critical discourse is to avoid the incoherences and weaknesses of a relativist position.

REFERENCES LIST

Abdel-Malek, Anouar. 1981. *Social Dialectics: Nation and Revolution*. Albany: State University of New York Press.

Amin, Samir. 1977. *Imperialism and Unequal Development*. New York: Monthly Review Press.

Amos, Valerie, and Pratibha Parmar. 1984 "Challenging Imperial Feminism." *Feminist Review* 17:3–19.

Baran, Paul A. 1962. *The Political Economy of Growth*. New York: Monthly Review Press.

Berg, Elizabeth. 1982. "The Third Woman." *Diacritics* (Summer):11–20.

Bhabha, Homi. 1983. "The Other Question—The Stereotype and Colonial Discourse." *Screen* 24, no. 6:23.

Boserup, Ester. 1970. *Women's Role in Economic Development*. New York: St. Martin's Press; London: Allen and Unwin.

Brown, Beverly. 1983. "Displacing the Difference—Review, *Nature, Culture and Gender*." *m/f* 8:79–89.

Cixous, Helene. 1981. "The Laugh of the Medusa." In Marks and De Courtivron (1981).

Cowie, Elizabeth. 1978. "Woman as Sign." *m/f* 1:49–63.

Cutrufelli, Maria Rosa. 1983. *Women of Africa: Roots of Oppression*. London: Zed Press.

Daly, Mary. 1978. *Gyn/Ecology: The Metaethics of Radical Feminism*. Boston: Beacon Press.

Deardon, Ann, ed. 1975. *Arab Women*. London: Minority Rights Group Report no. 27.

de Lauretis, Teresa. 1984. *Alice Doesn't: Feminism, Semiotics, Cinema*. Bloomington: Indiana University Press.

———. 1986. *Feminist Studies/Critical Studies*. Bloomington: Indiana University Press.

Deleuze, Giles, and Felix Guattari. 1977. *Anti-Oedipus: Capitalism and Schizophrenia*. New York: Viking.

Derrida, Jacques. 1974. *Of Grammatology*. Baltimore. Johns Hopkins University Press.

Eisenstein, Hester. 1983. *Contemporary Feminist Thought*. Boston: G. K. Hall and Co.

Eisenstein, Zillah. 1981. *The Radical Future of Liberal Feminism*. New York: Longman.

Eldhom, Felicity, Olivia Harris, and Kate Young. 1977. "Conceptualising Women." *Critique of Anthropology "Women's Issue"*, no. 3.

el Saadawi, Nawal, Fatima Mernissi, and Mallica Vajarathon. 1978. "A Critical Look at the Wellesley Conference." *Quest* 4, no. 2 (Winter):101–107.

Foucault, Michel. 1978. *History of Sexuality: Volume One*. New York: Random House.

———. 1980. *Power/Knowledge*. New York: Pantheon.

Gunder-Frank, Audre. 1967. *Capitalism and Underdevelopment in Latin America*. New York: Monthly Review Press.

Haraway, Donna. 1985. "A Manifesto for Cyborgs: Science, Technology and Socialist Feminism in the 1980s." *Socialist Review* 80 (March/April):65–108.

Harris, Olivia. 1983a. "Latin American Women—An Overview." In Harris (1983b).

———. 1983b. *Latin American Women*. London: Minority Rights Group Report no. 57.

Hosken, Fran. 1981. "Female Genital Mutilation and Human Rights." *Feminist Issues* 1, no. 3.

Huston, Perdita. 1979. *Third World Women Speak Out.* New York: Praeger.

Irigaray, Luce. 1981. "This Sex Which Is Not One" and "When the Goods Get Together." In Marks and De Courtivron (1981).

Jahan, Rounaq, ed. 1980. *Women in Asia.* London: Minority Rights Group Report no. 45.

Jeffery, Patricia. 1979. *Frogs in a Well: Indian Women in Purdah.* London: Zed Press.

Joseph, Gloria, and Jill Lewis. 1981. *Common Differences: Conflicts in Black and White Feminist Perspectives.* Boston: Beacon Press.

Kishwar, Madhu, and Ruth Vanita. 1984. *In Search of Answers: Indian Women's Voices from Manushi.* London: Zed Press.

Kristeva, Julia. 1980. *Desire in Language.* New York: Columbia University Press.

Lazreg, Marnia. 1988. "Feminism and Difference: The Perils of Writing as a Woman on Women in Algeria." *Feminist Issues* 14, no. 1 (Spring):81–107.

Lindsay, Beverley, ed. 1983. *Comparative Perspectives of Third World Women: The Impact of Race, Sex and Class.* New York: Praeger.

Lorde, Audre. 1983. "An Open Letter to Mary Daly." In Moraga and Anzaldua (1983), 94–97.

Marks, Elaine, and Isabel De Courtivron. 1981. *New French Feminisms.* New York: Schocken Books.

Mies, Maria. 1982. *The Lace Makers of Narsapur: Indian Housewives Produce for the World Market.* London: Zed Press.

Minces, Juliette. 1980. *The House of Obedience: Women in Arab Society.* London: Zed Press.

Modares, Mina. 1981. "Women and Shi'ism in Iran." *m/f* 5 and 6:61–82.

Mohanty, Chandra Talpade. 1987. "Feminist Encounters: Locating the Politics of Experience." *Copyright* 1, "Fin de Siecle 2000," 30–44.

Mohanty, Chandra Talpade, and Biddy Martin. 1986. "Feminist Politics: What's Home Got to Do with It?" In de Lauretis (1986).

Mohanty, S. P. 1989. "Us and Them: On the Philosophical Bases of Political Criticism." *Yale Journal of Criticism* 2 (March):1–31.

Moraga, Cherríe. 1984. *Loving in the War Years.* Boston: South End Press.

Moraga, Cherríe, and Gloria Anzaldúa, eds. 1983. *This Bridge Called My Back: Writings by Radical Women of Color.* New York: Kitchen Table Press.

Morgan, Robin, ed. 1984. *Sisterhood Is Global: The International Women's Movement Anthology.* New York: Anchor Press/Doubleday; Harmondsworth: Penguin.

Nash, June, and Helen I. Safa, eds. 1980. *Sex and Class in Latin America: Women's Perspectives on Politics, Economics and the Family in the Third World.* South Hadley, Mass.: Bergin and Garvey.

Rosaldo, M. A. 1980. "The Use and Abuse of Anthropology: Reflections on Feminism and Cross-Cultural Understanding." *Signs* 53:389–417.

Said, Edward. 1978. *Orientalism.* New York: Random House.

Sen, Gita, and Caren Grown. 1987. *Development Crises and Alternative Visions: Third World Women's Perspectives.* New York: Monthly Review Press.

Smith, Barbara, ed. 1983. *Home Girls: A Black Feminist Anthology.* New York: Kitchen Table Press.

Spanos, William V. 1984. "Boundary 2 and the Polity of Interest: Humanism, the 'Center Elsewhere' and Power." *Boundary 2* 12, no. 3/13, no. 1 (Spring/Fall).

Spivak, Gayatri Chakravorty. 1987. *In Other Worlds: Essays in Cultural Politics.* London and New York: Methuen.

Strathern, Marilyn, and Carol McCormack, eds. 1980. *Nature, Culture and Gender*. Cambridge: Cambridge University Press.

Tabari, Azar. 1980. "The Enigma of the Veiled Iranian Women." *Feminist Review* 5:19–32.

Tinker, Irene, and Michelle Bo Bramsen, eds. 1972. *Women and World Development*. Washington, D.C.: Overseas Development Council.

Young, Kate, Carol Walkowitz, and Roslyn McCullagh, eds. 1981. *Of Marriage and the Market: Women's Subordination in International Perspective*. London: CSE Books.

VIOLENCE IN THE OTHER COUNTRY

China as Crisis, Spectacle, and Woman*

Rey Chow

On June 4, 1989, after weeks of peaceful demonstrations by Chinese civilians for reform and democracy, the Chinese government sent troops and tanks to massacre hundreds at Beijing's Tiananmen Square. In the following weeks, Chinese armies were ordered to clean up the mess they had created; soldiers became so socially constructive that they cut civilians' hair on the streets of Beijing. Meanwhile, hundreds were arrested and tried, and an unknown number executed.[1]

Benedict Anderson (1983, 68), in a footnote in his book *Imagined Communities: Reflections on the Spread of Nationalism*, says: "So, as European imperialism smashed its insouciant way around the globe, other civilizations found themselves traumatically confronted by pluralisms which annihilated their sacred genealogies. The Middle Kingdom's marginalization to the Far East is emblematic of this process." The fact of China's marginalization in the twentieth-century world is obvious; it is a marginalization that makes us think of it as the "other country."[2] However, Anderson's remarks contain another, equally important point, if only in passing, in the word *traumatically*. The trauma faced by Chinese people in the whole process of "modernization" has yet to be properly understood. The Tiananmen incident confronts us with this fact.

*This essay is drawn, in part, from *Woman and Chinese Modernity: The Politics of Reading between West and East*, by Rey Chow (Minneapolis: University of Minneapolis Press, 1990).

The first point about this trauma is the futility of intellectual discourse at the moment of shock. There is nothing subtle, nothing reflexive, about a government gunning down its own, or for that matter any, people. This experience shocks us out of our assumed categories of thinking. All of a sudden, those of us who are academics cannot see the world as scholars, but rather become journalists. We become suddenly aware of the precarious, provisional nature of our discourse. The unreliability of conventional sources of information, the limitations of our reasoning instruments, the repetitive narratives to which we are subjected—all these raw aspects of our representational machinery suddenly become acute, plunging our perception into crisis.

I heard a feminist ask: "How should we read what is going on in China in terms of gender?" My immediate response to that question was, and is: "We do not, because at the moment of shock Chinese people are degendered and become simply 'Chinese.' " To ask how we can use gender to "read" a political crisis such as the present one is to insist on the universal and timeless sufficiency of an analytical category, and to forget the historicity that accompanies all categorical explanatory power. In her essay "Explanation and Culture: Marginalia," Gayatri Spivak (1987, 105; emphasis in original) writes:

> The will to explain was the symptom of a desire to have a self and a world. . . . the possibility of explanation carries the presupposition of an explainable (even if not fully) universe and an explaining (even if imperfectly) subject. These presuppositions assure our being. Explaining, we exclude the possibility of the *radically* heterogeneous.

Any analytical discourse on the Chinese situation in terms of a single category, when Chinese prodemocracy protesters are being arrested, punished, or killed for having demonstrated peacefully for freedom, is presumptuous. The problem is not how we should read what is going on in China in terms of gender, but rather: what do the events in China tell us about gender as a category, especially as it relates to the so-called Third World? What are gender's limits, where does it work, and where does it not work? How do these events help us recognize the anger often voiced by non-Western women about the singular priority that is given to "woman" by bourgeois liberal feminism? The roots of this anger do not simply lie in the need, neglected by bourgeois liberal feminism's agenda to put the female sex in the forefront of all battles, to *pluralize* the term *woman*. *Women*, often used as remedy for that neglect, leaves most problems of social inequity intact. If the more trendy *women* itself is, at best, an unstable category, it is because, as Denise Riley (1988, 5) tells us, "this instability has a historical foundation." The anger felt by non-Western women is never simply that they have been left out of bourgeois liberal

feminism's account "as women," but, more important, that their experiences as "women" can never be pinned down to the narrowly sexualized
aspect of that category, as "women" versus "men" only. What is often
assumed to be the central transaction between women and culture—wom-
en's heterosexual relation to men—has little relevance to the China crisis.

China Watching

Rather than a purely analytical discourse on the China situation, I
want to raise a set of questions that pertain more closely to us in the U.S.,
where most of us participate in "China watching" as TV audiences and
newspaper readers. China is, in this instance as it has been for the past
several decades, a spectacle for the West. Our condemnation of the military violence in Beijing must go hand in hand with the understanding
that the deaths of the thousands of Chinese people were an overdetermined event. In many respects, the media all over the world perform the
function of urging those protesters on; our cameras lie in wait for the next
"newsworthy" event to unfold before us. When I say "overdetermined,"
therefore, I mean to include the complicity of our technology, which does
much more than enable us to "see."

Since the week of June 11, 1989, for instance, the focus on the China
crisis has shifted to how the Chinese government is controlling the dissemination of the news and how it is, after the military crackdown, instituting the control of thought and speech through propaganda. The
Chinese authorities *are* ruthless in their deployment of camera networks
and other mass communication channels to track down "dissidents." The
crudity of their technologies of indoctrination is transparent: they kill,
and then they lie. But what role do the media play on our side? There
have been instances in which Chinese people cautioned photographers
not to take their picture for fear they would be arrested, and what happens
to them? We see their pictures with their cautioning as "explanation" of
the "China crisis," either in the form of a silent caption (in the newspapers) or in the voiced commentary of our reporters (on television). This
happened even in the same reports that criticized the Chinese government
for issuing telephone numbers so that people could turn others in. Even
though some newscasters now take the trouble to obscure the faces of
the people they interview, in some cases it is too late. Meanwhile, these
newscasts continue to take us to more remote places such as villages,
where they continue to film people and try to make them talk.

To use a familiar narrative from the archives of imperialism, we are
still locked within the political structure of the movie *King Kong* (1933),
with our media always ready to venture out to "make a movie" about
the unknown jungle with its dark, abominable secrets. Much like Director

Denim's film crew, our cameras capture the inhuman monster and present it to us in the "civilized" world as a spectacular sight on display. King Kong was mounted on a rack for a well-dressed theater audience in New York City; China is served to us on the television screen at home.

Describing what she calls "the civilizing power of socialized capital," Spivak (1987, 90) says: "The irreducible search for greater production of surplus-value (dissimulated as, simply, 'productivity') through techno-logical advancement; the corresponding necessity to train a consumer who will need what is produced and thus help realize surplus-value as profit . . . all conspire to 'civilize.' " Recast in the realm of *ideological* production alone, Spivak's remarks explain the frantic simulation of information/knowledge in what I'd call the King Kong syndrome. This is the cross-cultural syndrome in which the "Third World," as the site of the "raw" material that is "monstrosity," is produced for the surplus-value of spectacle, entertainment, and spiritual enrichment for the "First World." The intensive productivity of the Western newsperson leads to the establishment of clear boundaries. Locked behind the bars of our television screens, we become repelled by what is happening "over there," in a way that confirms the customary view, in the U.S. at least, that ideology exists only in the "other" (anti-U.S.) country.

In *King Kong*, the white woman, Ann (Fay Wray), is the point of struggle between the film crew and the "natives." Within her society Ann occupies the position of the underprivileged. Herself the victim of patriarchal oppression (an oppression that includes her being "lifted" into the role of heroine as a result of hunger and thus made part of the profit-making film industry), the white woman becomes the hinge of the narrative of progress, between enlightened instrumental reason and barbarism-lurking-behind-the-Wall. The white woman is what the white man "produces" and what the monster falls for. If her body is, in filmic language, the place of "suture," what it sews together—what it "coheres"—are the white man's production and the monster's destruction.

The "King Kong syndrome" surfaces in the China crisis in the way the "goddess of liberty" is reproduced across Chinese communities as a defiant emblem of what China "lacks": democracy. The first replica of the Goddess of Liberty was constructed at the Beijing Academy of Arts at the height of the Tiananmen demonstrations. After the statue was mowed down with the protesters on the morning of June 4, Chinese groups in Taiwan, Hong Kong, and the U.S. produced other replicas in a concerted effort to attack the Chinese communist government's scandalizing acts. *King Kong* ends with the statement "Beauty killed the Beast." In the China crisis this sounds like a prophecy for the future, and Chinese people in particular, with little intellectual choice of any kind left, feel obligated to condone the statement's prescriptive as well as descriptive meaning.

In the age of electronic and mechanical reproductions, the Chinese government's resort to political repression should make us think not only in terms of their current violence, but of the global roots of that violence, and the similar gestures of repressive *veiling* we have already encountered in other non-Western countries. What the Western media reenact is the whole issue of extraterritoriality that has been present in Sino-Western relations since the mid-nineteenth century. For those who are not familiar with the term, extraterritoriality was one of the many concessions China was forced to grant to foreign powers in the "unequal treaties" signed during the nineteenth and early twentieth centuries. It meant that nationals and subjects of the "treaty powers" were subject to the civil and criminal laws of their own countries and not to Chinese law. Foreigners were thus protected for their undertakings on Chinese soil—against the Chinese.

From the days of England's gunboat diplomacy to the present day, the question of human rights, when it is raised in China in relation to the West, has never been separable from the privilege of extraterritoriality demanded by the Western diplomat, trader, or missionary. If you think of a person such as Ted Koppel or Tom Brokaw standing on the street in Beijing, speaking a language which is not Chinese, condemning the Chinese government, and how fantastic a spectacle *that* is, then the issue of "journalistic freedom" that is presented as the grounds for intrusive filming and reporting becomes much more problematic than what it purports to be. This is not the same as criticizing such "freedom" by endorsing the Chinese government's facile, misleading charge that the West is "meddling with China's internal affairs." What it means is that it forces us to question the presuppositions that underlie such "freedom," revealing it to be *not* a basic existential condition to which all are entitled (though this is the claim that is made) but a network of demands, negotiations, and coercions that are themselves bound by historical determinants constructed on slaughter and bloodshed.

The tragedy of the China crisis lies in the polarization, which is still inscribed in nativist and nationalistic terms (the Chinese vis-à-vis the rest of the world), between an obsolete cultural isolationism, currently supported by military violence and the paternalistic ideology of the governing regime, and a naive, idealistic clamor for democracy "American style," produced from a plethora of discourses ranging from the astrophysicist Fang Lizhi, to workers, intellectuals, and students, and to the overseas communities, all of which converge on the symbolism of the white-woman-as-liberty. This polarization leaves everyone little to choose from, and that is why the emotional and moral stand taken by Chinese "representations" around the globe, myself included, is unanimously supportive of the "white woman" symbolism. Only a united front, oblivious of the differences in class, gender, education, and profession, can cope with the violence experienced as ethnic trauma.

But the polarization between "traditionalism" or what I have called cultural isolationism (represented by the Party official line), on the one hand, and "democracy," on the other, means that extraterritoriality—the exemption from local jurisdiction—becomes itself exempted from the history of its own role, not in the promotion of freedom and rights but in the subjugation of other peoples in the course of colonial conquests. To return to the theme of the production of knowledge as surplus-value: the production of knowledge about the non-West was possible, in the past, because the producers were exempted from local jurisdiction even as they committed crimes on "local territory." Nowadays, instead of guns, the most effective instruments that aid in the production of the "Third World" are the technologies of the media. It is to these technologies—the bodies of the Western journalist and cameraperson, their voices, their images, their equipment, and the "reality" that is broadcast in the U.S. and then "faxed" back to China—that extraterritoriality is extended, and most of all by Chinese communities overseas who must, under the present circumstances, forget the history of extraterritoriality in Sino-Western relations.

The fetish of the white woman is a serious one, even though it is not, unlike some interpretations of *King Kong*, about sex. Here woman is not the heterosexual opposite of man, but the symbol of what China is not/ does not have. In the eyes of many U.S. leftist intellectuals, it is disturbing to see young Chinese students fighting for their cause with this symbolism. Don't they know what atrocities have been committed in the name of liberty and democracy? we ask implicitly or explicitly. For instance, Ronald Reagan's comments on the current Chinese situation, heard during the week of June 11, sound more like an unconscious description of his own foreign policies: "They have something elemental to learn: you cannot massacre an idea; you cannot run tanks on hope. . . ."

And couldn't the Chinese students learn about "democracy" from the way Margaret Thatcher's British government is treating the citizens of Hong Kong? From 1842, when Hong Kong (Island) was, by the Treaty of Nanking, ceded to Britain as a result of the Opium War (which British historians nowadays prefer to call, euphemistically, the "First Anglo-Chinese War"), to the present, when Hong Kong (the British crown colony that includes the Hong Kong Island, the Kowloon Peninsula, and the leased New Territories) is an international city, Britain's policy toward its colonized peoples has remained untouched by history and motivated by pure self-interests. A century and a half ago, self-interests (monetary profit derived from opium, produced in India and sold in China) were justified in terms of Chinese people's desire for opium, in the sense of "they asked for it"; now, self-interests (the need to protect England from being "colonized" by the peoples from its previous and current "dependent territories") are expressed pointblank by members of the British public in the following way: "The thought of three and a half million people coming over to the island of Britain is quite horrifying."[3] Three and a half million is the number of Hong Kong people whose national status is, as their passports specify, "British Dependent Territories citizen."

Such elaborations of the contradictory nature of the claims of democracy remain, as yet, inaccessible to the Chinese who grew up on the Mainland in the past twenty to thirty years. They have been, precisely because of the cultural isolationism implemented by the government at different levels, deprived of the intellectual space that would allow them the kind of critical understanding I am suggesting. An emotional idealism which arises from desperation and which is displaced onto a fetish such as the Goddess of Liberty is the closest they could come to a taste of freedom. There is as yet no room—no intellectual room, no reflexive mobility—to understand the history in which the ideal of "democracy" deconstructs itself in the West. Instead of focusing only on the problematic nature of their fetishizing (and thereby implicitly sneering at their naiveté), it is necessary for us to ask why these students are doing this, what their frustrations are, and what the causes of those frustrations are in their own as well as world history.

Because as intellectuals we do the kind of work that is by necessity reflexive, more likely to have effects in the long run than in the immediate future, responses to these questions can be only preliminary at a moment such as this. And yet, as well, we must respond. The image of the Chinese intellectual I often have in mind is that of a tiny person weighed down with a millstone, much heavier and much older than she is, as she tries to fight her way into the "international" arena where, if only perfunctorily, she can be heard. This millstone is "China." My choice of the feminine pronoun is deliberate. If, as I said, "woman" and "women" become rather pointless categories if they refer only to the dominant sexual transaction of woman-versus-man, then there are other ways in which the oppressed and marginalized status of the "Third World" woman can be instructive. China as a spectacle, as what facilitates the production of surplus-value in the politics of knowledge-as-commodity—this China becomes, in its relation to the West, "woman": in the sense that it is the "Other" onto which the unthinkable, that which breaks the limits of civilized imagination, is projected.

"Woman" in the Other Country

In an event such as the present one, the Chinese woman, who is
forever caught between patriarchy and imperialism, disappears as a matter
of course. Where she appears, she does not appear as "woman" but as
"Chinese"; this is the message we learn from the twenty-three-year-old
student leader Chai Ling. The issues that the figure of the Chinese woman
brings, the issues of gender and sexuality *and* their enmeshment in politics,
are here intercepted and put on hold by the outbreak of military violence—
even though it is precisely these issues that have to be probed in order
for us to get to the roots of violence in patriarchal Chinese culture. What
are the links between what is currently happening and a tradition that
emphasizes order and harmony, but that also consistently crushes the
openness brought to it by intellectuals, students, and young people? Time
and again in the past few decades, when things have just begun to be
open enough for such issues of liberation to come into their own, we see
a crackdown of the kind that immediately requires the postponement of
the consideration of such issues. As a result, Chinese women, like their
counterparts in many other patriarchal "Third World" countries, are required to sacrifice and postpone their needs and their rights again and
again for the greater cause of nationalism and patriotism. As one of the
most oppressed sectors of Chinese society, they get short shrift on both
ends: whenever there is a political crisis, they stop being women; when
the crisis is over and the culture rebuilds itself, they resume their more
traditional roles as wives and mothers as part of the concerted effort to
restore order.

To my mind, it is sexuality and gender, and the challenge to the bases
of traditional authority they bring, which would provide the genuine
means for undoing the violence we witness today. This is because this
violence cannot be understood apart from the long-privileged status that
is conferred upon paternalistic power among the Chinese, be that power
exercised in the home, in channels of education, and in civil as well as
military administration. If this sounds like a contradiction to my opening
remarks, it is because the very efficacy with which we can use gender
and sexuality as categories for historical inquiry is itself historical; this
efficacy is a result of the relative political stability and material well-being
that are available to us as an intellectual community in North America.
The battle *we* fight is thus a different, albeit concurrent, one.

Closer to home, we see how the challenge to authority posed by gender
and sexuality is resisted in a field such as sinology, which is much more
interested in protecting the timeless treasures of the Chinese tradition. In
the practices of sinology we see not the barbaric but the beautiful China,
which occupies a highly revered place among world intellectuals as the

"Other" that satisfies the longing for exotic ancient civilizations. Alternatively, China was also the Other that provided, for Western leftists in the 1960s—precisely at the height of what have since then been revealed as the horrors of the Cultural Revolution—a hopeful different route to communism. Both the specialist and the amateur China admirer have the tendency to attribute to "China" *absolute* differences from the West. In this tendency lies a suppression of thought: if, as historians tirelessly tell us, modern East Asian history is the history of "Westernization," and if "Westernization" is not merely a "theme" but the materiality of daily life for modern Asian peoples, then how could it be possible to insist on the idealist demarcation between "East" and "West" that we still so often encounter?

"This is Chinese" and "this is not Chinese" are modes of description and criticism which we constantly hear, from journalists, to business people, to academic "China specialists." These modes of description and criticism, which are articulated on the presumed certainty of what *is* "Chinese," use the notion "Chinese" as a way to legitimize the authority of tradition and thus exclude the fundamental instability of any ethnic category. The suppression of thought through authoritarianism, even when the "authority" of tradition has become, literally, corrupt, is therefore not limited to the blatant policies of the Chinese communist government, although at this point that government is making a spectacle of what is a long process of cultural trauma and collapse. When we move our attention away from the short-term brutality, which we must remember and condemn, we will see that repressive politics is a general problem pertaining to (the understanding of) modern China as a part of the "Third World," a problem whose roots cannot be confined to a single incident.

If the immediate cases of military violence are translatable into the paradigm of "King Kong breaks loose," then the problems posed by sinology and China studies find a revealing analysis in a more recent film, *Gorillas in the Mist* (1988).[4] In many ways, *Gorillas* is the antipode to *King Kong:* whereas in the latter movie we see the "Other" world depicted as being uncivilized, a condition that leads to its death, in the former we see the good and gentle nature of the gorillas in contrast to the brutality of those who hunt them down for profit. Thanks to the pioneering work of primatologists such as Dian Fossey, the film's ending credits tell us, this "Other" world is allowed to live. Mediating between the civilized and uncivilized worlds is once again the white woman, whose bravery and foolhardiness "create" the story. This time, instead of King Kong holding a screaming Ann in his gigantic paw, we see the Dian Fossey character (Sigourney Weaver) responding to Nature's call and holding hands with the gorillas. Instead of the gorilla, it is the white woman who is killed. The destruction of King Kong affirms civilization; the white woman in *Gorillas* is seen to have "gone off the deep end" in her battle against civilization, a battle which results in her mysterious death.

In the present context, I propose to recast *Gorillas* in the logic of Edward Said's argument about "Orientalism," even though that logic may appear rigid and predictable at times. What the Orientalism argument enables us to see is this: the white female primatologist, like the great Orientalists, knows the language of the "natives" and speaks to/of/on behalf of them with great sympathy. But in her doing so, the "native culture" also becomes her possession, the site of her spiritual war against the "home" that is the Western world. We are thus confronted with what is perhaps the ugliest double bind in the history of imperialism: while the kind, personal intent behind many a missionary exploration of the "Other" world must be recognized—as a benign humanism extended pluralistically across not only nations and cultures but species—such explorations are implicated in colonialism and neocolonialism in their romantic insistence that the "wild" stay "alive" in their original, "natural" habitat. This double bind is, I believe, the thorniest issue that our progressive discourses, in dealing with the "others" as part of a self-consciousness–raising program, have yet to acknowledge fully.

China Studies and the Problem of Westernization

Where do these ape narratives lead us with regard to modern China and Chinese women? "Letting the natives live where they belong," transcribed into a field such as sinology and China studies, becomes another way of reaffirming the authority of the Chinese tradition to the exclusion of other, "non-Chinese" modes of inquiry. Who gets to defend that authority? Where does it leave the "native"? The answers to this question form the remaining part of my argument, which I shall introduce with the help of a personal scenario.

Since one of my primary areas of research is modern Chinese literature, I often meet sinologists and China historians, some male and some female, who ask me this question directly or indirectly: "Why are you using Western theory on Chinese literature?" Since I happen to work with questions of femininity in modern Chinese literature, I am also asked from time to time, "Why are you using Western feminist theory on Chinese women?"

The contradictions about modern China as a site of the production of knowledge-as-surplus-value are revealingly demonstrated in these simple interrogations. The questions put to me are clearly based on sets of oppositions: the West versus the non-West; dominant versus "other" national or ethnic traditions; dominant theories of women versus "other" women; the subjectivities of "Western" versus "non-Western" feminist critics. Although the point that we must not be trapped within dichotomies is a familiar one, many of us, especially those who experience racial, class, or gendered dichotomies from the unprivileged side, are still within the power of dichotomization as an epistemological weapon. The above kind of interrogation slaps me in the face with the force of a nativist moralism, precisely through a hierarchical dichotomy between West and East that enables my interrogators to disapprove of my "complicity" with the West. Such disapproval arises, of course, from a general context in which the criticism of the West has become mandatory. However, where does this general critical imperative leave those ethnic peoples whose entry into culture is, precisely because of the history of Western imperialism, already "Westernized"? For someone with my educational background, which is British colonial and American, the moralistic charge of my being "too Westernized" is devastating; it signals an attempt on the part of those who are specialists in "my" culture to demolish the only premises on which I can speak.

This personal scenario brings to the fore the cultural predicament that faces all of those who have to negotiate their way into dominant channels of representation. As my earlier image of the Chinese intellectual suggests, the millstone around our necks—"China" and the "Chinese tradition"— is huge and crippling; as it weighs us down it also gives shape to our movements and gestures. Over a long period of time the millstone becomes, for many, their only attitude toward the world. On the other hand, the Chinese intellectual knows that she must fight her way into the world precisely because she is already, in one way or another, "Westernized." In what ways can she speak?

Once again, I pose the question in the feminine form because I think in the shifting boundaries implied by the term *Chinese women* lie the clues to the *general* stakes that are involved for Westernized Chinese intellectuals entering the international "field." The instabilities of the categories "Chinese" and "women" are multiplied by their juxtaposition, allowing for questions such as: Who are Chinese women? What do they tell us about "China"? What do they tell us about "woman" and "women"? What does it mean when China historians study them as one entity? What are the relations between "Chinese women" and "China studies"?

Basically, how have the stories of Chinese women been told "internationally"? I would address this question in the area I know best—academia. In the wake of interests of "women" across the disciplines, investigations of Chinese women are quickly establishing themselves, through what Chandra Mohanty ("Under Western Eyes," this volume) calls "the third world difference"—"that stable, ahistorical something that apparently oppresses most if not all the women in these countries"—as a viable area of research among historians, anthropologists, sociologists, and film critics, as well as sinologists who specialize in the classical texts.[5] The objects of such investigations vary from female peasants in remote Chinese villages to the heroines of premodern as well as modern Chinese political history, to the "feminine turn of rhetoric" in literary texts, and to female mystics in less well researched parts of prominent dynasties. At the university where I teach this year, for instance, a couple of other junior faculty and I were put in charge of a conference sponsored by the Department of East Asian Studies when the authorities decided it was time we had a conference "on women." It is obvious that in the eyes of academic administrators, whose roles in the production and circulation of "knowledge" cannot be slighted even though many of them have no interest in scholarship, "women" is now a profitable theme, on a par with such others as "calligraphy," "time," or "water" (in the particular department concerned). But more alarming is, once again, a homologous situation between "woman"–"women" and "First World"–"Third World": if "woman" is now a category of inquiry in well-established disciplines, then the "other woman" is attached to well-established methodologies of investigation in the so-called non-Western fields.

To sinology and the mammoth U.S. enterprise of "Chinese history," the emergence of "Chinese women" is now a new addition which often brings with it the emphases of the "Chinese tradition": the understanding of Chinese women must, it is implied, take place within the parameters of Chinese texts and Chinese history. Returning the natives to their natural habitat, perhaps? We are faced here not with the blatant imperialistic acts of capture and murder that describe the King Kong syndrome, but with the lofty spiritual ideal, typified by *Gorillas in the Mist*, of "letting the Other live in their place and my love."

What can be said about the complex meanings that cluster around the "white woman" here? "Letting the Other live," when it is cast in terms of the relation between white female sinologists/China historians and Chinese women, calls forth, first of all, the questions that have been raised about the paradigmatic relation between white and nonwhite women as "investigator" and "investigatee." This relation is often foregrounded by nonwhite women's indignation at the universalism of "womanhood" as suggested by dominant feminist discourses. In an attempt to raise women's status in the West, liberal feminism, like all alternative ideologies which seek to overthrow those previous to them, spoke on behalf of all women. The error of this universalism lies in the fact that it disguises a more fundamental relation between white and nonwhite women, which is mediated by legacies of a very different kind. After all, "beyond sisterhood there are still racism, colonialism and imperialism!" (Mohanty, this volume).

Vis-à-vis the non-Western woman, the white woman occupies the position, with the white man, as investigator with "the freedom to speak." This relation, rather than the one that says "we are all women," is particularly evident in disciplines such as anthropology and ethnography. What has become untenable is the way Western feminism imposes its own interests and methodologies on those who do not inhabit the same sociohistorical spaces, thus reducing the latter to a state of reified silence and otherness. This criticism informs Audre Lorde's (1984) famous "Open Letter to Mary Daly." A similar kind of criticism is voiced by Aihwa Ong (1988, 80), who puts it this way: "when feminists look overseas, they frequently seek to establish *their* authority on the backs of non-Western women, determining for them the meanings and goals of their lives" (emphasis in original).

In China studies, where the understanding of China is institutionally organized around notions such as "tradition" and "modernity," the spaces allocated to Chinese women fall into two large categories. First, among historians and social scientists, Chinese women figure prominently in "case studies." Ong (1988, 85) puts it succinctly:

> By portraying women in non-Western societies as identical and interchangeable, and more exploited than women in the dominant capitalist societies, liberal and socialist feminists alike encode a belief in their own cultural superiority. . . . For instance, studies on women in post-1949 China inevitably discuss how they are doubly exploited by the peasant family and by socialist patriarchy, reflecting the more immediate concerns of American socialist feminists than perhaps of Chinese women themselves. By using China as a "case study" of the socialist experiment with women's liberation, these works are part of a whole network of Western academic and policy-making discourses on the backwardness of the non-Western, non-modern world.

The case study belongs to the rhetoric of instrumental reason. Unlike the sinologist, the social scientist may not be fluent in the language, but then her project is not exactly that of becoming "submissive" to Chinese culture (in the way Fossey learned to be "submissive" to the gorillas). Rather, it is to use Chinese women—and the more remote they are from Western urban civilization, the better—for the production of the types of explanations that are intelligible (*valuable*) to feminism in the West, including, in particular, those types that extend pluralism to "woman" through "race" and "class." To be sure, documentary films such as *Small Happiness* (by Carma Hinton, who speaks Chinese fluently) help push Chinese women into the international field where they would be recognized as victims. The question is: how would Chinese women be recognized beyond the victim status? What would a film by Chinese women about American female China scholars be like?

As Ong goes on to suggest about non-Western women in general, the second space in which Chinese women are allowed to appear is—to borrow from Johannes Fabian's concept of "coevalness"[6]—of an absolute "other time." This is the time of classical history and literature, which renders Chinese women *speechless* even as they offer innumerable enticements to scholarly study. I have attended lectures by women sinologists who research well-known classical Chinese texts for their themes on women and who recall with great relish the details of those texts as if they were the details of an exotic jungle. In this case, like a Fossey, the sinologist "submits" to the language of the gorillas. The point, however, is this: once Chinese women, like Chinese texts, are confined to the "culture garden" (Fabian 1983, 47) that is "their past," everything that is said about them can be labeled "different" in an absolute sense: they are "Chinese" and hence cannot and should not be touched by Western methodologies.

These two main spaces, the case study and the culture garden, that are available to Chinese women follow from the institutional division of Chinese studies into the modern and the traditional. This division is clearly felt in the incompatibility between those who are immersed in the labyrinths of classical textual hermeneutics and those who are propelled by the post-Enlightenment goals of "knowing" (in this case, a backward nation) with rational tools. The problem of modernity, because it is always approached by way of such taxonomic divisions, remains caught in them. Subsequently, Chinese people, too, are classified according to their proximity to tradition or to modernity. Those from Mainland China are, implicitly, more "authentic," while those from Taiwan and especially those from Hong Kong are "contaminated." Even as it is inextricable from the daily experience of Asian peoples, the materiality of Westernization as an irreducible part of Asian modern self-consciousness remains unrecognized and inarticulate in the paradigms set down by China specialists.

And yet it is precisely the materiality of this self-consciousness which would provide the clues to the protests against the spectacular violence that we see breaking out in China today. What are the sources of such violence? Great dangers lie ahead if we simply equate it with the present regime. What are some of the justifications used by the ultra-conservative Party leaders at this point?—that these are China's "internal" affairs; that the students are not "patriotic" or "loyal" to the Party; that the soldiers were trying to restore "order" in Beijing. These outrageous distortions of fact are, ideologically, in keeping with the reverence for established authority and for "tradition" that is required in all Chinese learning. Violence here is the other side of "culture"; it is what underlies the cherished notion of civilization in which China is more than heavily invested. Dealing with this violence means that a different kind of self-consciousness, one that refuses to seek legitimation in terms of facile unities or taxonomic divisions, has to be sought for long-term political intervention. This consciousness is, to quote Teresa de Lauretis, the "consciousness of ideological complicity." De Lauretis (1988, 136) defines it in specific relation to the feminist subject:

> The feminist subject, which was initially defined purely by its status as colonized subject or victim of oppression, becomes redefined as much less pure— and *not unified* or *simply divided* between positions of masculinity and femininity, but *multiply organized* across positionalities along several axes and across mutually contradictory discourses and practices.

As more and more non-Western women participate in feminist discourses, this "consciousness of ideological complicity" is bound to become an unavoidable political as well as theoretical issue, forcing upon each of us the following questions: How do I speak? In what capacity and with whose proxy? Therefore, while it is important that we continue to acknowledge the necessity of the kind of work that elaborates the unequal relationship between Western feminism and non-Western women along the lines of "investigator versus investigatee," it is also crucial that we recognize the emergence of a different, still marginalized, mode of articulation—that of the non-Western, but Westernized, feminist subject, whose existence epitomizes the stakes involved in this "complicity." A productive use of feminism in the non-Western context would imply feminism's capacity to respond to the ways these "other" feminist subjects speak.

Chinese Women and/as the Subject of Feminism

Because it is "multiply organized," the space of the Westernized, non-Western feminist subject is an elusive one and as such always runs the risk of being elided. The China crisis shows us such an elision: at the moment of political shock, Chinese women become degendered, and join everyone else as "Chinese." In the long run, however, when the roots of violence can be probed more leisurely and analytically, the problems *embodied* by Chinese women with regard to the Chinese tradition and China scholarship in the West would serve as focal points through which the reverence for authority must be attacked. In a field where such reverence is, in the foreseeable future at least, clearly immovable, and where investments in heritage are made with strong patriarchal emphases, the emergence of Chinese women as feminist subjects (rather than as objects of study) is difficult. This is because feminist self-consciousness, even when it is recognized, easily becomes the latest support for "heritage" and "tradition."

Here the work of Ding Ling (1904–1986) is instructive. What I would like to point out, as an elaboration of my argument about the relation between Western feminism and non-Western women as it surfaces in China studies, are some of the ways Ding Ling's works are typically read. These readings are, to my mind, problematic because, in a way that reflects the larger problems in the field, they partake of the specular political structures of "othering" that I have been describing—structures that block the emergence of the "other women" as historical subjects.

In its different stages, Ding Ling's writing career exemplifies contrasts that are portrayed in this description of the difference *between white and nonwhite women*: "Verisimilitude, realism, positive images are the demands that women of color make of their own writing as critical and political practice; white women demand instead simulation, textual performances, double displacements" (de Lauretis 1986, 17). Although Ding Ling is one of the most well known modern Chinese women writers, her works from the twenties and early thirties are generally considered to be immature; they revolve around themes of sexuality and femininity, and the "female subjectivity" that is evident in them is usually fraught with contradictions, illusions, and a great sense of despair. Her later works, notably *The Sun Rises over the Sanggan River* (1948) and those produced after her punishment and imprisonment during the Cultural Revolution, are much more "patriotic," suggesting a conscious repudiation of the interests in her more youthful period through a devotion to the Chinese tradition and the Chinese people.

This construction of Ding Ling's development as a writer is the one most favored by Chinese communist critics, but it is also popular among Ding Ling scholars in the West, especially in the U.S. The gist of it is: Ding Ling, as a woman writer, turned from the contamination of being "white" to the purity of being colored; from being concerned with "performance" in her youthful years, she became concerned with "realism" the way a Chinese (colored) woman writer *should be*.

What is interesting is that, when American China scholars who are interested in "women" study modern Chinese literature, it is often to a Chinese woman writer such as Ding Ling that they turn, in order to gauge their measurements of sexuality and gender in what they emphasize as a "non-Western" culture. Ding Ling passes the tests of these scholars with flying colors. The trajectory of her career fits extremely well with the essentializing tendencies that already dominate the field of China studies. Her increasingly patriotic leanings make it possible for some to regard her work in terms of so-called Chinese feminism.

The nationalizing, or *nativizing*, of feminism in this case springs from a need to decenter the West, and as such it is a type of critique of the hegemony of Western discourse. However, what does it mean when non-

Chinese scholars insist on the "Chinese-ness" of Chinese texts and writers, and with that, the implied judgment of what is "not Chinese"? If nativism per se is problematic, then a nativism prescribed by the non-Chinese scholar on the "native" is even more so. History books tell us that modernization in Asia means "Westernization." Why is it that, if Chinese texts and writers exhibit "symptoms" (as they well should) of having been affected/infected, they are by and large viewed with concern, suspicion, and disapproval?

As in the interrogation of my work that I described earlier, what is left out is precisely the material reality of a Westernized subjectivity that is indelibly present in the non-Western intellectual's entrance into the world. Ding Ling's development, like that of all writers, especially women writers, in "Third World" countries, was complex. I do not think it can in any way be evaluated teleologically, in terms of progress from "immaturity" to "maturity," from being "Westernized" to being "Chinese." The "return" to her traditional origins in her later years has to be understood in terms other than those of idealist nativism. (This point necessitates a close reading of her works and can be substantiated only elsewhere.) It is highly problematic, then, when feminist China scholars simply build on a nationalistic teleological construction by adding to it the label of "feminism." Conversely, the attempt to deconstruct the hegemony of patriarchal discourses through feminism is itself foreclosed by the emphasis on "Chinese" as a mark of absolute difference.

Paradoxically, then, the "authority" that feminism exercises on non-white women as they look overseas is evident even when these other women are given their "own" national and ethnic identity in the manner I just described. The introduction of sinocentrism—what I in the early part of this essay described as cultural isolationism—as a way to oppose the West is far from being the solution to the problems created by Western centrism itself. The attempts to champion a "Chinese feminism" on the part of some feminist China scholars do not really create avenues for modern Chinese women to come forth on their own terms, but rather compound deep-rooted patriarchal thinking to which "woman" is now added as the latest proof of, once again, the continuity and persistence of a pure indigenous "tradition." For Chinese women who go through the most mundane parts of their lives with the knowledge that it is precisely this notion of an "originary" Chinese tradition to which they cannot cling, the advocacy of a "Chinese feminism" in the nativist sense is exclusionary in nature; what it excludes are their lived relations to Westernization and the role played by these relations, however contradictory, in their subject-positions.

The idealism of those in the West who specialize in "Third World" cultures, and the charges they lay against members of those cultures for being "too Westernized" are the twin aspects of the "cultural predicament" that, as I suggest, confronts the Westernized feminist critic. Because it is irreversible, this predicament is oppressive. But perhaps this is precisely where feminism can be best used in a non-Western context. In the words of Kamala Visweswaran (1988, 29), the fundamental reconstitutive value of feminism and the potential of a feminist ethnography which has yet to be expressed consist in that which "locates the self in the experience of oppression in order to liberate it."

The development of any theory typically requires a period in which the space which that theory marks off for its own emergence is elaborated to the point at which it must give way to its own critique. Western feminism, I think, is at such a point. Its continued relevance to other oppressed groups would depend on its understanding of its own historicity: having derived much of its strength and sophistication from the basis of women's experiences of oppression, it needs to ask itself how it can open up similar avenues for others without assuming the "master discourse" position. These others cannot be responded to simply with words such as *pluralism* and *cosmopolitanism*. Feminism needs to face up to its own history in the West. It belongs to a juncture in time when Western thought's efforts at overcoming itself are still, relatively speaking, supported by a high level of material well-being, intellectual freedom, and personal mobility. This historical juncture at which feminism has come to the fore in every facet of Western knowledge is not an accidental one. Even though it often, if not always, speaks the language of oppression and victimization, Western feminism owes its support to the existence of other populations who continue to experience daily exclusions of various kinds, many of which are performed at territorial borders. It is the clear demarcation of such borders which allows us the comfort and security in which to theorize the notion of "exclusion" itself. While some of us enjoy this comfort and security through the accident of birth, others, like myself, do so through "naturalization," which often means that we speak with "native fluency" our oppressor's language. The task of the Westernized feminist is not to unlearn that language but to ask that her accented interventions be understood properly, not as an excuse for nativism but as the demand, put to feminism, for "a willingness, at times, to shred this 'women' to bits" (Riley 1988, 114)—so that other histories can enter.

To bring in the non-Western woman and feminist in the manner I have done is to append a nexus of problems which is not recognizable in the immediate crisis in China. As such, this essay is asymmetrical; my end does not fit my beginning. But "other women" speak without good manners as a rule. For them, articulation means the crude assembling of what is presently and urgently at hand, in order to stockpile provisions for the longer fight.

NOTES

1. During this time I was to deliver a paper at a conference called "Nationalisms and Sexualities" at Harvard University. I had planned to discuss work of the controversial modern Chinese writer Yu Dafu. Watching the events in China unfold in the U.S. media, I felt more and more that, at that moment in Chinese history, a talk devoted to "sexuality" was out of place. I therefore decided to speak about the current events. This essay is, in part, the talk I gave.

2. "The Other Country" was the title of the panel on which I was speaking.

3. At a teleconference via satellite entitled "Hong Kong: A Matter of Honor?", held between Hong Kong and England during June 1989.

4. I am grateful to Giuliana Menozzi's Ph.D. dissertation, "Aspects of the Discourse of Wildness within Modernity" (Comparative Literature, University of Minnesota, 1989). Menozzi's juxtaposition of *King Kong* and *Gorillas in the Mist* alerts me to the Bakhtinian dialogic nature of their making, even though I am using that "dialogue" for a different purpose.

5. Readers who are interested in having a general view of the critical treatment of Chinese women as historical figures, fictional characters, or authors may consult the following sources: Margery Wolf and Roxanne Witke, eds., *Women in Chinese Society* (Stanford: Stanford University Press, 1975); Marilyn B. Young, ed., *Women in China: Studies in Social Change and Feminism* (Ann Arbor: Center for Chinese Studies, The University of Michigan, 1973); Richard W. Guisso and Stanley Johannesen, eds., *Women in China: Current Directions in Historical Scholarship* (Youngstown: Philo Press, 1981); Angela Jung Palandri, ed., *Women Writers of Twentieth-Century China* (Asian Studies Program, University of Oregon, 1982); Anna Gerstlacher, Ruth Keen, Wolfgang Kubin, Margit Miosga, and Jenny Schon, eds., *Women and Literature in China* (Bochum: Studienverlag Brockmeyer, 1985). Significant recent coverage of Chinese women in journals includes *Modern Chinese Literature*, Fall 1988; *Camera Obscura*, no. 18; *Wide Angle* 11, no. 2. This, of course is by no means an exhaustive list.

6. See Fabian, *Time and the Other: How Anthropology Makes Its Object* (New York: Columbia University Press, 1983).

REFERENCES

Anderson, Benedict. 1983. *Imagined Communities: Reflections on the Spread of Nationalism.* London: Verso and New Left Books.
Camera Obscura, no. 18.
de Lauretis, Teresa. 1986. "Feminist Studies/Critical Studies: Issues, Terms, and Contexts." In *Feminist Studies/Critical Studies.* Bloomington: Indiana University Press. 1–19.
————. 1988. "Displacing Hegemonic Discourses: Reflections on Feminist Theory in the 1980s." *Inscriptions,* no. 3/4:127–41.
Fabian, Johannes. 1983. *Time and the Other: How Anthropology Makes Its Object.* New York: Columbia University Press.
Gerstlacher, Anna, Ruth Keen, Wolfgang Kubin, Margit Miosga, and Jenny Schon, eds. 1985. *Women and Literature in China.* Bochum: Studienverlag Brockmeyer.
Guisso, Richard W., and Johannesen, Stanley, eds. 1981. *Women in China: Current Directions in Historical Scholarship.* Youngstown: Philo Press.

Lorde, Audre. 1984. *Sister Outsider: Essays and Speeches.* Trumansburg, N.Y.: The Crossing Press.

Menozzi, Giuliana. 1989. "Aspects of the Discourse of Wildness within Modernity." Ph.D. dissertation, Comparative Literature, University of Minnesota.

Modern Chinese Literature. Fall 1988.

Mohanty, Chandra Talpade. "Under Western Eyes: Feminist Scholarship and Colonial Discourses." In this volume.

Ong, Aihwa. 1988. "Colonialism and Modernity: Feminist Re-presentations of Women in Non-Western Societies." *Inscriptions,* no. 3/4:79–93.

Palandri, Angela Jung, ed. 1982. *Women Writers of Twentieth-Century China.* Asian Studies Program, University of Oregon.

Riley, Denise. 1988. *"Am I That Name?: Feminism and the Category of "Women" in History.* Minneapolis: University of Minnesota Press.

Spivak, Gayatri. 1987. *In Other Worlds: Essays in Cultural Politics.* New York and London: Methuen.

Visweswaran, Kamala. 1988. "Defining Feminist Ethnography." *Inscriptions,* no. 3/4:27–44.

Wide Angle 11, no. 2.

Wolf, Margery, and Roxanne Witke, eds. 1975. *Women in Chinese Society.* Stanford: Stanford University Press.

Young, Marilyn B., ed. 1973. *Women in China: Studies in Social Change and Feminism.* Ann Arbor: Center for Chinese Studies, The University of Michigan.

THE TRUTH
THAT NEVER
HURTS

Black Lesbians in Fiction in the 1980s*

Barbara Smith

In 1977 when I wrote "Toward a Black Feminist Criticism," I wanted to accomplish several goals. The first was simply to point out that Black women writers existed, a fact generally ignored by white male, Black male, and white female readers, teachers, and critics. Another desire was to encourage Black feminist criticism of these writers' work, that is, analyses that acknowledged the reality of sexual oppression in the lives of Black women. Probably most urgently, I wanted to illuminate the existence of Black lesbian writers and to show how homophobia ensured that we were even more likely to be ignored or attacked than Black women writers generally.

In 1985 the situation of Black women writers is considerably different from what it was in 1977. Relatively speaking, Black women's literature is much more recognized, even at times by the white male literary establishment. There are a growing number of Black women critics who rely upon various Black feminist critical approaches to studying the literature. There has been a marked increase in the number of Black women

*This essay previously appeared in *Wild Women in the Whirlwind: The Afra-American Women's Literary Renaissance,* edited by Joanne Braxton and Andree Nicola-McLaughlin (N.J.: Rutgers University Press, 1989).

who are willing to acknowledge that they are feminists, including some who write literary criticism. Not surprisingly, Black feminist activism and organizing have greatly expanded, a precondition which I cited in 1977 for the growth of Black feminist criticism. More writing by Black lesbians is available, and there has even been some positive response to this writing from nonlesbian Black readers and critics. The general conditions under which Black women critics and writers work have improved. The personal isolation we face and the ignorance and hostility with which our work is met have diminished in some quarters, but have by no means disappeared.

One of the most positive changes is that a body of consciously Black feminist writing and writing by other feminists of color actually exists. The publication of a number of anthologies has greatly increased the breadth of writing available by feminists of color. These include *Conditions: Five, the Black Women's Issue* (1979); *This Bridge Called My Back: Writings by Radical Women of Color* (1981); *All the Women Are White, All the Blacks Are Men, but Some of Us Are Brave: Black Women's Studies* (1982); *A Gathering of Spirit: North American Indian Women's Issues* (1983); *Cuentos: Stories by Latinas* (1983); *Home Girls: A Black Feminist Anthology* (1983); *Bearing Witness/Sobreviviendo: An Anthology of Native American/Latina Art and Literature* (1984); and *Gathering Ground: New Writing and Art by Northwest Women of Color* (1984). First books by individual authors have also appeared, such as *Claiming an Identity They Taught Me to Despise* (1980) and *Abeng* (1984) by Michelle Cliff; *Narratives: Poems in the Tradition of Black Women* (1982) by Cheryl Clarke; *For Nights Like This One* (1983) by Becky Birtha; *Loving in the War Years: Lo Que Nunca Paso Por Sus Labios* (1983) by Cherríe Moraga; *The Words of a Woman Who Breathes Fire* (1983) by Kitty Tsui; and *Mohawk Trail* (1985) by Beth Brant (*Degonwadonti*). Scholarly works provide extremely useful analytical frameworks, for example, *Common Differences: Conflicts in Black and White Feminist Perspectives* (1981) by Gloria I. Joseph and Jill Lewis; *Black Women Writers at Work* (1983), edited by Claudia Tate; *When and Where I Enter: The Impact of Black Women on Race and Sex in America* (1984) by Paula Giddings; and *Black Feminist Criticism: Perspectives on Black Women Writers* (1985) by Barbara Christian.

Significantly, however, "small" or independent, primarily women's presses published all but the last four titles cited, and almost all the authors and editors of these alternative-press books (although not all of the contributors to the anthologies) are lesbians. In his essay "The Sexual Mountain and Black Women Writers," critic Calvin Hernton (1985, 7) writes,

> The declared and lesbian black feminist writers are pioneering a black feminist criticism. This is not to take away from other writers. All are blazing new

trails. But especially the declared feminists and lesbian feminists—Barbara Smith, Ann Shockley, Cheryl Clarke, Wilmette Brown, and the rest—are at the forefront of the critics, scholars, intellectuals, and ideologues of our time.

Yet Hernton points out that these writers are "subpopular," published as they are by nonmainstream presses. In contrast, nonlesbian Black women writers have been published by trade publishers and are able to reach, as Hernton explains, a "wider popular audience."

In an excellent essay, "No More Buried Lives: The Theme of Lesbianism in Audre Lorde's *Zami*, Gloria Naylor's *The Women of Brewster Place*, Ntozake Shange's *Sassafras, Cypress and Indigo*, and Alice Walker's *The Color Purple*," critic Barbara Christian (1986, 188) makes a similar observation. She writes:

> Lesbian life, characters, language, values are *at present* and *to some extent* becoming respectable in American literature, partly because of the pressure of women-centered communities, partly because publishers are intensely aware of marketing trends. . . . I say, *to some extent*, because despite the fact that Walker received the Pulitzer for *The Color Purple* and Naylor the American Book Award for *The Women of Brewster Place*, I doubt if *Home Girls*, an anthology of black feminist and lesbian writing that was published by Kitchen Table Press, would have been published by a mainstream publishing company.

Significantly, Christian says that "lesbian life, characters, language, values" are receiving qualified attention and respectability, but lesbian writers themselves are not. No doubt this is why she suspects that no trade publisher would publish *Home Girls*, which contains work by women who write openly as lesbians and which defines lesbianism politically as well as literarily.

The fact that there is such a clear-cut difference in publishing options for out Black lesbian writers (who are published solely by independent presses) and for nonlesbian and closeted Black women writers (who have access to both trade and alternative publishers) indicates what has *not* changed since 1977. It also introduces the focus of this essay.[1] I am concerned with exploring the treatment of Black lesbian writing and Black lesbian themes in the context of Black feminist writing and criticism.

Today, not only are more works by and about Black women's writing available, but a body of specifically Black feminist writing exists. Although both the general category of Black women's literature and the specific category of Black feminist literature can be appropriately analyzed from a Black feminist critical perspective, explicitly Black feminist literature has a unique set of characteristics and emphases which distinguish it from other work. Black feminist writing provides an incisive critical perspective on sexual political issues which affect Black women—for example, the issue of sexual violence. It generally depicts the significance of Black women's relationships with each other as a primary source of support. Black feminist writing may also be classified as such because the author identifies herself as a feminist and has a demonstrated commitment to women's issues and related political concerns. An openness in discussing lesbian subject matter is perhaps the most obvious earmark of Black feminist writing, and not because feminism and lesbianism are interchangeable, which of course they are not.

For historical, political, and ideological reasons, a writer's consciousness about lesbianism bears a direct relationship to her consciousness about feminism. It was in the context of the second wave of the contemporary feminist movement, influenced by the simultaneous development of an autonomous gay liberation movement, that the political content of lesbianism and lesbian oppression began to be analyzed and defined. The women's liberation movement was the political setting in which antilesbian attitudes and actions were initially challenged in the late 1960s and early 1970s and where at least in theory, but more often in fact, homophobia was designated unacceptable, at least in the movement's more progressive sectors.

Barbara Christian (1986, 199–200) also makes the connection between feminist consciousness and a willingness to address lesbian themes in literature. She writes:

> Some of the important contributions that the emergence of the lesbian theme has made to Afro-American women's literature are: the breaking of stereotypes so that black lesbians are clearly seen as *women*, the exposure of homophobia in the black community, and an exploration of how homophobia is related to the struggle of all women to be all that they can be—in other words to feminism.

> That is not to say that Afro-American women's literature has not always included a feminist perspective. The literature of the seventies, for example, certainly explored the relationship between sexism and racism and has been at the forefront of the development of feminist ideas. One natural outcome of this exploration is the lesbian theme, for society's attack on lesbians is the cutting edge of the anti-feminist definition of women.

Black feminist writers, whether lesbian or nonlesbian, have been aware of and influenced by the movement's exploring of, struggling over, and organizing around lesbian identity and issues. They would be much more likely to take Black lesbian experience seriously and perhaps to explore Black lesbian themes in their writing, in contrast with authors who either have not been involved in the women's movement or are antifeminist. For example, in her very positive review of *Conditions: Five, the Black*

Women's Issue, originally published in *Ms.* magazine in 1980, Alice Walker (1984, 288-89) writes:

> Like black men and women who refused to be the exceptional "pet" Negro for whites, and who instead said they were "niggers" too (the original "crime" of "niggers" and lesbians is that they prefer themselves), perhaps black women writers and non-writers should say, simply, whenever black lesbians are being put down, held up, messed over, and generally told their lives should not be encouraged, *We are all lesbians.* For surely it is better to be thought a lesbian, and to say and write your life exactly as you experience it, than to be a token "pet" black woman for those whose contempt for our autonomous existence makes them a menace to human life.

Walker's support of her lesbian sisters in real life is not unrelated to her ability to write fiction about Black women who are lovers, as in *The Color Purple.* Her feminist consciousness undoubtedly influenced the positiveness of her portrayal. In contrast, an author such as Gayle Jones, who has not been associated with or seemingly influenced by the feminist movement, has portrayed lesbians quite negatively.[2]

Just as surely as a Black woman writer's relationship to feminism affects the themes she might choose to write about, a Black woman critic's relationship to feminism determines the kind of criticism she is willing and able to do. The fact that critics are usually also academics, however, has often affected Black women critics' approach to feminist issues. If a Black woman scholar's only connection to women's issues is via women's studies, as presented by white women academics, most of whom are not activists, her access to movement analyses and practice will be limited or nonexistent. I believe that the most accurate and developed theory, including literary theory, comes from practice, from the experience of activism. This relationship between theory and practice is crucial when inherently political subject matter, such as the condition of women as depicted in a writer's work, is being discussed. I do not believe it is possible to arrive at fully developed and useful Black feminist criticism by merely reading about feminism. Of course every Black woman has her own experiences of sexual political dynamics and oppression to draw upon, and referring to these experiences should be an important resource in shaping her analyses of a literary work. However, studying feminist texts and drawing only upon one's *individual* experiences of sexism are insufficient.

I remember the point in my own experience when I no longer was involved on a regular basis in organizations such as the Boston Committee to End Sterilization Abuse and the Abortion Action Coalition. I was very aware that my lack of involvement affected my thinking and writing *overall.* Certain perceptions were simply unavailable to me because I no longer was doing that particular kind of ongoing work. And I am referring to missing something much deeper than access to specific information about sterilization and reproductive rights. Activism has spurred me to write the kinds of theory and criticism I have written and has provided the experiences and insights that have shaped the perceptions in my work. Many examples of this vital relationship between activism and theory exist in the work of thinkers such as Ida B. Wells-Barnett, W. E. B. Du Bois, Lillian Smith, Lorraine Hansberry, Frantz Fanon, Barbara Deming, Paolo Freire, and Angela Davis.

A critic's involvement or lack of involvement in activism, specifically in the context of the feminist movement, is often signally revealed by the approach she takes to lesbianism. If a woman has worked in organizations where lesbian issues were raised, where homophobia was unacceptable and struggled with, and where she had the opportunity to meet and work with a variety of lesbians, her relationship to lesbians and to her own homophobia will undoubtedly be affected. The types of political organizations in which such dialogue occurs are not, of course, exclusively lesbian and may focus upon a range of issues, such as women in prison, sterilization abuse, reproductive freedom, health care, domestic violence, and sexual assault.

Black feminist critics who are lesbians can usually be counted upon to approach Black women's and Black lesbian writing nonhomophobically. Nonlesbian Black feminist critics are not as dependable in this regard. I even question at times designating Black women—critics and noncritics alike—as feminist who are actively homophobic in what they write, say, or do, or who are passively homophobic because they ignore lesbian existence entirely.[3] Yet such critics are obviously capable of analyzing other sexual and political implications of the literature they scrutinize. Political definitions, particularly of feminism, can be difficult to pin down. The one upon which I generally rely states: "Feminism is the political theory and practice that struggles to free *all* women: women of color, working-class women, poor women, disabled women, lesbians, old women—as well as white, economically privileged, heterosexual women. Anything less than this vision of total freedom is not feminism, but merely female self-aggrandizement" (Smith 1981, 49).

A Black gay college student recently recounted an incident to me that illustrates the kind of consciousness that is grievously lacking among nonfeminist Black women scholars about Black lesbian existence. His story indicates why a Black feminist approach to literature, criticism, and research in a variety of disciplines is crucial if one is to recognize and understand Black lesbian experience. While researching a history project, he contacted the archives at a Black institution which has significant holdings on Black women. He spoke to a Black woman archivist and explained that he was looking for materials on Black lesbians in the 1940s. Her immediate response was to laugh uproariously and then to say that the collection contained very little on women during that period and nothing at all on lesbians in any of the periods covered by its holdings.

Not only was her reaction appallingly homophobic, not to mention impolite, but it was also inaccurate. One of the major repositories of archival material on Black women in the country of course contains material by and about Black lesbians. The material, however, is not identified and defined as such and thus remains invisible. This is a classic case of "invisibility [becoming] an unnatural disaster," as feminist poet Mitsuye Yamada (1981, 35–40) observes.

I suggested a number of possible resources to the student, and in the course of our conversation I told him I could not help but think of Cheryl Clarke's (1982, 15) classic poem "Of Althea and Flaxie." It begins:

In 1943 Althea was a welder
very dark
very butch
and very proud
loved to cook, sew, and drive a car
and did not care who knew she kept company with a woman

The poem depicts a realistic and positive Black lesbian relationship which survives Flaxie's pregnancy in 1955, Althea's going to jail for writing numbers in 1958, poverty, racism, and, of course, homophobia. If the archivist's vision had not been so blocked by homophobia, she would have been able to direct this student to documents that corroborate the history embodied in Clarke's poem.

Being divorced from the experience of feminist organizing not only makes it more likely that a woman has not been directly challenged to examine her homophobia, but it can also result in erroneous approaches to Black lesbian literature, if she does decide to talk or write about it. For example, some critics, instead of simply accepting that Black lesbians and Black lesbian writers exist, view the depiction of lesbianism as a dangerous and unacceptable "theme" or "trend" in Black women's writing. Negative discussions of "themes" and "trends," which in time may fade, do not acknowledge that for survival, Black lesbians, like any oppressed group, need to see our faces reflected in myriad cultural forms, including literature. Some writers go so far as to see the few Black lesbian books in existence as a kind of conspiracy, and bemoan that there is "so much" of this kind of writing available in print. They put forth the supreme untruth that it is actually an advantage to be a Black lesbian writer.

For each lesbian of color in print there are undoubtedly five dozen whose work has never been published and may never be. The publication of lesbians of color is a "new" literary development, made possible by alternative, primarily lesbian/feminist presses. The political and aesthetic strength of this writing is indicated by its impact having been far greater than its actual availability. At times its content has had revolutionary implications. But the impact of Black lesbian feminist writing, to which Calvin Hernton refers, should not be confused with access to print, to readers, or to the material perks that help a writer survive economically.

Terms such as *heterophobia*, used to validate the specious notion that "so many" Black women writers are depicting loving and sexual relationships between women, to the exclusion of focusing on relationships with men, arise in the academic vacuum, uninfluenced by political reality. "Heterophobia" resembles the concept of "reverse racism." Both are thoroughly reactionary and have nothing to do with the actual dominance of a heterosexual white power structure.

Equating lesbianism with separatism is another error in terminology, which will probably take a number of years to correct. The title of a workshop at a major Black women writers' conference, for example, was "Separatist Voices in the New Canon." The workshop examined the work of Audre Lorde and Alice Walker, neither of whom defines herself as a separatist, either sexually or racially. In his introduction to *Confirmation: An Anthology of African American Women,* coeditor Imamu Baraka is critical of feminists who are separatists, but he does not mention that any such thing as a lesbian exists. In his ambiguous yet inherently homophobic usage, the term *separatist* is made to seem like a mistaken political tendency, which correct thinking could alter. If "separatist" equals lesbian, Baraka is suggesting that we should change our minds and eradicate ourselves. In both these instances the fact that lesbians do not have sexual relationships with men is thought to be the same as ideological lesbian "separatism." Such an equation does not take into account that the majority of lesbians of color have interactions with men and that those who are activists are quite likely to be politically committed to coalition work as well.

Inaccuracy and distortion seem to be particularly frequent pitfalls when nonlesbians address Black lesbian experience because of generalized homophobia and because the very nature of our oppression may cause us to be hidden or "closeted," voluntarily or involuntarily isolated from other communities, and as a result unseen and unknown. In her essay "A Cultural Legacy Denied and Discovered: Black Lesbians in Fiction by Women," Jewelle Gomez (1983, 122) asserts the necessity for realistic portrayals of Black lesbians:

> These Black lesbian writers . . . have seen into the shadows that hide the existence of Black Lesbians and understand they have to create a universe/home that rings true on all levels. . . . The Black Lesbian writer must throw

> herself into the arms of her culture by acting as student/teacher/participant/ observer, absorbing and synthesizing the meanings of our existence as a people. She must do this despite the fact that both our culture and our sexuality have been severely truncated and distorted.

> Nature abhors a vacuum and there is a distinct gap in the picture where the Black Lesbian should be. The Black Lesbian writer must recreate our home, unadulterated, unsanitized, specific and not isolated from the generations that have nurtured us.

This is an excellent statement of what usually has been missing from portrayals of Black lesbians in fiction. The degree of truthfulness and self-revelation that Gomez calls for encompasses the essential qualities of verisimilitude and authenticity that I look for in depictions of Black lesbians. By verisimilitude I mean how true to life and realistic a work of literature is. By authenticity I mean something even deeper—a characterization which reflects a relationship to self that is genuine, integrated, and whole. For a lesbian or a gay man, this kind of emotional and psychological authenticity virtually requires the degree of self-acceptance inherent in being out. This is not a dictum but an observation. It is not a coincidence, however, that the most vital and useful Black lesbian feminist writing is being written by Black lesbians who are not caught in the impossible bind of simultaneously hiding identity yet revealing self through their writing.

Positive and realistic portrayals of Black lesbians are sorely needed, portraits which are, as Gomez states, "unadulterated, unsanitized, specific." By positive I do not mean characters without problems, contradictions, or flaws, mere uplift literature for lesbians, but instead writing that is sufficiently sensitive and complex, which places Black lesbian experience and struggles squarely within the realm of recognizable human experience and concerns.

As African Americans, our desire for authentic literary images of Black lesbians has particular cultural and historical resonance, since a desire for authentic images of ourselves as Black people preceded it long ago. After an initial period of racial uplift literature in the nineteenth and early twentieth centuries, Black artists during the Harlem Renaissance of the 1920s began to assert the validity of fully Black portrayals in all art forms including literature. In his pivotal 1926 essay "The Negro Artist and the Racial Mountain," Langston Hughes (1976, 309) asserted:

> We younger Negro artists who create now intend to express our individual dark-skinned selves without fear or shame. If white people are pleased we are glad. If they are not, it doesn't matter. We know we are beautiful. And ugly too. The tom-tom cries and the tom-tom laughs. If colored people are pleased we are glad. If they are not, their displeasure doesn't matter either.

We build our temples for tomorrow, strong as we know how, and we stand
on top of the mountain, free within ourselves.[4]

Clearly, it is not always popular or safe with either Black or white
audiences to depict Black people as we actually are. It still is not. Too
many contemporary Blacks seem to have forgotten the universally de-
based social-political position Black people have occupied during all the
centuries we have been here, up until perhaps the civil rights era of the
1960s. The most racist definition of Black people was that we were not
human.

Undoubtedly every epithet now hurled at lesbians and gay men—
"sinful," "sexually depraved," "criminal," "emotionally maladjusted,"
"deviant"—has also been hurled at Black people. When W. E. B. Du Bois
described life "behind the veil," and Paul Laurence Dunbar (1971, 184)
wrote:

We wear the mask that grins and lies,
It hides our cheeks and shades our eyes,—
This debt we pay to human guile;
With torn and bleeding hearts we smile,
And mouth with myriad subtleties.
Why should the world be overwise,
In counting all our tears and sighs?
Nay, let them only see us, while
　　We wear the mask. . . .

what were they describing but racial closeting? For those who refuse to
see the parallels because they view blackness as irreproachably normal,
but persist in defining same-sex love relationships as unnatural, Black
lesbian feminist poet Audre Lorde reminds us, "Oh," says a voice from
the black community, "but being Black is NORMAL!" "Well, I and many
Black people of my age can remember grimly the days when it didn't
used to be!" Lorde is not implying that she believes that there was ever
anything wrong with being Black, but points out how distorted "majority"
consciousness can cruelly affect an oppressed community's actual treatment and sense of self. The history of slavery, segregation, and racism
was based upon the assumption by the powers that be that blackness
was decidedly neither acceptable nor normal. Unfortunately, despite legal
and social change, large numbers of racist whites still believe the same
thing to this day.

The existence of lesbianism and male homosexuality is normal, too,
traceable throughout history and across cultures. It is a society's *response*
to the ongoing historical fact of homosexuality that determines whether
it goes unremarked as nothing out of the ordinary, as it is in some cultures,

or if it is instead greeted with violent repression, as it is in ours. At a time when Acquired Immune Deficiency Syndrome (AIDS), a disease associated with an already despised sexual minority, is occasioning mass hysteria among the heterosexual majority (including calls for firings, evictions, quarantining, imprisonment, and even execution), the way in which sexual orientation is viewed is not of mere academic concern. It is mass political organizing that has wrought the most significant changes in the status of Blacks and other people of color and which has altered society's perceptions about us and our images of ourselves. The Black lesbian feminist movement simply continues that principled tradition of struggle.

A Black woman author's relationship to the politics of Black lesbian feminism affects how she portrays Black lesbian characters in fiction. In 1977, in "Toward a Black Feminist Criticism," in order to analyze a Black woman's novel with a woman-identified theme, I had to rely upon Toni Morrison's *Sula* (1974), which did not explicitly portray a lesbian relationship. I sought to demonstrate, however, that because of the emotional primacy of Sula and Nel's love for each other, Sula's fierce independence, and the author's critical portrayal of heterosexuality, the novel could be illuminated by a lesbian feminist reading. Here I will focus upon three more recent works—*The Women of Brewster Place, The Color Purple,* and *Zami: A New Spelling of My Name*—which actually portray Black lesbians, but do so with varying degrees of verisimilitude and authenticity, dependent upon the author's relationship to and understanding of the politics of Black lesbian experience.

Gloria Naylor's *The Women of Brewster Place* (1983) is a novel composed of seven connecting stories. In beautifully resonant language, Naylor makes strong sexual political statements about the lives of working poor and working-class Black women and does not hesitate to explore the often problematic nature of their relationships with Black men—lovers, husbands, fathers, sons. Loving and supportive bonds between Black women are central to her characters' survival. However, Naylor's portrayal of a lesbian relationship in the sixth story, "The Two," runs counter to the positive framework of women bonding she has previously established. In the context of this novel, a lesbian relationship might well embody the culmination of women's capacity to love and be committed to each other. Yet both lesbian characters are ultimately victims. Although Naylor portrays the community's homophobia toward the lovers as unacceptable, the fate that she designs for the two women is the most brutal and negative of any in the book.

Theresa is a strong-willed individualist, while her lover, Lorraine, passively yearns for social acceptability. Despite their professional jobs, Lorraine and Theresa have moved to a dead-end slum block because of

Lorraine's fears that the residents of their two other middle-class neighborhoods suspected that they were lesbians. It does not take long for suspicions to arise on Brewster Place, and the two women's differing reactions to the inevitable homophobia they face are a major tension in the work. Theresa accepts the fact that she is an outsider because of her lesbianism. She does not like being ostracized, but she faces others' opinions with an attitude of defiance. In contrast, Lorraine is obsessed with garnering societal approval and would like nothing more than to blend into the straight world, despite her lesbianism. Lorraine befriends Ben, the alcoholic building superintendent, because he is the one person on the block who does not reject her. The fact that Ben has lost his daughter and Lorraine has lost her father, because he refused to accept her lesbianism, cements their friendship. Naylor writes,

> "When I'm with Ben, I don't feel any different from anybody else in the world."
> "Then he's doing you an injustice," Theresa snapped, "because we are different. And the sooner you learn that, the better off you'll be."
> "See, there you go again. Tee the teacher and Lorraine the student, who just can't get the lesson right. Lorraine who just wants to be a human being—a lousy human being who's somebody's daughter or somebody's friend or even somebody's enemy. But they make me feel like a freak out there, and you try to make me feel like one in here. The only place I've found some peace, Tee, is in that damp ugly basement, where I'm not different."
> "Lorraine." Theresa shook her head slowly. "You're a lesbian—do you understand that word?—a butch, a dyke, a lesbo, all those things that kid was shouting. Yes, I heard him: And you can run in all the basements in the world, and it won't change that, so why don't you accept it?"
> "I have accepted it!" Lorraine shouted. "I've accepted it all my life, and it's nothing I'm ashamed of. I lost a father because I refused to be ashamed of it—but it doesn't make me any *different* from anyone else in the world."
> "It makes you damned different!"
>
> "That's right! There go your precious 'theys' again. They wouldn't understand—not in Detroit, not on Brewster Place, not anywhere! And as long as they own the whole damn world, it's them and us, Sister—them and us. And that spells different!"[5]

Many a lesbian relationship has been threatened or destroyed because of how very differently lovers may view their lesbianism—for example, how out or closeted one or the other is willing to be. Naylor's discussion of difference represents a pressing lesbian concern. As Lorraine and Theresa's argument shows, there are complicated elements of truth in both their positions. Lesbians and gay men are objectively different in our sexual orientations from heterosexuals. The society raises sanctions against our sexuality that range from inconvenient to violent and which render our social status and life experiences different. On the other hand, we would like to be recognized and treated as human, to have the basic rights enjoyed by heterosexuals, and if the society cannot manage to support how we love, we would like to at least be left alone.

In "The Two," however, Naylor, sets up the women's response to their identity as an either/or dichotomy. Lorraine's desire for acceptance, although completely comprehensible, is based upon assimilation and denial, while Naylor depicts Theresa's healthier defiance as an individual stance. In the clearest statement of resistance in the story, Theresa thinks:

> If they practiced that way with each other, then they could turn back to back and beat the hell out of the world for trying to invade their territory. But she had found no such sparring partner in Lorraine, and the strain of fighting alone was beginning to show on her. (P. 136)

A mediating position between complete assimilation and alienation might well evolve from some sense of connection to a lesbian/gay community. Involvement with other lesbians and gay men could provide a reference point and support that would help diffuse some of the straight world's power. Naylor mentions that Theresa socializes with gay men and perhaps lesbians at a bar, but her interactions with them occur outside the action of the story. The author's decision not to portray other lesbians and gay men, but only to allude to them, is a significant one. The reader is never given an opportunity to view Theresa or Lorraine in a context in which she is the norm. Naylor instead presents them as "the two" exceptions in an entirely heterosexual world. Both women are isolated, and although their relationship is loving, it also feels claustrophobic. Naylor writes:

> Lorraine wanted to be liked by the people around her. She couldn't live the way Tee did, with her head stuck in a book all the time. Tee didn't seem to need anyone. Lorraine often wondered if she even needed her.

> She never wanted to bother with anyone except those weirdos at the club she went to, and Lorraine hated them. They were coarse and bitter, and made fun of people who weren't like them. Well, she wasn't like them either. Why should she feel different from the people she lived around? Black people were all in the same boat—she'd come to realize this even more since they had moved to Brewster—and if they didn't row together, they would sink together. (P. 142)

Lorraine's rejection of other lesbians and gay men is excruciating, as is the self-hatred that obviously prompts it. It is painfully ironic that she considers herself in the same boat with Black people in the story who are heterosexual, most of whom ostracize her, but not with Black people who are lesbian and gay. The one time that Lorraine actually decides to go to the club by herself, ignoring Theresa's warning that she won't have a good time without her, is the night that she is literally destroyed.

Perhaps the most positive element in "The Two" is how accurately Naylor depicts and subtly condemns Black homophobia. Sophie, a neighbor who lives across the airshaft from Lorraine and Theresa, is the "willing carrier" of the rumor about them, though not necessarily its initiator. Naylor writes,

> Sophie had plenty to report that day. Ben had said it was terrible in there. No, she didn't know exactly what he had seen, but you can imagine—and they did. Confronted with the difference that had been thrust into their predictable world, they reached into their imaginations and, using an ancient pattern, weaved themselves a reason for its existence. Out of necessity they stitched all of their secret fears and lingering childhood nightmares into this existence, because even though it was deceptive enough to try and look as they looked, talk as they talked, and do as they did, it had to have some hidden stain to invalidate it—it was impossible for them both to be right. So they leaned back, supported by the sheer weight of their numbers and comforted by the woven barrier that kept them protected from the yellow mist that enshrouded the two as they came and went on Brewster Place. (P. 132)

The fact of difference can be particularly volatile among people whose options are severely limited by racial, class, and sexual oppression, people who are already outsiders themselves.

A conversation between Mattie Michaels, an older Black woman who functions as the work's ethical and spiritual center, and her lifelong friend, Etta, further prods the reader to examine her own attitudes about loving women. Etta explains,

> "Yeah, but it's different with them."
> "Different how?"
> "Well . . ." Etta was beginning to feel uncomfortable.
> "They love each other like you'd love a man or a man would love you—I guess."
> "But I've loved some women deeper than I ever loved any man," Mattie was pondering. "And there been some women who loved me more and did more for me than any man ever did."
> "Yeah." Etta thought for a moment. "I can second that but it's still different, Mattie. I can't exactly put my finger on it, but . . ."
> "Maybe it's not so different," Mattie said, almost to herself. "Maybe that's why some women get so riled up about it, 'cause they know deep down it's not so different after all." She looked at Etta. "It kinda gives you a funny feeling when you think about it that way, though."
> "Yeah, it does," Etta said, unable to meet Mattie's eyes. (Pp. 140-41)

Whatever their opinions, it is not the women of the neighborhood who are directly responsible for Lorraine's destruction, but six actively homophobic and woman-hating teenage boys. Earlier that day Lorraine and Kiswana Browne had encountered the toughs, who had unleashed their sexist and homophobic violence on the two women. Kiswana had verbally bested their leader, C. C. Baker, but he was dissuaded from physically retaliating because one of the other boys reminded him: "'That's Abshu's woman, and that big dude don't mind kickin' ass'" (p. 163). As a lesbian, Lorraine did not have any kind of "dude" to stand between her and the violence of other men. Although she was completely silent during the encounter, C. C.'s parting words to her were, "'I'm gonna remember this, Butch!'" That night when Lorraine returns from the bar alone, she walks into the alley which is the boys' turf. They are waiting for her and gang-rape her in one of the most devastating scenes in literature. Naylor describes the aftermath:

> Lorraine lay pushed up against the wall on the cold ground with her eyes staring straight up into the sky. When the sun began to warm the air and the horizon brightened, she still lay there, her mouth crammed with paper bag, her dress pushed up under her breasts, her bloody pantyhose hanging from her thighs. She would have stayed there forever and have simply died from starvation or exposure if nothing around her had moved. (P. 171)

She glimpses Ben sitting on a garbage can at the other end of the alley sipping wine. In a bizarre twist of an ending, Lorraine crawls through the alley and mauls him with a brick she happens to find as she makes her way toward him. Lorraine's supplicating cries of "'Please. Please.'... the only word she was fated to utter again and again for the rest of her life," conclude the story (p. 173).

I began thinking about "The Two" because of a conversation I had with another Black lesbian who seldom comes into contact with other lesbians and who has not been active in the feminist movement. Unlike other women with whom I had discussed the work, she was not angry, disappointed, or disturbed by it, but instead thought it was an effective portrayal of lesbians and homophobia. I was taken aback because I had found Naylor's depiction of our lives so completely demoralizing and not particularly realistic. I thought about another friend who told me she had found the story so upsetting she was never able to finish it. And of another who had actually rewritten the ending so that Mattie hears Lorraine's screams before she is raped and saves her. In this "revised version," Theresa is an undercover cop who also hears her lover's screams, comes into the alley with a gun, and blows the boys away. I was so mystified and intrigued by the first woman's defense of Naylor's perspective that I went back to examine the work.

According to the criteria I have suggested, although the lesbian characters in "The Two" lack authenticity, the story possesses a certain level of verisimilitude. The generalized homophobia that the women face, which culminates in retaliatory rape and near-murderous decimation, is quite true to life. Gay and lesbian newspapers provide weekly accounts, which sometimes surface in the mainstream media, of the constant violence leveled at members of our communities. What feels disturbing and inauthentic to me is how utterly hopeless Naylor's view of lesbian existence is. Lorraine and Theresa are classically unhappy homosexuals of the type who populated white literature during a much earlier era, when the only alternatives for the "deviant" were isolation, loneliness, mental illness, suicide, or death.

In her second novel, *Linden Hills* (1985), Naylor indicates that Black gay men's options are equally grim. In a review of the work, Jewelle Gomez (1985, 224) writes:

> One character disavows a liaison with his male lover in order to marry the appropriate woman and inherit the coveted Linden Hills home. . . . We receive so little personal information about him that his motivations are obscure. For a middle-class, educated gay man to be blind to alternative lifestyles in 1985 is not inconceivable but it's still hard to accept the melodrama of his arranged marriage without screaming "dump the girl and buy a ticket to Grand Rapids!" Naylor's earlier novel [*The Women of Brewster Place*] presented a similar limitation. While she admirably attempts to portray black gays as integral to the fabric of black life she seems incapable of imagining black gays functioning as healthy, average people. In her fiction, although they are not at fault, gays must still be made to pay. This makes her books sound like a return to the forties, not a chronicle of the eighties.

Gomez's response speaks to the problems that many lesbian feminists have with Naylor's versions of our lives, her persistent message that survival is hardly possible. I do not think we simply want "happy endings"—although some do occur for lesbians both in literature and in life—but an indication of the spirit of survival and resistance which has made the continuance of Black lesbian and gay life possible throughout the ages.

In considering the overall impact of "The Two," I realized that because it is critical of homophobia, it is perhaps an effective story for a heterosexual audience. But because its portrayal of lesbianism is so negative, its message even to heterosexuals is ambiguous. A semisympathetic straight reader's response might well be: "It's a shame something like that had to happen, but I guess that's what you get for being queer." The general public does not want to know that it is possible to be a lesbian of whatever color and not merely survive but thrive. And neither does a

heterosexual publishing industry want to provide them with this information.

The impact of the story upon lesbian readers is quite another matter.
I imagine what might happen if a Black woman who was grappling with
defining her sexuality and who had never had the opportunity to read
anything else about lesbians, particularly Black ones, were to read "The
Two" as a severely cautionary tale. Justifiably, she might go no further
in her exploration, forever denying her feelings. She might eventually
have sexual relationships with other women, but remain extremely closeted. Or she might commit suicide. Naylor's dire pessimism about our
possibilities lies at the crux of the problems I, a Black lesbian reader, have
with "The Two."

Alice Walker's portrayal of a lesbian relationship in her novel *The
Color Purple* (1982) is as optimistic as Naylor's is despairing. Celie and
Shug's love, placed at the center of the work and set in a rural southern
community between the world wars, is unique in the history of African
American fiction. The fact that a book with a Black lesbian theme by a
Black woman writer achieved massive critical acclaim, became a bestseller,
and was made into a major Hollywood film is unprecedented in the
history of the world. It is *The Color Purple* to which homophobes and
antifeminists undoubtedly refer when they talk about how "many" books
currently have both Black lesbian subject matter and an unsparing critique
of misogyny in the Black community. For Black lesbians, however, especially writers, the book has been inspirational. Reading it, we think it
just may be possible to be a Black lesbian and live to tell about it. It may
be possible for us to write it down and actually have somebody read it
as well.

When I first read *The Color Purple* in galleys in the spring of 1982, I
believed it was a classic. I become more convinced every time I read it.
Besides great storytelling, perfect Black language, killingly subtle Black
women's humor, and an unequivocal Black feminist stance, it is also a
deeply philosophical and spiritual work. It is marvelously gratifying to
read discussions of nature, love, beauty, God, good, evil, and the meaning
of life in the language of our people. The book is like a jewel. Any way
you hold it to the light, you will always see something new reflected.

The facet of the novel under consideration here is Walker's approach
to lesbianism, but before I go further with that discussion, it is helpful to
understand that the work is also a fable. The complex simplicity with
which Walker tells the story, the archetypical and timeless Black southern
world in which she sets it, the clear-cut conflicts between good and evil,
the complete transformations undergone by several of the major characters, and the huge capacity of the book to teach are all signs that *The
Color Purple* is not merely a novel but a visionary tale. That it is a fable

may account partially for the depiction of a lesbian relationship unencumbered by homophobia or fear of it and entirely lacking in self-scrutiny about the implications of lesbian identity.

It may be Walker's conscious decision to deal with her readers' potentially negative reactions by using the disarming strategy of writing as if women falling in love with each other were quite ordinary, an average occurrence which does not even need to be specifically remarked. In the "real world" the complete ease with which Celie and Shug move as lovers through a totally heterosexual milieu would be improbable, not to say amazing. Their total acceptance is one clue that this is indeed an inspiring fable, a picture of what the world could be if only human beings were ready to create it. A friend told me about a discussion of the book in a Black writers' workshop she conducted. An older Black woman in the class asserted: "When that kind of business happens, like happened between Shug and Celie, you know there's going to be talk." The woman was not reacting to *Purple* as a fable or even as fiction, but as a "real" story, applying her knowledge of what would undoubtedly happen in real life, where most people just aren't ready to deal with lesbianism and don't want to be.

Because the novel is so truthful, particularly in its descriptions of sexual oppression and to a lesser extent racism, the reader understandably might question those aspects of the fable which are not as plausible. Even within the story itself, it is conceivable that a creature as mean-spirited as Mr. _____ might have something to say about Shug, the love of his life, and Celie, his wife, sleeping together in his own house. For those of us who experience homophobia on a daily basis and who often live in fear of being discovered by the wrong person(s), like the teenage thugs in "The Two," we naturally wonder how Celie and Shug, who do not hide their relationship, get away with it.

Another fabulous aspect of Celie's and Shug's relationship is that there are no references to how they think about themselves as lesbian lovers in a situation where they are the only ones. Although Celie is clearly depicted as a woman who at the very least is not attracted to men and who is generally repulsed by them, I am somewhat hesitant to designate her as a lesbian because it is not a term that she would likely apply to herself, and neither, obviously, would the people around her. In a conversation with Mr. _____ in the latter part of the book, Celie explains how she feels:

He say, Celie, tell me the truth. You don't like me cause I'm a man?
I blow my nose. Take off they pants, I say, and men look like frogs to me.
No matter how you kiss 'em, as far as I'm concern, frogs is what they stay.
I see, he say.[6]

Shug, on the other hand, is bisexual, another contemporary term that does not necessarily apply within the cultural and social context Walker has established. There is the implication that this is among her first, if it is not her only, sexual relationship with another woman. The only time within the novel when Shug and Celie make love, Walker writes:

> She say, I love you, Miss Celie. And then she haul off and kiss me on the mouth.
> Um, she say, like she surprise. I kiss her back, say, um, too. Us kiss and kiss till us can't hardly kiss no more. Then us touch each other.
> I don't know nothing bout it, I say to Shug.
> I don't know much, she say. (P. 109)

Despite her statement of inexperience, Shug is a wonderfully sensual and attractive woman who takes pleasure in all aspects of living, from noticing "the color purple in a field" to making love with whomever. When Shug tries to explain to Celie why she has taken up with a nineteen-year-old boy, the two women's differing perspectives and sexual orientations are obvious. Walker writes:

> But Celie, she say. I have to make you understand. Look, she say. I'm gitting old. I'm fat. Nobody think I'm good looking no more, but you. Or so I thought. He's nineteen. A baby. How long can it last?
> He's a man. I write on the paper.
> Yah, she say. He is. And I know how you feel about men. But I don't feel that way. I would never be fool enough to take any of them seriously, she say, but some mens can be a lots of fun.
> Spare me, I write. (P. 220)

Eventually Shug comes back to Celie, and Walker implies that they will live out their later years together. The recouplings and reunions that occur in the novel might also indicate that the story is more fantasy than fact. But in Celie and Shug's case, the longevity of their relationship is certainly a validation of love between women.

The day Shug returns, Celie shows her her new bedroom. Walker writes:

> She go right to the little purple frog on my mantelpiece.
> What this? she ast.
> Oh, I say, a little something Albert carve for me. (P. 248)

Not only is this wickedly amusing after Celie and Mr. _____'s discussion about "frogs," but Mr. _____'s tolerance at being described as such to the point of his making a joke gift for Celie seems almost too good to be true. Indeed, Mr. _____'s transformation from evil no-account to a sen-

sitive human being is one of the most miraculous one could find any-
where. Those critics and readers who condemn the work because they
find the depiction of men so "negative" never seem to focus on how
nicely most of them turn out in the end. Perhaps these transformations
go unnoticed because in Walker's woman-centered world, in order to
change, they must relinquish machismo and violence, the very thought
of which would be fundamentally disruptive to the nonfeminist reader's
world view. It is no accident that Walker has Celie, who has become a
professional seamstress and designer of pants, teach Mr. _____ to sew,
an ideal way to symbolize just how far he has come. In the real world,
where former husbands of lesbian mothers take their children away with
the support of the patriarchal legal system and in some cases beat or even
murder their former wives, very few men would say what Mr. _____
says to Celie about Shug: "I'm real sorry she left you, Celie. I remembered
how I felt when she left me" (p. 238). But in the world of *The Color Purple*,
a great deal is possible.

One of the most beautiful and familiar aspects of the novel is the
essential and supportive bonds between Black women. The only other
person Celie loves before she meets Shug is her long-lost sister, Nettie.
Although neither ever gets an answer, the letters they write to each other
for decades and Celie's letters to God before she discovers that Nettie is
alive constitute the entire novel. The work joyously culminates when
Nettie, accompanied by Celie's children who were taken away from her
in infancy, returns home.

Early in the novel Celie "sins against" another woman's spirit and
painfully bears the consequences. She tells her stepson, Harpo, to beat
his wife, Sofia, if she doesn't mind him. Soon Celie is so upset about
what she has done that she is unable to sleep at night. Sofia, one of the
most exquisitely defiant characters in Black women's fiction, fights Harpo
right back, and when she finds out Celie's part in Harpo's changed behavior, she comes to confront her. When Celie confesses that she advised
Harpo to beat Sofia because she was jealous of Sofia's ability to stand up
for herself, the weight is lifted from her soul, the women become fast
friends, and she "sleeps like a baby."

When Shug decides that Celie needs to leave Mr. _____ and go with
her to Memphis, accompanied by Mary Agnes (Squeak), Harpo's lover
of many years, they make the announcement at a family dinner. Walker
writes:

> You was all rotten children, I say. You made my life a hell on earth. And
> your daddy here ain't dead horse's shit.
> Mr. _____ reach over to slap me. I jab my case knife in his hand.
> You bitch, he say. What will people say, you running off to Memphis like
> you don't have a house to look after?

Shug say, Albert. Try to think like you got some sense.

Why any woman give a shit what people think is a mystery to me.

Well, say Grady, trying to bring light. A woman can't git a man if peoples talk.

Shug look at me and us giggle. Then us laugh sure nuff. Then Squeak start to laugh. Then Sofia. All us laugh and laugh.

Shug say, Ain't they something? Us say um *hum,* and slap the table, wipe the water from our eyes.

Harpo look at Squeak. Shut up Squeak, he say. It bad luck for women to laugh at men.

She say, Okay. She sit up straight, suck in her breath, try to press her face together.

He look at Sofia. She look at him and laugh in his face. I already had my bad luck, she say. I had enough to keep me laughing the rest of my life. (P. 182)

This marvelously hilarious scene is one of the countless examples in the novel of Black women's staunch solidarity. As in *The Women of Brewster Place,* women's caring for each other makes life possible; but in *The Color Purple* Celie and Shug's relationship is accepted as an integral part of the continuum of women loving each other, while in the more realistic work, Lorraine and Theresa are portrayed as social pariahs.

If one accepts that *The Color Purple* is a fable or at the very least has fablelike elements, judgments of verisimilitude and authenticity are necessarily affected. Celie and Shug are undeniably authentic as Black women characters—complex, solid, and whole—but they are not necessarily authentic as lesbians. Their lack of self-consciousness as lesbians, the lack of scrutiny their relationship receives from the outside world, and their isolation from other lesbians make *The Color Purple*'s categorization as a lesbian novel problematic. It does not appear that it was Walker's intent to create a work that could be definitively or solely categorized as such.

The question of categorization becomes even more interesting when one examines critical responses to the work, particularly in the popular media. Reviews seldom mention that Celie and Shug are lovers. Some critics even go so far as to describe them erroneously as good friends. The fact that their relationship is simply "there" in the novel and not explicitly called attention to as lesbian might also account for a mass heterosexual audience's capacity to accept the work, although the novel has of course also been homophobically attacked.[7] As a Black lesbian feminist reader, I have questions about how accurate it is to identify Walker's characters as lesbians per se, at the same time that I am moved by the vision of a world, unlike this one, where Black women are not forced to lose their families, their community, or their lives because of whom they love.

A realistic depiction of African American lesbian experience would be neither a complete idyll nor a total nightmare. Audre Lorde terms *Zami: A New Spelling of My Name* (1983) a "biomythography," a combination of autobiography, history, and myth. I have chosen to discuss it here because it is the one extended prose work of which I am aware that approaches Black lesbian experience with *both* verisimilitude and authenticity. *Zami* is an essentially autobiographical work, but the poet's eye, ear, and tongue give the work stylistic richness often associated with well-crafted fiction. At least two other Black women critics, Barbara Christian (1986, 187-210) and Jewelle Gomez (1983, 118-19), have included *Zami* in their analyses of Black lesbians in fiction. Because *Zami* spans genres and carves out a unique place in African American literature as the first full-length autobiographical work by an established Black lesbian writer, it will undoubtedly continue to be grouped with other creative prose about Black lesbians.

The fact that *Zami* is autobiographical might be assumed to guarantee its realism. But even when writing autobiographically, an author can pick and choose details, can create a persona which has little or nothing to do with her own particular reality, or she might fabricate an artificial persona with whom the reader cannot possibly identify. A blatant example of this kind of deceptive strategy might be an autobiographical work by a lesbian which fails to mention that this is indeed who she is; of course, there are other, less extreme omissions and distortions. Undoubtedly, Lorde selected the material she included in the work, and the selectivity of memory is also operative. Yet this work is honest, fully rounded, and authentic. It is not coincidental that of the three works considered here, *Zami* has the most to tell the reader about the texture of Black lesbian experience, and that it was written by an out Black lesbian feminist. The candor and specificity with which Lorde approaches her life are qualities that would enhance Black lesbian writing in the future.

Zami is a Carriacou word for "women who work together as friends and lovers."[8] Just as the title implies, *Zami* is woman-identified from the outset and thoroughly suffused with an eroticism focusing on women. Lorde connects her lesbianism to the model her mother, Linda, provided— her pervasive, often intimidating, strength; her fleeting sensuality when her harsh veneer was lifted—and also to her place of origin, the Grenadian island of Carriacou, where a word already existed to describe who Linda's daughter would become. As in *The Color Purple* and *The Women of Brewster Place*, in *Zami* relationships between women are at the center of the work. Here they are complex, turbulent, painful, passionate, and essential to the author's survival.

Although Lorde continuously explores the implications of being a Black lesbian and she has an overt consciousness about her lesbianism which is missing from Naylor's and Walker's works, she does not define lesbianism as a problem in and of itself. Despite homophobia, particularly in the left of the McCarthy era; despite isolation from other Black women because she is gay; and despite primal loneliness because of her many levels of difference, Lorde assumes that her lesbianism, like her blackness, is a given, a fact of life which she has to neither justify nor explain. This is an extremely strong and open-ended stance from which to write about Black lesbian experience, since it enables the writer to deal with the complexity of lesbianism and what being a Black lesbian means in a specific time and place. Lorde's position allows Black lesbian experience to be revealed from the inside out. The absence of agonized doubts about her sexual orientation and the revelation of the actual joys of being a lesbian, including lust and recognizable descriptions of physical passion between women, make *Zami* seem consciously written for a lesbian reader. This is a significant point, because so little is ever written with us in mind, and also because who an author considers her audience to be definitely affects her voice and the levels of authenticity she may be able to achieve. Writing from an avowedly Black lesbian perspective with Black lesbian readers in mind does not mean that a work will be inaccessible or inapplicable to nonblack and nonlesbian readers. Works such as *Zami*, which are based in the experiences of writers outside the "mainstream," provide a vitally different perspective on human experience and may even reveal new ways of thinking about supposedly settled questions. Or, as Celie puts it in *The Color Purple*: "If he [God] ever listened to poor colored women the world would be a different place, I can tell you" (P. 175). It would be more different still if "he" also listened to lesbians.

The fact that *Zami* is written from an unequivocally Black lesbian and feminist perspective undoubtedly explains why it is the one book of the three under discussion that is published by an alternative press, why it was turned down by at least a dozen trade publishers, including one that specializes in gay titles. The white male editor at that supposedly sympathetic house returned the manuscript saying, "If only you were just one," Black or lesbian. The combination is obviously too much for the trade publishing establishment to handle. We bring news that others do not want to hear. It is unfortunate that the vast majority of the readers of *The Women of Brewster Place* and *The Color Purple* will never have the opportunity to read *Zami*.

Lorde's description of Black "gay-girl" life in the Greenwich Village of the 1950s is fascinating, if for no other reason than that it reveals a piece of our cultural history. What is even more intriguing is her political activist's sense of how the struggles of women during that era helped shape our contemporary movement and how many of our current issues, especially the desire to build a Black lesbian community, were very much a concern at that time. The author's search for other Black lesbians and her lovingly detailed descriptions of the fragments of community she finds give this work an atmosphere of reality missing in "The Two" and *The Color Purple*. Unlike Lorraine and Theresa and Celie and Shug, Lorde is achingly aware of her need for peers. She writes:

> I remember how being young and Black and gay and lonely felt. A lot of it was fine, feeling I had the truth and the light and the key, but a lot of it was purely hell.
> There were no mothers, no sisters, no heroes. We had to do it alone, like our sister Amazons, the riders on the loneliest outposts of the kingdom of Dahomey.
>
> There were not enough of us. But we surely tried. (Pp. 176–77)
>
> Every Black woman I ever met in the Village in those years had some part in my survival, large or small, if only as a figure in the head-count at the Bag on a Friday night.
> Black lesbians in the Bagatelle faced a world only slightly less hostile than the outer world which we had to deal with every day on the outside—that world which defined us as doubly nothing because we were Black and because we were Woman—that world which raised our blood pressures and shaped our furies and our nightmares.
>
> All of us who survived these common years have to be a little proud. A lot proud. Keeping ourselves together and on our own tracks, however wobbly, was like trying to play the Dinizulu War Chant or a Beethoven sonata on a tin dog-whistle. (P. 225)

The humor, tenacity, and vulnerability which Lorde brings to her version of being in "the life" are very precious. Here is something to grab hold of, a place to see one's face reflected. Despite the daily grind of racism, homophobia, sexual and class oppression, compounded by the nonsolutions of alcohol, drugs, suicide, and death at an early age, some women did indeed make it.

Lorde also describes the much more frequent interactions and support available from white lesbians, who were in the numerical majority. Just as they are now, relationships between Black and white women in the 1950s were often undermined by racism, but Lorde documents that some women were at least attempting to deal with their differences. She writes:

> How imperfectly, we tried to build a community of sorts where we could, at the very least, survive within a world we correctly perceived to be hostile to us: we talked endlessly about how best to create that mutual support which twenty years later was being discussed in the women's movement as a brand new concept. Lesbians were probably the only Black and white women in New York City in the fifties who were making any real attempt to com-

municate with each other; we learned lessons from each other, the values of which were not lessened by what we did not learn. (P. 179)

Lorde approaches the meaning of difference from numerous vantage points in *Zami*. In much of her work prior to *Zami* she has articulated and developed the concept of difference which has gained usage in the women's movement as a whole and in the writing of women of color specifically. From her early childhood, long before she recognizes herself as a lesbian, the question of difference is *Zami*'s subtext, its ever-present theme. Lorde writes: *"It was in high school that I came to believe that I was different from my white classmates, not because I was Black, but because I was me"* (p. 82). Although Lorde comes of age in an era when little, if any, tolerance exists for those who do not conform to white-male hegemony, her stance and that of her friends is one of rebellion and creative resistance, including political activism, as opposed to conformity and victimization. *Zami* mediates the versions of lesbianism presented in *The Women of Brewster Place* and *The Color Purple*. It is not a horror story, although it reveals the difficulties of Black lesbian experience. It is not a fable, although it reveals the joys of a life committed to women.

Since much of her quest in *Zami* is to connect with women who recognize and share her differences, particularly other Black lesbians, it seems fitting that the work closes with her account of a loving relationship with another Black woman, Afrekete. Several years before the two women become lovers, Lorde meets Kitty at a Black lesbian house party in Queens. Lorde writes:

One of the women I had met at one of these parties was Kitty.
When I saw Kitty again one night years later in the Swing Rendezvous or the Pony Stable or the Page Three—that tour of second-string gay-girl bars that I had taken to making alone that sad lonely spring of 1957—it was easy to recall the St. Alban's smell of green Queens summer-night and plastic couch-covers and liquor and hair oil and women's bodies at the party where we had first met.
In that brick-faced frame house in Queens, the downstairs pine-paneled recreation room was alive and pulsing with loud music, good food, and beautiful Black women in all different combinations of dress. (P. 241)

The women were fifties dyke-chic, ranging from "skinny straight skirts" to Bermuda and Jamaica shorts. Just as the clothes, the smells, the song lyrics, and food linger in the author's mind, her fully rendered details of Black lesbian culture resonate within the reader. I recalled this party scene while attending a dinner party at the home of two Black lesbians in the Deep South earlier this year. One of the hostesses arrived dressed impeccably in white Bermuda shorts, black knee-socks, and loafers. Her hair straightened 1980s-style, much like that of the 1950s, completed my sense of déjà vu. Contemporary Black lesbians are a part of a cultural tradition which we are just beginning to discover through interviews with older women such as Mabel Hampton and the writing of authors such as Ann Allen Shockley, Anita Cornwell, Pat Parker, and Lorde.

When she meets Afrekete again, their relationship helps to counteract Lorde's loneliness following the breakup of a long-term relationship with a white woman. The bond between the women is stunningly erotic, enriched by the bond they share as Black women. Lorde writes:

> By the beginning of summer the walls of Afrekete's apartment were always warm to the touch from the heat beating down on the roof, and chance breezes through her windows rustled her plants in the window and brushed over our sweat-smooth bodies, at rest after loving.
> We talked sometimes about what it meant to love women, and what a relief it was in the eye of the storm, no matter how often we had to bite our tongues and stay silent.
>
> Once we talked about how Black women had been committed without choice to waging our campaigns in the enemies' strongholds, too much and too often, and how our psychic landscapes had been plundered and wearied by those repeated battles and campaigns.
> "And don't I have the scars to prove it," she signed. "Makes you tough though, babe, if you don't go under. And that's what I like about you; you're like me. We're both going to make it because we're both too tough and crazy not to!" And we held each other and laughed and cried about what we had paid for that toughness, and how hard it was to explain to anyone who didn't already know it that soft and tough had to be one and the same for either to work at all, like our joy and the tears mingling on the one pillow beneath our heads. (P. 250)

The fact that this conversation occurs in 1957 is both amazing and unremarkable. Black lesbians have a heritage far older than a few decades, a past that dates back to Africa, as Lorde (1984, 45–52) herself documents in the essay "Scratching the Surface: Some Notes on Barriers to Women and Loving." Lorde's authentic portrayal of one segment of that history in *Zami* enables us to see both our pasts and our futures more clearly. Her work provides a vision of possibility for Black lesbians surviving whole, despite all, which is the very least we can demand from our literature, our activism, and our lives.

Despite the homophobic exclusion and silencing of Black lesbian writers, the creation of complex, accurate, and artistically compelling depictions of Black lesbians in literature has been and will continue to be essential to the development of African American women's literature as a whole. The assertion of Black women's rights to autonomy and freedom,

which is inherent in the lives of Black lesbians and which is made politically explicit in Black lesbian feminist theory and practice, has crucial
implications for all women's potential liberation. Yet far too many nonlesbian Black women who are actively involved in defining the African
American women's literary renaissance as critics, teachers, readers, and
writers completely ignore Black lesbian existence or are actively hostile
to it.

Black women's homophobia in literary and nonliterary contexts ne-
gates any claims that they might make to honoring Black feminist principles or to respecting the even older tradition of Black women's sisterhood from which Black feminism springs. Ironically, excluding or
attacking Black lesbians often marginalizes the very women who have
built the political and cultural foundations that have made this renaissance
possible.

Ultimately, the truth that never hurts is that Black lesbians and specifically Black lesbian writers are here to stay. In spite of every effort to
erase us, we are committed to living visibly with integrity and courage
and to telling our Black women's stories for centuries to come.

NOTES

1. Audre Lorde and Ann Allen Shockley are two exceptions. They have published with both commercial and independent publishers. It should be noted that
Lorde's poetry is currently published by a commercial publisher, but that all of
her works of prose have been published by independent women's presses. In
conversation with Lorde I learned that *Zami: A New Spelling of My Name* was
rejected by at least a dozen commercial publishers.

2. In her essay "The Black Lesbian in American Literature: An Overview,"
Ann Allen Shockley summarizes Jones's negative or inadequate treatment of Lesbian themes in her novels *Corregidora* and *Eva's Man* and in two of her short
stories. Ann Allen Shockley, "The Black Lesbian in American Literature: An Overview," in *Home Girls: A Black Feminist Anthology*, ed. Barbara Smith (Latham, NY:
Kitchen Table, 1983), p. 89.

3. In her essay, "The Failure to Transform: Homophobia in the Black Community," Cheryl Clarke comments: "The black lesbian is not only absent from
the pages of black political analysis, her image as a character in literature and her
role as a writer are blotted out from or trivialized in literary criticism written by
black women." Clarke also cites examples of such omissions. In *Home Girls*, ed.
Smith, pp. 204–205.

4. It is interesting to note that recent research has revealed that Hughes and
a number of other major figures of the Harlem Renaissance were gay. See Charles
Michael Smith, "Bruce Nugent: Bohemian of the Harlem Renaissance," in *In the
Life: A Black Gay Anthology*, ed. Joseph F. Beam (Boston: Alyson, 1986), pp. 213–
214, and selections by Langston Hughes in *Gay and Lesbian Poetry in Our Time:*

An Anthology, ed. Carl Morse and Joan Larkin (New York: St. Martin's, 1988), pp. 204–206.

5. Gloria Naylor, *The Women of Brewster Place* (New York: Penguin, 1983), pp. 165–166. All subsequent references to this work will be cited in the text.

6. Alice Walker, *The Color Purple* (New York: Washington Square, 1982), p. 224. All subsequent references to this work will be cited in the text.

7. In his essay "Who's Afraid of Alice Walker?" Calvin Hernton describes the "hordes of . . . black men (and some women)" who condemned both the novel and the film *The Color Purple* all over the country. He singles out journalist Tony Brown as a highly visible leader of these attacks. Brown both broadcast television shows and wrote columns about a book and movie he admitted to have neither read nor seen. Hernton raises the question "Can it be that the homophobic, nitpicking screams of denial against *The Color Purple* are motivated out of envy, jealousy and guilt, rather than out of any genuine concern for the well-being of black people?" Calvin Hernton, *The Sexual Mountain and Black Women Writers* (New York: Anchor, 1987), pp. 30–36.

8. Audre Lorde, *Zami: A New Spelling of My Name* (Freedom, Calif.: Crossing, 1983), p. 255. All subsequent references to this work will be cited in the text.

REFERENCES

Baraka, Imamu, and Bibi Amina Baraka. 1983. *Confirmation: An Anthology of African American Women.* New York: Quill.

Bethel, Lorraine, and Barbara Smith, eds. 1979. *Conditions: Five, The Black Women's Issue.*

Birtha, Becky. 1983. *For Nights like This One.* San Francisco: Frog in the Well.

Brant, Beth. 1984. "A Gathering of Spirit." *Sinister Widsom* 23/24.

———. 1985. *Mohawk Trail.* Ithaca, N.Y.: Firebrand.

Christian, Barbara. 1986. *Black Feminist Criticism: Perspectives on Black Women Writers.* New York: Pergamon.

Clarke, Cheryl. 1982. *Narratives: Poems in the Tradition of Black Women.* New York: Kitchen Table: Women of Color Press.

———. 1983. "The Failure to Transform: Homophobia in the Black Community." In Smith, ed., *Home Girls.* 197–208.

Cliff, Michelle. 1980. *Claiming an Identity They Taught Me to Despise.* Watertown, Mass.: Persephone Press.

———. 1984. *Abeng.* Freedom, Calif.: Crossing Press.

Cochran, Jo, et al., eds. 1984. *Gathering Ground.* Seattle: Seal Press.

Dunbar, Paul. 1971. "We Wear the Mask." In Wiggins, ed., *The Life and Works of Paul Laurence Dunbar.* New York: Kraus. 184.

Giddings, Paula. 1984. *When and Where I Enter: The Impact of Black Women on Race and Sex in America.* New York: Bantam Press.

Gómez, Alma, Cherríe Moraga, and Mariana Romo-Camona, eds. 1983. *Cuentos: Stories by Latinas.* New York: Kitchen Table: Women of Color Press.

Gomez, Jewelle. 1983. "A Cultural Legacy Denied and Discovered: Black Lesbians in Fiction by Women." In Smith, ed., *Home Girls.* 110–123.

———. 1985. "Naylor's Inferno." *The Women's Review of Books* 2, no. 11 (August).

Hernton, Calvin. 1985. "The Sexual Mountain and Black Women Writers." *The Black Scholar* 16, no. 4 (July/August).

———. 1987. "Who's Afraid of Alice Walker?" In *The Sexual Mountain and Black Women Writers*. New York: Anchor Press. 30–36.

Hughes, Langston. 1976. "The Negro Artist and the Racial Mountain." In Nathan Higgins, ed., *Voices from the Harlem Renaissance*. New York: Oxford.

Hull, Gloria, Patricia Bell Scott, and Barbara Smith. 1982. *All the Women Are White, All the Blacks are Men, But Some of Us Are Brave: Black Women's Studies*. New York: The Feminist Press.

Joseph, Gloria I., and Jill Lewis. 1981. *Common Differences: Conflicts in Black and White Feminist Perspectives*. New York: Anchor Press.

Lorde, Audre. 1983. *Zami: A New Spelling of My Name*. Freedom, Calif.: Crossing Press.

———. 1984. *Sister Outsider*. Freedom, Calif.: Crossing. 46–52.

Moraga, Cherríe, and Gloria Anzaldúa. 1981. *This Bridge Called My Back: Writings by Radical Women of Color*. Watertown, Mass.: Persephone Press.

Naylor, Gloria. 1983. *The Women of Brewster Place*. New York: Penguin Press.

Shange, Ntozake. 1982. *Sassafras, Cypress and Indigo*. New York: St. Martin's Press.

Shockley, Ann Allen. 1983. "The Black Lesbian in American Literature: An Overview." In Smith, ed., *Home Girls*.

Smith, Barbara. 1977. *Toward a Black Feminist Criticism*. Freedom, Calif.: Crossing.

———. 1981. "Racism and Women's Studies." In Hull et al., eds., *All the Women Are White, All the Blacks are Men, But Some of Us Are Brave: Black Women's Studies*. 83–93.

———, ed. 1983. *Home Girls: A Black Feminist Anthology*. New York: Kitchen Table: Women of Color Press.

Tate, Claudia, ed. 1983. *Black Women Writers at Work*. New York: Continuum Publishing Co.

Tsui, Kitty. 1983. *The Words of a Woman Who Breathes Fire*. New York: Kitchen Table.

Walker, Alice. 1982. *The Color Purple*. New York: Washington Square.

———. 1984. "Breaking Chains and Encouraging Life." In *In Search of Our Mother's Gardens: Womanist Prose*. New York: Harcourt Brace Jovanovich.

Yamada, Mitsuye. 1981. "Invisibility Is an Unnatural Disaster: Reflections of an Asian American Woman." In Moraga et al., eds., *This Bridge Called My Back: Writings by Radical Women of Color*.

2 Public Policy, the State, and Ideologies of Gender

REDRAFTING MORALITY

The Postcolonial State and the Sexual Offences Bill of Trinidad and Tobago

M. Jacqui Alexander

In the contemporary period, morality has become an important mechanism for disciplining and regulating the social. Its political agenda has taken shape in the ideologies of international capital that attempt to legitimate the exploitation of a predominantly female Third World workforce through symbols of docile and submissive womanhood. It manifests itself in the fundamentalist right that has diffused its brand of morality in terms of the monogamous conjugal family and has reified motherhood at a time when its material base is being dramatically undermined, when it is downright unsafe to be a mother for the majority of women in the Third World. It manifests itself also in political parties and a wide range of state practices that are visibly linked to the right, utilizing legal and bureaucratic apparatuses to legislate norms. *Morality* has become a euphemism for *sex*. To be moral is to be asexual, (hetero)sexual, or sexual in ways that presumably carry the weight of the "natural." The political struggle to redraft morality requires feminist engagement. In this essay, I use the Sexual Offences Bill that was signed into law in Trinidad and Tobago in 1986 to suggest certain trajectories for such an engagement. The legislation is an important site where the struggle to link sexuality with morality was particularly fierce. I suggest important markers for the project of historical reconstruction and future political organizing.

Attempts to manage sexuality through morality are not without historical precursors. They are inextricably bound to colonial rule. In fact, the very identity and authority of the colonial project rested upon the racialization and sexualization of morality. Clearly one aspect of the project was carried out in the overt articulation at both institutional and discursive levels, but there was also another, perhaps mystified element that was expressed as the self-attributing superiority of the colonizer and the attribution of inferiority to the colonized. The moves to usurp the consciousness of the colonized by attempts to remake the self, evidenced, for instance, in the active suppression of indigenous systems of metaphysics or in the constant preoccupation with manners and "the Character of the Negro" detailed in travelogues and buried deep in the presuppositions of colonial historiography, were simultaneously aimed at dislodging resistance, reorganizing daily life, reconstituting identity, indeed remaking the sexual identity of those subjected to colonial rule.[1] This is why unmasking these presuppositions forms an important dimension of any counterproject.

In the case of the Caribbean, the embeddedness of the colonial state in the slave plantation economy assured state managers a central role in managing Black labor, on which the very existence of that economy rested. And the management of Black labor within a racially complex class system comprising free coloreds, Black slaves, and a white planter class (with close links to metropolitan capital and tenuous links to the indigenous free coloreds) rested on several simultaneous strategies, each relying upon the formal and informal enforcement of certain racialized sexual codes of conduct. In a study of the sexual complexities of race and class and the curious pattern of morality that developed during the colonial period in the Caribbean, Barbara Bush traces the simultaneous construction of womanhood through notions of "white ladies, coloured favourites and Black wenches," and concludes the following:

> By the mid-eighteenth century, sugar monoculture was consolidated, and crucial and damning contrasts between Black and white women reinforced a developing racialist ideology. Their economic and sexual roles became strongly differentiated. The now leisured white women became the embodiment of modesty and respectability, but also the victims of a rigid double-standard of morality which allowed men full sexual licence. Black concubinage became "de rigueur" and white women were artificially elevated as Black women were unfairly debased.[2]

Conjugal marriage was actively encouraged among slaves but was actively discouraged between white men and colored women because it interrupted the accumulation of private property and wealth by the white father and his "natural" heirs. According to the planter class, "free coloreds were acquiring property and wealth by inheriting land from their natural white fathers," so active measures were put in place to discourage it.[3] An Elizabethan statute of rape institutionalized and legitimized violent colonial masculinity which took the form of rape but criminalized Black masculinity, thereby solidifying the cult of true womanhood and its correlates the white Madonna and the Black whore.[4]

This "rigid double-standard" of morality was again applied by the planter class during the labor crisis which the official end of slavery produced (the period often referred to as indentureship). Indian women who were recruited from Calcutta and Madras to work on sugar plantations and came without conjugal families were defined by colonial state and migrant men alike as "prostitutes," "social outcasts," and "prone to immoral conduct." According to Rhoda Reddock, who has examined the historical construction of the "Indian Woman Problem" in Trinidad and Tobago, "it was the historical conflation of interests between migrant Indian men, struggling to improve their socio-economic and caste position within a new and hostile environment, colonial capital, and the state's desire for a stable . . . self-reproducing and cheap labor force" that worked to generate ideologies rooted in particular notions of morality aimed at curtailing women's autonomy.[5] Although never historically stable, the complicity of the state in regulating sex and managing sexuality through certain norms of morality is not a new dimension of state practice.

However, it is difficult to recall in recent years a piece of legislation that has generated such intense interest and debate as the Sexual Offences Bill: "An Act to Repeal and Replace the Laws of Trinidad and Tobago Relating to Sexual Crimes, to the Procuration, Abduction and Prostitution of Persons and to Kindred Offences."[6] It was not unusual that the regulation of sex was managed through a juridical framework, for as we saw, this was an integral element of state practice from its inception in the slave economy. But the Act represents the first time that the coercive arm of the postcolonial state had confronted the legacy of its colonial trauma and attempted "to bring all laws dealing with sexual offences under one heading."[7] This gesture of consolidation not only brought different elements of the state apparatus into direct opposition (the Law Commission and central parliamentarians, for example) but engaged the entire array of institutional mechanisms that historically had a stake in regulating sexuality, particularly women's sexuality, such as the church, the "family," the law, and state managers themselves. The Act originated within the Law Commission that was formed in 1971 with a mandate from the Ministry of Legal Affairs to suggest new areas for legislation. A working committee had spent three years examining the sexual laws of other Commonwealth countries. But for our purposes, it will be more useful to read the bill not through its origins but in terms of its contextual emergence. In this way, one can understand the ways in which state managers came to construct the societal imperatives they confronted in terms of prohibitions and punishments regarding certain kinds of sex.

Fifteen of the nineteen provisions constituting the legislation had prior lives and were being reconsolidated under a different schedule of punishments. Prohibitions regarding sex within one's family, whether biological or adopted ("incest"), and against women who exchanged sex for money ("prostitutes") and those who aided them, such as brothel keepers, or who exploited them, such as pimps, had long been established in the emendations to the Offences against the Person Acts—all variants of British law. What was new was that the commission moved to criminalize new areas of sexual activity. It established prohibitions against employers who took sexual advantage of their "minor" employees at the workplace and made sex with a girl age fourteen to sixteen a statutory offense. In addition, for the first time, rape within marriage was criminalized: any "husband" who had forceful intercourse with his "wife" without her consent could be convicted and imprisoned under a new offense called "sexual assault." This came to be known popularly as Clause 4. Buggery committed in private between consenting adults (two men or husband and wife) was decriminalized.

Clause 4 and the proposal to decriminalize gay sex created such a public furor and posed such a dilemma for central parliamentarians that under the direction of the deputy prime minister and chief parliamentarian, Kamaluddin Mohammed, the House suspended its customary procedures of hearing and convened a select committee of *all* of its members to study the bill in private. Proceedings remain, as yet, unavailable for public scrutiny, but the redrafted provisions of the final bill bore little resemblance to their precursor. As it currently stands, rape in marriage can be proven only under certain, very restrictive conditions: only where there has been some legal action taken to indicate a "breakdown" of the marriage, such as a judicial separation, the initiation of divorce proceedings, or evidence that the couple now live in separate households. According to the legislation, no proceedings shall be instituted except by or with the consent of the director of public prosecutions. Homosexual sex was recriminalized; and lesbian sex became punishable under a new offense called "serious indecency" if "committed on or towards a person sixteen years of age or more."

But how did state managers come to frame this discourse on sex in the ways in which they did? What was at stake that made it necessary for some state managers to regulate violent areas of domestic patriarchy? What set of conditions prompted legislators to ensnare and to specifically control lesbian sex? And why at this historical juncture?

In a self-generated commentary, the commission stated explicitly that the bill's aim was to "bring back morality within the fabric of society."[8] It stated that it wished to grapple with the knotty relationships among sexual behaviors, moral rectitude, and the criminal law and posed the central problematic by gauging the extent to which the criminal law ought to have reflected the *fact* that certain kinds of sexual conduct were *"commonly* thought to be *morally wrong* or an outrage to public standards of decency." Avoiding entirely the question about who constructs facts and "common knowledges" about morality, it borrowed its definitions from the Wolfenden Committee on Homosexual Offences and Prostitution, which convened in Britain in 1954 and established morality as the preservation of "public order and decency, protection of the young from sexual exploitation by adults while at the same time deterring the young from indulging in sexual activities, and providing sufficient safeguards against [sexual] exploitation and corruption of others, particularly those who are specifically vulnerable because they are young, weak in body or mind, inexperienced or in a state of special physical, official or economic dependence."[9] While this gesture symbolizes the ongoing dependent relationship between Britain and its former colony, it actually provides no clear definitions of morality.

Central parliamentarians, on the other hand, used data indicating that Trinidad and Tobago had the highest incidence of AIDS per capita in the Caribbean as the basis for recriminalizing homosexual sex and restoring morality. So what initially appeared as a liberal gesture on the part of law commissioners to decriminalize gay sex actually converged with the final text produced by the parliamentarians as a treatise on morality. What Foucault observes about the self-justification of the criminal justice system through its "perpetual reference to something other than itself, [and its] increasing reinscription in non-juridical systems" is applicable here, for the contested terrain of morality is just one such nonjuridical system. Morality has become entangled with what he has identified as the "practice of the power to punish," and in this instance, has been conflated with sex and sexuality, thereby obscuring the state's complicity in sexual politics.[10] For state managers, the codification of sexual behaviors lies rooted in an ostensibly fledgling morality in a society that has been overtaken by all the defining signs of Western decadence: AIDS, promiscuity, prostitution, lesbian sex, and overall sexual intemperance. It is unclear whether any of the penalties attached to incest, prostitution, or lesbian and gay sex would fulfill the promise of moral restoration, but this normative stance is less significant here than the desire and ability of state managers to construct a productive discourse which draws on certain notions of morality and naturalness and ultimately takes its cues from a gendered and racialized social order while appearing to have no political interest at stake. It is only within the context of the legal framework and a close examination of the sexual boundaries it draws and solidifies that one can truly grapple with the meanings and definitions of morality that state managers intend. How morality is produced, then, is of crucial analytical and ideological import.

This essay focuses, therefore, on the trajectory of the discursive production of morality in the legal text and demonstrates that state managers reinscribe sex (albeit forbidden, "amoral," and "unnatural" sex) as the basis of relationships between women, between men, between men and women, and between adults and "minors" by constructing maleness and femaleness in terms of sexualized categories. But this sexual reinscription is not based on relationships of equivalency. A hierarchy is established within the discourse and manifests itself in two simultaneous gestures, one that draws boundaries around licit sex (boundaries that become isomorphic with the right morality) and thereby creates a category of illicit or criminalized sex to enforce licit sex. The right morality cannot be established without what managers construct as illicit.

Analytically, I will unify two dimensions of the official discourse that have been treated separately and held in discrete suspension: the one that draws parameters around legitimate heterosexual sex, and the other that criminalizes lesbian sex and recriminalizes homosexual sex. They are enjoined here not because they are to be conflated politically or ideologically—eroticized domination in the form of marital rape is not the same as sex between lesbians—but because, as I demonstrate later, their location and timing within a singular discursive frame are significant, related, and therefore not coincidental. In a curious encounter, they derive from the force of a constructed morality that resides in nature, where the only sanctioned form of sex is identified as procreative. Biology and procreation sanction nature and morality to such an extent that when eroticized violence threatens to dissolve heterosexual conjugal marriage, a textual restoration is enacted by criminalizing lesbian sex and sex among gay men—an act of reasserting the conjugal bed. Indeed, the reinscription of the conjugal bed occurs precisely because no alternative sexualities are permissible; by legally outlawing other alternatives that "reject the obligation of coitus," the power of marriage is reinscribed, and with it the reinforcement of "the obligatory social relationship between 'man' and 'woman'."[11] The heterosexual contract is textually restored by criminalizing lesbian sex and sex between men. I follow, therefore, a general dialectic approach which, in the case of the criminalizing of lesbian sex, brings into stark relief that which state managers define as threatening and banish to the underground.

I am not attempting, however, a methodological move which privileges the authority of the legal text and which might, therefore, mask the real material effects discourses engender. The legislation is an act of power, but it is also a site for contestation, for the state, while being one of the major actors in institutionalizing sexual politics, is not the *only* actor. Textually, women become the ground upon which certain notions of virile masculinity, family, and sexuality are argued, but in contrast to other discourses where women's subjectivity is entirely muted, women are not missing from or silenced in the public discourse.[12] Moreover, the definitions of sexuality which "wives" and women construct interrupt those definitions of sexualities deployed by state managers, and so they will be made central to my analysis.

In focusing on constructed meaning, one can sever the bond which state managers establish between sex and morality, and between morality and nature. It will help to shift the terms of interpretation away from a narrow focus on the "mechanisms of the power to punish"—the linchpin of state strategy—to locate these developments within wider spheres of power. If discourses are read as the instruments for the exercise of power (and, as Biddy Martin suggests, the "paradigmatic enactments of those struggles over meaning"),[13] discourses must therefore be situated contextually. In this instance, it is necessary to explode the negotiated and contested meanings about sexuality, and their relation to a racialized class field. I want to use the instance of the bill, then, to demonstrate the ways in which certain ideologies about sexuality were formed. In the discussion that follows, I use the text of the legislation to lay out and foreground the construction of morality and the conflation of morality with hegemonic conjugal sexuality. Then, within the public arena I trace the major political struggles over the contending meanings and definitions of erotic autonomy deployed therein. I end with some questions about future trajectories for feminist inquiry and politics.

Negotiating and Suspending "Consent": The Law as Moral Arbiter

A close reading of the constitutive elements of the legal text and its interpretations indicates that it took shape within an established hierarchy of punishments, stipulations, and injunctions. It is through this schedule that state managers establish what they deem to be an appropriate morality and, correspondingly, the set of practices which fall outside its purview and therefore require policing of some kind. But what are the ways in which the text functions as moral authority, the definitive moral arbiter of sexual practices?

Textually, morality gets codified through the enactment of three simultaneous gestures: (1) the central positioning of legitimate, naturalized sex within the conjugal arena, and with it particular notions of procreative sex; (2) the establishment of a sexual standoff, as it were, between that form of naturalized sex and other forms of amoral, forbidden sex: incest, prostitution, sex with "minors," and lesbian and gay sex; and (3) the construction of an unnatural underworld of lesbian and gay sex by a textual association with bestiality. These textual strategies must be read simultaneously because there is no absolute set of commonly understood or accepted principles called "the natural" which can be invoked except as they relate to what is labeled "unnatural." Heterosexual sex, even while dysfunctional (as in rape in marriage), assumes the power of natural law only in relation to sex which is defined in negation to it (what natural sexual intercourse is not) and in those instances where desire presumably becomes so corrupt that it expresses itself as bestiality. Here is the definition of sexual intercourse that was attached as a supplementary note to the Act: "[The Clauses] do not necessarily define 'sexual intercourse' but give a characteristic of it. 'Sexual intercourse' means natural sexual intercourse in the clauses relating to rape and other offences of sexual intercourse with women, whereas the clause concerned with buggery relates to unnatural sexual intercourse." In other words, heterosexual practices carry the weight of the natural only in relational terms and ultimately, one might argue, only in its power to designate as amoral and unnatural those practices which disrupt marriage and certain hegemonic notions of family. What is fundamentally at stake, therefore, in consolidating these moral claims is the institution of marriage and its patriarchal correlates: hegemonic masculinity, procreative sex, subordinated femininity, and vague but powerful notions of "consent."

In laying out the terms of "serious indecency" that criminalized lesbian sex, legislators faced quite a dilemma about language. The first clause stated broadly: "a *person* who commits an act of serious indecency on or towards another is guilty of an offence." It is unclear at this point for whom the penalties are intended, except that in the second clause it is noted that a "husband," a "wife," or a "male" or "female" who is "sixteen years of age or more" is exempted. The definition becomes somewhat more explicit in the final clause: "an act of serious indecency is an act *other than sexual intercourse* (whether *natural* or unnatural) by a person involving the use of the genital organs for the purpose of arousing sexual desire." Clearly the definition of what is natural or unnatural is predicated on a heterosexual conjugal contract; by default, an act other than sexual intercourse (natural, i.e., between men and women) defines lesbian sex! State managers are unable to draw on any widely understood category to describe lesbian sex. Instead, they seize upon the body, women's *sexual* organs, which is constructed and essentialized as an autonomous force, insensitive to all morality and in single-minded pursuit of arousing and gratifying sexual desire.[14] This is what is to be curbed and placed within the confines of a prison. So, unlike religious discourse which gives no room to experience sexual desire, this discourse acknowledges desire, but it is the form of desire and presumably the objectionable ways in which it is expressed that defy explanation and must, therefore, be outlawed.

"Buggery," "bestiality," and "serious indecency" occupy contiguous spaces in the unnatural world of the legal text. The term *buggery* itself supersedes the term *sodomy*, which evokes the scriptural metaphor in which God and nature punish sexual deviation and restore order. In a close analysis of ecclesiastical writings, Alan Bray offers a useful reading of the textual union between buggery and the unnatural:

> Homosexuality was not part of . . . the law of nature. It was not part of the chain of being, or the harmony of the created world or its universal dance. It was not part of the Kingdom of Heaven or its counterpart the Kingdom of Hell (although that could unwittingly release it). It was none of these things because it was not conceived of as part of the created order at all; it was part of its dissolution. . . . And as such it was not a sexuality in its own right, but existed as a potential for confusion and disorder in one undivided sexuality. . . . What sodomy and buggery represented . . . was . . . the disorder in sexual relations that, in principle at least, could break out anywhere.[15]

Bray is pointing here to the presumed synchrony among order, the natural, and the (hetero)sexual. Heterosexuality promotes order while homosexuality, its antithesis, promotes chaos or the very dissolution of the natural. What is suggested is that some interest might well intervene to establish order out of chaos. The state is one such interest, which rules by normalizing chaotic relations, and in this instance does so through a set of narrowly crafted notions of morality which inform its gestures. The significance here is that it sets the stage for the kind of repressive state rule clearly evidenced in this piece of legislation.

Taken together, the set of practices that were legally defined as sexual crimes and kindred offenses are offset by a notion of consent and a schedule of punishments that operate in sometimes unclear, sometimes idiosyncratic, and even contradictory ways. And even within these spheres of consent, hierarchies operate. Certain types of consent are more legitimate than others; at times adulthood serves as proxy for consent, while at others it is suspended and infantilized, especially when it operates within the arena of forbidden sex. Consent was also transferred from the domestic to the public sphere, where it was defined as the power of the state apparatus to prosecute. Within the legislation, the terrain of consent and distributive justice is uneven, and indeed sticky.[16] In what follows, I examine the contradictory manner in which they operate and intersect with the definitions of morality framed earlier.

The legislative provision on rape draws a distinction between marital rape ("sexual assault"), which can be committed only by "husbands" and for which the penalty is fifteen years' imprisonment, and real rape, which can be committed only by men—ostensible strangers—and for which the penalty is imprisonment for life. The defining element here is that a husband "forcefully has sexual intercourse with [his wife] *without* her consent." But if it is the violence attendant with sex and the protection of women which state managers insist are the focus of the rape penalty, then there is really no compelling reason for them to distinguish between marital rape and other forms of rape. In this legal sphere, the horror of rape rests not so much in its violence but in a moment where a wife withholds her consent. The issue of consent works, therefore, to obscure the actuality of violence. In contrast, a woman's consent, which presumably acts to prevent rape within "normal" marital relations, is eclipsed when she is actually raped. Thereafter, consent resides in an official of the state (the director of public prosecutions), whose authority determines the admissibility of the charge for trial. According to the legislation, no proceedings shall be instituted except by or with the consent of the director of public prosecutions.

Further, the state's notion of consent is ideologically bound to the enforcement of morality and permissible, procreative sex, and is exemplified in the case of prostitution and lesbian and gay sex. In the case of the former, the provision reads: "a person who, (a) knowingly lives wholly or in part on the earnings of prostitution, or (b) in any place solicits for *immoral* purposes is guilty of an offence and is liable on conviction to imprisonment for five years." That an adult woman consents to earn her livelihood by exchanging sex for money is defined as "immoral," and abrogates her rights to give consent.

A similar suspension of consent operates in the case of lesbian and gay sex, which are simultaneously stigmatized and criminalized. Buggery between "consenting" adults carries with it a sentence of ten years. It is presumably as serious a sexual infraction as heterosexual incest between adults and unconsenting heterosexual sex either with "minors" in the workplace or with "mentally subnormal" women. Gay sex between minors appears more serious than incest between minors and carries with it the same five-year penalty as lesbian sex. "Mentally subnormal" women and girls are deemed incapable of providing consent. (Ironically, the text eroticizes girls from the outside by sexualizing them and constructing them as untouchable, but criminalizes them for any expression of sexual agency.) In all instances, however, morality acts to regulate consent, and in keeping with its position of power within the text can either dispense it or revoke it. It acts to penalize women who consent to intercourse with anyone except their husbands, to suppress the sexual agency of women (particularly prostitutes, lesbians), girls, and gay men who stand outside conjugal marriage. And this is what became the primary point of contestation within the public arena. I outline the elements of the political struggle in what follows.

Sacrilegious Sex within Sanctimonious Marriage? Or Is Legitimized Masculinity in Question?

For almost two years, the Sexual Offences Bill remained in the public arena while certain popular consciousnesses about domestic violence and contending definitions of male power crystallized. The political struggle was evidenced in public spaces: the courtroom, the streets, popular cultural forms such as the calypso, a variant of Black working-class men's humor called "picong," and various forms of media. Multiple constituencies emerged: the organized feminist community (the Rape Crisis Center, the Caribbean Association for Feminist Research and Action [CAFRA], Working Women, Concerned Women for Progress, and the Group), which made alliances with feminist activist lawyers; a coalition of women in public services and trade unions (the Sexual Offences Bill Action Committee); women who appeared not to have an organizational base; the Bar Association, the Southern Assembly of Lawyers, and the Law Society, invited by state managers to provide formal responses to the bill; and a group of several religious organizations in which the Catholic church was the major respondent. In the absence of any record of the internal deliberations of state managers, it is important methodologically to reconstruct the developments that took shape within the public arena and to map the broad trajectories defined by these different constituencies. After all, this public contestation will be the only memory of this experience to interrupt the official history which presents itself as monolithic.

At this point I will utilize the set of problematics that framed the public debate and developed in the press particularly, because it was through this medium that public interpretations of the event were mediated and at the same time reinforced in editorials supporting those definitions of morality deployed by state managers.[17] I use here verbatim quotations from newspaper articles to stage an encounter among the constituencies.

Apart from religious beliefs, the main reason people get married is to have sexual intercourse freely and at their convenience. (Hendrickson Seunath, chair of the Southern Assembly of Lawyers)

There is nothing in the marriage contract that states: "I promise to give my husband unlimited rights to intercourse with or without my consent." (Ann Holder)

The [sexual assault] clause will destroy the very essence of marriage. (Lee Renwick, columnist, *Guardian*)

If allowing a wife to charge her husband with rape is tantamount to destroying the very basis of marriage, then, in this vein, the very basis of marriage must be rape. . . . The offence of rape seeks to destroy sexual intercourse without consent. If destroying sexual intercourse without consent is the same as destroying marriage, "the very essence of marriage" then, must be rape. (B. C. Pires)

I am bitterly opposed to this on religious grounds; the law has no place in the bedroom. (Kamaluddin Mohammed, deputy prime minister)[18]

Taken together, these voices, although differentially located, map some clear distinctions between the meanings men and women attach to conjugal relations and erotic autonomy within those relations. Women foregrounded the notion that a certain kind of masculinized violence had found legitimacy within marriage but went beyond the focus on marriage to examine the wider sphere of sexual politics. That it was men who crafted the discourse, the men with power, was central to their argument; and even when women cast their objections in terms that resembled those of state managers (in this case the contractual language of consent), they displaced the terms of submission and of implied consent inherent in the domestic structures in which they live. Male discourse, on the other hand, centered on the defense of marriage and an appeal on religious grounds to preserve its sanctity and ward off any threats to morality and family that might have been posed by legitimizing lesbian and gay sexualities. Men wished to retain the "private" character of domestic marital relations and, through it, unlimited sexual access to women.

In this regard, then, this discourse was a gendered one. I do not wish to suggest that all men denied the existence of violence in marriage, that no men supported Clause 4, and that all women were in favor of the Clause, for this would amount to an essentializing move which constructs men and women solely in terms of sexual difference. What I suggest, however, is that women are able to see themselves as victims of violence, if you will, because of an institutionalized history of violence which sanctions their subordination within fundamentally asymmetrical power relationships. It is the location that women occupy and the challenge they pose to the ideological obliteration of violence that heighten the very moment of contestation. Marriage is less at stake for women, therefore, than the ideologies regarding passive, compliant womanhood which such a location has inspired.

For B. C. Pires, as her statement indicates, marriage is often anchored in a violent masculinity that expresses itself through coercion and forced sexual dominance. Pires perceives the *actual experience* of domination and substitutes for it the *ideology* of the sanctity, the solemnity, and inviolability of marriage. It is this *experience* of domestic violence which feminists placed on the political agenda, challenging the problematic conflation of the religious and the secular which state managers and church dogma had presented and exposing the ways in which state managers redrafted morality on the basis of partial notions that excluded knowledge about sexual violence. For when the sanctity of marriage privileges and defines morality, it acts to suppress women's experiences and alternative definitions of morality. Women came to voice in politicizing their experiences of violence. This violence was expressed in one palpably moving story in which a woman described the physical and sexual violation her mother confronted in a culture of complicity: "she had no help, no help in a culture that says that a man has unlimited access to *his* woman's body . . . including the right to beat her into submission. . . ." Her formulation of violence and the veiled reference to autonomous desire differs markedly from that of Hendrickson Seunath and later found collective expression in the organized mobilization to reinstate Clause 4 after it had been hastily withdrawn from public debate by the General Council of the ruling party.

The ironic reinscription of religious metaphors in this secular debate requires some scrutiny. Only the Presbyterian and Catholic sects entered the political arena, and they did so in official support of Clause 4. But buried in the pages of the *Catholic News*, the publication of the Catholic church, one Hugh Cameron argued that the Clause had become a threatening Sword of Damocles and called on the authority of "natural justice" and the "Rules of Evidence" which derive therefrom "to preclude the taking of Evidence from one spouse against the other partner."[19] But through which set of beliefs could one come to understand this surprisingly liberal gesture given the church's historical role in regulating women's desire and its struggles with the state to carve out its own domain of influence? The positioning of the body as sacrosanct in ecclesiastical teachings provides certain important clues. For the Catholic church, the body remains "the temple of the holy spirit," to be used only in the service of procreation, in "proper circumstances, i.e., with the context of marriage."[20] Rape, then, is a violation of that temple, a violation of sacred marriage. It is sacrilegious sex and as sacrilege is one of those sins of the flesh which ought to be punished by God (or priests whom God has designated to mediate earthly punishments and forgiveness on His behalf) and in this instance through the courts. The church's objection rests, therefore, not in the defense of women's erotic autonomy but in the belief that rape is a violation of *the* only legitimate ground for enacting procreative sex.

It is in asserting the primacy of procreative sex and the defense of marriage and the family that the interests of state managers and church pundits intersect. They converge as well because both church and state managers continue to exert control over women's sexuality by regulating access to the material bases of procreation: to contraception, health-care services, and abortion by legislating through secular law and religious dictate the circumstances under which these services are to be distributed, if at all. Both understand the power of religious appeal in a context in which religion and scripture provide important understandings of the social world. When Kamaluddin Mohammed, as the central state player, opposes the inclusion of Clause 4 and rests his objection on the cultural authority of religion, his claim lies on somewhat contradictory yet potentially compelling grounds. Unlike other claimants in the discourse, he locates this authority not on hegemonic Judeo-Christian claims of morality, chastity, and submission but on principles of Islam which he leaves undefined. In the absence of a formal response from the Muslim community, however, this gesture might be read as an attempt to link the material and constitutive effects of the discourse: mobilizing the Muslim community to the very fact of producing a discourse based in Islam.

It is in this sense that the act of representation is simultaneously an exercise of power. Which world is Mohammed representing when he states that the law has no place in the bedroom? He is actually articulating three worlds but appears to be representing only one. For he speaks as a powerful member of state who is able to shift the site and shape the terms and trajectories of the discourse. He speaks also as the putative representative of Islam; and, thirdly, he speaks as a patriarch residing within a particular domestic sphere. While he insists on the privacy of domesticity and on the inappropriate influence of public law, he is still able to shift the terms of the legal debate publicly. The same can be said about Sampat Metha who, as an influential lawyer with formalized links to the Law Commission and informal links to state managers, can insist on privacy (according to Metha, "any reasonable man or woman would not want to go to the police station and report the details of their sex . . . or what happened in the privacy of their bedrooms") with appeals to common sense, rationality, and a notion of egalitarianism which are vastly at odds with what B. C. Pires elucidated earlier and which find little correspondence in the prevailing cultural codes and practices regarding masculine sexualized violence within conjugal relations.

I have marked the emergence of this gendered discourse, charted not in an essentialized way but grounded within an understanding of women's *differential* experience of violence and power within sexual relationships. I have argued that such a location makes the moment of contestation possible: when state managers produce a discourse rooted in morality, or based in the defense of marriage and the legitimation of a masculinized violence, women assert their sexual agency in order to define the terms of female subjectivity. Clearly, contemporary feminist political praxis is not as marginal as it appears. It has turned morality into a feminist issue and challenged the state on the very ground it has constructed. It faces an ongoing political challenge, however, to contest the criminalization and marginalization of lesbian sex and to politicize the conflation of morality with heterosexuality.

My intent throughout this essay has been to foreground the complicity of the state in sexual politics, demonstrating that the state is active in sexualizing relations between men and women, in normalizing and regulating relations within civil society while simultaneously diffusing those relations with partial definitions of morality. The state is not the neutral or dispassionate interest as it negotiates relationships between itself and civil society that pluralists would have us believe, nor is it a neutered state as some Marxist analyses suggest. The state actively sexualizes relationships between men and women and has a major stake in promoting and defending conjugal masculinity. It also has the capacity to create new political constituencies (in this instance, a category called lesbians) and has chosen to exercise power within "the family."[21] (So far, there is no evidence that the two most significant provisions of the legislation have been implemented.) "Wives" can potentially be protected by the state, but in a context where marriage is class-specific and the majority of intimate relationships are institutionalized outside this domain, women, not "wives," are the ones at greater risk of not being protected.[22] In the debate and in the legal text, morality was cast on narrow conjugal familial grounds, and women were incorporated into the debate but only to the extent that they are wives, not women who could exercise both political and sexual agency. The potentialities of women's agency get collapsed into "wives" and ultimately into a subordinated position. The importance, therefore, of examining both elements of the discourse on morality (rape and marriage and criminalizing lesbian sex) was to demonstrate the complex way in which women's agency is being recast when morality is predicated on women as "wives." It is only in their capacity as "wives" that women can make certain claims on the state. Nonwives, prostitutes, lesbians can make no such claims.

So whom do state managers believe they are representing by institutionalizing morality within a racialized class context? Are the political appeals directed toward Black middle-class "wives" who have become increasingly economically independent in the last decade, and who might potentially erode the Black "family" on which the existence of nationalism relies? Nationalism has historically defined women as guardians of culture whose cultural, even national, responsibility was to bear and raise children.[23] But how will East Indian "wives" and the constructions of their femininity figure in these political strategies?[24] On what terms will women and "wives" of different sexualities express a mutual solidarity and define their own subjectivities?

The significance of the Sexual Offences Bill is that it moves beyond a discrete case study to provide a point of entry to think about the recasting of morality and its implications for feminist methodology and political praxis. Morality is a feminist issue not only because women who are "wives" become the ground on which some very narrow definitions of womanhood are redrawn, but also because the very formulation of morality is underwritten in fundamentally gendered terms assigning women to a subordinated position while invoking some higher religious or natural principles in order to do so. The terms are consonant with a mode of sexuality that would reproduce labor power and a conjugal heterosexual norm. The postcolonial state has moved to suppress women's autonomy and women's political organizing by attempting to disrupt the praxis of feminist and radical progressive movements that has focused on the politics of everyday life as a terrain of struggle. By linking morality to sexuality, and to conjugal marriage in particular, the postcolonial state is able to produce a hegemonic discourse that is strikingly similar to the Victorian cult of true womanhood and the moral reform movements of its day, and to the religious and secular fundamentalists of the contemporary period. Its actions dovetail well with the global diffusion of fundamentalism.

But the terrain of morality is highly contested terrain, in spite of the ability of the state to mobilize its forces of coercion in order to suppress feminist popular struggle, and in spite of its insistence on locating the structures of cathexis in the private sphere. What this suggests for feminist politics and cross-cultural modes of inquiry is the centrality of linking the domain of the public and private, and exposing the ways they are ideologically bound. Such linkages pose a threat to the state. Both spheres are constituted through productive discourses. One of the major tasks at hand is to theorize from the point of view and contexts of marginalized women not in terms of a victim status or an essentialized identity but in terms that push us to place women's agency, their subjectivities and collective consciousness, at the center of our understandings of power and resistance. Moreover, the postcolonial state has had to face the reality of women's autonomous organizing in other arenas. Since feminists have linked sexual violence to structural economic violence, the struggle to redefine sexuality in narrow terms will become more fierce within state agencies and the economy, as well as in popular culture.[25] Structural adjustment policies—the new realignments between the International Monetary Fund, the World Bank, and the postcolonial state organized around export-oriented privatized production—have both exacerbated the debt and simultaneously increased the burden for women whose unpaid labor compensates for retrenchments in health and social services.[26] These are the central moral questions which women have politicized and which the state works to displace as it attempts to solve the crisis of legitimacy by restricting the range of sexualities that are permissible and by acting to limit the kinds of questions which can conceivably fit within a moral frame.

NOTES

I wish to thank Chandra Talpade Mohanty, Honor Ford Smith, Kum Kum Bhavnani, and Cynthia Enloe, whose insights and support have taught me plenty about political solidarity and collective struggle. I remain deeply indebted to the women of the Caribbean whose active struggles around sexuality have made this analysis possible.

1. For a discussion of some of the problems that emerge from a historical reconstruction which relies on a colonial standpoint, see Lucille Mathurin Mair, "Reluctant Matriarchs," *Savacou* 13 (1977):1–6. Three instructive accounts in this regard are Mrs. A. C. Carmichael, *Domestic Manners and Social Condition of the White, Coloured and Negro Population of the West Indies* (New York: Negro Universities Press, 1969; original publication 1833); Nicholas Guppy, ed., *Yseult Bridges, Child of the Tropics: Victorian Memoirs* (Trinidad and Tobago: Scrip-J Printers, 1980); Evangeline Walker Andrews, ed., *Journal of a Lady of Quality: Being the Narrative of a Journey from Scotland to the West Indies, North Carolina, and Portugal, in the Years 1774 to 1776* (New Haven: Yale University Press, 1934).

2. Barbara Bush, "White 'Ladies,' Coloured 'Favorites' and Black 'Wenches:' Some Considerations on Sex, Race and Class Factors in Social Relations in White Creole Society in the British Caribbean," *Slavery and Abolition* 2 (1988):248–63.

3. Lorna McDaniel, "Madame Phillip-O: Reading the Returns of an 18th Century 'Free Mulatto Woman' of Grenada" (unpublished manuscript, 1986). Madame Phillip-O migrated from Grenada to Trinidad, and it is in this context that McDaniel makes her analysis.

4. Mair, p. 6.

5. Rhoda Reddock, "Indian Women and Indentureship in Trinidad and Tobago: 1845-1917," *Economic and Political Weekly* 20 (1985):80, 84. David Trotman has also analyzed the colonial construction of black working-class women as criminals in nineteenth-century Trinidad. See David Vincent Trotman, *Crime in Trinidad: Conflict and Control in a Plantation Society, 1838-1900* (Knoxville: The University of Tennessee Press, 1968).

6. Laws of Trinidad and Tobago, *The Sexual Offences Bill: "An Act to Repeal and Replace the Laws of Trinidad and Tobago Relating to Sexual Crimes, to the Procuration, Abduction and Prostitution of Persons and to Kindred Offences"* (Port-of-Spain: Government Printing Office, 1986). Subsequent references, unless otherwise indicated, are taken from the legislation.

7. Law Commission of Trinidad and Tobago, *Explanatory Note to the Sexual Offences Bill* (Internal Document, 1985).

8. Ibid. There is a thorough discussion of the politics of the passage of the legislation and those elements that central parliamentarians suppressed after their deliberations. For instance, two proposals barring "evidence" about the sexual reputation of the survivor and a stipulation that no corroboration was required for conviction of a rapist were eliminated. See Tina Johnson, *The Impact of Women's*

Consciousness on the History of the Present Case of Clause Four, Concerning Women and Development Series (Barbados: University of the West Indies, 1988).

9. The Wolfenden Commission was convened by the Church of England in 1954. See *The Wolfenden Report: Report of the Committee on Homosexual Offences and Prostitution* (New York: Lancer Books, 1964). This discourse on the protection of children seems more in keeping with Victorian notions of childhood than with the actual experiences of children in the Caribbean, whose chronological years belie the range of adult responsibilities they assume. For a discussion of the former, see Deborah Gorham, "The 'Maiden Tribute of Modern Babylon' Re-examined: Child Prostitution and the Idea of Childhood in Late Victorian England," *Victorian Studies* 21 (1978):353–79.

10. Michel Foucault. *Discipline and Punish: The Birth of the Prison* (New York: Random House, 1979), pp. 16–31.

11. Monique Wittig. "The Straight Mind," *Feminist Issues* (Summer 1980):103–10.

12. This formulation has been persuasively argued by Lata Mani for the Indian context. See Lata Mani, "The Construction of Women as Tradition in Early Nineteenth-Century Bengal," *Cultural Critique* 7 (1987):119–56; for a contemporary account of the imbrication of religious and secular discourse and their implication for women's subjectivity, see Zakia Pathak and Rajeswari Sunder Rajan, "Shabano," *Signs* 14, no. 3 (1989):558–83.

13. Biddy Martin, "Feminism, Criticism and Foucault," in Irene Diamond and Lee Quinby, eds., *Feminism and Foucault: Readings on Resistance* (Boston: Northeastern University Press, 1988), p. 18.

14. For a similar analysis of the inscription of erotic and legal discourses on the female body in Muslim societies, see Fatna A. Sabbah, *Woman in the Muslim Unconscious* (New York: Pergamon Press, 1984).

15. Alan Bray, *Homosexuality in Renaissance England* (London: Gay Men's Press, 1988), p. 25. Ed Cohen provides an incisive account of the shifting meanings of sodomy within religious, political, cultural, and literary contexts. See Cohen, "Legislating the Norm: From Sodomy to Gross Indecency," *Southern Atlantic Quarterly* 88, no. 1 (1989):181–218. Between 1873 and 1930 there were 78 imprisonments for sodomy in Trinidad and Tobago. These seem, however, to have been tried in magistrates' courts so that proceedings would not ordinarily be available (David Trotman of Toronto, interview by author, March 1990). The precise ways in which British redefinitions were grafted onto the colonial context and the specific debates about sodomy in the earlier period in Trinidad and Tobago go beyond the purview of my essay. There is a general discussion of the transplantation of British law in Henry Alcazar, "Evolution of English Law in Trinidad," *Minutes of the Canadian Bar Association* 12 (1927):159–67. The extent to which law enabled and solidified the colonial project is superbly summarized in Alcazar's closing discussion: "the evolution of English law in Trinidad . . . presents some interesting features. I regard it as a monument to the colonizing genius of the British race which stood out in the past in relation to the development of many Colonies and Dominions and is still helping the British Government to develop, to the mutual advantage of the native races which inhabit them and the rest of the Empire, those vast territories in Africa and elsewhere which form part of our Empire."

16. The ideological manipulation of the terrain of consent is an important area for consideration. Its link to a rational objective state apparatus in an advanced capitalist context is provided by Catherine A. Mackinnon, "Feminism, Marxism, Method, and the State: Toward Feminist Jurisprudence," *Signs* 8, no. 4 (1982):635–

58. For its application in a British colonial context, see Dagmar Engels, "The Age of Consent Act of 1891: Colonial Ideology in Bengal," *South Asia Research* 3, no. 2 (November 1984):107–34.

17. Cohen, p. 210.

18. All newspaper references are taken from the *Trinidad Guardian* (1985, 1986) and the *Trinidad Express* (1985, 1986).

19. *Catholic News*, 20 April 1986.

20. *Catholic News*, 14 May 1989.

21. For an excellent discussion of the state in sexual politics, see "The Structure of Gender Relations," in R. W. Connell, *Gender and Power* (Stanford, Calif: Stanford University Press, 1987), pp. 119–41. See also Connell, "The State in Sexual Politics: Outline of a Theory" (unpublished manuscript).

22. "Bastardy" and "illegitimacy" are two sites where the construction of "proper womanhood" has been encoded historically. In the last decade, between 40% and 50% of children did not live in nuclear families. In 1935 the figure was 70.6%, and these children were defined as "illegitimate." See Stephanie Daly, *The Developing Legal Status of Women in Trinidad and Tobago* (Port-of-Spain: The National Commission on the Status of Women, 1982), p. 26. See also Gordon Rohlehr, "The Sociology of Food Acquisition in a Context of Survivalism," in Patricia Mohammed and Catherine Shepherd, eds., *Gender in Caribbean Development* (Barbados: University of the West Indies, 1988).

23. This relationship between nationalism and sexuality is a knotty one indeed. See Joan French and Honor Ford Smith, *Women's Movements and Organizations in an Historical Perspective: Women, Work and Organizations in Jamaica, 1900-1944* (Netherlands: The Hague, 1985). Rhoda Reddock, "Women, Labour and Struggle in Twentieth-Century Trinidad and Tobago" (Ph.D. thesis, Netherlands: The University of Amsterdam, 1984). See also Cynthia Enloe, "Nationalism and Masculinity," in *Bananas, Beaches and Bases: Making Feminist Sense of International Politics* (Los Angeles: University of California Press, 1989).

24. Solidarity politics among East Indian and African Women are taking shape within the context of contemporary political struggle in the Caribbean. However, the history of the state's ambivalent relationship to East Indian women requires further analysis. See note 5 above. See also Stephanie Daly, "The Development of Laws Affecting East Indians in Trinidad and Tobago" (unpublished manuscript, 1984); Noor Kumar Mahabir, *The Still Cry: Personal Accounts of East Indians in Trinidad and Tobago during Indentureship (1845-1917)* (Trinidad: Calaloux Publications, 1985).

25. Peggy Antrobus, *Structural Adjustment, Cure or Curse? Implications for Caribbean Development* (Barbados: University of the West Indies, 1989). For a lucid and comprehensive account of the systemic economic crises under conditions of increased militarization and violence in the Third World, see Gita Sen and Caren Grown, *Development, Crises, and Alternative Visions: Third World Women's Perspectives* (New York: Monthly Review Press, 1987). They argue that "peace and justice cannot be separated from development just as equality cannot, because the conditions that breed violence, war, and inequality are themselves often the results of development strategies harmful or irrelevant to the poor and to women" (74). An excellent analysis of the implications of underdevelopment and structural adjustment for cultural workers is provided by Honor Ford Smith, *Ring Ding in a Tight Corner: A Case Study of Funding and Organizational Democracy in Sistren, 1977-1988* (Toronto: International Council for Adult Education, 1989).

26. Much more needs to be understood about the ways in which sexual politics come to be codified around particular issues in order to flesh out the political

emergence of sexual violence. Sistren, a working-class group of Jamaican women, has done so through popular theater. See also their testimonies in Sistren with Honor Ford Smith, *Lionheart Gal: Life Stories of Jamaican Women* (London: The Women's Press, 1986).

BUILDING POLITICS FROM PERSONAL LIVES

Discussions on Sexuality among Poor Women in Brazil*

Carmen Barroso and Cristina Bruschini

Thousands of small groups of poor women in the large cities of Brazil have been fighting for their most urgent needs. Sex education has been one of these needs, in spite of the resistance of the traditional political parties—on both the right and the left. In responding to this demand, a group of researchers developed a project of action research which aimed to construct a collective knowledge about sexuality based on the experience of these women. This essay reports on this project against the background of the ongoing political and ideological debates on family planning and sex education in Brazil.

The Politics of Family Planning in Brazil

Population policies have been the subject of heated debate for the past three decades. The issue of population control first appeared on the political scene during the 1960s when the Kennedy administration tried to link its economic aid to Latin America with policies aimed at checking the so-called demographic explosion (Gondin and Hackert 1982). The policies had a very clear neomalthusian ring: population control was con-

*This essay was previously published in *Third World, Second Sex: Women's Struggles and National Liberation*, Vol. 2, edited by Miranda Davies (London: Zed Press, 1987).

ceived as the solution to the problem of poverty and underdevelopment. Vice-President Johnson himself stated that "less than 5 dollars invested in population control is worth a hundred dollars invested in economic growth" (Wiarda and Helzner 1981).

Population control soon found supporters among the Brazilian elite, who were adept at using very conservative political arguments. In 1965, for instance, a leading economist argued that population control should be the government's main objective and added: "The economic situation is due, not to Yankee exploitation but rather to the unwanted child." An influential newspaper argued in 1977 that the continuing tendency of the proletariat to multiply more rapidly than the middle class would bring "somber consequences to the political and social order. In Brazil, as in the world as a whole, it is very hard to check the tremendous growth of the proletariat. As a result the proletariat is unable to rise to the middle class in sufficient numbers, which is fundamental to capitalism."

In spite of this support by sectors of the conservative elite, the U.S. policy of imposing population-control programs was, on the whole, self-defeating. The fact that it was presented as a requirement for economic assistance implied that it was a price to be paid. Its imposition from the top down, without consulting Brazilian public opinion, made rightists and leftists alike agree that it was a serious threat to national autonomy, and that it represented a foreign intrusion into the nation's internal affairs. The prevailing idea that the existence of a large population was not a problem but rather an important resource, both economically and strategically, was thereby reinforced.

Perhaps the most important pressure group against the government support of population control was the Catholic church. Although no longer linked to the state, Catholicism is still the dominant religion, insofar as it is the religion of both the majority and the upper classes. The church has attempted to respond to the demands of the antagonistic social classes represented in its clientele. Under the influence of liberation theology, the church's top hierarchy has identified itself with the interests of the lower classes on several different occasions, thus becoming a special target of repression by the authoritarian government. At the same time, the Brazilian church is highly dependent on the Vatican, and thus it has avoided making any statement favorable to birth control for a long time, even when European churchmen were doing so. These factors allowed for a curious combination of a great tolerance for birth-control practices at the individual level and, up until recently (when two influential foreign theologians, Charbonneau and Lepargneur, spoke out against the general trend), an absolute rejection of any kind of official family-planning policy.

This rejection is a point of consensus in a church otherwise quite divided with regard to political and doctrinal issues; since, as pointed out by Gramsci, unity is a major source of strength for the Catholic church, the importance of the issue of family planning is correspondingly inflated in order to overshadow disagreements in other areas. Even the progressive wing of the church holds conservative views in matters that directly challenge the church's own authority over personal lives: sexuality, reproduction, women's rights. The tolerance at the individual level can also be understood within the overall strategy to maintain the church's authority. To assert that birth control is a sin and at the same time to hold the monopoly over forgiveness is a powerful way to keep control over the "psychology of the masses," as Reich called it.

The main arguments the church used against government support for birth control were: (1) population control is not a solution for the problems of underdevelopment and poverty; (2) each couple has the right to choose the size of its family, without interference from the state; and (3) Brazil should avoid yielding to foreign pressures to limit its population. These reasons were all political, rather than religious, arguments. The use of political arguments seemed both an authentic concern of the church in its "option for the poor" and a strategy to avoid resorting to moral objections to family planning, known to enjoy little popularity among Brazilians of all classes.

The Brazilian government showed no sign of willingness to implement an official program to curb population growth given the resistance to it by diverse constituencies including some members of the military government. As a result, the International Planned Parenthood Federation—IPPF, an international agency largely financed by the U.S. government—adopted a different strategy. IPPF created a private institution, Bemfam, which provided free family-planning services through "community distribution of pills" and clinics. Bemfam was created in 1965 with two main objectives: (1) to have a "demonstration effect," that is, to be a pilot program that showed the feasibility of this kind of service; and more important, (2) to act as an advocacy group for an official wide-scale program.

On the one hand, one cannot deny that Bemfam has been partially successful in meeting both aims. By the mid-seventies, in spite of strong criticism from groups as diverse as church representatives, the military, and nationalists from the right and left, it had established an extensive network of services in many states. The first sign of change in the government's opinion appeared during the 1974 Conference on Population in Bucharest. Whereas in 1968 the president had sent a strong natalist message to the Pope, stating that the country's demographic density was compatible with its global needs for development and defense, in 1974 Brazil's statement at the UN conference, although still favoring population growth, recognized the government's responsibility for providing the information and means of birth control demanded by low-income families. Bemfam claims that this change was largely due to its own efforts. This is obviously an exaggeration, but Bemfam did play some role in shaping these policies. More important, however, are the social and economic changes in Brazilian society which brought about a 24 percent decline in the birth rate in the seventies, in spite of the absence of a government program (Merrick 1983).

Rural-urban migration has kept a steady pace: the percentage of the population living in urban areas, which was 45.1 in 1960, reached 67.6 in 1980. It is well known that in subsistence agriculture the low cost of childrearing and children's early participation in production make large families a useful survival strategy. In the seventies, the widespread introduction of export crops and sugar cane (used as a substitute for gasoline after the oil crisis) expelled small land tenants and turned a large proportion of rural workers into salaried ones, with no access to land for food production. For them, as for urban workers, large families became less viable. In the urban areas, the expansion of state sector employment and the service sector in general resulted in increased participation of middle-class women in the labor market, with no corresponding decrease of their responsibility for child care: an added incentive for birth control. Cultural factors also played a role: although feminism is far from being a mass movement, its ideas, albeit diluted or even distorted, have reached large portions of the population through the mass media. The number of TV sets tripled in the seventies, reaching 75 percent of the urban population. The main thrust of the mass media, of course, has been not the dissemination of new women's roles but the stimulus to consumerism, which is also incompatible with large families.[1]

More recently, Bemfam in its advocacy of family planning has tried to use different arguments for different audiences. It has, on occasion, even resorted to discourses based on the human right to decide the number of children, and women's right to control their own bodies, as well as relied upon arguments concerning the prevention of public health problems resulting from uncontrolled fertility, and the separation of sexual pleasure from procreation. However, since the 1960s, the main emphasis has been neomalthusian, which links the economic problems of the country with the high birth rate. This conservative ideology permeates Bemfam's educational program. It is designed to increase motivation by convincing poor people that the reason for their poverty is the large number of children they have. Bemfam was keen to state "everybody's duty to control birth," since women were conceived as irresponsible baby-producers who needed to be convinced of the need to avoid large families, regardless of what women themselves thought about desired family size.

This campaign about duties managed to keep alive the fears of authoritarian programs which established demographic goals with no respect for the individual's autonomy. Poor women's needs and motives were largely ignored, and their active participation was discouraged. Although these fears were justified to some extent, both by the example of grotesque incentives offered for sterilization in some countries and by the compulsory establishment of family size advocated by some of the most enthusiastic population-control supporters, the net result was that family planning came to be conceived only in terms of coercion and was therefore thoroughly rejected by democratic forces.

In general, progressive forces have not been very progressive with regard to birth control. Historical circumstances did not allow for any concerted action other than the resistance to attempts to impose birth-control and population-control programs. The authoritarian government, on the one hand, and the private organizations identified with population control, on the other, were not to be entrusted with the provision of high-quality services geared to women's needs. The establishment of self-help groups was unthinkable owing to a lack of resources and the threats from the repressive regime. The problem was that these objective limits to action were not clearly conceptualized and resulted in a sort of all-embracing antimalthusian thinking. The left position became a much broader rejection of birth control per se as if it were inherently neomalthusian rather than an adequate response to particular historical circumstances.

This mirror-image thinking is now being revised in some left circles, but in the seventies it had an absolute hegemony in all progressive currents. As has been analyzed by Gondin and Hackert (1982), antineomalthusianism is not really a theory, it is the negation of an obsolete dogma. Much of the literature produced by the left was concerned only with the ideology and the underlying motives of the bourgeois thinking behind population control. Concrete consequences of different policies and the content of these policies received little attention. The class interests of the proletariat were sometimes defined merely in terms of the negation of the interests of the bourgeoisie. The economic advantages of large families observed in some contexts were uncritically generalized as if they applied to all sectors of the poor, rural and urban alike, and the costs of high fertility to women and children were ignored, as if they were shared equally among all members of the family.

In some cases, the left-wing strategy of simply reversing the right's argument resulted in equally authoritarian arguments: for national security reasons, the country's population should grow as fast as possible, and therefore legislation prohibiting abortion should be strictly enforced, and the distribution of pills banned. The net result of the simplistic reasoning of the left was that it did not develop any alternative proposal for the solution of real problems faced by Brazilian women: the lack of adequate information, the limited access to safe contraception, the brutal reality of clandestine abortion.

The Women's Movement and Birth Control

In the late seventies, after a long period of demobilization due to the repressive military government, grassroots social movements emerged on the Brazilian scene. The women's movement has been one of the most widespread of these movements, with a wide array of aims and forms. In the large cities, thousands of small groups of low-income women have been fighting for water, sanitation, daycare centers, and other urgent neighborhood needs.

This process is well described by Schmink (1981), Alvarez (1986), and Blay (1985). Working-class women mobilized as women to defend their rights as wives and mothers, rights which were affected by the regressive wage policies, rises in the costs of living, and the low priority accorded to social sectors in state policies. The basis for this politicization of motherhood was provided by a large network of apolitical women's organizations promoted by the Catholic church: the mothers' clubs. Their political action within an authoritarian regime was made possible by the very ideology of this regime: by confining women to motherhood, it made it difficult to be openly repressive against mothers, who were exerting their legitimate rights to defend their children.

Initially, the women did not challenge gender power arrangements, but contrary to the expectations of the traditional political parties—on both the right and the left—soon one of the most frequently voiced needs was for sex education and for discussion of the relationships between women and men. Given the strong prejudice against the subject, insofar as it is considered to be both immoral and nonpolitical, one can attribute its emergence only to the deep conflicts women confront when dealing with their own sexuality.

These conflicts have been exacerbated by the social changes that have narrowed affective life to couple relationships and have brought sexual pleasure to play a central role in what came to be thought of as personal fulfillment. The charge of *non*political is still frequently voiced by the left, although not so unanimously in the last few years. This charge is based both on a narrow view of politics which considers irrelevant anything that is not directly concerned with the class struggle, or the fight against imperialism, and also paradoxically on a fear that a power struggle between the sexes may override class interests and undermine the fight around common causes.

The importance of the emergence of this demand for sex education by poor women was not immediately acknowledged by the feminist movement, which was reemerging within the middle class.[2] A whole process of social change was transforming the status of women inside and outside the family and setting the scenario for new ideas: increased participation in the modern sectors of the economy, higher levels of university attendance, wider dissemination of feminist ideas coming from the North, the legitimacy afforded by the UN International Women's Year, and disenchantment with the position of women in leftist parties. Many factors helped to create the environment in which feminist groups started to grow, initially in the learned middle classes of the large cities. When this movement reemerged in 1975, it felt compelled to assert its basic solidarity with the newly revived general struggle for democracy. It was defined as a struggle for civil liberties and against the high cost of living.

It was only after a few years that specifically feminist issues began to appear, although still in a very timid way. During the 1978 election campaign, five women's organizations and several women scholars from São Paulo signed a letter of women's rights that included the demand for information and access to contraception with medical assistance and for the legalization of abortion. In Rio, however, the Brazilian Women's Center did not dare to support anything more than "the opening of discussions on family planning policies." In 1979, in the final recommendations made at the First Congress of Women of São Paulo, which was organized by a coalition of twelve women's organizations, reproductive rights were simply stated in terms of the right to choose to have children, and a protest was made against the government's program to prevent high-risk pregnancies. The right *not* to have children was not mentioned, even though it was well known that millions of Brazilian women were resorting to desperate solutions to avoid the birth of unwanted children.[3]

In 1980, the Feminist Front of São Paulo published *What Is Abortion?*, a book which presents the case for legal abortion linked with global social change. Its tactic is to emphasize the health and welfare problems of illegal abortions and to downplay a woman's right to control her own body. Only one paragraph is devoted to control over female sexuality. The authors felt the need to examine in detail the Catholic arguments about the origin of life, and also the left's suspicion of the alleged neo-malthusian ring attached to the abortion struggle.

In 1981, when the government was studying a new basic health program which included family planning, feminist organizations of São Paulo put forth a statement called "No to the Government's ambiguous and vague proposal." Although the document clearly asserted women's right to control their own bodies and sexuality, and their decision to fight for legal abortions, its main emphasis was against the potential for coercive contraception and in favor of better living and working conditions.

In that same year, a group of feminist researchers at the Chagas Foundation began a project of action research on women's sexuality. This was an attempt to build a collective knowledge of sexuality based on the experiences of women living in the poor peripheries of the industrialized city of São Paulo. This project is described below.

Building Collective Knowledge of Sexuality in a Nonauthoritarian Way

The origin of the project was tied to the demand for discussions on sex education and gender relations voiced by women in the grassroots movements, and to the political contradictions surrounding the history of feminism and population policies in Brazil. The aims were to construct a collective knowledge about sexuality and to share this knowledge immediately among all the participants. Participant methodology was chosen in order to help small groups of women discuss the meaning of sexuality in their intimate relationships, as well as in the broader social context. Their discussions served as a basis for a series of booklets to be created and used both as discussion guides for similar groups and as a reference for all interested women.

The project was developed by the Chagas researchers in conjunction with the Mother's Club of Diadema, whose members are low-income housewives, most of them in their twenties and early thirties, some of them older, who take care of their homes and small children. Most of their husbands are unskilled workers in the neighborhood factories or have other manual occupations in the service sector. The club holds weekly meetings and offers sewing, painting, and knitting courses. The women read and write with great difficulty. They are the recipients of free distributions of food provided by government agencies. When asked about group discussions of sexuality, the members showed great enthusiasm. Although they had had previous experience in group activities and courses in infant care, they had not had any experience of the kind suggested.

TEACHING WHILE LEARNING. In the first meetings they asked many questions about body functions and anatomy. At times it was difficult not to lecture in order to provide all the information requested. One way we tried to avoid lecturing was to start from drawings they made in their small groups. If the aim was to help critical thought, understanding, and reflection on daily life, the starting point had to be aspects of daily life. But we also had to go beyond them to reach the real connections among these apparently chaotic elements. Thus, while each person's individual experience was valued, we also tried to locate sexuality within the context of social relations.

Five booklets were created from these discussions. The first booklet describes male and female bodies in a simple and direct way. Photographs of naked people were used to avoid the coldness of schematic drawings. The idea is to link physiology with flesh and blood, in a body that not only ovulates, but also desires and is able to feel pleasure. Pictures of common people were used to counterfight the dominant esthetic standards, and help women to accept and love their own figures.[4] The production of the first pictures was not easy, for at the beginning, inhibition resulted in rigid positions and artificial smiles. Furthermore, in our search for nonprofessional models, at first only young, beautiful, and middle-class friends were willing to be pictured. After a while we found a wider range of volunteers, including a middle-aged physician and a black domestic worker.

The second booklet presents information on birth control and a discussion of the social and political conditions of childbearing and child-rearing. The third one is geared to helping mothers accept and respond positively to the sexuality of their children, in order to avoid the reproduction of ignorance and shame of which they themselves were victims. The fourth booklet teaches self-examination of the breasts and genitals, and at the same time encourages the fight for the right to good-quality public medical services. Similarly, strong criticism of the authoritarianism of the medical profession is presented side by side with an acknowledgment of the bad working conditions of doctors in the public system. In the last booklet sexual pleasure is integrated with the whole gamut of life's pleasures. Issues discussed include the role of fantasy, similarities and differences between men and women, and the variability of individual preferences and behavior. A concerted attempt is made to avoid the presentation of ready-made recipes, or the imposition of new patterns of right and wrong. Rather, the aim is to instill in each woman respect for her own experiences and values, and for those that differ from hers.

Some pages of the leaflets illustrate the general tone. In dealing with pleasure, we discussed the difficulty of enjoying sex in situations where the whole family lives in a single room or in which the couple is threatened by unemployment (photo 1). At the same time, it was stressed that pleasure and sexual fulfillment are threatened not only by material conditions but also by the ignorance, shame, or distaste for their own bodies which women have had since early childhood (photo 2). Problems with the gynecological exam were discussed in relation to authoritarian attitudes from doctors and our repressive education about our bodies and sexuality in general (photo 3). We also discussed how women's subordination within the family reproduces the power structure of society as a whole, and thus how the family becomes a mechanism for developing

Nem sempre sentimos desejo ou prazer quando estamos cansadas por ter trabalhado muito ou aflitas porque a família dorme toda num só quarto.

Se estamos preocupadas com dinheiro, com filhos, saúde, emprego, ou se estamos com algum problema emocional, talvez fiquemos com menos disposição para transar.

Para que tenhamos mais direito ao prazer, não precisamos lutar para mudar esta sociedade?

1. The banner shown in the picture reads, "Pleasure for all. Feminist Collective of Campinas." (*Great Pleasure,* p. 6)

Temos dificuldade para sentir prazer sexual.

Temos medo de falar de sexo.

Sentimos vergonha de algumas partes de nos- so próprio corpo.

Como fazer para acabar com isso?

2. At the bottom of the page, a question asks: "How can we end all this?" (*Understanding Our Bodies*, p. 9)

Nem todos os médicos nos dão a atenção necessária.
Muitos não ouvem o que queremos falar e às vezes nem examinam direito.

Temos ou não o direito de aprender a cuidar melhor do nosso corpo?

3. Deluged by scientific jargon, the woman asks: "Do we have a right to learn about our own bodies?" (*The Gyn Exam*, p. 3)

Dentro da família, nos ensinaram somente a obedecer, a não pensar por nós mesmas. Isto acontece porque em nossa sociedade algumas pessoas tomaram para si o poder de decidir sobre a vida da maioria das pessoas.

4. (1) The boss asserts his power, rejecting a pay-raise request. (2) The husband-employee forbids his wife to have a job. (3) The wife-mother tells her son: "I give orders; you obey them." (4) The son repeats that to the cat. (5) The poor rat has nowhere to go but to escape. (*When the Children Ask for Certain Things,* p. 6)

Se as mulheres não se organizarem para lutar por seus direitos, as leis não serão cumpridas.

Nair Benedicto

Quais são os direitos da mulher, segundo as leis?

5. The sign says, "We want daycare." (*Do I Want to Be a Mother?* p. 10)

submissive individuals (photo 4). The need for women to organize to fight for their rights was discussed as well, although in a timid way (photo 5).

In helping the group to arrive at a critical understanding of their own situation, as being part of a structure of social relations, we too were learning, and had a chance to change our minds. We were convinced, for instance, that contrary to neomalthusian teachings, the most important thing about birth control was that it could not be used as a solution to economic problems. Although we still believe that the primary cause of poverty is structural, the women's resistance to our arguments and their daily behavior gradually convinced us that information about and access to contraception are also important elements for the improvement of their living conditions on a short-term basis. This improvement is clearly quite limited, both because the structural causes of poverty may remain unchanged and because inadequate health care renders high-technology contraception particularly risky. However, given these limits, contraception is seen by them as an immediate need to which they attach great priority, and which they do not see as incompatible with the struggle for a better health system and against the roots of poverty. What may seem obvious from the outside was, in fact, an arduous learning experience for us, given the whole history of heated political debate over this issue in Latin America.

Between Indoctrination and Neutrality

We tried to avoid false neutrality as well as the authoritarian imposition of our values. Laura, one of the participants, said, "In other courses, we remained quiet, listening to the teachers. But you don't come to give lectures." Their active participation gave them greater self-confidence to speak, because they knew they would be listened to. This does not mean that the researchers were romanticizing popular knowledge and experience or expecting to find a pure absolute truth among the participants. These women's discussions reproduced to varying degrees the ideology that ensures their domination.

Since the values of the dominant class are internalized by every class, and given that there is no pure and entirely autonomous popular culture, we had to ask ourselves about our role as participant researchers. When they said, for instance, that "a woman is a woman when she becomes a mother," "abortion is a crime," or "homosexuality is sickness," it was impossible to remain quiet. We felt that they had a right to information about what our opinions were, and that attempting to disguise them would be neither very effective nor ethically justifiable, since it did not seem fair to expect them to be candid while we withheld our own candid expressions. In dealing with controversial values, we gradually came to the point where we could state our point of view with no fear of imposing our opinions. In the groups we came to respect each other's convictions, and agreed that a point of view is nothing more than a point of view: to be accepted if it makes sense for us, to be rejected if it does not.

The most important thing is that the women always felt free to disagree with any one of us. While some raised concerns about the preservation of lower-class values and the danger of exposing women to middle-class feminist values, the women are not at all defenseless, naive beings, ready to swallow any new value mentioned, as one would believe from the overconcern voiced in some quarters with preservation of lower-class values, supposedly endangered by the exposure to middle-class feminist values. As long as it was made explicit that we did not claim to be the guardians of "Truth," and that our opinions were the result of our personal histories, which differed from theirs, this exchange of ideas seemed to increase their autonomy, much more than their previous lack of access to knowledge in the area.

We also found that these women disagree among themselves: for instance, when Ana said she thought it was her duty to have sex any time her husband wanted, Suely disagreed immediately, and a heated discussion followed. It did not take long for the naive researchers to discover that the mythical "Poor Woman" did not exist. Their shared common experiences and opinions did not exhaust the richness of their different lives and ideas.

New Challenges

After one year in which the Chagas researchers had given a series of seminars on the booklets to groups of feminists, grassroots communities, and women in left parties, requests started to come from civil servants—mostly women—in the education, welfare, and health systems. These were received mostly from the lower echelons at the local level; for instance, nurses at a city health clinic, facing the needs of poor women every day, asked for seminars to learn our methodology in order to replicate it with their clientele. It soon became clear that women doctors, nurses, teachers, and social workers came to the discussion groups with the same histories of doubts, fears, hopes, and strengths we found in militant and grassroots groups. This "womanity" had difficulty emerging in some groups when there was a rigid hierarchy in the workplace or an authoritarian personality in the leadership. But on the whole, it was surprisingly easy for women to share their common concerns and intimate experiences. Of course, these groups, who took upon themselves the extra responsibility of developing activities in sex education with their clientele, are not the typical civil servants settled within a system that breeds inertia and gives no recognition to special efforts. However, such groups are growing in number: by June 1984, we had worked with thirty-three of them (as compared with thirty-five non-state-related groups).

The transition to democracy presented new opportunities and new risks for Brazilian feminists. A growing crisis of legitimacy and a deepening economic collapse brought a gradual end to the military regime, starting with the election of opposition state governors in 1982. The coalition now in power is a blend of disparate political forces, including some progressive sectors. Some feminists have entered party politics and are lobbying from inside for gender-specific issues. Others are very reluctant to do so, either because they have joined the other progressive party which has remained in the opposition, or because their view of feminism attaches no relevance to state policies. Some of the "opposition feminists" work in middle-level posts of the government bureaucracy, where they have been trying to implement items of a feminist agenda. This has been facilitated by the need of the current regime to maintain its broad social basis of support, and the resulting courtship of the women's movement.

When state policy papers on women's health were drawn up for the first time in 1983, the reproductive-rights discourse of the women's movement featured prominently in them. Regardless of that, many feminist groups voiced strong opposition to them. This opposition expressed several trends: a generalized mistrust of government rhetoric more often used to disguise inertia or unpopular policies than to set guidelines for policy implementation; an unclear conceptualization of opposition-government relationships and the resulting fear that support for any specific policy would imply loss of independence and weakening of the opposition; an incipient development of the theory of reproductive autonomy and its relationship with state provision of sex education and family-planning services.

Continuing discussions and further developments at the institutional level dispelled some of these fears. It became clear that, while the postauthoritarian regime was not immune to rhetoric, this could now be used to support popular demands, organized to press the government to live up to its lofty declared intentions. Also, feminists became increasingly convinced that the crucial differences between population control and support for women's reproductive rights lay not in hidden motivations of policy makers but in the actual practices of health services. In the postauthoritarian regime, the greater threat to women's autonomy lies more in the lack of quality health services than in coerciveness. (Under the military regime, the proposal for the establishment of population-control policies constituted a real threat; therefore the fight against them went so far as to downplay the other side of women's right to control their own bodies. With "redemocratization," the demand for access to birth-control methods came to order.) So the women's health policies ended up gaining the support of the women's movement. Our main criticism now is the slow pace of implementation and the low priority accorded to participatory sex education.[5]

The programs of the Ministry of Health and two state secretaries of health have included in their activities the distribution of a small number of Chagas booklets. Although small (20,000), this number is much larger than what could be distributed directly through the women's groups. This has not occurred without resistance, of course. A conservative deputy has made a speech against the leaflets' "immorality," and other similar episodes have occurred. On the whole, however, they have been well accepted, and this is largely a result of the replication in its distribution of the small group methodology.

The project is now over. It was funded by the Ford Foundation, which has supported many progressive initiatives in Brazil, including some of the most radical feminist groups. During the early period of military dictatorship in the sixties, the Ford Foundation established a liberal reputation for supporting professors who had been expelled from the universities under the accusation of being leftists; in spite of that, in the seventies, most feminists were hesitant to approach the foundation, fearing that its interest in the women's movement was motivated by a desire to act as an intelligence service or to control, coopt, or neutralize the movement. In recent years, these doubts have given way to a more pragmatic approach. Given the fact that Ford officials have made no attempts to intervene in the groups' policies and practices, and that the information collected through grants' reports is public anyway, many feminist groups feel that there is no reason not to accept foundation support for projects that otherwise would not be feasible. In later phases of this project, the Pathfinder Fund provided support.

From the enthusiastic evaluations by participants, we know that the discussions have provided women with information and with a forum to critically question certain values. The warm contact we maintain with an extended network is both worrisome and gratifying. On the one hand, it is clear that the participants consider it to have been very positive for their personal growth, even if conflicts and contradictions in their daily life may have been exacerbated. On the other hand, the degree to which this new awareness is translated into commitment to collective efforts for change is not clear.

Nevertheless, some facts are reassuring. First, these women are taking the initiative of holding discussion groups all by themselves. Second, the booklets generated from the discussion have been shared with thousands of women, assembled in small groups throughout Brazil and other countries. Third, the asserted interest in sexual politics is part of a movement that is spreading throughout Latin America. By 1985, the issues of female sexuality and reproductive rights had come out of the closet in Brazil. Several groups (SOS Body, Recife, Women's House, Sexuality and Health, etc.) have chosen them as their central concern. National meetings have developed specific proposals for better health-care systems and methods of promoting women's autonomy. The linkages with general social conditions are presented as mutually reinforcing realms of change, not as excuses for paralysis. All of this was possible because the women of the poor peripheries of the cities asserted their needs, with no respect for the hierarchy of needs established by the well-meaning but misguided "bread first" school of thought.

NOTES

1. There is an extensive literature on fertility decline in Brazil (Paiva 1984; Merrick and Berquó 1983; Martine and Camargo 1984). Fertility has declined at all income levels, but more so among low-income urban women. As Merrick and Berquó stress, given the range of changes in fertility observed at both the regional and socioeconomic class levels, it is likely that recent experience reflects a combination of reinforcing factors rather than any single mechanism.

2. What we refer to as "the feminist movement" is thought of as that part of the women's movement which accords greater priority to the fight against gender subordination. In the seventies, there were great discussions about the distinction between "feminist" and "feminine" groups, which were conceived (by more conservative analysis) as contrary to each other. After ten years of coordinated work, in spite of recurring tensions among the groups, they are not seen as radical opposites. Also, there is not a clear-cut class division among them: although most feminist groups had a middle-class origin, there are middle-class groups which are not clearly feminist, and there are feminist working-class groups. The Third Latin American Feminist Encounter, held in August 1985, had 160 participants who did not have a college education, 166 who were nonwhite. For a good historical analysis of the interclass nature of feminism in Brazil, see Schmink (1981).

3. Research carried out in nine states of Brazil has shown high percentages of undesired pregnancies. In some states, less than half of the most recent pregnancies of married women were planned. Even in the most developed states, not more than 70 percent of them were planned (Rodrigues et al. 1984). In all likelihood the reported pregnancies refer to those carried to term, to which should be added those interrupted by abortion. The widespread recourse to abortion is reflected in the high number of complications requiring hospitalization: 200,000 a year, paid by the social security system (Mello 1982). Considering that the majority of abortions do not present sequelae requiring hospital care, and that data analyzed cover only about 40 percent of hospital care in Brazil, it is estimated that more than three million abortions are performed yearly.

4. In this we were not entirely successful. For some women, instead of broadening their concept of beauty, they were happy to verify that those pictured were "as ugly as we are"! In any case, the identification made learning easier.

5. See *Carta de Itapecirica,* a manifesto that came out of a national meeting of eighty women's groups in October 1984.

REFERENCES

Alvarez, Sonia. 1986. "Politicizing Gender and Engendering Democracy." In Alfred Stepan, ed., *Democratizing Brazil.* New Haven: Oxford University Press.

Blay, Eva. 1985. "Social Movements and Women's Participation in Brazil." *International Political Science Review* 6, no. 3:297–305.

Gondin, Linda M., and Ralph Hackert. 1982. "A Questão Populacional e a Esquerda Brasileira." Mimeo.

Martine, George, and Liscio Camargo. 1984. "Crescimento e Distribuicão da População Brasileira." *Revista Brasileira de Estudos de População* 1, no. 2:145-70.

Mello, Hildete Pereira. 1982. *Sequelas do Aborto, Custos e Implicações Sociais.* Fundação Carlos Chagas. INAMPS. Rio de Janeiro.

Merrick, Thomas W. 1983. "Fertility and Family Planning in Brazil." *International Family Planning Perspectives* 9, no. 4:110–18.

Merrick, Thomas, and Elza Berquõ. 1983. *The Determinants of Brazil's Recent Rapid Decline in Fertility.* Washington: National Academy Press.

Paiva, Paulo de Tarso Almeida. 1984. "The Process of Proletarianization and Fertility Transition in Brazil." Paper presented at the Annual Meeting of the Population Association of America.

Rodrigues, Walter, Leo Morris, and Barbara Janowitz. 1984. *Pesquisa Sobre Saúde Materno-infantil e Planejamento Familiar. Região Sul.* 1981. BEMFAM. Rio de Janeiro.

Schmink, Marianne. 1981. "Women in Brazilian Abertura Politics," *Signs* 7, no. 1:115-34.

Wiarda, Ieda Siqueira, and Judith Helzner. 1981. "Women, Population and International Development in Latin America: Persistent Legacies and New Perceptions for the 1980's." *Program in Latin American Studies,* Occasional Papers Series, no. 13. University of Massachusetts at Amherst.

WOMEN IN JAMAICA'S URBAN INFORMAL ECONOMY

Insights from a Kingston Slum*

Faye V. Harrison

The West Indian legacy of colonialism and imperialism is the world's oldest and possibly the world's harshest.[1] The work, adaptations, and struggles of Caribbean women, particularly poor Afro-Creole[2] women, warrant scholarly attention, for these experiences can reveal much about the part gender inequality, especially in its intersection with race and class oppression, plays in colonial and postcolonial domination and in dependent forms of national development.

Much of the material that exists on gender and on women in Caribbean societies can be found embedded in the many studies of lower-class family structure and in the works on internal marketing among peasants.[3] However, over the past decade or so, increasing attention has been more directly focused on the sociocultural, political, and economic underpinnings of women's lives.[4] The purpose of this essay is not to provide a general framework for analyzing the varying statuses of women across class boundaries in West Indian societies, but to offer a perspective on the positions occupied and roles played by women within what is sometimes called the "informal economy" of urban Jamaica, specifically the Kingston Metropolitan Area.[5] Drawing upon ethnographic data from "Oceanview," a slum in downtown Kingston, the ensuing discussion at-

*An earlier version of this essay is in *Nieuwe West Indische Gids/New West Indian Guide* 62, nos. 3 and 4 (1988). Reprinted with permission.

tempts to elucidate and provide a context for understanding important facets of the everyday lives and struggles of those women who occupy the lowest strata of the Jamaican class structure: women who represent some of the most marginal segments of the working class and petty bourgeoisie; and who, together with their young and aged dependents, constitute the largest proportion of their nation's poor.

A basic premise of this essay is that the problem of sexual inequality as it obtains in Jamaica today is integrally related to the broader processes of uneven development within the Caribbean periphery of the world capitalist system. That is, sexual oppression must be viewed in the national and international contexts of class and regional disparities which condition the specificity of women's everyday lives (Nash and Safa 1980, x–xi). The world capitalist system embodies a structure of labor-market segmentation wherein workers in peripheral countries receive no more than one-sixth of the wages received by their counterparts in the advanced industrial center (Amin 1980). Since female workers receive considerably less than male labor, Third World women represent a *cheaper than cheap* segment of the international work force (Lim 1983, 80; Nash 1983, 3). Capital accumulation and transfer on a world scale are based upon relations of superexploitation, the brunt of which Third World women bear. The interplay of class and gender is, therefore, integral to capitalist development at both national and international levels.

Patterns of Uneven Development in Jamaica

Jamaica, formally independent since 1962, has historically been one of the most politically and economically important countries in the Caribbean. Its current population is approximately 2.2 million, one-half of which is urban and one-third of which is situated in the primary city, Kingston (Department of Statistics 1978b, 3). The Jamaican economy is marked by uneven development or "underdevelopment," i.e., historically constituted processes that distort and subordinate domestic production and exchange to the accumulation interests of metropolitan capital (Mamdani 1976, 6). Based largely on the production of sugar and bananas, the mining and partial refining of bauxite, tourism, and manufacturing, Jamaica's economic structure is extroverted in that its dominant enterprises and sectors are largely foreign-owned or -controlled and oriented toward an export market. The economy is internally disjointed, for there are few organic links between domestic sectors (Beckford and Witter 1980, 66, 81). Instead, the major linkages are vertical; that is, agriculture, bauxite, tourism, and branch-plant manufacturing are integrated into North American (and largely U.S.) corporations. Accordingly, all inputs—raw materials, services, technology, and skilled personnel—are imported, and virtually all outputs from these industries are exported.

However, not all of the economy is directly controlled by corporate capital. Jamaica's peripheral capitalism encompasses variant forms of production and exchange which are subordinate to the dominant capitalist pattern. Some of these subordinate economic forms, e.g., subsistence agriculture, have their origins in earlier, noncapitalist modes of production/ exchange that have been absorbed into the domestic capitalist system as a result of the consolidation and widespread penetration of large-scale and primarily foreign capital (cf. Post 1978). Other patterns, such as many of those found within the small-scale, unlicensed sphere of the urban economy, have developed out of contradictions and complexities endemic to peripheral capitalism itself (cf. Kowarick 1979, 83).

Crisis of the Seventies and Eighties

During the fifties and sixties foreign investment, principally American, propelled a rapid and sustained growth in the economy (Jefferson 1972). This capital-intensive growth benefited the national bourgeoisie and middle class while it engendered a rise in unemployment and a decline in the poor's share in national income (Girvan and Bernal 1982, 37). In sharp contrast to the boom period, the 1970s brought two world recessions, quadrupled oil prices, sharp price increases for manufactured imports, and acute price and demand instability for Third World exports (National Planning Agency 1978, 6). The People's National Party (PNP), the ruling party of the 1972–80 period, instituted various reforms to redistribute national income and to secure greater "Jamaicanization" or sovereignty over the economy. One of the most dramatic actions the government took in response to international conditions and pressures from segments of the national bourgeoisie was the imposition of a production levy on the bauxite companies in 1974. Following the levy and Jamaica's part in the formation of the International Bauxite Association, the PNP announced its commitment to democratic socialism and to liberating itself from imperialism.

Fearing that Jamaica would move further leftward and expropriate investments, foreign and domestic capitalists, largely through the agency of the Jamaica Labour Party (JLP) opposition, mobilized a destabilization campaign to undermine the legitimacy of the PNP administration and oust it from office (Keith and Girling 1978, 29). Bauxite companies cut back production and filed a litigation suit; the American press discouraged tourism, Jamaica's second-largest foreign-exchange earner; local capitalists cut back production and, in many cases, closed down businesses and fled the island with their capital; and international commercial banks ceased making loans to Jamaica.

Facing an economic collapse, in 1977 the country was compelled to seek foreign exchange from the International Monetary Fund (IMF), whose restrictive policies exacerbated the island's economic slump as well as its volatile political climate (Girvan and Bernal 1982, 39, 40). In order to gain eligibility for IMF loans, the government had to undertake a number of drastic readjustments, among them cuts in real wages and retrenchment in the public sector. Initially the administration resisted the IMF strategy, but a severe credit squeeze forced it to reopen negotiations. Adhering to the terms of a standby loan, in April 1977 the government was forced to devalue its currency by almost 50 percent, impose indirect taxes, lift price controls, and limit wage increases. These measures resulted in a 35 percent decline in real wages and a 50 percent rise in the price level (Girvan and Bernal 1982, 43). After failing fiscal performance tests for two consecutive years, in early 1980 the government called for general elections in order to determine the nation's economic path. A month later the negotiations with the IMF were discontinued. The continuous shortages of basic commodities (even food staples), the rising unemployment (35 percent in 1980) especially affecting young adults and women, the constant currency devaluations and sharp price increases, and the unprecedented wave of political violence accompanying the campaign demoralized the population and eroded its confidence in the PNP government. Within several months the opposition party had electorally ousted the PNP as the country's ruling party and returned the economy to the orbit of Western banks, transnationals, and the IMF.

In spite of massive support from the United States government and international institutions, principally the IMF and the World Bank, the "deliverance" that the current prime minister, Edward Seaga, promised Jamaicans has yet to materialize. The balance-of-payments deficit grew from $200 million in 1980 to $600 million in 1986–87, and debt repayments have exceeded the inflow of loan funds since the JLP assumed power (Headley 1985, 26, 27). For the vast majority of ordinary Jamaicans, the current administration's strategy for economic recovery has been devastating. Living standards have fallen below what they were in 1980 as a consequence of "cutbacks in public sector employment, reductions in health and education expenditures, massive increases in the cost of public utilities, and the scaling down of local government services" (Stone 1987, 29). Although recent government data indicate a growth trend (*Jamaican Daily Gleaner* 1987; *Jamaican Weekly Gleaner* 1987), this increase in Gross National Product has not been converted into a mode of resource distribution favoring the majority of the populace. Similar to trends of the 1950s and 1960s, this more modest pattern of economic growth is accompanied by widening class disparities.

The Urban Informal Economic Sector

Since the consolidation of the capitalist mode at the turn of the century, Jamaica, like many Third World countries, has been unable to offer secure and stable employment opportunities for most of its working-age population. The chronic problem of "surplus" population, severely aggravated by the balance-of-payments crisis, is manifest in high rates of unemployment, immeasurably rampant underemployment, and successive waves of emigration, and is the consequence of the displacement of labor from both subsistence and modern sectors of the national economy. Much of the surplus working population—the dislocated peasants, displaced and landless wageworkers, and the marginally self-employed—is absorbed into the urban informal economic sector, which encompasses income-producing activities outside formal-sector wages, pensions, and gratuities (Portes 1981, 87).[6]

Within the urban informal economic sphere are myriad productive, marketing, and service activities and enterprises, most of which are unlicensed, untaxed, and able to circumvent the expenses imposed by state safety and sanitary regulations. This petty-scale sector of the economy is dependent upon large-scale and capital-intensive industry and complements it by taking on tasks that the latter generally neglects because of unprofitability (Roberts 1978) or illegality. Because of the export orientation of capitalist production in most of the Third World, the dominant economic spheres are not organized to satisfy all market demands. Whereas the formal, corporate sector meets the demands of the export market, the informal sector caters to many of the requirements of the domestic market. For example, owing to the gravity of economic conditions during the latter years of the PNP administration (when I collected most of my field data), the importation of a wide range of consumer and capital goods virtually ceased. A premium was therefore placed on items that had become scarce or unobtainable in the formal domestic market. The informal economy, particularly its illegal segments, became a major source of many goods and services, including such staple foodstuffs as rice, milk, flour, and cheese.

An integral and fairly stable component of Jamaica's illegitimate economic sphere is the production of and trade in ganja, or marijuana. While the local and national trade is important, the international distribution of "herb" is even more economically significant (Lacey 1977). In fact, at the height of the balance-of-payments crisis of the seventies, ganja production and trade was "the only healthy [sector] of the Jamaican economy. The 1.1 billion dollar business [was] the economic lifeline of Jamaica . . . after traditional segments of the economy failed" (*Newsweek* 15 Dec., 1980, 86). This starkly illustrates how integral informal-sector activities often are in peripheral capitalist economies.

While it may be clear that informal economic processes are subordinate to and dependent upon formally recognized economic sectors, it is also important to realize that capitalist accumulation itself is dependent upon the subsistence-oriented and other petty-scale activities of the informal sphere. The largely unlicensed and unregulated small-scale domain plays a critical role in subsidizing part of the costs of transnational corporations operating in Third World nations, enabling these firms to enforce comparatively low wages on their labor (Portes 1978, 37). Moreover, by lowering the costs of reproduction, informal economic activities indirectly subsidize workers in core nations, e.g., the United States, and thereby help maintain the rate and transfer of profit (Portes 1981, 106). The urban informal sector helps reduce labor costs for corporations in two major ways: first, by providing relatively cheap and/or accessible goods and services and, hence, reducing some of the costs of subsistence for the urban population, particularly wageworkers; and second, by decreasing the relative size of the formal labor force with its abundant labor available for casual and disguised forms of wagework.

"Self-employment" or "own-account" work represents a pattern of concealed wagework which permits capital to extract surplus labor from petty producers and traders. Several scholars, e.g., Portes (1981), Birkbeck (1979), and Scott (1979), have shown that much informal-sector activity is actually work done for the benefit of formal-sector firms. For example, the informal marketing of formal-sector goods constitutes a well-organized business ultimately controlled by capitalist firms. Rather than invest in retail chains, distributing firms utilize "independent" traders. In this case, informal trading represents an efficient and profitable means of circulating both national and imported goods in the domestic market. The character of this intersectoral linkage is concealed, because capital does not intervene directly in the informal labor process, which is generally organized around personalized, often familial, relationships. The informal labor process, therefore, should be distinguished from the underlying social relations of production and appropriation which permit capital to superexploit informal labor (cf. Amin 1980, 25).[7]

Informal economic relations, which are typically embedded in kinship and peer networks, permit the use of free or nominally paid labor and, consequently, "an output of goods and services at prices lower than those which could be offered under formal productive arrangements" (Portes 1981, 86). While such a system reduces the costs of reproduction for the petty-scale sphere, and therefore permits its viability, ultimately these very conditions maximize surplus extraction by reducing the costs that the dominant sector must pay to reproduce labor power.

The "Feminization" of the Informal Economy

The part the informal sector plays in lowering the general costs of reproducing labor power for formal-sector capital is also the role attributed to a reserve army of labor.[8] Saffioti (1978) bases her theoretical discourse on women in class societies upon the premise that intrinsic to capitalism is the existence of a reserve resulting from the exclusion of considerable segments of the working population from a secure position in the labor market. Under capitalist social conditions, a large proportion of women, particularly housewives who have been displaced from what are socially defined as productive economic roles, constitute a reserve labor force, whose surplus labor power is absorbed into the domestic domain of the social economy.

While women as housewives, working to reproduce their mates' labor power without the benefit of wages, may indeed represent an important and, in analytic terms, neglected component of the labor reserve, the quintessential reserve in peripheral societies such as Jamaica, where women constitute a sizeable component (47 percent) of the work force as well as of the displaced work force (i.e., informal workers),[9] includes those women who, as breadwinners and quite often as heads of households, must operate within the context of an insecure and informal opportunity structure to eke out a livelihood for themselves and for their young and aged dependents. From these segments of the reserve, middle- and upper-class housewives recruit and hire their domestic helpers, who for pitiably low wages perform most of the functions necessary for maintaining privileged households. From this informal labor force also come many of the female street vendors, called "higglers," who are responsible for distributing staple foodstuffs throughout the urban population, particularly to the poor.

The rate of formal unemployment for Jamaican women (39 percent) is more than twice as high as that for men (16 percent), resulting in more than twice as many women (167,900) being unemployed as compared to men (79,200) (Department of Statistics 1978b, 26). The relative feminization of unemployment and poverty is manifested in the informal economy wherein females participate in survival and subsistence activities in comparatively larger numbers and proportions. Moreover, in view of the pivotal position women occupy within familial and domestic configurations,[10] they tend to play principal mobilizational roles in "scuffling" ventures, i.e., small-scale income-generating processes.

The Sexual Division of Labor in the Informal Sphere

The urban informal economy consists of an expansive, competitive tertiary sector, a small sphere of secondary production or petty manufacture, and, in light of the physical constraints of the urban economy, a restricted sector of primary production, e.g., gardening and animal husbandry. The principal focus of informal-sector activity in the Kingston

Metropolitan Area, therefore, tends to be commodity circulation and services rather than production. The latter process is concentrated largely within the formal sphere of the urban economy. That is to say that petty producers have been substantially displaced by large-scale capital, and this displacement has affected women more drastically than men.

According to government data for the late 1970s and early 1980s, approximately 70 percent of all female workers in Jamaica were employed in the tertiary sector (i.e., commerce and services), while only about 32–33 percent of all male workers were active in this sector (Department of Statistics 1978b, 27; 1984, 308; Statistical Institute of Jamaica 1984, 10). Only 7–8 percent of the female work was in manufacture, whereas on average 14 percent of the male work force was concentrated there.

The respective distributions of female and male workers in the informal sector of one neighborhood's economic structure (that of Oceanview) indicate that both women and men shared exceedingly large concentrations in the tertiary sector of the locality and metropolitan economy. Still, the percentage of women workers in this sector exceeded that of men by about 11 percent.[11] Moreover, while a substantial percentage of men worked as producers (35 percent), a much lesser percentage of women (20 percent) were engaged in productive labor. It seems, therefore, that although most informal-sector participants were involved in commercial and service activities, the concentration of women's work in this particular domain was especially high (88 percent). This evidence suggests that compared with women, men tended to have access to income opportunities across a wider range of occupations, activities, and sectors. Furthermore, the income opportunities accessible to men, e.g., those in construction, provided higher levels of remuneration than female-specific jobs. Many of the higher-paying jobs available to males, however, tended to be insecure, or available only on a temporary, casual basis.

Nelson (1979) shows that within the informal economic sector of Nairobi, Kenya, women by and large are restricted to marketing skills (e.g., preparing beverages, cooking, caring for children, and washing clothes) practiced in the home, whereas men market a much wider range of skills and services.[12] Evidence from Oceanview confirms this kind of sexual division of labor. For instance, close to 33 percent of the working women in my sample were engaged in some sort of domestic service, while about 26 percent were employed in general services (e.g., casual streetcleaning, hairstyling, and spiritual healing). In contrast, 40 percent of the men in the sample were engaged in general services (e.g., taxi driving, vehicle repair, and photography).

Approximately 46 percent of all the women sampled were involved in either or both the marketing of domestic services (33 percent) and the marketing of domestic or household consumer goods (24 percent), e.g., foodstuffs, cooking utensils, and clothing. Few (3 percent) of the men were engaged in services (e.g., baking and cooking) that could be classified as domestic; nonetheless, approximately 18 percent were involved in marketing domestic commodities—food, durable domestic goods, and clothing. It is important to realize that the majority (78 percent) of these female marketers were "higglers," i.e., street vendors selling fresh, and therefore perishable, vegetables and fruits, and only about 22 percent of the female retailers were shopkeepers.[13] Conversely, 64 percent of the male retailers were proprietors of small grocery shops, stores, or restaurants, while only about 36 percent were street vendors. Male retailers were more likely to manage larger-scale enterprises. Furthermore, whereas these male proprietors generally benefited from the labor of their spouses and/or kinswomen, their female counterparts were less inclined to have adult males as regular sources of labor. Although perhaps the large higgler category may evince salient management and organizational skills among women as instrumental actors, these abilities and achievements were not widely channeled into other important areas. Men were more likely to hold supervisory positions and to market leadership skills and services, for example, as foremen of construction and public works crews and as informal labor recruiters and political party brokers. Further, a larger proportion of men than women were engaged in productive and service activities (e.g., vehicle repair, electrical work, plumbing, carpentry, masonry, welding, etc.) which demanded some readily recognized degree of technical expertise.

It is also noteworthy that male and female informants had different patterns of participation in the small urban primary sector. Women, for instance, tended to raise fowl and tree fruits for household and domestic subsistence, while men were more inclined to produce for commodity exchange. Half of the men involved in primary production were engaged in raising pigs or goats for the market. Women's involvement in secondary production, viz., petty manufacture, was largely restricted to the production of children's and women's clothing, while men produced men's clothing, shoes, furniture, and woodcarvings, and were involved in building construction. Women's work across all sectors was linked largely to domestic needs and functions.

Another discernible category of informal economic activity is that related to entertainment or recreation.[14] Approximately 22 percent of the males in my sample admittedly participated in this sphere as barkeepers (5 percent), ganja traders (14 percent), and gambling vendors/brokers (3 percent). Approximately 31 percent of the women were involved in often multiple and interrelated occupations within this sphere as barkeepers (13 percent), ganja traders (7 percent), gambling vendors and housemistresses (11 percent), and "sportin' gals" or prostitutes (5 percent). Of course, these percentages, which represent only what informants were willing to divulge, grossly underestimate the extent of involvement in illegal activities, particularly in the ganja trade and prostitution. These two illegal spheres seem to reflect a division of labor by gender, in that although women are indeed active in the production and exchange of ganja, the trade is a domain in which males predominate. On the other hand, prostitution at the local level is largely organized by women, who tend not to have pimps or male superiors. This relative autonomy, however, is absent in the major tourist zones, where commoditized sexual exchanges are typically mediated by male brokers.

Nelson (1979) treats prostitution and those serial mating practices in which an economic motive or dimension is apparent as instances of the marketing of services that women practice and perform within the domestic domain.[15] Although she places prostitution and those mating practices which, for all intents and purposes, represent an economic survival strategy into the same category, the two behaviors should not be equated. The sexual services embodied in mating behavior are not commodities, as are the services prostitutes market, but use-values.

In view of this conceptual distinction between commodities and use-values, it is necessary to underscore the fact that the informal economy is not limited to the production and exchange of petty commodities. Of great significance is the production and nonmarket exchange—what Lomnitz (1977) calls "reciprocal exchange"—of such resources as information and any good or service which contributes in some way to subsistence and economic viability. Nonmarket exchange is especially crucial for the subsistence of a considerable proportion of ghetto (i.e., slum and shantytown) populations that cannot regularly engage in monetary transactions.

The Social Organization and Construction of Gender

Social networks—or very fluid and diffusely structured social relationships organized primarily around kinship, coresidential, and/or peer ties—constitute the basis for much of the socioeconomic activity within the informal economy. Kinship groupings extend beyond individual residential units, and the embeddedness of these households in broader domestic configurations is critical given the absence of state aid or welfare benefits for the formally unemployed or the nonwage working poor.

The primacy of extended consanguineal ties characterizes the situations of both women and men; however, ghetto women tend to be comparatively more reliant on or committed to kin and domestic groupings for salient and sustained social relationships. Women informants (particularly those in the 18–30-year range) tended to express distrust for friend-

ship and marriage,[16] suggesting that investments in such nonkin relationships would lead to additional demands on limited resources,
"trouble" and "war" over gossip and men, and, in the case of legal marriage, constraints on female independence and autonomy. "Me naa keep
friends" was the claim of several women who restricted most of their
intimate, reciprocal interactions to relatives. Women who were higglers
with relatively stable retail enterprises, officers in local-level political party
associations or mutual aid societies, or "bankers" in rotating credit networks called "partners" tended to have more intense relationships outside
the domestic sphere. For these women, peer relationships were often
significant; nonetheless, kin ties were viewed as much more reliable and
valuable.

While the idiom and organization of kinship are key in the everyday
lives of poor urban women, among ghetto men peer bonds are highly
valued and play a central role on the street corners where male networks
are based (cf. Brana-Shute 1976; Lieber 1976; Wilson 1971). The peer
networks of men between the ages of fifteen and thirty-five often assume
the form of gangs which may combine into gang hierarchies extending
over the territory of an entire neighborhood or an even more inclusive
district or zone (see Harrison 1987). Street corners and their associated
gangs provide the context within which subsistence-related information
is exchanged, material resources are redistributed, casual labor is recruited
for government-sector employment, and legitimate and illegitimate hus-
tling strategies are devised and carried out.

Interestingly, in the way that both women and men talked about their
lives and survival struggles, women seemed to place greater emphasis on
independence and autonomy than did men. Despite their actual dependence on the "babyfathers" (i.e., consensual mates), mothers, sisters, and
special neighbors of their active networks, women underscored the importance and necessity of independent action in surviving Kingston's
slums and shantytowns. They viewed their participation in familial networks, which extend and contract according to need and circumstance,
as the outcome of their individual strategies and negotiations rather than
as the result of group obligations and duties. "Networking," even among
kinspeople, was described as voluntary and instrumental, and it involved
no fixed, long-term commitments to a clearly defined social unit.

The assertion of female independence is not at all controverted by kin
alignments. In fact, the extended organization of kinship and domesticity,
with its internal division of labor and forms of cooperation, frees some
women for work and other activities outside the home. Those women
remaining at home and in the immediate neighborhood supervise and
care for the children as well as carry out other household-based tasks,
some of which generate income. Independence does not, therefore, imply

"a shedding of social attachments . . . [but] is linked to a strong sense of interpersonal connectedness" (Sutton and Makiesky-Barrow 1981, 496).

Manifestations of female autonomy, particularly in the economic domain as evidenced by the high rate of female participation in the labor force, have sometimes been taken by the public and by scholars to mean that women enjoy sexual equality (cf. Mintz 1981; Sutton and Makiesky-Barrow 1981). However, evidence indicating that women indeed suffer from underemployment, unemployment, low-paying jobs, and de facto disenfranchisement more disproportionately than their male counterparts serves to dispel this conception. Sexual inequality is also reflected in the incidence of wife battering and sexual violence as well as in ideological representations in, for instance, mass media advertisements and popular music (Antrobus and Gordon 1984, 120; Henry and Wilson 1975, 193–94). Male resentment against female competence and assertiveness is expressed in song lyrics which often encourage men to control or dominate women lest the latter's alleged cleverness, deviousness, and promiscuity endanger men's standing in the home and community (cf. Henry and Wilson 1975, 193).

Despite the ambivalence men may feel toward women's presence outside the home, women's work is expected and tolerated. The tolerance for female independence and for individual independence regardless of gender originated during the slavery era when both sexes were equally involved and exploited in the "public" domain of plantation work (Sutton and Makiesky-Barrow 1981). Mintz (1981) hypothesizes that since enslaved men could not assert "paterfamilial" domination over female slaves, and since slave masters relegated both male and female Africans to the status of chattel property, respect for individual rights and prerogatives for both men and women was strong among Afro-Jamaicans.

Historically, the masses of Jamaican women have been conspicuous as workers not (wholly) dependent on their kinsmen and mates for their sustenance and security. During the postemancipation period, peasant women complemented the work of male producers through a system of internal marketing controlled largely by the market women themselves. However, with the expansion and consolidation of capitalist social relations at the turn of the century, the autonomy of Afro-Jamaican women—and that of peasants, artisans, and traders on the whole—diminished. Owing to the entrenchment of colonial state power over the hitherto independent peasantry,[17] male dominance gained further legitimacy and was imposed on the society by established churches, schools, laws, and a system of job segregation and wage differentials.[18]

Gender and Politics

In the mid-seventies, a government redevelopment agency charged with upgrading housing, utilities, and social services in the Oceanview vicinity conducted a survey in order to identify the neighborhood's leadership on the basis of reputation. These "area leaders" were then to form an advisory committee that would aid in implementing the government program's objectives. Out of the twenty-three persons identified, only one was a woman. In a locality where women are quite visible in the economic arena and where their membership and work keep alive and active local-level political party groups and branches, why were women underrepresented as area leaders?

On the one hand, the term *leader* tends to connote authority and official status and is typically applied to middle-class political party functionaries. In this sense, Oceanview respondents would claim that there are no leaders among the locality's residents. With a qualified, expanded definition of *leader* as one with the respectability, personal influence, mobilizational skills, and resources to determine and implement local or factional goals (Swartz 1968, 1), respondents would generate a list of persons strategically situated in grassroots sociopolitical fields. The redevelopment program sought to identify the latter persons; yet the survey results yielded a predominantly male pool.

Contrary to the impression the neighborhood survey may have given, and although females may be denied legitimate recognition, it is not at all unusual for women to be principal political agents, i.e., de facto protagonists, catalysts, directors, and sustainers of sociopolitical action at the local level. Beckford and Witter (1980, 99) confirm this observation by pointing out that women are the main party workers in groups and branches. They maintain the party machinery during terms of government office, and they are the most committed campaigners during electoral contests. Their activism is manifested not only in association membership but also in the leadership of neighborhood party organs, for they often appear as secretaries, vice-presidents, and presidents. Nonetheless, by and large, despite various exceptions, women's power is largely confined to the lowest levels of political party structure and the inclusive state apparatus; they are not highly visible in the decision-making echelons. Even at the local level, the power and leadership of party women may be preempted by gang brokers who are often more strategically placed in the party machine.

In view of the constraints on their political role and participation, women are inclined and, in some respects, encouraged to assert their unevenly formed power by manipulating and influencing those men who are authorized or empowered actors in parties, government, street gangs, and mainstream churches.[19] For example, a former female group president recounted how she was pressured to become "friendly" with higher-level party brokers in order to gain access to important information and job opportunities for her local area. Another woman, who never joined a party association, used her acquaintance and intimacy with a party broker and a police officer to acquire favors which were crucial in securing and expanding her ganja trade business. In another case, a former group leader resigned from party activism because of the sexual harassment she encountered. She claimed that sexual services were often expected of women in exchange for party patronage. While women may sometimes gain power, influence, and control over resources through their relationships with male brokers, this dependent access to political capital leaves them vulnerable to manipulation and abuse.

The greatest proportions of women are found in informal fields of power, e.g., revival churches, school associations, and markets, wherein there arise opportunities for women as individuals and as groups to define and implement strategic local goals—Swartz's definition of politics (1968, 1). Generally, this sphere of activity is not typically perceived or designated as political, despite its intrinsic political dimensions and its articulation or interpenetration with formal political domains. Henry and Wilson suggest that because of the subservient role women play in society, they predominate in lower-class religious cults or sects: "religion is one of the few areas . . . where women find some measure of equality with significant others. It is also an area where women have free access and the fact that they can hold positions of office gives them a measure of status outside the religious group which they might not otherwise be able to achieve" (1975, 190).

In localities such as Oceanview, where interparty rivalry often attains volatile and life-threatening proportions, a large percentage of residents tend to retreat from "polytricks" and are distrustful of partisan activities and activists (see Harrison 1987, 1988). Parent Teacher Associations, mutual aid societies, and churches are more likely to be perceived as nonpartisan and therefore potentially more reflective of the interests and needs of a broader cross-section of the neighborhood. It is in such extradomestic situations that many women are able to mobilize their limited resources for the survival of their families and neighborhoods as well as for a sense of collective defense and autonomy.

Through their involvement in these often predominantly female spheres of action, women produce an emergent praxis of sisterhood marked by ambiguity and contradiction. The sisterhood engendered in certain informal fields can be seen as a constructive reaction to the constraints women confront as single parents, formal and informal workers, and political constituents. For example, many of the members of Oceanview's PTA consider that organization an alternative to the local party associations that have been unable to promote community development, peace, and unity. The PTA (whose agenda encompasses much more than educational objectives) represents a nonpartisan vehicle for actively resisting the various forms of victimization and oppression its members experience in their everyday lives.

Nonetheless, sisterhood may also comprise elements of collusion (cf. Westwood 1985) and escapism. Some Oceanview women believe that politics is intrinsically "wicked" and not a righteous means of meaningful change. The recurring statement "Me naa deal in politics; only God can save Jamaica" sometimes reflects this retreatist view. For women with this perspective, any politician or political activist, leftist or rightist, sincere or opportunist, is suspect and unworthy of support; and churches, friendly societies, or other associations provide a refuge. Whereas the informal sphere may provide women with alternative outlets for constructive political expression, it can also offer a means of retreat, suppressing effective opposition and resistance.

An informal organized sector of Oceanview's social organization not readily open to women's mobilization and empowerment is that of the Rastafari. Local followers of Rastafari, particularly the more senior and devoted "true Rastas," organize their religious worship, economic activities, and domestic life along clear lines of male dominance.[20] Rastafari represents one of the most culturally and politically significant mass movements in contemporary Jamaica.[21] Its ideology and idiom of protest and rebellion have permeated the slums and shantytowns, where displaced wageworkers and the marginally self-employed dwell. In Rastafarian views and practices, women are essentially spiritual and political dependents (Kitzinger 1969, 260; 1971, 588; Rowe 1980). Men must guide women in order for the latter to achieve spiritual wholeness and "sight," the "I/eye."[22] I broach this issue of patriarchy among Rastafari simply to highlight the sexist character of important elements in Jamaican culture and to suggest some of the contradictions within sociocultural forces that exert considerable influence on the uneven and often contradictory patterns of opposition, protest, and accommodation within some of the most alienated segments of Jamaican society.

The sexism that shapes and inhibits the political behavior of women active in the informal economy impedes the political development of the entire informal and casual work force. While this relationship between the social construction of gender and political underdevelopment holds also for the organized working class as well as for any class, it is especially critical for informal workers, because women are disproportionately represented among them.

I raise this question of the political character of informal labor because anthropologists and other social scientists have questioned whether the urban informal sector functions as a safety valve reinforcing the status quo or whether it represents a potential source of prerevolutionary rebellion (McGee 1971; Worsley 1972). Roberts (1978, 135) claims that the fragmented organization of small-scale socioeconomic enterprises, combined with the present-day survival orientation of the actors themselves, gives rise to sporadic and inhibited patterns of political action. Elsewhere I have argued that supralocal or state-level political processes also contribute to the containment of rebellion. Patronage-clientelism undermines solidarity among grassroots constituents; police and army repression thwarts efforts to disrupt or challenge the social order; and by labeling many forms of protest and rebellion as crime, the state delegitimates certain political behaviors and isolates rebels from potential allies in, for instance, the formal working class (Harrison 1982, 326–35).

An additional factor that contributes to the underdeveloped political character of the informal labor force, and one that has not been pinpointed, let alone accentuated, is the suppression of women's participation in politics, particularly in those fields most strategically aligned with or embedded in national (and international) level political structures. These most strategic fields, arenas, and institutions are male-dominated and conditioned largely by middle- and upper-class interests.

Sexual or gender inequality represents an essential and integral feature of social relations and cultural construction in Jamaica, where for the past four hundred years colonial and imperialist exploitation has governed the development of economic, political, and sociocultural patterns and structures. Although the focus of this essay has been on women and, more generally, on gender differentials within the urban petty-scale sphere of the Jamaican economy, it is extremely important to further contextualize the subordination and oppression characterizing these women's position by taking into account the pervasive impact of racism. During the course of Jamaica's history, the exploitation of the masses has been legitimized and rationalized by a system of ideas and symbols which has elaborated the allegedly inherent and functional inferiority of Africans as a distinct racial grouping and as bearers of a peculiar, "cultureless" culture. Racist ideology and institutional arrangements have historically supported and permitted the superexploitation of Afro-Jamaicans as a labor force, the violation of black and brown women as objects of sexual indulgence, and the political alienation and repression of the island's majority.

The many segments of the working-age population which, to varying extents, are absorbed into the urban informal economy may represent a surplus labor force from the point of view of their surface relationship to corporate capitalist spheres; however, the casual workers, scufflers, hustlers, and the petty producers and traders who fill the streets, lanes, and yards (i.e., communal residences) with their daily survival struggles are vertically integrated into peripheral capitalist structures that depend upon the articulation and interpenetration of variant socioeconomic patterns, the asymmetrical conjuncture of which constitutes a socioeconomic formation specific to the complexities and contradictions of Jamaica's historical development within a world system.

In a central way, the feminization of key sectors of the informal sphere contributes to the reproduction of a cheap, casual, and concealed work force accessible to capital for performing its temporary and largely unskilled tasks. Although responsible for supporting appreciable proportions of the nation's dependents and for organizing their non-wage-compensated work into minimally lucrative household-based ventures, women have the most limited access to income and capitalization opportunities. Despite the indisputable existence of substantial numbers of higglers, visible with the results of their mobilization of petty capital, the informal sector is not ruled by matriarchs. The economic status higglers have rests upon the marketing of domestic and household-use goods, and therefore on a sexually segregated system of economic opportunities which confines women to spheres related to domestic consumption. Moreover, whatever status and power individual higglers and other female retailers may in fact have within their communities, their associations, and their primary networks of kinspeople, friends, and clients, this power and status cannot be generalized to depict the situation of the majority of women in the slums and shantytowns of urban Jamaica. These latter women scuffle under fluctuating and unpredictable circumstances to eke out minimal subsistence for themselves and their "pickney" (children), either with or without sustained support from their "babyfathers," and under diffuse and ambiguous contracts of support and alliance with kin and fictive kin.

The mass of Jamaican women, who in some form or another operate as informally organized workers, have a legacy to inform their lives and struggles. On one hand, that legacy is long with the pain and blood of "sufferation" and "downpression," but on the other hand, it is also marked by the integrity of a people at some levels conscious of their potential power as resisters, rebels, and rulers of their own destiny. Despite obstacles and constraints, Afro-Jamaican women have historically made their footprints in paths of struggle on both economic and political planes. In light of the critical current state of affairs in Jamaica, it is becoming increasingly obvious that for "deliverance"[23] and change to come, Jamaica has to mobilize all of its people, men and women. How exactly this proposition will be translated into political discourse and applied to organization and praxis is a question for which only the unfolding of social history can provide answers.

Notes

1. Williams (1944) and Knight (1978) have written on political and economic aspects of Caribbean history. For studies of underdevelopment and dependency,

see Beckford (1972; 1975), Beckford and Witter (1980), Girvan (1973; 1976), Mintz (1977), and Thomas (1974).

2. The term *Creole* refers to the Caribbean-born descendants of the Africans and Europeans who peopled the West Indies during the colonization and slavery era. The category is not applied to postemancipation immigrants such as the Chinese and East Indians.

3. For examples of classic family studies, see Blake (1961), Clarke (1957), and Gonzalez (1969). See Bolles (1983) for a more current analysis of urban working-class households in crisis-torn Jamaica. For work on internal marketing, see Mintz (1955; 1964; 1981).

4. Henry and Wilson (1975) have addressed the general status of Caribbean women, Moses (1981) treats women's status in Montserrat, and Sutton and Mak-iesky-Barrow (1981) focus on Barbadian women. Bolles (1981; 1983) deals with Jamaican women's family and (both formal and informal) work responsibilities in the context of the economic austerity exacerbated by the International Monetary Fund. D'Amico-Samuels (1986) illuminates the relationship gender has to class and color in the development of the tourist economy in Negril, Jamaica.

5. My perspective is based largely on fieldwork done on political and eco-nomic processes in a locality in the Kingston Metropolitan Area in 1978–79. This research was made possible by a Fulbright-Hays Predoctoral Fellowship. The period of data analysis was supported by a grant-in-aid from the Wenner-Gren Foundation for Anthropological Research and a Danforth-Compton Fellowship from the Danforth Foundation. Comments and support from Louise Lamphere, Deborah D'Amico-Samuels, and Chandra Talpade Mohanty were invaluable in the rewriting of this essay.

6. It is impossible to directly measure the actual extent of participation in the informal sphere of an economy, because informal activities and enterprises tend, for the most part, not to be recorded or registered. We can assume, however, that this sector absorbs the unemployed (defined as those actually seeking wage-work or those willing to do wagework) and those segments of the population which have never sought formal wage employment. It is also important to note that, to varying extents, formal workers—even members of the established middle class—are involved in informal economic activities as a means of supplementing their income. While the informal economy acts as a buffer against unemployment, it also provides capitalization opportunities for petty entrepreneurs and petty capitalists. In fact, Stone (1977) claims that an indeterminate number of busi-nesspeople from the most precarious segments of Jamaica's petty bourgeoisie commonly engage in informal and sometimes illegal means of capitalization and appropriation (e.g., gambling and ganja ventures) in order to maintain and expand their legitimate enterprises.

7. This distinction between labor process and social relations of production is pertinent in light of the argument that the informal sector represents a distinct mode of production (cf. Davies 1979).

8. The reserve, surviving under tenuous and insecure social and economic circumstances, consists of unemployed workers, casual workers moving from job to job, displaced peasants and agroproletarians forced into cities, and long-term "scufflers" and the marginally self-employed. See Braverman (1974, 388) for a discussion of Marx's formulation of surplus population.

9. In 1978 women represented approximately 47 percent of Jamaica's total recorded labor force (Department of Statistics 1978b, 26). Over 65 percent of all women above the age of fourteen were part of this force. In light of the fact that in 1978 38 percent of the female labor force was formally unemployed, and an

even larger percentage underemployed, it appears that women are dislocated and excluded from formal labor-market opportunities at a higher rate than men, who suffered a 16 percent rate of unemployment in 1978.

There is a history of relatively high rates of both formal and informal employment among women in former plantation slave societies such as Jamaica. During the slavery era, both men and women were fully employed as slave labor. Scholars (e.g., Patterson 1967; Mintz and Price 1977) have suggested that at this juncture the sexual division of labor was slight; however, women experienced a double drudgery in that they were responsible for both field and household tasks (Davis 1981). Women also played pivotal roles in the "protopeasant" sphere of the slave economy, and were partly responsible for marketing their agricultural surplus. The peasant economy of the postemancipation period was organized around a clear sexual division of labor in which men were primarily responsible for cultivation while women were largely responsible for marketing.

10. One-third of all households in Jamaica are headed by women (Department of Statistics 1978a, 10).

11. The data for this discussion were collected from a small sample of forty-five women and fifty-six men. These data were gathered as part of a broader investigation of the organization of socioeconomic and political life in Oceanview. Although the sample is limited, the data it yielded are consistent with the results of government surveys conducted in the 1970s (e.g., those done by the Urban Development Corporation).

12. This pattern of sexual segregation in work (domestic vs. nondomestic) has been noted by anthropologists such as Rosaldo (1974) who underscore the relevance of the domestic vs. public dichotomy in a wide variety of sociocultural cases.

13. Of all of the women sampled, 16 percent were higglers and 5 percent shopkeepers (e.g., grocers). Among the men, 7 percent were street vendors and 12 percent grocers and restaurateurs. Interestingly, outside this domestic-goods realm, female proprietors outnumbered their male counterparts. For instance, 13 percent of the women in the sample were barkeepers, compared to only five percent of the men. Most of the regular clientele of neighborhood bars are men and their guests. I am suggesting that women play an important role in entertaining men, for whom public drinking and, perhaps less openly, gambling are regular features of peer-related socializing and recreation.

14. This category which Nelson uses in her Kenya study is misleading in the sense that ganja traders may also be seen as providing a product necessary for religious rituals and healing, and gamblers may consider their activity hard work rather than mere recreation.

15. Nelson's conception of prostitution as a domestic activity is consistent with the generally held definition of domesticity or domestic functions, which involve all those activities involved in the production or preparation of food, in child-rearing, in consumption, and in sexual reproduction or mating (Yanagisako 1979).

16. Most women in the sample as well as in the population at large were not legally married but were involved in common-law unions and visiting relationships.

17. In the aftermath of emancipation, a reconstituted peasantry arose in opposition to the declining plantation system. This peasantry emerged before the formation of a capitalist mode of production and the consolidation of a class of agrarian capitalists. At this juncture peasants were in a strong position relative to large landholders. The former usually owned their own plots and paid little or nothing in taxes to the state. Furthermore, they were able to circumvent the

expropriation of some part of the product of their labor by controlling exchange relations through networks of higglers—the mothers, wives, sisters, and daughters of peasant households (Post 1978).

18. See Henry (1983, 100–107) for a discussion of the postemancipation cultural colonization of Afro-Jamaicans, and Post (1978, 34–35) for a treatment of the role of colonial state policies in thwarting the development of a free peasantry and enhancing the power of an emergent capitalist class. I have extended this line of argument to the realm of gender.

19. Henry and Wilson (1975) bring out that in the popular view, women are often depicted as devious, manipulative, and conniving. It is noteworthy that these stereotypes apply as well to perceptions of lumpenproletarians who also commonly activate strategies of manipulation when dealing with politicians.

20. Whereas a large number of "youts" (i.e., male adolescents and adult males under thirty-five) wear their hair in dreadlocks and claim to be Rastafarian, I am concerned with that minority of males who are committed to Rastafari religious beliefs and lifestyle, and who are designated as "true Rastas" within the locality. This segment exerts considerable influence over the secular "dreads."

21. See Smith, Augier, and Nettleford (1960), Nettleford (1970), Barrett (1977), Chevannes (1981), and Campbell (1987) for analyses of the Rastafari in Jamaica. See Austin (1983, 236) for comments on the routinization of the movement during the past two decades.

22. Within the past decade, however, women have become more visible and vocal within the Rastafari movement. For instance, in 1980 three women's organizations were established. While "daughters" claim not to challenge the patriarchal tenets and structure of the movement, their very mobilization and "reasonings" (i.e., consciousness-raising rituals) seem to be generating new perspectives on women and on Rastafari itself.

The concept of "sight" refers to spiritual vision and knowledge of truth. That of the "I" refers to vision as well, but "I" also signifies the collective Rastafari, the "I and I," whose shared "reasonings" and sacramental rituals (ganja smoking and Nyabingi) lead to heightened transcendence.

23. "Deliverance" is a religious concept applied to popular political discourse in Jamaica. During the 1980 electoral campaign against Michael Manley and the PNP, Edward Seaga, the present prime minister, promised deliverance to Jamaica. Politicians commonly manipulate popular religious symbols when mobilizing the electorate. The PNP made use of Rastafarian and revivalist (i.e., syncretist Christian) symbols in earlier campaigns.

REFERENCES

Amin, Samir. 1980. "The Class Structure of the Contemporary Imperialist System." *Monthly Review* 31, no. 8:9–26.
Antrobus, Peggy, and Lorna Gordon. 1984. "The English-speaking Caribbean: A Journey in the Making." In Robin Morgan, ed., *Sisterhood Is Global: The International Women's Movement Anthology*. Garden City: Anchor Books/Doubleday. 118–26.
Austin, Diane J. 1983. "Culture and Ideology in the English-speaking Caribbean: A View from Jamaica." *American Ethnologist* 19:223–40.

Barrett, Leonard. 1977. *The Rastafarians: Sounds of Cultural Dissonance.* Boston: Beacon Press.

Beckford, George L. 1972. *Persistent Poverty: Underdevelopment in Plantation Economics of the Third World.* New York: Oxford University Press.

———, ed. 1975. *Caribbean Economy: Dependence and Backwardness.* Mona: Institute of Social and Economic Research, University of the West Indies.

Beckford, George, and Michael Witter. 1980. *Small Garden . . . Bitter Week: The Political Economy of Struggle and Change in Jamaica.* London: Zed Press.

Birkbeck, Chris. 1979. "Garbage, Industry, and the 'Vultures' of Cali, Colombia." In Ray Bromley and Chris Gerry, eds., *Casual Work and Poverty in Third World Cities.* Chichester: John Wiley and Sons. 161–84.

Blake, Judith. 1961. *Family Structure in Jamaica: The Social Context of Reproduction.* Glencoe, Ill.: Free Press.

Bolles, A. Lynn. 1981. "Household Economic Strategies in Kingston, Jamaica." In Naomi Black and Ann Baker Contrell, eds., *Women and World Change: Equity Issues in Development.* Beverly Hills: Sage Publications. 83–96.

———. 1983. "Kitchens Hit by Priorities: Employed Working-class Jamaican Women Confront the IMF." In June Nash and María Fernández-Kelly, eds., *Women, Men and the International Division of Labor.* Albany: State University of New York Press. 138–60.

Brana-Shute, Gary. 1976. "Drinking Shops and Social Structure: Some Ideas on Lower-class Male Behavior." *Urban Anthropology* 5:53–68.

Braverman, Henry. 1974. *Labor and Monopoly Capital: The Denigration of Work in the Twentieth Century.* New York: Monthly Review Press.

Campbell, Horace. 1987. *Rasta and Resistance: From Marcus Garvey to Walter Rodney.* Trenton: Africa World Press.

Chevannes, Barry. 1981. "The Rastafari and Urban Youth." In Carl Stone and Aggrey Brown, eds., *Perspectives on Jamaica in the Seventies.* Kingston: Jamaica Publishing House. 392–422.

Clarke, Edith. 1957. *My Mother Who Fathered Me.* London: George Allen and Unwin.

D'Amico-Samuels, Deborah. 1986. "You Can't Get Me Out of the Race: Women and Economic Development in Negril, Jamaica, West Indies." Unpublished doctoral dissertation, City University of New York.

Davies, Rob. 1979. "Informal Sector or Subordinate Mode of Production?" In Ray Bromley and Chris Gerry, eds., *Casual Work and Poverty in Third World Cities.* Chichester: John Wiley and Sons. 87–104.

Davis, Angela. 1981. *Women, Race, and Class.* New York: Random House.

Department of Statistics, Jamaica. 1978a. *The Labour Force.* Kingston.

———. 1978b. *Statistical Abstract.* Kingston.

———. 1984. *Statistical Yearbook of Jamaica, 1982.* Kingston.

Girvan, Norman. 1973. "The Development of Dependency Economics in the Caribbean and Latin America: Review and Comparison." *Social and Economic Studies* 22:1–33.

———. 1976. *Corporate Imperialism: Conflict and Expropriation. Transnational Corporations and Economic Nationalism in the Third World.* New York: Monthly Review Press.

Girvan, Norman, and Richard Bernal. 1982. "The IMF and the Foreclosure of Development Options: The Case of Jamaica." *Monthly Review* 33, no. 9:34–48.

Gonzalez, Nancie L. Solien. 1969. *Black Carib Household Structure: A Study of Migration and Modernization.* Seattle: University of Washington Press.

Harrison, Faye V. 1982. "Semiproletarianization and the Structure of Socioeconomic and Political Relations in a Jamaican Slum." Unpublished doctoral dissertation, Stanford University.

———. 1987. "Gangs, Grassroots Politics, and the Crisis of Dependent Capitalism in Jamaica." In David Hakken and Hanna Lessinger, eds., *Perspectives in U.S. Marxist Anthropology*. Boulder, Colo.: Westview Press. 186–210.

———. 1988. "The Politics of Social Outlawry in Urban Jamaica." *Urban Anthropology and Studies in Cultural Systems and World Economic Development* 17, nos. 2–3:259–77.

Headley, Bernard D. 1985. "Mr. Seaga's Jamaica: An Inside Look." *Monthly Review* 37, no. 4:35–42.

Henry, Frances, and Pamela Wilson. 1975. "The Status of Women in Caribbean Societies: An Overview of Their Social, Economic and Sexual Roles." *Social and Economic Studies* 24:165–98.

Henry, Paget. 1983. "Decolonization and Cultural Underdevelopment in the Commonwealth Caribbean." In Paget Henry and Carl Stone, eds., *The Newer Caribbean: Decolonization, Democracy, and Development*. Philadelphia: Institute for the Study of Human Issues. 95–120.

"Jamaica: Back in Business." 1980. *Newsweek* (15 December):86.

Jamaican Daily Gleaner. 1987. 1987 Annual.

Jamaican Weekly Gleaner. 1987. "Growth: Fiction or Reality?" Carl Stone column (26 October):10.

Jefferson, Owen. 1972. *The Post-war Economic Development of Jamaica*. Mona: Institute of Social and Economic Research, University of the West Indies.

Keith, Sherry, and Robert Girling. 1978. "Caribbean Conflict: Jamaica and the United States." *NACLA Report on the Americas* 12, no. 3:3–36.

Kitzinger, Sheila. 1969. "Protest and Mysticism: The Rastafari Cult of Jamaica." *Journal for the Scientific Study of Religion* 8:240–62.

———. 1971. "The Rastafarian Brethren of Jamaica." In Michael Horowitz, ed., *Peoples and Cultures of the Caribbean*. New York: Natural History Press. 580–88.

Knight, Franklin W. 1978. *The Caribbean: The Genesis of a Fragmented Nationalism*. New York: Oxford University Press.

Kowarick, Lucio. 1979. "Capitalism and Urban Marginality in Brazil." In Ray Bromley and Chris Gerry, eds., *Casual Work and Poverty in Third World Cities*. Chichester: John Wiley and Sons. 69–85.

Lacey, Terry. 1977. *Violence and Politics in Jamaica, 1960–1970*. Manchester: Manchester University Press.

Lieber, Michael. 1976. " 'Liming' and Other Concerns: The Style of Street Embedments of Port-of-Spain, Trinidad." *Urban Anthropology* 5:319–34.

Lim, Linda, Y. D. 1983. "Capitalism, Imperialism, and Patriarchy: The Dilemma of Third World Women Workers in Multinational Factories." In June Nash and María Fernández-Kelly, eds., *Women, Men and the International Division of Labor*. Albany: State University of New York Press. 70–91.

Lomnitz, Larissa Adler. 1977. *Networks and Marginality: Life in a Mexican Shantytown*. New York: Academic Press.

Mamdani, Mahmood. 1976. *Politics and Class Formation in Uganda*. New York: Monthly Review Press.

McGee, T. G. 1971. "Revolutionary Change and the Third World City." In T. G. McGee, *The Urbanization Process in the Third World*. London: G. Bell and Sons. 64–93.

Mintz, Sidney W. 1955. "The Jamaican Internal Marketing Pattern." *Social and Economic Studies* 4:95–103.

———. 1964. "The Employment of Capital by Market Women in Haiti." In Raymond Firth and B. S. Yamey, eds., *Capital, Savings and Credit in Peasant Societies*. Chicago: Aldine Publishing Co. 256–86.

———. 1977. "The So-called World System: Local Initiative and Local Response." *Dialectical Anthropology* 2:253–70.

———. 1981. "Economic Role and Cultural Tradition." In Filomina Chioma Steady, ed., *The Black Woman Cross-culturally*. Cambridge: Schenkman Publishing Co. 515–34.

Mintz, Sidney W., and Richard Price. 1977. *An Anthropological Approach to the Afro-American Past: A Caribbean Perspective*. Philadelphia: ISHI Occasional Papers in Social Change.

Moses, Yolanda T. 1981. "Female Status, the Family, and Male Dominance in a West Indian Community." In Filomina Chioma Steady, ed., *The Black Woman Cross-culturally*. Cambridge: Schenkman Publishing Co. 499–514.

Nash, June. 1983. "The Impact of the Changing International Division of Labor on Different Sectors of the Labor Force." In June Nash and María Fernández-Kelly, eds., *Women, Men, and the International Division of Labor*. Albany: State University of New York Press. 3–38.

Nash, June, and Helen I. Safa, eds. 1980. *Sex and Class in Latin America: Women's Perspectives on Politics, Economics and the Family in the Third World*. South Hadley, Mass.: Bergin and Garvey Publishers.

National Planning Agency. 1978. *Five Year Development Plan, 1978–82*. Kingston: Ministry of Finance and Planning, Jamaica.

Nelson, Nici. 1979. "How Women and Men Get By: The Sexual Division of Labor in the Informal Sector of a Nairobi Squatter Settlement." In Ray Bromley and Chris Gerry, eds., *Casual Work and Poverty in Third World Cities*. Chichester: John Wiley and Sons. 283–302.

Nettleford, Rex. 1970. *Mirror, Mirror: Identity, Race and Protest in Jamaica*. Kingston: William Collins and Sangster (Jamaica).

Patterson, Orlando. 1967. *The Sociology of Slavery: An Analysis of the Origins, Development and Structure of Negro Slave Society in Jamaica*. Rutherford: Fairleigh Dickinson University Press.

Portes, Alejandro. 1978. "The Informal Sector and the World Economy: Notes on the Structure of Subsidized Labor." *Institute of Development Studies Bulletin* 9:35–40.

———. 1981. "Unequal Exchange and the Urban Informal Sector." In Alejandro Portes and John Walton, eds., *Labor, Class, and the International System*. New York: Academic Press. 67–106.

Post, Ken. 1978. *Arise Ye Starvelings: The Jamaican Labour Rebellion of 1938 and Its Aftermath*. The Hague: Martinus Nijhoff.

Roberts, Bryan. 1978. *Cities of Peasants: The Political Economy of Urbanization in the Third World*. Beverly Hills: Sage Publications.

Rosaldo, Michelle. 1974. "A Theoretical Overview." In Michelle Rosaldo and Louise Lamphere, eds., *Woman, Culture, and Society*. Stanford, Calif.: Stanford University Press. 17–42.

Rowe, Maureen. 1980. "The Women in Rastafari." *Caribbean Quarterly* 26, no. 40:13–21.

Saffioti, Heleieth I. B. 1978. *Women in Class Society*. New York: Monthly Review Press.

Scott, Alison MacEwen. 1979. "Who Are the Self-employed?" In Ray Bromley and Chris Gerry, eds., *Casual Work and Poverty in Third World Cities*. Chichester: John Wiley and Sons. 105–29.

Smith, M. G., F. R. Augier, and Rex Nettleford. 1960. *The Rastafari Movement in Kingston, Jamaica*. Mona: Institute of Social and Economic Research, University College of the West Indies.

Statistical Institute of Jamaica. 1984. "The Labour Force, 1983 Preliminary Report." Kingston.

Stone, Carl. 1977. "The Political Economy of Gambling in a Neo-colonial Economy." In Carl Stone and Aggrey Brown, eds., *Essays on Power and Change in Jamaica*. Kingston: Jamaica Publishing House. 58–64.

———. 1987. "Running Out of Options in Jamaica: Seaga and Manley Compared." *Caribbean Review* 15, no. 3:10–12, 29–32.

Sutton, Constance, and Susan Makiesky-Barrow. 1981. "Social Inequality and Sexual Status in Barbados." In Filomina Chioma Steady, ed., *The Black Woman Cross-culturally*. Cambridge: Schenkman Publishing Co. 469–99.

Swartz, Marc J. 1968. "Introduction." In Marc J. Swartz, ed., *Local-level Politics: Social and Cultural Perspectives*. Chicago: Aldine Publishing Co. 1–52.

Thomas, Clive Y. 1974. *Dependence and Transformation: The Economics of the Transition to Socialism*. New York: Monthly Review Press.

Westwood, Sallie. 1985. *All Day, Every Day: Factory and Family in the Making of Women's Lives*. Urbana: University of Illinois Press.

Williams, Eric. 1944. *Capitalism and Slavery*. Chapel Hill: University of North Carolina Press.

Wilson, Peter. 1971 "Caribbean Crews: Peer Groups and Male Society." *Caribbean Studies* 10, no. 4:18–34.

Worsley, Peter. 1972. "Frantz Fanon and the Lumpenproletariat." In Ralph Miliband and John Saville, eds., *The Socialist Register*. London: The Merlin Press. 193–230.

Yanagisako, Sylvia J. 1979. "Family and Household: The Analysis of Domestic Groups." *Annual Review of Anthropology* 8:161–205.

WOMEN AND CRIME
IN THE UNITED STATES

Juanita Diaz-Cotto

During the last decade several theories have emerged which attempt to explain the increase in the number of women arrested in the United States since the 1960s.[1] Many of these theories assert that women are becoming more aggressive and violent as a result of their changing roles in society and the impact of the women's movement. This essay challenges these claims and presents a realistic interpretation of the economic, social, and political forces which shape women's lives and may lead to their increasing arrest and incarceration. I suggest further that many of these women are among those in our society who dare challenge the limited roles and opportunities available to women in general.

In order to set the context for my arguments, I will present a brief history of the women's prison-reform movement and discuss the assumptions that led to the creation of separate women's prisons. I will also give an overview of traditional rehabilitation methods within this historical framework and posit their modern-day ramifications.

The Women's Prison-Reform Movement

During the 1820s, Protestant women prison reformers in the United States began to visit incarcerated females. These Christian women were appalled by the conditions that female prisoners were forced to endure (Freedman 1981, 15–17, 59–60). The prisons were designed to detain male prisoners only, and women, sometimes with their children, were crowded into small sections of the institutions, overwhelmed by disease, hunger, and physical and sexual abuse. The reformers' initial aims were to help imprisoned women repent for their "sins" (meaning crimes) and to convert them to Christian ways of living. However, they soon found themselves providing services such as sewing and writing classes within the institutions and opening halfway houses where released women could live temporarily while acquiring legal work skills.

Several events took place during the second half of the nineteenth century which led women prison reformers to demand the creation of separate prisons for women to be administered by women. The most important of these was the increase in arrests of women and their conviction to penal institutions. This increase was related to the various economic, social, and political changes which took place after the Civil War and which culminated in rapid industrialization of the country and increasing rural migration (and foreign immigration) to the cities (Freedman 1981, 13–15).

Separate Women's Prisons

The argument that women's prisons, if administered and staffed by women, could be used to rehabilitate (that is, reform) female offenders was based on a series of erroneous assumptions. The first assumption was that all imprisoned women need to be rehabilitated. The second was that prisons could be used to rehabilitate. The third was that rehabilitation could be accomplished without the complete transformation of all institutions in society. The fourth was that women's prisons could fulfill the goals of rehabilitation because the administrators, the staff, and the prisoners would all be women. And finally, reformers, or women like them (white, middle- and upper-class), believed themselves to be the best fit to lead female prisoners (disproportionately poor and working-class black and immigrant white women) on the road to rehabilitation (Freedman 1981, 46–64).

Women reformers argued that a woman usually resorted to crimes such as prostitution and petty larceny after being abandoned (alone or with her children) by a man who had taken sexual advantage of her. In a woman's prison, they suggested, this "fallen woman," far from the influence and abuse of men, could be taught to fulfill her expected social roles of wife and mother (Freedman 1981, 44–45). She could become a lady rather than continue to act as a "criminal." Thus a major goal of many of the female prison reformers was the perpetuation of the traditional sex roles assigned to women by society.

The transformation of the "fallen woman" would be accomplished by using women's prisons to teach Bible classes, cooking, sewing, cleaning, washing clothes, and other skills which would prepare her to fulfill these roles and support herself financially. Hence, since the opening of the first women's prison in Indiana in 1873, the focus of rehabilitation has been on teaching work skills in traditional low-paying women's occupations in the service sector. These occupations offer women minimal opportunities for social and economic advancement and, more often than not, make it difficult for them to meet their basic financial needs and those of their dependents.[2]

Women's institutions almost from their inception have been more preoccupied with punishment and security concerns than with realistic rehabilitation. In the best of cases rehabilitation has meant focusing on changing individuals. Prison administrators, for the most part, have not seriously questioned the social, economic, racial, and political conditions which lead women to be arrested and incarcerated. Even when economic factors (i.e., poverty, the state of the economy) have been discussed as possibly influencing the nature of illegal behavior, very little is said except that the individual has been unable to adapt to her environment in a socially acceptable manner. Failure to adapt is then blamed on the prisoner for not having the proper family life or friends while growing up, and/or the right attitude toward work and authority, both of which would have prevented her from breaking the law.

A look at the sociodemographic profile of incarcerated women will allow us to see the type of woman most likely to be arrested and imprisoned in the United States in any one year. Additionally, a look at the types of offenses for which women were arrested in 1965, 1978, and 1984 will give us some insight into the major causes leading to women's arrests.

Profile of Incarcerated Women

In 1880, 75.06 percent of women imprisoned in the United States were classified as white. By 1890 this number had decreased to 62.42 percent (Freedman 1981, 82). Surveys conducted in 1978 reveal that white women constituted 46.4 percent of the total (see Table 1).[3] The overrepresentation of black women within local jails and state and federal prisons is corroborated by the fact that between 1880 and 1985, blacks made up only 12 to 13 percent of the country's population (U.S. Bureau of the Census 1987, 16). In states such as New York, where Latino men and women constitute close to 10 percent of the population, Latinas make up 23.4 percent of women incarcerated in state prisons (Hispanic Inmate Needs Task Force 1986, 162).

It is particularly instructive to examine the characteristics of women incarcerated in local jails throughout the United States. A study in 1978 demonstrates that, at the time of their arrest, 72.9 percent of the women were under the age of thirty (see Table 2). Although four out of every five, or 80.5 percent, of the women were single,[4] 47.1 percent had dependents. Almost half of the women, 49.5 percent, earned an income of

TABLE 1 Women Prisoners Held in Federal and State Prisons and Local Jails, by Race, 1978

Institution	Total[a] Population	Total Number of Women	Percentage[b] of Total Prisoners	White Women	Percentage of Total Women	Black Women	Percentage of Total Women	Other Women	Percentage of Total Women	Not Known	Percentage of Total Women
Jails	158,394	9,555	6.0	4,666	48.8	4,630	48.5	259	2.7	n/a	n/a
Federal Prisons	29,803	1,828	6.1	727	39.8	974	53.3	24	1.3	103	5.6
State Prisons	276,799	10,892	3.9	4,947	45.4	5,509	50.6	169	1.6	267	2.5
TOTAL	464,996	22,265	4.8	10,340	46.4	11,113	49.9	452	2.0	370	1.7

Sources: Adapted from U.S. Department of Justice, Bureau of Justice Statistics, *Prisoners in State and Federal Institutions on December 31, 1978, National Prisoner Statistics Bulletin*, May 1980, p. 20; and U.S. Department of Justice, Bureau of Justice Statistics, *Profile of Jail Inmates: Sociodemographic Findings from the 1978 Survey of Inmates in Local Jails, National Prisoner Statistics Report*, October 1980, p. 13.

[a]Includes the total of male and female prisoners in these institutions.
[b]Percentages may not add to 100 due to rounding off.

$3,000 a year or less, while another 21.6 percent earned between $3,000 and $5,999. The median income was $2,416, and the median level of education was tenth grade. At the time of the survey, 42.6 percent of the women had not been convicted of any previous crime.

From these data we can conclude that women in local jails are predominantly single, poor, and working-class white and minority women under the age of thirty. Almost half of them have dependents, and an equal proportion have not completed a high-school education. Therefore, even if these women did not suffer the effects of direct employment discrimination on the basis of their sex and/or race-ethnicity, many had not acquired the educational or vocational skills which would allow them access to decent-paying jobs.[5]

Crimes for Which Women Are Arrested

Up until the late 1970s, the phenomenon of female criminality had been largely ignored by social scientists, criminologists, lawyers, and penologists. Traditional studies and observations of female criminality such as those of Lombroso and Ferrero (1895), Thomas (1907), Pollack (1961), and Freud (1933) argued that women's crimes are the result of the women's inability to adapt to their "natural feminine roles." The implication of these studies is that women who commit crimes are masculine, and therefore, aggressive.

Recent studies of female criminality, as Carol Smart and Dorie Klein have argued, have done little to dispel this myth. In fact, the increase in the number of arrests for women since the 1960s has led some criminologists and sociologists to contend that female offenders are becoming increasingly more aggressive and violent. Supporters of this argument, such as Freda Adler (1975), assert that an increase in women's economic and psychological independence, allegedly brought about by the women's movement, has led more women to commit violent crimes such as robbery, murder, and assault. These are crimes traditionally associated with male offenders.

The data used to support these arguments are drawn from the *FBI Uniform Crime Reports* (1984) and are based on increases in the "rate of arrests." As Table 3 demonstrates, between 1965 and 1984 the rate of arrests for women involved in all offenses increased 148.4 percent, while that for males increased 67.7 percent. Arrests for women have increased more rapidly than arrests for men.

The fact is that when we look at the actual numbers involved (Table 3), we see that over 3 million more men were arrested in 1984 than in 1965, while 889,332 more women were arrested during the same period. In order for men to have experienced an increase in the rate of arrests

TABLE 2 Women Prisoners Held in Local Jails, by Selected Sociodemographic Characteristics, 1978

Characteristic	Total Women	Percentage[a] of Total Women	White Women	Percentage of Total Women	Black Women	Percentage of Total Women	Other Women	Percentage of Total Women
Total	9,555[b]	100.0	4,666	48.8	4,630	48.5	259	2.7
Age								
Under 30	6,962	72.9	3,259	46.8	3,497	50.0	205	2.9
Median Age	25.45		25.40		25.65		23.49	
Marital Status[c]								
Separated, Never Married, Divorced, or Widowed	7,693	80.5	3,473	45.1	4,026	52.3	195	2.5
Dependents at Time of Admission[c]								
With Dependents	4,503	47.1	1,703	37.8	2,678	59.5	122	2.7
Highest Grade of School Completed[c]								
Less than 12	5,557	58.2	2,573	46.3	2,834	51.0	151	2.7
Median Grade	10.5		10.6		10.3		10.4	
Convicted	5,476	42.6	2,035	49.9	1,934	47.5	105	2.6

Employment Status								
Not Working	6,331	66.3	2,897	45.8	3,268	51.6	166	2.6
Annual Income								
Less than $3,000	4,725	49.5	2,198	46.5	2,417	51.2	110	2.3
$3,000–$5,999	2,065	21.6	1,090	52.8	911	44.1	65	3.1
Without Income	852	8.9	439	51.5	387	45.4	26	3.1
Median Income	2,416		2,594		2,254		2,566	
Main Source of Income[c]								
Wages & Salaries	3,397	35.6	1,875	55.2	1,432	42.2	89	2.6
Transfer Payments[d]	2,866	30.0	995	34.7	1,785	62.3	86	3.0
No. Independent Income[e]	2,350	24.6	1,332	56.7	954	40.6	64	2.7
Illegal	585	6.1	292	49.9	288	49.2	5	0.9

Source: Adapted from the U.S. Department of Justice, Bureau of Justice Statistics, *Profile of Jail Inmates: Sociodemographic Findings from the 1978 Survey of Inmates of Local Jails, National Prisoner Statistics Report*, October 1980, pp. 12–14.

[a]Percentages may not add to 100 due to rounding off.

[b]Women prisoners were 6.0 percent or 9,555 of the 158,394 persons held in local jails.

[c]This category does not include the sublisting of "Not Reported."

[d]Social Security, unemployment benefits, education grants, and welfare.

[e]Includes borrowing from and support by family or friends.

TABLE 3

Arrest, Trends by Sex, 1965, 1978, and 1984[a]

Arrests for	1965	1978	1984
TOTAL ARRESTS MALE/FEMALE	5,031,393	9,775,087	8,921,708
TOTAL OFFENSES			
Male	4,431,625	8,227,228	7,432,608
(Rate of arrest compared to 1965			+67.7)
TOTAL PERCENTAGE OF ALL ARRESTS			
Male	88.1	84.2	83.3
VIOLENT CRIMES[b]			
Male			
total number	133,238	400,697	341,388
percentage	89.8	89.8	89.3
PROPERTY CRIMES[c]			
Male			
total number	592,251	1,352,656	1,112,327
percentage	85.9	77.7	76.6
TOTAL OFFENSES			
Female	599,768	1,547,859	1,489,100
(Rate of arrest compared to 1965			+148.4)
TOTAL PERCENTAGE OF ALL ARRESTS			
Female	11.9	15.8	16.7
VIOLENT CRIMES			
Female			
total number	15,127	45,425	40,858
percentage	10.2	10.2	10.7
PROPERTY CRIMES			
Female			
total number	97,052	388,598	339,775
percentage	15.1	22.3	23.4

Source: Adapted from U.S. Department of Justice, Federal Bureau of Investigations, *FBI Uniform Crime Reports* (Washington, D.C.: U.S. Government Printing Office), 1965 (p. 115), 1978 (p. 197), and 1984 (p. 179).
[a]Percentages may not add up to 100 due to rounding off.
[b]Violent crimes—murder, forcible rape, robbery, aggravated assault.
[c]Property crimes—burglary, larceny-theft, motor vehicle theft, and, as of 1979, arson.

similar to that for women, over 6 million more men would have had to be arrested in 1984 compared to 1965! As Laura Crites (1976) states, "The implication is clear: because traditionally fewer women have been arrested than men, any increase in female arrests is likely to result in a higher percentage of 'rate of increase'"(35).

In order to verify whether this increase in the number of arrests for women does in fact indicate that women are becoming increasingly violent, we can examine those crimes considered the most serious by the FBI. This category of crimes, which makes up what is called the "crime index," is divided into two subcategories: violent and property crimes. Under the subcategory of violent crimes are included murder, forcible rape, robbery, and aggravated assault. Property crimes include burglary, larceny-theft, motor vehicle theft, and, as of 1979, arson.

The statistics show that although more women were arrested for violent crimes in 1984 than in 1965, women still accounted for only 10.7 and 10.2 percent respectively of all violent offenses committed during those years (Table 3). Additionally, the overwhelming increase in arrests for women within the crime index category has taken place not in violent crimes but in property crimes. While 14.1 percent of all persons arrested for property crimes in 1965 were women, in 1984 this number had increased to 23.4 percent.

There are two additional ways of disproving the argument that women's crimes are becoming increasingly violent. The first approach is to look at the "Rank Ordering of the Most Frequent Arrests for Women, by Offense" as Crites (1976) has done. Table 4 indicates the top ten crimes for which women were arrested in 1965, 1978, and 1984. During these years, none of the top ten crimes for which women were arrested were violent crimes.[6] In 1984, three of the top ten offenses were economic crimes,[7] with one out of every five women arrested for larceny-theft and another one in ten arrested for embezzlement, prostitution, or commercialized vice. While at least five of the top ten offenses could be considered "victimless crimes,"[8] four offenses involved drugs or alcohol.

The second approach to refute the argument that women are becoming increasingly violent is to look at the "Female Percentage of Total Arrests, by Offense" (Table 5). This table lists the top ten offenses most often committed by women in comparison with men. It is important to note that while the offenses of murder and nonnegligent manslaughter as well as aggravated assault were included in the top ten offenses in 1965, they do not appear in the top ten in either 1978 or 1984. In fact, the data indicate that not only are women not becoming increasingly violent, but they seem to be less violent.

Moreover, many women may be arrested for victimless crimes, such as prostitution, running away, and drunkenness, because they have violated traditional stereotypes about how women in our society should behave rather than because they are breaking the law. In 1984, women's arrests exceeded those for men in only two categories, prostitution and commercialized vice, and running away. While four of the top ten offenses

TABLE 4

Rank Ordering of the Most Frequent Arrests for Women, by Offense, 1965, 1978, and 1984

1965	
Offense	Percentage of Arrests
Drunkenness	19.8
Larceny-theft	14.2
Disorderly conduct	12.1
Running away	7.1
Prostitution & commercialized vice	4.4
Other assaults	3.7
Liquor law violations	3.5
Driving under the influence	2.5
Curfew & loitering law violations	2.3
Vagrancy	1.9
1978	
Larceny-theft	22.2
Disorderly conduct	7.0
Driving under the influence	6.5
Running away	6.5
Fraud	5.9
Drunkenness	5.4
Drug-abuse violations	5.3
Other assaults	3.9
Prostitution & commercialized vice	3.9
Liquor law violations	3.4
1984	
Larceny-theft	20.5
Driving under the influence	10.5
Disorderly conduct	6.0
Embezzlement	5.5
Drug-abuse violations	5.2
Drunkenness	5.1
Running away	4.4
Liquor law violations	4.2
Other assaults	4.2
Prostitution & commercialized vice	4.1

Source: Adapted from U.S. Department of Justice, Federal Bureau of Investigations, *Uniform Crime Reports* (Washington, D.C.: U.S. Government Printing Office), 1965 (p. 115), 1978 (p. 197), and 1984 (p. 179).

TABLE 5

Female Percentage of Total Arrests, by Offense, 1965, 1978, and 1984

1965	
Offense	Percentage of Arrests
Prostitution & commercialized vice	77.5
Running away	47.1
Larceny-theft	22.1
Fraud	20.3
Curfew & loitering law violations	18.9
Forgery & counterfeiting	18.4
Murder & nonnegligent manslaughter	17.6
Embezzlement	17.2
Sex offenses (except forcible rape & prostitution)	14.9
Aggravated assault	13.5
1978	
Prostitution & commercialized vice	67.7
Running away	57.4
Fraud	36.8
Larceny-theft	31.7
Forgery & counterfeiting	29.7
Vagrancy	29.4
Embezzlement	25.1
Curfew & loitering law violations	21.6
Disorderly conduct	16.1
Liquor law violations	14.7
1984	
Prostitution & commercialized vice	69.9
Running away	57.8
Fraud	40.4
Embezzlement	36.9
Forgery & counterfeiting	33.7
Larceny-theft	30.2
Curfew & loitering law violations	23.7
Disorderly conduct	17.2
Liquor law violations	16.4
Other assaults	15.1

Source: Adapted from U.S. Department of Justice, Federal Bureau of Investigations, *Uniform Crime Reports* (Washington, D.C.: U.S. Government Printing Office), 1965 (p. 115), 1978 (p. 197), and 1984 (p. 179).

were victimless crimes,[9] five of the top six offenses were economic crimes[10] (Table 5).

The overall importance of focusing on arrests for economic crimes is that it leads us to question whether women may be increasingly forced to turn to these types of crimes because of worsening economic conditions. The number of arrests involving drugs and alcohol could indicate both an attempt on the part of women to increase their income through illegal means, and/or an increase in drug and alcohol addiction among women trying to escape from societal conditions they feel powerless to change or control.

What Does the Women's Movement Have to Do with This Anyway?

It has been argued that women offenders are becoming increasingly violent and that this tendency is the result of the influence of the women's rights movement. The movement contributes to women's criminality, the argument goes, because it questions their traditional roles in society and so leads them to act in a more independent manner. In the process, this growing independence causes women to "act like men," meaning aggressive and violent. We must remember that during the second half of the nineteenth century, when arrest rates for women rose in comparison to those of previous centuries, the women's rights movement was also blamed. At that time traditional voices such as those of Lombroso and Ferrero (1895) argued that the cause of increasing crimes among women lay in women's growing "emancipation" (Smart 1976).

Within this context, the women's movement played a key role in pointing out that the increase in arrests of women was the result of deteriorating economic conditions and the repression unleashed on women who dared step outside their traditional feminine roles (Freedman 1981, 41–42). The offense most often used to illustrate this argument is prostitution, traditionally considered the result of wanton behavior by women. In fact, women work as prostitutes to support themselves and their families. Crites (1976) makes the added argument that it has been women least involved and identified with the women's movement, that is, poor and working-class white and minority women, who are increasingly subject to arrests.

Traditional studies such as those of Lombroso and Ferrero (1895), Thomas (1907), Pollack (1961), and Freud (1933), and more recent studies such as that of Adler (1975) have included little or no discussion of female crimes in relation to the state of the economy, the educational and occupational opportunities available to women, or the division of labor along sexual and/or racial-ethnic lines. Rather, the causes of women's arrests and crimes have been seen as the result of women's inability to conform to their "natural feminine roles." It is within this context that the women's rights movement is seen as the cause of the increase in women's arrest rates during the past twenty years, as the movement promotes women's independence and the breaking down of cultural barriers which keep women in their place.

Recent studies by feminist social scientists such as Crites (1976), Klein (1976), and Smart (1976) have sought to demonstrate that the increase in women's arrests is due not to pathological factors such as the failure of women offenders to conform to their socially determined roles, but to economic, social, and political factors. Feminists have also been key in demonstrating that the increase in arrest rates for women does not indicate that women are becoming more violent. On the contrary, the rise in arrests for economic crimes indicates that women's economic position is worsening and that they are more willing to risk being arrested in order to be able to support themselves and their dependents.

Additionally, we must look at why the state chooses to focus on enforcing laws which penalize the types of actions taken by poor and working-class white and minority women while ignoring the more destructive white-collar and corporate crimes (Wickman and Dailewy 1982). These women not only are the victims of economic, sexual, and/or racial-ethnic discrimination, but many are being penalized for taking actions which challenge the limited roles and opportunities available to them.

Thus the rehabilitation model espoused by women prison reformers since the 1820s and its application in women's prisons today need to be examined within (a) the context of economic inequalities which place poor and working-class white and minority women at the lowest end of the economic spectrum, (b) racial/ethnic discrimination which leads to a disproportionate number of minority women incarcerated in penal institutions, (c) sexual discrimination which punishes women for stepping outside traditionally assigned female roles, and (d) state policies which define what actions in a society are labeled criminal, what type of offenses the criminal justice system focuses on enforcing at any one time, and what communities and social classes are targeted for incarceration as a result of these policies.

NOTES

I would like to thank Lourdes Torres for her great editing suggestions and encouragement.

1. In 1965 women constituted 11.9 percent of those arrested. By 1978 and 1984 this number had increased to 15.8 percent and 16.7 percent respectively (see Table 3).

2. Today these occupations include secretarial work, domestic service, and waitressing. However, even this minimal concern with the fate of women in prison is irrelevant for the 50 percent of the women who are incarcerated in local jails in the United States on any one day. In these cases women tend to be locked up in their cells for up to twenty-three and a half hours a day, while men in these institutions may have access, although limited, to educational, vocational, and work programs.

3. Until recently government statistics did not include the category of "Hispanic" in their studies. Even now, Latina women are sometimes classified as either black or white depending on the color of their skin and who is conducting the survey.

4. Never married, separated, widowed, or divorced.

5. This sociodemographic profile of women in local jails in 1978 still describes the type of women most likely to be incarcerated in both local jails and state prisons in 1989.

6. The "other assaults" category included in the top ten offenses in 1965, 1978, and 1984 had been defined by the *FBI Uniform Crime Reports* as "assaults and attempted assaults where no weapons were used and which did not result in serious or aggravated injury to the victim." Other assaults, or simple assaults, as they are also called, are not considered serious enough to include them in the crime index category.

7. Crimes economically motivated, such as prostitution, fraud, embezzlement, forgery and counterfeiting, and larceny-theft.

8. Crimes in which there is no official complainant or victim. In this case, prostitution, running away, drug-abuse violations, drunkenness, and violation of the liquor laws.

9. Prostitution, running away, violations of liquor laws, curfew, and loitering laws.

10. Prostitution, fraud, embezzlement, forgery and counterfeiting, and larceny-theft.

REFERENCES

Adler, F. 1975. *Sisters in Crime*. New York: McGraw-Hill Books.

Crites, L. 1976. "Women Offenders: Myth vs. Reality." In Laura Crites, ed., *The Female Offender*. Lexington, Mass.: D. C. Heath and Co.

FBI *Uniform Crime Reports, Crime in the U.S.* 1984. Washington, D.C.: Department of Justice.

Freedman, E. 1981. *Their Sister's Keepers: Women's Prison Reform in America, 1830–1930*. Ann Arbor: University of Michigan Press.

Freud, S. 1933. *New Introductory Lectures on Psychoanalysis*. New York: W. W. Norton.

Hispanic Inmate Needs Task Force. 1986. *A Meeting of Minds, An Encounter of Hearts: 1986 Action Plan*. Albany: New York State Department of Correctional Services, Division of Hispanic and Cultural Affairs.

Klein, Dorie. 1976. "The Etiology of Female Crime: A Review of Literature." In Laura Crites, ed., *The Female Offender*. Lexington, Mass.: D. C. Heath and Co.

Lombroso, C., and W. Ferrero. 1895. *The Female Offender*. London: Fisher Unwin.

Pollack, O. 1961. *The Criminality of Women*. New York: A. S. Barnes.

Simon, R. 1975. *Women and Crime*. Lexington, Mass.: D. C. Heath and Co.

Sims, Patsy. 1976. "Women in Southern Jails." In Laura Crites, ed., *The Female Offender*. Lexington, Mass.: D. C. Heath and Co. 137–47.

Smart, C. 1976. *Women, Crime, and Criminology: A Feminist Critique*. London: Routledge and Kegan Paul.

Thomas, W.I. 1907. *Sex and Society*. Boston: Little Brown.

———. 1967. *The Unadjusted Girl*. New York: Harper and Row.

U.S. Bureau of the Census. 1987. *Statistical Abstracts of the United States*. 108th ed. Washington, D.C.

Wickman, P., and T. Dailewy, eds. 1982. *White-Collar and Economic Crime: Multidisciplinary and Cross-National Perspectives*. Lexington, Mass.: D. C. Heath and Co.

3 National Liberation and Sexual Politics

WOMEN'S EQUALITY AND NATIONAL LIBERATION

Angela Gilliam

O ne of the major challenges for those people concerned with women's equality is the development of a unifying theoretical focus that connects local concerns with national *and* international issues. Since so much of the social analysis in our society is based on the local qua individualistic approach, it is necessary to attempt to devise "ways of seeing" and knowing that incorporate the previously excluded—or to put it another way, that turn "mankind" into "humankind." For those also interested in national liberation in today's world, this means going beyond the problem of Eurocentricity in contemporary social theory. In order to do this, "it is imperative that the absent . . . be made present because the greater part of the truth, as is shown by the continuing revolutions in the Third World, is in that which is absent" (Mafeje 1981). This essay, then, intends to examine two issues—national liberation and women's equality—from the perspective of that which has been previously excluded. Inherent in such a paradigm is the imperative of integrating a sensitivity to global issues with an awareness that women around the world may have different priorities. Such a sensitivity is cognizant of the fact that the discourse of the U.S. women's movement, as well as the national and international representation of it, is controlled by elites.

Nonetheless, it is reasonable to assert that the women's movement in the United States has made two significant contributions. First, it has highlighted the relationship between reproductive rights and an equitable health-care-delivery system (e.g., Dreifus 1978; Frankfort 1972). Second, the women's movement has also challenged the idealized roles and concepts about family structure that have been held up as models by which to measure and oppress those women who are structurally denied access to that idealization (Davis 1981; Andreas 1971).

Yet, the major portion of the mainstream women's movement in the United States—and, by extension, the Western women's movement in general—has been hampered by characteristics that limit its international relevance. First, it has been essentially a struggle for *equal access*. In this way, the women's movement replicates the problems of the U.S. civil rights movement. Neither movement has as its basis the transformation of the system at its roots; the major concern has been to open up the system so that "women could also be policemen," or, "blacks could be promoted in the army." To challenge the system itself would be to confront *what* the police or the army actually does. Another problem of both the civil rights struggle and the women's movement is that the elites in those movements have become the officially recognized leadership, channels through which the lesser-privileged are expected to voice their grievances. This not only leads to tokenism as a solution but also to a clear reduction in economic concerns.

In the place of economic issues, cultural or gender identity has become the major focus. In the case of African American men and women, cultural nationalism has become one of the central themes of the civil rights battle, sometimes based on a longing to find African kings and queens in the African past. More often it has been related to reconstructing long-lost links to Africa—a noble goal. Thus, the problems of African people are defined as primarily cultural, and rarely are they tied to political economy. As Stanislas Adotevi (1972) warned, the black poet who did not participate in his or her people's total struggle merely exercised in "negritation" and ultimately proved to be a member of a comfortable elite connecting to the people's movement exclusively through song. Furthermore, a critical component of this dynamic is posing "all white people"—irrespective of economic or social condition—as the enemy.

The women's movement in the United States has a similar paradigm. For many, gender and sexual identity has become the major focus of women's concerns, rather than economics. The reification of gender propels the movement into identifying women and men as two distinct classes (Atkinson 1974). All men therefore are transformed into oppressors of all women, and hence the former are declared the enemy; this tendency is evident in a lecture once given at the College at Old Westbury, whose title may be paraphrased as "There is no such thing as a rich woman." This conveniently permitted the elite women spokespersons to avoid the question of their participation in the economic oppression of many of their sisters in the nation and throughout the world. Such an inquiry of necessity would have linked women's oppression worldwide with the role the U.S. government plays in the international economic order. Instead, the standard position of some Western feminists was that all women were natural allies. An extreme version of this line of thought is that Margaret Thatcher, prime minister of Great Britain, and Jeanne Kirkpatrick, former U.S. ambassador to the United Nations and architect of militaristic U.S. policies in Central America, are more deserving of solidarity—because they are women—than the men who fought against those policies.

Female chauvinism is an outgrowth of a primarily gender-oriented struggle because it operates on the assumptions that women are more "human" than men, and that this is biologically determined (Johnston 1973). The projection of sexualism, which focuses on sex and sexuality separate from economics and politics, not only has made it difficult for many national minority women in the United States to identify with the more privileged sectors of the women's movement, but such a perspective is also in the interests of the ruling class. For one thing, it prevents the women's movement in the United States from becoming a powerful force for positive and creative change, because a unified approach to women's issues is avoided. A unified approach must simultaneously integrate the questions of racism, class oppression, and sexism.

Sexualism, by concentrating on sexual identity, has also permitted the Far Right to appropriate concerns about the family. Instead of analyzing the impact of unemployment, lack of child care, and militarism on women and their families, the movement made the right to participate in and define one's sexuality take primacy in the women's struggle for equality.

Hence, the divisions in the women's movement, as reflected in the "Common Differences" conference, are between those who believe that the major struggle for women is increasing their access to, and control over, the world's resources and those who believe that the main issue is access to, and control over, orgasms. Although sexuality is important, it *must* be tied to the political and the economic; otherwise, women set themselves up for another kind of domination. It is my position that the global class question must be central in the struggle for the world's resources, goods, and services, and that women's equality should be defined within this overall struggle.

It is important to note that both heterosexual and lesbian women fall prey to sexualism. This phenomenon emerges as a natural factor in a society that has traditionally been sex-obsessed. On the one hand, sex is utilized as a marketing concept to sell all types of commodities from automobiles to toothpaste. On the other hand, the notion that sex is a

normal physiological process about which children should be informed
at all levels has never really taken hold in all sectors of U.S. society, given
the Calvinistic ethic that is at the root of the country's values. It is not
totally illogical that some women should have reached a conclusion that
their struggle should net as a result the right to the sexual behavior to
which men feel they are entitled. This is bourgeois ideology for many
reasons, however.

First of all, it concentrates on the *individual* and is narcissistic. Such
a definition of women's true dimensions for struggle pulls away from the
collective or shared concerns—except with one's own class. Sexualism
becomes the new elitism, the new expression of class struggle within the
movement, since most of the world's working women—including many
poor women in the United States—identify survival issues to be food,
housing, health care, and employment, not sexuality.

The 1980 Women's Mid-Decade Meeting in Copenhagen offers a particularly germane illustration of this point. One of the most tendentious
and divisive points raised by Western women during that conference
concerned clitoridectomy and the practice of infibulation of female genitalia, which still exist in parts of Africa and the Middle East. This became
a rallying point for Western women, and as they promoted this issue, it
seemed to establish a hierarchical relationship to their Third World sisters
through intellectual neocolonialism. It revealed latent racism, because the
form in which the issues were articulated was in terms of those "savage
customs" from "backward" African and Arab cultures. Underlying this
formulation was the implicit evidence of a rising anti-Arab and anti-
Islamic fervor that was starting to emanate from Western countries. As
Edda Gachukia (one of the Kenyan organizers of the 1985 End of the
Decade Meeting in Nairobi) told those attending a pre-Nairobi session at
the World Division Office of the United Methodist church, this action in
Copenhagen forced Arab and African women—who had always fought
against female circumcision on health grounds—to feel compelled to defend it. In addition, the women attending this meeting saw a consolidation
of the schism between the issues set forth by Third World women and
those of interest to Western women.

Nawal el Saadawi, an Egyptian writer who described her own clitoridectomy as part of her book on sexuality in the Arab world (1980), has
mentioned elsewhere (1982; 1983) that Western women often go to countries such as the Sudan and "see" only clitoridectomy, but never notice
the role of multinational corporations and their exploited labor. And Rose
Catchings, whose office sponsored the May 1985 meeting with Gachukia,
pointed out that it was the way in which this theme emerged at the 1980
meeting in Copenhagen that forced minority women from the United

States to question their relationship to this type of advocacy for Third World women's rights.

A careful examination of this issue demonstrates how sexualism can serve as a paradigm or "lens" for Western feminists to measure women in other parts of the world. In an interview done at the "Common Differences" conference with Patterson and Gilliam, el Saadawi (1983) pointed to the work of Fran Hosken as a case in point, "[She] came to my home in Cairo . . . I gave her information regarding the political and historical aspects, and she didn't use it." And Patterson (1983) observed that at the 1982 African Studies Association meeting, many objected to "[Hosken's] using clitoridectomy as the only point for defining women's oppression in Africa and the Middle East." A careful perusal of the quarterly of which Hosken is editor—*Women's International Network News* (*WINN*)—and its regular column entitled "Female Circumcision: Genital and Sexual Mutilation" demonstrates an unusually single-minded preoccupation with this issue, and confirms el Saadawi's assertion that Hosken is ahistorical. In affirming that *WINN* is the only journal to address this question, Hosken—now recognized in the West as an expert on the question of clitoridectomy—exotifies Egypt and the subject in general. This lack of a horizontal, nonvertical approach produces a hierarchical discussion in which the "expert" looks at an aspect of another culture from "up above."

An egalitarian focus, on the other hand, which embodies a methodological principle of "parallel process," makes clear that many "traditional practices" in U.S. culture—child sexual abuse immediately comes to mind—also threaten the lives and limbs of children. Yet *WINN* "pursues" the Third World in a quasi-titillating way, eschewing a more global approach.

What became clearer after 1980 was that the issue of sexuality should be neither divorced from the political and the economic, nor take primacy over the question of reproductive rights. As Sally Mugabe (wife of Zimbabwe's prime minister, Robert Mugabe) said in her press conference at the Nairobi Meeting in July 1985, there are two issues of power that are central to women, and without which women's equality is impossible: (1) independent access to money or resources that enable women to contribute to their own and their children's livelihood, and (2) control over the reproductive decisions that relate to their bodies.

And increasingly, U.S. women are losing not only the principle of affirmative action in the workplace, but also the rights to manage their bodies with regard to reproduction. Moreover, the trend toward arbitrary male custody in litigation affects all women in the U.S., and is fundamentally an economic question. As lesbian anthropologist Renee Llanusa-Cestero elucidates, "it is this trend towards the reinvestment of male dominance around which lesbian and heterosexual women can be united as a group—but *not* as a class."[2] The very concept of "class" itself is more exact as a component of the Marxian paradigm. However, the precision of a definition of class that is rooted in the Marxian theory of socioeconomic formations has rarely been given importance other than in intellectual circles. Ethel Tobach, series editor of Genes and Gender, explains that the reason for this lies in the relationship of the women's movement to the larger society of which it is a part: "It is not that women do not find dialectical materialism a useful method for analysis, but that they have incorporated the same anti-Marxist stance that is projected in the U.S. society as a whole."[3]

Moreover, the voices of U.S. women appear to have become muted, in part by the mythology that women in the United States have realized more freedom than women in other countries—especially those of the Third World. Women in the U.S. all too infrequently challenge the definitions of "freedom" that are bandied about. What a multinational corporation defines as a "most favorable investment climate—cheap labor, abundant resources, new markets, and the *political climate to guarantee the first three*" (*Controlling Interest* 1978)—is often the bottom line in the definition of "freedom" that U.S. soldiers are sent to defend. That cheap and exploited labor includes women. Whether in urban or rural areas, women are frequently the ones most likely to be employed in tasks involving minute detail, long hours, and repetitive work that is undervalued, lesser-paid, and temporary (Bisilliat and Fieloux 1983). Multinational companies oppose national liberation movements because they challenge a status quo that is in the interest of big business.

There are compelling interlocking relationships connecting natural resources, national liberation struggles, multinational corporations, and women's oppression worldwide. For example, the struggle for power in Namibia and South Africa certainly involves critical control over mineral resources. Few U.S. citizens realize how many of the minerals found in abundance in southern Africa—including cadmium, chromium, vanadium, cobalt, and uranium—are used in the production of turbine jet engines, nuclear reactors, and other military components (Nabudere 1977). For many in the U.S., the liberation of the black majority in southern Africa is secondary to the question of whether we can "keep the minerals flowing to us" without paying more. The profit motive is key to U.S. definitions of freedom. Yet, until recently the U.S. government told its citizens that the struggle is against "an evil empire" presumably doing the Devil's work (Lewis 1983). Although Namibia's pending independence is being touted in the U.S. media, the effect of the Reagan administration's policy of "constructive engagement" with the South African government has been the creeping apartheidization of U.S. culture and the gradual labeling of those of the world's peoples who dare to challenge the transnationals' definition of "freedom" and "liberty" as "communists" and "terrorists."

The main influence of apartheid on U.S. society is the acceptance and legitimation of the Pretoria regime's view that anyone who would transform South Africa as it is now is a "terrorist." Apartheid's jails are filled with women serving long sentences and who actively worked against that system, such as Teresa Ramashamola of the United Democratic Front or Marion Sparg of the African National Congress (ANC). ANC freedom fighters are routinely executed for high treason in a country where they cannot vote, own land, or have political rights.

Apartheid also affects family structure; for instance, childrearing practices must accommodate the system of labor control. According to Ona Jirira (1982), Zimbabwean scholar in economics, the relationship between women's reproductive rights and economic factors under apartheid bears scrutiny. Women under apartheid bear the brunt of having to feed the family as a consequence of the forced separation of men from their families. In other parts of southern Africa, women in the past were often forced into a seasonal labor migration process. Whereas formerly they were, say, subsistence weavers, as land was taken away by multinational corporations, women were forced to pick a crop which would interrupt the lactation process. Family life thus became distorted by the needs of production, especially when production was controlled by those unconcerned with the interests of laborers.

Apartheid is the most pernicious form of social and productive order in existence. Such a system clearly demonstrates the need to merge the issues of political, economic, and racial oppression (UN Centre against Apartheid 1978). In this context, what southern African woman could identify with a women's struggle that did not address the issue of the oppression of men workers as well? Yet this is precisely what some women in the U.S. do, maintaining that the problem of men workers is not a "woman's issue."

Yet another example of a national liberation question that resembles apartheid, and which confronts women in a particularly difficult way, is the situation existing in the West Bank and Gaza—a reality that I witnessed myself. On February 20, 1988, eleven women from the United States embarked on a fact-finding trip to the West Bank and Gaza. We were the first all-woman delegation from the U.S. to visit the region after the Intifadah began in December 1987. The delegation was sponsored by the Union of Palestinian Women in the U.S., and was a pluralistic group including educators, writers, Catholic nuns, and Jews. (I was the only African American participant.) Our group witnessed beatings by the Israeli army; we visited men, women, and children in hospitals who had had

their limbs amputated or broken, or had been shot; and we also met some
of the families of those killed since December.

For example, on February 25, 1989, in a widely reported incident, the
Israeli army invaded the Al Ittihad Hospital in Nablus, where they beat
thirty doctors and nurses, dragged six patients from their beds, and beat
them and their families. This occurred within ninety minutes of a visit
by our delegation to the hospital, and it forever transformed the way we
viewed the trip. The very day of our visit to Al Ittihad Hospital, before
the invasion, we talked to patients, and saw the x-rays of multiple wounds
to limbs fractured with dum dum bullets (banned presumably according
to the Geneva Accords). Women and men both struggled to overcome
traditional Muslim modesty about the body in order to tell our women's
delegation that they were being wounded in their reproductive organs.
The night before the hospital was attacked, we interviewed a doctor whose
area of expertise was the intrauterine deaths caused by a poison "tear"
gas (produced in the U.S. at Federal Laboratories in Saltzburg, Pennsylvania).[4] He confirmed that there was a high incidence of attacks to the
genitalia of Palestinian men. From the depths of my African American
heritage and collective memory of lynchings, the attacks on the reproductive organs of Palestinian men and women seemed part of a deliberate
policy. Reports of such attacks also gave new meaning to the 7 A.M.
February 24, 1988, "Voice of Israel" news program recommending that
Israeli Jewish couples increase their families from 2.8 to 3.5 children.

As I visited that region, what struck me was the consolidation of
policies that were similar to what I had learned about apartheid. Just as
in South Africa, funerals are banned in the Occupied Territories. Our
delegation was turned away from one village on Monday, February 22,
as we tried to attend a service. We did visit a family whose teen-age
daughter had been killed in her kitchen by the bullet of a settler; the
body was returned to the family at midnight for immediate burial only,
and no women were allowed to attend the funeral. Nothing can convey
what it was like to hold the hand of, and try to provide comfort and
solidarity to, a mother whose child had been buried the week before.

Also as in South Africa, even religious services are controlled and
subject to army invasion. The February 22, 1988, issue of the *Jerusalem
Post* cites the Right Wing Tehiya party's call to the Israeli Defense Force
to "cleanse the mosques of those who incite to rebellion." Palestinians
must carry ID cards at all times under threat of imprisonment. No one
from the West Bank or Gaza could be in Jerusalem after midnight. The
U.S. women's delegation was made to feel the curfew that applies to
Palestinians. We had to stop all gatherings with Palestinians at a certain
time in the evening so the people we were talking with could return to
their towns in time for the curfew.

In spite of the increased restrictions, Palestinian women are more and more in the forefront of the resistance, and they are increasingly among the dead and wounded. Women have organized into neighborhood groups throughout the West Bank and Gaza. These committees are an integral part of the Union of Palestinian Women's Committees in the Occupied Land. This new militance of women is matched by the commitment of the Palestinian communities as a whole throughout the West Bank and Gaza.

On the night before the return to the United States, our delegation met with Palestinian women leaders from all over the region. Not only these women but everyone the delegation talked to about the situation insisted that *their* representative in the international community and to the world is the Palestine Liberation Organization (PLO). Just as in South Africa, where even the colors of the African National Congress are strictly forbidden, so too *any* symbol connected to Palestinian nationhood and sovereignty—or to the PLO—is inimical to the Israeli government. And just as important, the U.S. delegation also brought back testimony from those anonymous Israeli army soldiers and doctors who believed that their orders to break bones and strategically inflict wounds represented a threat to their humanity.

Such conditions are not unique to the Middle East or southern Africa. The question of the relationship between mineral resources and independence is also a central one to the people of the South Pacific French colony of New Caledonia, which is one of the world's largest suppliers of nickel. Many U.S. citizens do not even know where this country is located. Yet, what goes on in this French colony encapsulates the issues of national liberation elsewhere. Strategic migration as a metropolitan weapon against an indigenous independence movement has been largely successful. The original inhabitants—Melanesians, or Kanaks according to their own self-definition—number 45,000; the European French, 30,000; French from Algeria, 5,000; Polynesians, 7,000; and Vietnamese refugees, 7,000.[5] Each of these groups receives rewards from French colonialism that the Kanaks do not. Therefore, the absolute numbers of people who want independence from France have been reduced. According to Dewe Gorodey, the first Kanak woman to receive a college education, the French government maintains that the nickel supply will run out in only twenty years. Presumably, independence will be easier to attain only as the nickel supply is increasingly depleted. The crisis in New Caledonia is linked to the struggle for a nuclear-free and independent Pacific, and the desire for the French to cease the ecologically destructive nuclear explosions in the Pacific. In addition, existence in New Caledonia is marked with reservations cum bantustans for the Kanak people. Even the open-air food market is virtually dominated by women of French descent whose families originally came from Algeria after the Algerian Revolution. Is this not a "woman's issue"?

The kind of activism that U.S. women promoted against the Nestle multinational corporation's advertisements for infant formula in the Third World could be initiated around the issue of mineral-resource plunder. At the very least, analyses of the relationship between liberation movements and labor exploitation in areas of strategic minerals should become themes that women examine, if only because women and their children are casualties. But U.S. women often frustrate attempts to give discussions a more global perspective.

An example of this very process is the experience of Domitila Barrios de Chungara at the International Women's Year Tribunal in Mexico in 1975. Here was a woman who, as an organizer of tin miners' wives against Bolivian state repression, had been jailed for being part of the struggle against exploitation of workers in her country. In *Let Me Speak* (Barrios de Chungara 1978), she maintains that U.S. women's-rights activist Betty Friedan accused her of being "manipulated by men" and thinking only "about politics" because she was concerned about underfed children, vomiting lungs, and underdevelopment. Domitila insisted that the "interests of the bourgeoisie really aren't our interests." In Bolivia, even issues such as population and birth control are not automatically guaranteed to be subjects of uniform agreement among women, and therefore have class-bound elements. On the one hand, women should have reproductive choice, but in racist, repressive governments with birth control as policy, what seems to be "choice" can be an instrument against women.

For example, though Bolivia is underpopulated, many Bolivian women have been forcibly sterilized.[6] Yet, the former Banzer regime was later to agree to a secret plan to resettle thirty thousand white families fleeing southern African liberation on the grounds that it would help ameliorate the "racial imbalance" in Bolivia, which was an Indian majority.[7] Birth control in this context is not automatically something one struggles to gain.

Another example of repressive state birth control involves Puerto Rican women—in a situation of colonial domination by the United States—who not only have been sterilized in large numbers, but also were the "guinea pigs" for contraceptive experimentation. How many U.S. women are concerned about this type of colonialist excess? Or, is there a general acceptance of the view that the Puerto Ricans who raise these questions are merely nationalists, and therefore terrorists?

To interpret every struggle for national equality in the Third World as a result of "Soviet clientism" is the ultimate in racist ideology. It assumes that oppressed peoples would be content to continue being the world's chattel were it not for "outside agitation." The latter phrase was frequently heard during the civil rights struggles of the sixties in the U.S. South, and in itself the concept demonstrates the merging of the dynamics of racism and economic oppression with sexual domination. These dynamics also coalesce in every major former plantation economy in the Western hemisphere, with the notable exception of Cuba.

At this point, it is useful to note that Cuba is the one former plantation economy that has seriously attempted to address—at the national level— the issues of racism and sexism. Not only are Cubans confronting the difficult task of redefining national identity, but this is done at all levels of society. Cuban leader Fidel Castro has proclaimed that Cuba is an Afro-Latin country, and he has affirmed the importance of integrating more blacks, women, and youth into its party leadership. Films such as *The Other Francisco* and *The Last Supper* also reflect the Cuban revolution's interest in the historical reinterpretation of the plantation past.[8] Moreover, writers such as Morejón (1981) demonstrate the need to reconstruct theory regarding the national formation of Cuban culture to include all of the country's people. The substantial gains that the Cuban people have made in free health care and free education have had an extraordinary impact on women, as well. As an African American woman, I was struck most as I traveled in Cuba by the fact that it was the only former slave society in the Western hemisphere where people cannot be found burrowing in garbage cans for food.

The Brazilian case is also instructive because there are certain similarities with the United States. Afro-Brazilian women share many of the same problems that African American women in the U.S. have with the mainstream women's movement. For one thing, the spokespersons in the women's movement in Brazil suffer from the same strategic tunnel vision about the intersection of race, gender, and class as occurs in the U.S. As González (1982) points out, "the black woman is practically excluded from the texts and discussion of the feminist movement in our country [Brazil]."

One example of this academic myopia can be found in the study of Bahian women in the labor force by Elizabeth Jelin (1977). A historical analysis demonstrates that fully 80 percent or more of the population of Bahia, which was once the seat of the plantation economy, appear to be West African, whether they acknowledge being "black" or not. Thus, the issue of racism is central to this discussion, as it is in any former plantation economy. Although Jelin clearly attempts to use a Marxist methodology, it seems that she has chosen to highlight the question of political economy and ignore that of race altogether. This becomes a classic problem of some Marxists, repeated over and over again, as though the issues of race *and* class did not need to be addressed concretely and simultaneously, especially as they intersect the issue of gender (which includes sexuality).

Often overlooked in such Marxist and/or feminist analyses is the fact that women of African or indigenous descent in the Western hemisphere have been forced to seek "whitening"—either of their phenotypes (physical appearance) or their cultural expression—as a process to gain social acceptance and/or employability (Gilliam 1988). In many of the countries with either indigenous or black majorities, the working woman experiences a particular oppression on the basis of gender. Not only has she been the unsung transformer and transmitter of national culture, but she has often not had the most elementary reproductive rights, in that she has not always been able to control access to her body. The race mixture and subsequent cultural synthesis that are described positively by many ruling-class intellectuals were primarily due to the effects of exploitative patterns of conjugal union (Martínez-Alier 1974). That is, the woman was from the dominated sector and belonged to a different ethnic group from that of the male, who more often than not was from the dominant class and had power over her. Race mixture and cultural contact have represented the concrete exploitation of women from less-privileged sectors. Although Martínez-Alier was writing about Cuba, the implication of her work is that there was a critical difference between white and black women as regards "honor." The black woman had to earn honor through her comportment; the white woman would lose honor (which was a priori ascribed) by her behavior. In historical reconstruction, then, there is the need to visualize the burden of slavery from the perspective of the slave woman. After all, responsibility is on the side of privilege. And, as Stetson (1982) has pointed out, many scholars treat slavery as a black male phenomenon.

In addition, male dominance in the social sciences can produce theoretical entrapments such as that which I call "the-Great-Sperm-Theory-of-National-Formation." Gilberto Freyre, one of the best-known Brazilian sociologists of the plantation economy, suffers from this "optic." To Freyre, the Portuguese *man* created a "Portuguese society in the tropics" through *his* creation of the mulata, or mixed-race woman. This ideology, called "Luso-tropicalism," has been challenged by Marxist intellectuals. But Brazilian feminists—whether Marxist or bourgeois in approach—have yet to challenge this racist sexism in Brazil.[9] This defective analysis is directly related to the fiction that "Iberian" slavery was more benign than Anglo-Saxon—a myth that has adherents in both the U.S. and South America. Freyre (1961, 261) himself elucidates this position amply for the reader:

> The growing importance of the civilization nee Portuguese and nowadays, according to some of us, Luso-tropical, for the entire modern system of relations of Europeans with non-Europeans—relations which only through the

Portuguese and the Spaniards seem to be able to develop into relations not only reciprocal but also of amply cultural and freely biological interpenetration, free from the Anglo-Saxon dread of "mongrelization."

Earlier Freyre revealed the root of this perspective, which would become part of the classic sociology of the plantation (1946, 279):

The truth is that the social conditions surrounding the development of the child on the old sugar plantation of Brazil as on the antebellum plantation of Virginia and the Carolinas—where the young one is constantly surrounded by the Negro or mulatto girl who is easily to be had—are in themselves sufficient to explain the predilection [for black women] mentioned.

Hence, the Afro-Brazilian woman is not even seen as an agent of transculturation and the subsequent creation of national culture. Yet, as the principal person who transmitted culture, language, and customs in the plantation system, the slave woman had a vital role. Thus, Freyre further degrades Afro-Brazilian women by postulating their roles as perennial sex objects. It is now possible to understand the sociohistorical frame of reference for the popular Brazilian parable that a Brazilian man's idea of heaven is "a black woman to work, a white woman to marry, and a brown-skinned woman to screw."[10]

In his vital exposé of Brazilian racism, Nascimento (1977) declares that the "myth of the innate tendency of the Portuguese to interbreed with the Black woman can be exposed on an examination of Portuguese behavior in Africa." French sociologist Roger Bastide (1972) also criticized the Luso-tropicologist's approach.

No culture responds differently to slavery. All slavery [in this hemisphere] resulted in the domination and exploitation by the white man . . . lusotropicology changes from a cultural, nonsociological description of events into a sentimental ideology of underdevelopment by ascribing value to the vestiges of a past era [slavery].

The significant critiques of this popular historiographical perspective have largely been made by men, because many Brazilian feminists are fragmented by the same problems that U.S. women's rights activists frequently have—the failure to acknowledge their own racial and class bias in looking at women's issues.

Hence, the problem of social and economic class in the very interpretation of class issues is at once relevant in this discussion, for it demonstrates another problem: Which Third World women speak for which Third World women? This question has relevance for the U.S. as well. One writer who has posed the questions of race, class, and gender together is Angela Davis. Yet, her pioneering work is sometimes treated narrowly by elite feminist writers in the United States (i.e., Willis 1982).

Conflict in interpretation about class versus national struggle has often been a source of debate in the African American community, especially pertaining to the position of women and the interpretation of events in Africa. As Urdang (1989) has pointed out, the national liberation struggle in Mozambique was the primary structure within which women's equality became possible. Yet, on one occasion immediately following independence in Mozambique in 1975, a member of FRELIMO spoke in the Afro-American community of Harlem. During the question-and-answer period, a young man asked, "What is the role of the woman in the national liberation struggle?" The answer was cogent: "If you have to ask the question, you are not in a liberation struggle."

Isabel Letelier went further in her keynote address at the "Common Differences" conference. She stated that the role a woman plays on the barricades will determine what she will be building (and the role she will play when the fighting has stopped). This was one of the points made by Rigoberta Menchú, a delegate of the exiled Unified Guatemalan Opposition to the United Nations in 1982, and a Quiché Indian woman. As she affirmed in a WBAI radio interview in New York City on December 6, 1982, women not only participate at all levels in the struggle, but they and their children are often labeled "communist terrorists" by the Guatemalan government, which so perceives the illiterate and poor majority in that country. In increasing numbers, women and their children are the actual casualties when the Guatemalan armed forces destroy villages. This is replicated in other situations where actual fighting takes place.

For Menchú, the struggle in Guatemala is merely a continuation of a 450-year-long battle against domination in Guatemala. To the Guatemalan people, the multinational corporation is the inheritor of the original invading armies from Spain. Hence, for Guatemalan women, the concept of "sisterhood"' is not the appropriate frame of reference, if it means ignoring class and ethnic barriers (Latin American and Caribbean Women's Collective 1980). In this connection, Burkett (1977) made the following comment while critiquing the vacuum in research which examines the relationship between Marxism and women's studies:

> And so we are left with the infrequently examined but blithely accepted assumption that sex is as important a force in the historical process as class ... and while we theorize endlessly about the oppression of women, we all too frequently forget that the position of the one is maintained only through the exploitation of the other and that such a relationship leaves little concrete room for sisterhood.

Burkett concludes that Indian and/or black women ask themselves: "If sexism was the cause of the discrimination against [me], why [do my]

Indian and black brothers live so poorly?" The separation of sexism from the political, economic, *and* racial is a strategy of elites. As such, it becomes a tool to confuse the real issues around which most of the world's women struggle. It is not enough to romanticize about the Guatemalan Indians' concept of Mother Earth and how that affects the way they view the world. Equally important is to realize that the Indian peoples in that country are being exterminated in this twentieth-century version of the "Indian Wars." Part of that realization is comprehending that the U.S. government gives military aid money to the Guatemalan regime.

As can be seen by some of the aforementioned examples, sex is often an instrument of oppression. Thus, sexual liberation *can* be a component of national liberation. But the liberation of women, and therefore the process of equality, is fundamentally tied to socioeconomic change. This lesson was elucidated by women from the People's Republic of Cabo Verde immediately after the triumph of PAIGC (the ruling party) in 1976. There is nothing more engaging that the newly developed attitude of a people's confidence to improve their lot and humanize their society through increasing control over their labor and resources. Such was the environment in 1976 when I was invited to the mountain town of Santa Catarina by a group of women on the island of Santiago. The purpose was for me to talk to their daughters in order to convince them to go on studying so that they would be better able to take part in the revolutionary process. There was no electricity in this part of Cabo Verde except between 7 and 11 P.M. because 1976 was a year of desperate power shortage in West Africa and even parts of Europe. As we sat in the candlelight, the determination of the woman who had called the meeting emphasized a certain intensity of the occasion. She affirmed that she had always believed that women were equal to men, and insisted that her focus on sexuality was germane to many women whose husbands live and work far away or in other countries.

> I want my daughter to take part in what is taking place in this country. If she gets married now, she will never participate in the change. I don't want her to be like me. I am married to a good man. As you know, about 40 percent of Cape Verdian men are laborers in Europe, and my husband is in Holland. That house over there that we are building brick by brick right next to this little cabin is being made with the money he sends home. Every two years he gets one month's vacation, and comes home to meet the baby he made the last time, and to make a new one. I don't want that for my daughter. I've heard that it is possible to prevent pregnancy by knowing the calendar. Please teach our girls how to count the days so that they can control their pregnancies.[11]

This issue was not about men's oppression of women, but about the impact of unequal and international labor structures on family relations.

Therefore, this analysis of sexuality as it relates to national liberation is different from the questions that U.S. women are accustomed to formulating, i.e., in this context sexuality is understood within the context of economics and politics, rather than simply male domination.

What are the implications of this discussion for U.S. women who also fight inequality? For one thing, women in this country have to struggle on the basis of *issues* rather than gender, ethnicity, or sexual preference. There are basic questions that can be raised which would enable women to develop informed theoretical positions about the relationship between the domestic and international context of class. If that battle is concerning who will control the access and distribution of the world's resources, then on what side does one fall? What is the relationship between societal rewards and punishments? Who is filling the prisons? In any given national liberation struggle, the latter question is the key to determining how one defines those who are the privileged in a society. In the current international economic order, U.S. citizens are privileged. As a result, U.S. women must ask themselves, "How does the way of life in the U.S. affect the way people look at women's equality and national liberation?" Are U.S. women agents for the very victimization against which they struggle? This is especially critical for those women who are members of oppressed minorities in the United States. During the "Common Differences" conference, a Mexican-American lesbian writer declared, "the only hunger that I have ever known is the hunger for sex and for freedom." In the "geopolitics of hunger"—to cite de Castro's book (1977)—that is the privileged situation of a select few. Indeed, freedom is a class concept, defined directly by one's access to resources. U.S. women must boldly abandon the paradigm—the constraining lens—of anticommunism if a mutual comprehensibility between us and other women throughout the world is an objective. The underside of anticommunism is the corollary that life as it is lived by the U.S. capitalist class represents the zenith in human existence.

In addition, U.S. women—regardless of race and irrespective of sexual preference—must reaffirm our collective struggle and move beyond the individualism projected by the wealthy of the world. We must confront the domination of other peoples that is often carried out in our name. Hence, U.S. women must be clear that merely proclaiming that one is a woman, or a lesbian, or a member of a particular ethnic or national group is not enough. Otherwise, it facilitates our becoming pawns in the moves by big business to dominate the women's movement.

It is not in the interests of big business for the women of this country to identify with the overwhelming majority of the world's women and to learn *from* them. The revolutionary potential of that convergence of forces is checked by concentrating on the sexual and the individual in framing research. But as Nawal el Saadawi put it, it is impossible to liberate women in countries that are economically dependent on the West.[12] Her position was somewhat in opposition to that of Rosario Morales (1981, 92), who defined as a "macho line" the perspective that the struggle against imperialism comes first.

Frequently, though, the attempts by some U.S. women to link "women's issues" to geopolitics are transformed into sexualism. Such is the case with Robin Morgan's treatise entitled *The Demon Lover: On the Sexuality of Terrorism* (1989). Although Morgan clearly grounds her argument in a critique of warmongering throughout the world, she omits an analysis that would take into account the *systemic* or structural properties of the domination of women *and* men. By masculinizing war and struggles for liberation, she not only excludes women from them but also delegitimizes those battles. Moreover, she absolves women from any responsibility in the reproduction of values that reinforce a culture of violence. For example, by isolating the problem of wifebeating and the abuse of children (especially females) around the globe, she ends up supporting the position that the Reagan administration took at the Nairobi Women's Meeting. The Administration's effort at that meeting was to concentrate on violence in the family and to discourage analyses that linked geopolitical power and family violence.

Morgan also implies that the "terrorist" is primarily male, though the U.S. military *application* of that word within the context of low-intensity conflict—from Vietnam to Nicaragua—has definitely included women and children. For Morgan, a terrorist is "the logical incarnation of patriarchal politics in a technological world" (1989, 33). Thus, Morgan defines womanhood as almost supranational and above culture, and hence produces an analysis that is simultaneously separatist and relativist. In calling for a "third politics altogether" removed from the facile positioning between Left and Right (327–28), Morgan avoids the inevitable necessity of acknowledging the responsibility that contemporary capitalism has for the miserable lives of so many women in the world. She claims, "The powers of female sexuality, in all of their expressions *and* redefinitions (maternal, celibate, bisexual, lesbian, and heterosexual) have the potential of forming completely different relationships in the twenty-first century" (327). Under the same system of profits before people?

The issue is redefining the nation away from a war—positive/peace-negative, bully state. Central to such transformation is the "restructuring of this country's economy so that we do not live off the lives and work of Third World women," as lesbian writer Minnie Bruce Pratt (1984, 54–55) affirmed. It is relatively easy for women in the U.S. to say that "machismo" dominates warlike foreign policy in the country. However, Margaret

Thatcher exists, if for no other reason than to prove that women leaders can also promote militaristic, proapartheid, and antilabor policies.

To many women in national liberation struggles, machismo and feminism are two sides of the same coin, because U.S. feminists have not integrated the political and economic aspects in their analysis of women's issues. Therefore, international feminism within the context of control by U.S. women—elites or nonelites—cannot, should not, exist.[13] U.S. women must boldly define a unifying perspective that integrates race, gender, and class. In addition, the impact of transnational banks and multinational corporations on most human beings must be confronted. After all, when corporations decide to transfer the U.S. jobs overseas, they invariably do so in order to avoid paying U.S. citizens decent wages. This affects the U.S. working class, and ties women in this country to women in the Third World. It also connects women to those men who struggle for equality, as well. To make a real contribution, women must work toward a more whole world for *all* humans. To quote African revolutionary Amilcar Cabral (1975), "We must build a society on a scientific basis; we can no longer afford to believe in imaginary things."

NOTES

This essay was originally written as a presentation for the conference "Common Differences: Third World Women and Feminist Perspectives" held at the University of Illinois, Champaign-Urbana, April 9–13, 1983. One of the stated goals for this controversial and historic meeting was to establish the basis for an "international feminism" prior to the 1985 World Conference to Review and Appraise the Achievements of the United Nations Decade for Women meeting to be held in Nairobi in 1985. I was concerned that under this rubric, the Nairobi meeting could be appropriated by parochial U.S. feminists. I feared that isolation from a global perspective might enable them to advance the Reagan administration's goals of separating the decade's themes of PEACE, DEVELOPMENT, AND EQUALITY from "women's issues" at that epic gathering in Africa. It is thus to U.S. feminists, and in the context of the above, that this essay was originally written. However, other data, including those provided as a result of attendance at the 1985 meeting in Nairobi, and as a consequence of participation in a 1988 fact-finding trip to the West Bank and Gaza, have been added to ensure the cogency of my original arguments.

1. Subsequent to my making this point during the original presentation at the "Common Differences" conference, others have also provided clarity about the limitations of the "equal access" paradigm. One brilliant example of such an analysis is the one published by Dietz (1987) in which she linked this formulation to a "rights-based" definition of citizenship.

2. Acknowledgment must be made of the critique of and commentary on this paper by sister-colleagues Debbie D'Amico-Samuels, Renee Llanusa-Cestero,

and Ethel Tobach. I am also indebted to Steve Kirkpatrick, librarian of the State University of New York, College at Old Westbury, for research support. Above all, I take this opportunity to express my heartfelt thanks to my sister and role model, Rose Catchings, under whose auspices at the World Division of the United Methodist church in New York I attended the United Nations End of the Decade for Women Meeting in Nairobi in 1985. Moreover, it was as a result of funding from her office that I traveled to the South Pacific and specifically to New Caledonia. Her moral and financial support to African American and Third World women throughout the world are herein gratefully acknowledged.

3. Ethel Tobach made this comment in her statements as cochair of a session entitled "Human Values and Scientific Literacy: Leacock's Multidisciplinary Approach" during the January 14–19, 1989, annual meeting of the American Association for the Advancement of Science. Together with Betty Rosoff, Tobach is series editor for Genes and Gender: A Series on Hereditarianism and Women.

4. The best report on this chemical warfare is by Wolf (1988), according to whom on May 6, 1988, the "California-based Trans-Technology Corporation through its Federal Laboratories subsidiary in Saltzburg, Pennsylvania—decided to suspend sales of [this weapon] to Israel."

I was the only woman participant to testify on this question before the Congressional Black Caucus Special Hearing on the Middle East on April 26, 1988 (shown on C-Span). The information presented in this chapter comprises components of that testimony.

5. These figures were approximations that I received from independence forces (Parti du Liberation des Kanaks—PALIKA) in the capital city of Noumea in 1978.

6. This problem was the subject of a Bolivian film entitled *Blood of the Condor*, which was directed by Jorge Sanjines in conjunction with the Ukamau Collective—a group of primarily indigenous Bolivians committed to disseminating Bolivian reality. This film was financed publicly by students, workers, and average Bolivians who wanted the truth to be told about the forced sterilizations of indigenous women, as well as U.S. complicity in this problem. It is distributed by New Yorker Films, 16 West 61st Street, New York City.

7. Information given here is detailed in a report entitled "Documents on Colonialist Export from South Africa to Latin America" (June 1977). It was compiled by the Africa Research Group, Uppsala University (Department of Peace and Conflict Research), Uppsala, Sweden. It was distributed by NACLA, which has offices in New York City.

8. Both of these films are distributed by New Yorker Films, 16 West 61st Street, New York City.

9. Racist sexism in Brazil is reflected in different ways, and has many corollaries. One example of this emerged during an interview that I had with renowned Brazilian archbishop Dom Helder Camara during his trip to New York City to attend the Spiritual Summit Conference VI, October 7–9, 1984, sponsored by the Temple of Understanding. Not only was he startled to see that a black woman had made the appointment to interview him, but in response to a question that alluded to racism in Brazil, he took great offense at the suggestion and denied that such could be possible, affirming—oblivious to the reaction his words caused—that there could be no racism in Brazil "because the entire country drank milk from the breasts of the black mammy [mae preta]."

10. The Portuguese version of this rhyme is as follows: "Preta p'ra trabalhar, branca p'ra casar, e mulata p'ra fornicar."

11. I reconstructed this commentary, which was originally in Crioulo and Portuguese.

12. This statement was made during a conference sponsored by the Arab-American Anti-Discrimination Council (ADC) on June 22, 1982, in New York City, and was reinforced during an interview with me (see references).

13. The hierarchization of issues was a complex one at the July 1985 End of the Decade for Women Meeting in Nairobi. For one thing, it was the first such meeting of its kind on the African continent. Many of the women from Latin America were concerned about the foreign debt; many Arab women were concerned about Palestinian national rights; African women were united in their stand against apartheid. That historic conference was divided into two segments—the nongovernmental (NGO) forum and the official, governmental component. For the U.S.-based Women for Racial and Economic Equality (WREE), who participated in the forum, it was gratifying to have our petition opposing Reagan administration policies signed by 1,300 out of 2,000 U.S. sisters. Above all, the majority of U.S. women who went to Nairobi rejected the Reagan administration's position (as articulated by U.S. State Department liaison Jean Berghaust in a pre-Nairobi NGO meeting at the UN) that "peace and disarmament are not women's issues."

That the U.S. government saw itself in an adversarial position to the concerns of the world's women is exemplified by the fact that the only man in the official delegation was Alan Keyes, an African American diplomat who fluently articulated U.S. government positions on South Africa. Although Maureen Reagan was the titular head of the delegation, it was perceived by many observers from around the world that the decisions were being made by Keyes. When I confronted him during a press conference as to which group of U.S. women he represented, he replied that such was beyond his purview; he was there to teach the other members of the official delegation how to "handle the UN system."

REFERENCES

Adotevi, S. S. 1972. *Negritude et Negrologues*. Collection Bibliotheque 10/18. Paris: Union Generale d'editions.
Andreas, C. 1971. *Sex and Caste in America*. Englewood Cliffs: Prentice Hall.
Atkinson, T. G. 1974. *Amazon Odyssey*. New York: Links Books.
Barrios de Chungara, D. 1978. *Let Me Speak: A Woman of the Bolivian Mines*. Written with Moema Viezzer. London: Monthly Review Press.
Bastide, Roger. 1972. "Lusotropicology, Race, and Nationalism, and Class Protest and Development in Brazil and Portuguese Africa." In R. Chilcote, ed., *Protest and Resistance in Angola and Brazil*. Los Angeles: University of California Press.
Bisilliat, J., and Fieloux, M. 1983. *Femmes du Tiers-Monde*. Paris: Le Sycamore.
Burkett, E. 1977. "In Dubious Sisterhood: Race and Class in Spanish Colonial South America." *Latin American Perspectives (Women and Class Struggle)* 4, nos. 1 and 2 (Winter and Spring).
Cabral, A. 1975. "Resistencia Cultural." In *Analise de Alguns Tipos de Resistencia*. Portugal: Seara Nova.

Controlling Interest: The World of the Multinational. 1978. Film directed by L. Adelman. Distributed by California Newsreel, San Francisco.

Davis, A. 1981. *Women, Race and Class.* New York: Random House.

de Castro, J. 1977. *Geopolitics of Hunger.* New York: Monthly Review Press.

Dietz, M. G. 1987. "Context Is All: Feminism and Theories of Citizenship." *Daedelus* 116, no. 4:1–24.

Dreifus, C. 1978. *Seizing Our Bodies: The Politics of Women's Health.* New York: Vintage Books.

el Saadawi, N. 1980. *The Hidden Face of Eve: Women in the Arab World.* London: Zed Press.

———. 31 May 1982 and 20 June 1982. Interview with Angela Gilliam on "*Everywoman's Space Special*," WBAI Radio, New York.

———. 1983. "Out of Egypt: A Talk with Nawal el Saadawi, T. Patterson, and A. Gilliam." *Freedomways,* Special Middle East Issue, Part 2, 23:3.

Frankfort, E. 1972. *Vaginal Politics.* New York: Bantam Books.

Freyre, G. 1946. *The Masters and the Slaves: A Study in the Development of Brazilian Civilization.* New York: Alfred A. Knopf.

———. 1961. *The Portuguese and the Tropics: Suggestions Inspired by the Portuguese Methods of Integrating Autochthonous Peoples and Cultures Differing from the European in a New, or Luso-Tropical Complex of Civilization.* Lisbon: Executive Committee for the Commemoration of the Vth Centenary of the Death of Prince Henry the Navigator.

Gilliam, A. 1988. "Telltale Language: Race, Class, and Inequality in Two Latin American Towns." In Johnnetta B. Cole, ed., *Anthropology for the Nineties.* New York: Free Press.

González, L. 1982. "O Papel da Mulher Negra na Sociedade Brasileira." In M. Luz, ed., *Lugar da Mulher.* Rio de Janeiro: Graal Editora.

Jelin, E. 1977. "The Bahiana in the Labor Force." In J. Nash and H. Safa, eds., *Sex and Class in Latin America.* New York: Praeger.

Jirira, O. 6 September 1982. "Women's Work in the Third World." Interview with Angela Gilliam on "Everywoman's Space," WBAI Radio, New York.

Johnston, J. 1973. *Lesbian Nation: The Feminist Solution.* New York: Simon and Schuster.

Latin American and Caribbean Women's Collective. 1980. *Slaves of Slaves: The Challenge of Latin American Women.* London: Zed Press.

Lewis, Anthony, 1983. "Onward, Christian Soldier." *New York Times,* 10 March.

Mafeje, A. 1981. "On the Articulation of Modes of Production: Review Article." *Journal of Southern Africa Studies* 8, no. 1 (October).

Martínez-Alier, V. 1974. *Marriage, Class, and Colour in Nineteenth Century Cuba: A Study of Racial Attitudes and Sexual Values in a Slave Society.* London: Cambridge University Press.

Menchú, R. 6 December 1982. "The National Liberation Struggle in Guatemala." Interview with Angela Gilliam on "Everywoman's Space," WBAI Radio, New York.

Morales, R. 1981. "We're All in the Same Boat." In C. Moraga and G. Anzaldúa, eds., *This Bridge Called My Back: Writings by Radical Women of Color.* Watertown, Mass.: Persephone.

Morejón, N. 1981. *Nación y Mestizaje en Nicolás Guillén* (Nation and Race Mixture in [the Poetry of] Nicolás Guillén). Havana: Union of Writers and Artists (UNEAC).

Morgan, R. 1989. *The Demon Lover: On the Sexuality of Terrorism.* New York: W. W. Norton and Co.

Nabudere, D. 1977. *The Political Economy of Imperialism.* London/Dar Es Salaam: Zed Press.

Nascimento, A. 1977. *Racial Democracy in Brazil: Myth or Reality?* Ibadan: Sketch.

Patterson, T. 1983. "Out of Egypt: A Talk with Nawal el Saadawi." With A. Gilliam. *Freedomways,* Special Middle East Issue, Part 2, 23:3.

Pratt, M. B. 1984. "Identity: Skin Blood Heart." In E. Bulkin, M. B. Pratt, and B. Smith, *Yours in Struggle.* Brooklyn, N.Y.: Long Haul Press. 9–64.

Stetson, E. 1982. "Studying Slavery: Some Literary and Pedagogical Considerations on the Black Female Slave." In G. Hull, P. B. Scott, and B. Smith, eds., *All the Women Are White, All the Blacks Are Men, but Some of Us Are Brave.* City University of New York: Feminist Press.

United Nations Centre against Apartheid. 1978. *The Effects of Apartheid on the Status of Women in South Africa,* no. 7/78.

Urdang, S. 1989. *And Still They Dance: Women, War and the Struggle for Change in Mozambique.* London: Monthly Review Press.

Willis, E. 1982. "Sisters under the Skin? Confronting Race and Sex." *Village Voice Supplement,* No. 8 (June 8):7–12.

Wolf, L. 1988. "Israel Wages Chemical Warfare with American Tear Gas." *Covert Action Information Bulletin,* Special Issue on Israel and the Middle East, no. 30 (Summer).

SEXUALITY AND SEXUAL POLITICS

Conflicts and Contradictions for Contemporary Women in the Middle East

Evelyne Accad

Sexuality seems to have a revolutionary potential so strong that many political women and men are afraid of it. They prefer, therefore, to dismiss its importance by arguing that it is not as central as other factors, such as economic and political determinations which are easily recognizable as the major factors that produce revolution—class inequalities, hunger, poverty, lack of job opportunities. In this essay, I would like to argue that sexuality is much more central to social and political problems in the Middle East than previously thought, and that unless a sexual revolution is incorporated into political revolution, there will be no real transformation of social relations.

By sexual revolution, I mean one which starts at the level of personal life, with a transformation of attitudes toward one's mate, family, sexuality, and society; specifically, a transformation of the traditional rapports of domination and subordination which permeate interpersonal, particularly sexual, relationships (such as power struggles, jealousy, possession). Change is fundamental at the level of sexual and familial intimacy. We need to develop an exchange of love, tenderness, equal sharing, and recognition among people. This would create a more secure and solid basis for change in other spheres of life—political, economic, social, re-

start w/
attitudes +
rapports of
domination

ligious, and national as they are often characterized by similar rapports of domination. By political revolution, I mean one primarily motivated by nationalism. I would argue that if all of the various political parties who are trying to dominate a small piece of territory in Lebanon were to unite and believe in their country as an entity not to be possessed and used, but to be loved and respected, much of the internal violence, destruction, and conflicts would begin to cease, and we could work more positively toward resolution. Nationalism—belief in and love of one's country—in this context seems a necessity.

In the Middle East, nationalism and feminism have never mixed very well. Women have been used in national liberation struggles—Algeria, Iran, Palestine, to name a few—only to be sent back to their kitchens after "independence" was gained. To those who believe that it is utopian to think that the two can ever blend, I would like to suggest first, that it has never been tried, since sexuality has never been conceptualized as being at the center of the problems in the Middle East. Second, if an analysis of sexuality and sexual relations were truly incorporated into the revolutionary struggle in Lebanon, nationalism could be transformed into a more viable revolutionary strategy.

In most discussions of third world feminism, sexuality and the privatized oppression of women by men are relegated to secondary issues. When sexuality and/or male domination is raised as a significant factor, conflicts arise over the validity of Marxism versus feminism, economic equality versus sexual equality, national revolution versus women's rights—as if these concepts must be opposed, as if the life of one means the death of the other. For instance, at the "Common Differences: Third World Women and Feminist Perspectives" conference (University of Illinois at Urbana-Champaign, April 1983), a major conflict arose between those women who believed sexuality and male domination to be central, and those who believed class and imperialism to be central. Mostly Marxist women, speaking in the name of *all* third world women, claimed that economic issues—such as food and shelter—were far more important than sex. They accused U.S. lesbians at the conference of overemphasizing sex, particularly lesbianism. As I listened, I felt that their arguments were very "paternalistic," and somewhat irrelevant: first, because sex is one of the basic needs—like food and sleep—in any culture; second, because no mention was made of the spiritual and/or psychological needs for love, affection, and tenderness, intimately connected with sexuality, which are felt by people in all cultures. To claim that some women live without these needs because of more pressing economic factors seems not only very unfair but an exercise which only some intellectuals can afford. And third, from my research and analysis, I believe that sexuality and sex-role socialization are intimately connected to the national conflicts and on-going war in Lebanon.

In the past five years, I have conducted extensive research throughout the Middle East, interviewing women in rural and urban areas about their sexuality, relations with men (husbands, brothers, sons), relations with other women, and the social conditions of their lives. I also attended a conference, "What Feminism for the Maghreb" (Tunisia, 1985), which addressed issues of feminism, nationalism, and, peripherally, sexuality, and taught a course on the role of Arab women at Beirut University College in 1985, living the war in Lebanon that year (as well as previous years). My research, teaching, discussing, and own thinking about these issues have helped me to clarify my perspectives on the role of feminism in nationalist struggles, and the centrality of sexuality to the social and political relations of whole groups of people. In this essay I would like to suggest the importance of sexuality and sexual relations to third world women's lives, and the centrality of sexuality and male domination to the political and national struggles occurring in the Middle East.

First of all, contrary to the perspectives of many intellectuals and political women and men involved in the U.S. and/or the Middle East, my interviews with rural and urban women indicate that sexuality is of utmost concern to women. In fact it is often women from the neediest levels of society who are the most outspoken on the subject of sex, love, and their relationships to their husbands and family, and who, contrary to what some intellectuals have expressed, see the need for change in these areas of their lives. Perhaps it is because they have not interpreted and analyzed their needs from within the framework of patriarchal ways of thinking (i.e., Marxism, nationalism, capitalism) that they can be so outspoken. For example, in Oran, Algeria (1984), I interviewed a group of maids at the hotel where I was staying. The majority of them lived in polygamous relationships and had to wear the veil when going out. Most of them expressed anger toward both customs—polygamy and the veil— and wished for different conditions for their daughters. Similarly, in 1978, I visited hospitals in the United Arab Emirates, and conducted interviews with women living in different oases and remote places. They too expressed to me their anger about the conditions of their lives—having to produce children every year under the threat of repudiation, or having to accept their husbands' taking younger wives if they did not, and having to wear the *burqa* (a mask-type leatherlike face cover which left purplish-blue marks from sweating).

Secondly, it seems clear to me that given the way in which political intellectuals have dealt with sexuality, at least at the conferences that I have attended, the issues are far more central than anyone is willing to admit. At the conference "What Feminism for the Maghreb" (1985) at the Club Taher in Tunisia, and at the "Common Differences" conference in Illinois, the topic of sexuality, with all of its ramifications, divided women and created enormous amounts of tension. In Tunisia, women who chose to speak out on sexuality were ostracized by the majority of other feminist intellectuals. The most open and frank woman on the subject decided to leave the country because she felt misunderstood and rejected even by the feminist movement. Some women asked me to shut off the cassette recorder when they talked about sexuality, and some burst into tears when talking about intimate experiences in their lives. I wondered as I listened and talked with women why there was so much pain in remembering past events in their lives connected with sexuality, yet so much resistance and denial around a political analysis of sexuality. Similarly at the conference in Illinois, women viciously attacked one another over the issues of sexuality and their place in the lives of third world women.

One of the participants at the conference in Tunisia provided some analysis of the centrality of sexuality, and yet its denial on the part of political women. Unfortunately, because of her analysis and her willingness to speak in such an environment, she felt she had to leave her country. When I wrote her, asking if I could mention her by name, or if she preferred to remain anonymous, she replied, "Please get me out of anonymity which weighs on me, and is slowly killing me. But what name should I use? Ilham Bint Milad—my father's? Bousseu—my mother's? Ben Ghadifa—my husband's? or just my surname which is not enough? How does one solve this problem?" At the conference, Ilham began her speech with a discussion of why she had decided to lift the veil of silence over her condition, to get rid of autocensorship (a word which acquired great significance when I lived in Tunisia, witnessing its way of killing creativity and freedom in several women I became close to), so that she would no longer be her own enemy.

She felt that the silence of Tunisian feminists had fallen over three spheres: (1) the feminine body, (2) women's personal relationships, and (3) sexual identity. Silence, she suggested, reigns over the subject of periods, virginity, masturbation, sexual pleasure in general, abortion, birth, and the feminine body as a whole. She recited poetry she had written about her period in French and in Arabic—noticing how it was harder to talk about it in Arabic. The following excerpts from her speech give a sense of her analysis:

> The myth of virginity is such an idiocy. The ritual takes place in pain. It is like a green bubble to be burst. And it is for this bubble, this hollowness, this emptiness, that women are taught repulsion, shame, disgust toward their bodies, and the fear of sexuality. . . .

The first sexual pleasure known by the child is masturbation. . . . In certain families, it is called "to do evil." We live in a situation where the body is morally neglected. In such a context, how can only learn to love one's body? How can one learn to read one's desires, and even more to let them rise in oneself? How can sexual pleasure, condemned for so long, exercise itself freely just because it has become approved by an institution on the basis of having a partner? . . . The child learns to associate pleasure with culpability. The body, instead of being an object of pleasure, becomes an enemy which hurts. . . . How can a body which never learns to love or to speak, develop in a harmonious sexual relationship? . . .

Silence prevails, not only on the topic of the feminine body but also, more generally, on everything that touches upon intimate relations, which are constantly shifting between dream and reality, between love and hate. . . . Why do my tears fall when my neighbor is beaten up? Why do I feel personally humiliated? The pain she experiences in her life affects me for many reasons. The life of such a woman is like a magnifying glass, which reflects back to me an exaggerated image of my own condition. Obtaining the respect of others is a constant struggle for women. The enslavement of other women sets limits to my own blossoming. . . . But above all, her life reminds me of another woman's suffering, to which I was for a long time a spectator—that of my mother. . . .

Ilham also raised the problem of women turning on each other when one or another brought up issues of sexuality. I found this particularly relevant because I have faced similar responses from feminist intellectuals. Fear and autocensorship are two key factors preventing women from wanting to explore these issues. The subject of sexuality is too close to home and to one's personal life. At this conference, when the topic was raised, women gossiped openly about each other, about individual sexualities and sexual practices, thereby widening the malaise and tensions. As Ilham herself suggested:

Women's hatred expresses itself in many ways. . . . Feminism and gossiping appear as a contradiction. Unfortunately, it is not so. I was a target of gossip by feminists, the preceding year, after my communication on "Femininity and Fecundity." They accused me of being a prostitute, a divorcee, a lesbian, a robber of husbands, and a scandal because I refused maternity! I would like to emphasize how all these accusations are related to sexuality.

While the purpose of gossiping is to alleviate what is bothersome, to make oneself feel more secure, it also expresses anxiety over marginality, and tries to disarm one's sense of culpability. . . . Apart from trying to repress the other, because one is not able to free oneself, gossip has two consequences: (1) It prevents the woman who pronounced it from fulfilling her own desires, therefore of knowing herself deeply, (2) it destroys the woman who uttered it, especially when one adds to it bad conscience, and the feeling—more or less diffused—of having made a dangerous concession to society, and to the mother. . . .

Gossiping and hostility between women upsets the followers of unconditional feminine love. But their protests do not go as far as defending or even pronouncing the word *homosexuality*. This would entail too much subversion. It is a point of no return, a path which society cannot forgive. At the personal level, it is too risky to return to the love affair with the mother. Homosexuality is also condemned by society because it shakes its foundations. Not only is it not productive—in terms of procreation, therefore threatening the survival of society—but it also shakes the foundation of capitalism where production is very much valued. Above all, it affirms the right to pure pleasure, a suspicious concept, because anarchist by essence. . . . Isn't the Third World characterized by a dangerous confusion between individuality and individualism, through a most repressive structure of duty? . . .

One more issue I wold like to address is jealousy in the context of love. The woman who arouses one's jealousy is one we feel is stealing something from us, as our mother stole from us, our in-depth being, our body. The more a person lives under repression, with no satisfaction, the greater his or her jealousy will be. In this context, love and pleasure are necessarily threatened if shared. When someone gives to another, she feels she has necessarily lost something of her own. Jealousy also increases when the person we envy also stirs our love and admiration. . . . Jealousy is the expression of a lack of confidence in oneself. . . . One can understand why intellectuals have kept silent in this domain: analysis and reasoning are hardly protections against jealousy. . . .

The topic of women's personal relations was charged with meaning. It brought to the surface much of the uneasiness I had felt in my relationships with some of the women at the conference. Because I had raised issues connecting sexuality to war, I had been the target of gossip by some of the women of the group, as if to make what I had to say less important and even suspect. I was accused of being CIA, engaging in orgies, and stealing boyfriends. Ilham's speech made me feel less isolated, and explained to me some of the problems we face as women who are committed to nationalism as well as to feminism and sexual freedom.

Ilham's speech is worthy of notice for a variety of reasons. It is important to note that there was no discussion of the issues she raised at the conference. Rather than take up her points, the talk centered on issues of language and Arab nationalism. Sexuality was hardly touched upon, despite the fact that the focus of the conference was to be "What Feminism for the Maghreb?" Only one other woman used a frank and personal approach, and when she gave testimony about what had led her to feminism, it was done with extreme uneasiness. Part of the malaise came from the split between the women themselves, their search for identity and the simultaneous realization of the political, economic, and social tensions created by the crisis the Arab world is undergoing.

Another method of silencing the discussion of sexuality and its relationship to political and social conflicts is through unquestioning adherence to dogmatic political systems of thinking. Many nationalist and leftist women at both conferences felt that women should rally behind already existing leftist movements and ideologies. Yet in these movements, traditional morality often filters through the dogmas, setting new barriers between women's sense of obligation and their search for truth and freedom. Yolla Polity-Charara (1980) provides an incisive analysis of this problem as exemplified in Lebanese politics. According to her, many Lebanese women joined political parties thinking that the condition of women would change. In 1975, during the activities organized for International Women's Year, the Democratic party invited the delegates of the political parties in Lebanon to a meeting aimed at weighing the possibilities for organizing a joint action. Women from the Phalangist party, the National Bloc, the Progressive Socialist party, the Ba'ath party, and the Communist party, as well as others from smaller groups, found themselves suspicious and indeed rivals because "how could it be possible with so many ideological differences and antagonisms, representing the whole range of political forces of Lebanon, not to be divergent on the details of women's demands" (p. 141)?

According to Polity-Charara, the party and ideological loyalties made women loath to complain about their fate to other unknown women, and even more so to rivals. The militants among them, when conscious of the discrimination women faced, when they were not themselves token women in the party, preferred to wash their dirty laundry within the family; they refused to publicly question the men of their party, to admit that their men were not the most advanced, the most egalitarian, and the most revolutionary. Thus, in such a context, loyalty and siding with a group become more important than discussing the issues with frankness and openness in order to find solutions to the problems.

It is obvious from all of my experiences in the Middle East, as well as in the United States, that sexuality stirs in people reactions that go much deeper than mere intellectual exercises. It brings out gut-feeling reactions that go far beyond conscious levels of explanation. It is also evident that sexuality often works together with what may appear as more tangible factors—political, economic, social, and religious choices. It is part of the psychological, physical, and spiritual aspects of human existence. As such, it seems quite obvious that if sexuality is not incorporated into the main feminist and political agenda, the struggles for freedom will remain on a very superficial level. A problem cannot be solved without going to its roots.

If women do not begin to see the necessity of dealing with issues of sexuality, more women will feel isolated, rejected, and misunderstood, even within a group leading the same struggle. More will feel pushed to leave for other places, or simply drop out of political struggle, in the hope of finding better acceptance and tolerance. Under the cover of progressive dogmas, some Western and Eastern feminists will continue to speak in the name of third world women, triggering in all women a retreat into a "national identity" or selfless and sexless socialist system, neither of which speaks to women's experience and struggles in their own lives. What happened at the "Common Differences" conference is an illustration of such reaction. In the name of leftist ideology, some feminists argued that for third world women, development, food, and shelter take precedence over issues of sexuality. This resulted in such violent arguments that many women felt caught and pressured into "taking sides," which led some to leave the conference altogether. These reactions are struggles for power and a repetition of male patterns of behavior. Many of the debates involve some women who speak on behalf of another group through an already existing dogma, rather than working toward an analysis which would incorporate the pain and suffering women are subjected to in all parts of our lives.

The importance of incorporating a discourse on sexuality when formulating a revolutionary feminist theory became even more evident as I started analyzing and writing about the Lebanese war. I have grown convinced that the war itself is closely connected with the way people perceive and act out their sense of love and power, as well as their sense of relationship to their partners, to the family, and to the general society. Usually the argument has been made that wars create such conditions of despair, and that within such a context women's issues are unimportant. Many argue that if the "right" side in a war were to win, then women's problems would automatically be solved. I would like to argue the reverse. I would suggest that if sexuality and women's issues were dealt with from the beginning, wars might be avoided, and revolutionary struggles and movements for liberation would become more effective. Justice cannot be won in the midst of injustice. Each of the levels is connected to the others.

The whole range of oppression women suffer in the Middle East, including forced marriage, virginity, and the codes of honor, claustration, the veil, polygamy, repudiation, beating, lack of freedom, and the denial of the possibility to achieve their aims and desires of life, etc.—practices that I ran away from in Lebanon at the age of twenty-two—are closely connected to the internal war in Lebanon (I am not referring to the Israeli and Syrian occupations, or the foreign interferences). There are at least eighteen—with many subdivisions—political parties fighting each other in Lebanon. Each of these parties has different interests; each tries to dominate a small piece of territory and impose its vision of Lebanon onto that territory; and each tries to dominate the others largely through the control of women.

One of the codes of Arab tribes is *sharaf* (honor), which also means the preservation of girls' virginity, to ensure that the women are kept exclusively for the men of their tribe. Women's lives are regulated not by national laws but by community ones. All legal questions related to individual status are legislated by denominational laws. Each creed has a different legislation according to its religion. For example, there is no civil marriage in Lebanon. Marriage, divorce, separation, custody of children, and inheritance are resolved according to one's confession—religious denomination. Each of the group's laws, rites, practices, and psychological and sexual pressures aims at keeping their women exclusively for the men of their community.

Arab society in general, and Lebanese in particular, has always had pride in the *za'im* (leader, chief, hero). The *za'im* is the macho man par excellence. Not only does he embody all the usual masculine values of conquest, domination, competition, fighting, boasting, etc., but also that of *shatara* (cleverness). *Shatara* means to succeed and get what one wants, even through lying and perfidy. *Za'im* and *shatara* are concepts much valued in tribal society. The Lebanese war has transformed the *za'im* into the *askari* (man with the gun, militiaman).

The *askari* has technical military training, and his goal is "self-preservation" of his group. In addition to his military and his economic-social functions, he has played and continues to play a role that is most violently destructive of his country, and therefore of his sexuality as well. He uses weapons of war to destroy and seize control of one region or of another group. He participates in looting to benefit his clientele and to extend the range of his influence. Given the extension of his influence, he builds a system of wealth distribution and gains more power. Material gains are obtained through his gun and other weapons of war. It is a "primitive" system, and a vicious destructive cycle, rather than a self-preserving one. The more men desire omnipotence and the control of others, the more weapons are used. The means of conquest are given a value in proportion to their success. The gun, the machine gun, the cannon—all of the masculine sexual symbols which are extensions of the phallus—are put forward and used to conquer and destroy.

The meaning and importance given to a military weapon and to the sexual weapon are equal. Man uses his penis in the same way he uses his gun: to conquer, control, and possess. The whole macho society must be unveiled and condemned because in the present system one tries to obtain material goods and territory, not in order to enjoy them, not out of need, but only to enlarge one's domain and authority. Similarly, sexual relations are not built on pleasure, tenderness, or love, but on reproduction, the preservation of girls' virginity (so-called "honor" of the family), the confinement and control of women for the increase in male prestige, and the overestimation of the penis.

Lebanese society, which is currently composed of these groups, values such individuals because people believe that they will save the society and guarantee its survival. Yet, in reality, they are leading the society more and more toward death and destruction. The Lebanese people are blinded by their immediate needs, and by values they have been taught to take pride in. The whole system must be rethought and changed.

If the attitude of the people does not undergo a profound transformation—a radical change in the way they perceive power and love—there can be no solution to the inextricable dilemma Lebanon is going through. Outside powers may continue to play with and on Lebanon, trying to impose their views and interests. If the Lebanese people were to successfully unite and believe in their country; if they would strive *not* to possess a small part of it, but could develop a love for it outside material interests; if nationalism could unite all the various factions fighting each other under a common aim and belief, it could move toward a real solution. In this respect, nationalism (although often mixed with sexism) may appear to be the more urgent need. But I would argue that if nationalism remains at a sexist stage, and does not move beyond ownership and possession as final goals, the cycle of hell will repeat itself and the violence will start all over again. In Lebanon, then, both nationalism and feminism are necessary: nationalism in order to save Lebanon, and feminism in order to change the values upon which social relationships are created and formed. Only with the two combined will salvation become more lasting. And thus the work must begin at the most personal levels: with a change in attitudes and behavior toward one's mates, one's family, one's sexuality, one's society. From such a personal beginning, at least some of the internal conflicts might work toward resolution. With a stronger nationhood based in real love, rather than domination, the strength might radiate and push out outside influences.

The analysis I have given is clearly not restricted to Lebanon, but involves most geographical areas afflicted with war. The ideas about sexuality, its centrality to the social relations among and between women and men, and its relationship to war and national interests, probably make sense to different degrees everywhere. What makes the situation in Lebanon unique is that these questions take on huge proportions and are more obvious than elsewhere. Lebanon is a Mediterranean country, highly dominated by Islamo-Arab influences. As such, it carries the codes of honor and women's oppression, as well as masculine-macho values, to their farthest limits. The tragedy of this situation holds its own answer.

In conclusion, I would like to stress that the conflicts and contradictions which contemporary Middle Eastern women face in their society, in their families, and even within feminist and political groups working for social change, have their roots in sexuality and sexual politics. Sexuality is at the core of most debates and choices of human existence. It is urgent to acknowledge this fact, and to start dealing with it openly, frankly, and probably painfully. It also must be incorporated into any analysis, theory, and/or practice of revolution. If the conflicts and tensions surrounding our sexual and emotional lives are not incorporated into our struggle for freedom, we are not likely to see tangible and lasting results.

I hope that my observations, analysis, and deductions will help women all over the world realize that their common struggle is far more important and binding than the differences that might lead some of them to want to disengage from the feminist movement. I also hope that sexuality—the right to sexual pleasure, the emotional relationship between two persons, as well as the problems connected with it: virginity, genital mutilation, etc., in the East, rape, pornography, etc., in the West—will grow to be recognized as an important element, as serious and as essential as food, shelter, jobs, and development in the struggles for revolutionary change.

REFERENCES

Abunasr, Junlinda. 1980. *The Development of the Three to Six Year-Old Lebanese Children and Their Environment*. Beirut: I.W.S.A.W.
Accad, Evelyne. 1978. *Veil of Shame: Role of Women in the Contemporary Fiction of North Africa and the Arab World*. Sherbrooke, Quebec: Naaman.
———. 1986. *Contemporary Arab Women Writers and Poets*. Beirut: Institute for Women's Studies in the Arab World.
———. 1988. *Coquelicot du Massacre*. [Novel on the war in Lebanon with a cassette of songs.] Paris: L'Harmattan.
———. 1989. *L'Excisée: The Mutilated Woman*. Washington: Three Continents Press.
———. 1989. *Women Unmask War Unveils Men: Sexuality, War and Literature in the Middle East*. New York: NYUP.
Adnan, Etel. 1982. *Sitt Marie Rose*. Sausalito, Calif.: Post-Apollo Press.
Ajami, Fouad. 1987. "The Silence in Arab Culture." *The New Republic* 6.
Al-Shaykh, Hanan. 1986. *The Story of Zahra*. London/New York: Readers International.
Antonius, Soraya. 1983. "Fighting on Two Fronts: Conversations with Palestinian Women." In Miranda Davies, ed., *Third World, Second Sex*. London: Zed Press.
Arbid, Marie Therese. 1980. *Ma Guerre, Pourquoi Faire?* Beirut: An-Nahar.
Awwad, Tawfiq Yusuf. 1976. *Death in Beirut*. London: Heineman.
Badinter, Elisabeth. 1986. *L'un est l'autre: Des Relations Entre Hommes et Femmes*. Paris: Odile Jacob.

Barakat, Halim. 1977. *Lebanon in Strife*. Austin: University of Texas Press.
———. 1983. *Days of Dust*. Washington: Three Continents Press.
Barry, Kathleen. 1984. *Female Sexual Slavery*. New York/London: New York University Press.
Boukhedenna, Sakinna. 1987. *Journal "Nationalité: Immigré(e)."* Paris: L'Harmattan.
Brownmiller, Susan. 1976. *Against Our Will: Men, Women, and Rape*. New York: Bantam.
Chedid, Andrée. 1976. *Cérémonial de la Violence*. Paris: Flammarion.
———. 1985. *La Maison sans Racines*. Paris: Flammarion.
———. 1987. *The Sixth Day*. London: Serpent's Tail.
Connell, Bob. 1985. "Masculinity, Violence and War." In Paul Patton and Ross Poole, eds., *War/Masculinity*. Sydney: Intervention.
Cooke, Miriam. 1987. *Women Write War: The Centering of the Beirut Decentrists*. Oxford: Center for Lebanese Studies.
———. 1988. *War's Other Voices: Women Writers on the Lebanese Civil War, 1975–1982*. Cambridge: Cambridge University Press.
Corm, Georges. 1986. *Géopolitique du Conflit Libanais*. Paris: La Decouverte.
Davies, Miranda, ed. 1983. *Third World—Second Sex: Women's Struggles and National Liberation, Third World Women Speak Out*. London: Zed Press.
Davis, Angela. 1983. *Women, Race and Class*. New York: Vintage Books.
Dworkin, Andrea. 1980. *Marx and Gandhi Were Liberals: Feminism and the "Radical" Left*. Palo Alto, Calif.: Frog in the Well.
———. 1980. *Pornography: Men Possessing Women*. New York: Perigee Books.
el Saadawi, Nawal. 1980. *The Hidden Face of Eve*. Boston: Beacon Press.
———. 1983. *Woman at Point Zero*. London: Zed Press.
———. 1984. *Douze Femmes dans Kanater*. Paris: Des Femmes.
Enloe, Cynthia. 1983. *Does Khaki Become You?: The Militarisation of Women's Lives*. London: Pluto Press.
Erlich, Michel. 1986. *La Femme Blessée: Essai sur Les Mutilations Sexuelles Féminines*. Paris: L'Harmattan.
Farrar, Adam. 1985. "War: Machining Male Desire." In *War/Masculinity*. Sydney: Intervention.
"Femmes et Violences." 1981. *Alternatives Non Violentes*, no. 40, Printemps.
Gadant, Monique, ed. 1986. *Women of the Mediterranean*. London: Zed Press.
Gebeyli, Claire. 1985. *Dialogue Avec le Feu* (Carnets du Liban). Caen: Le Pave.
———. 1975. *Mémorial d'exil*. Paris: St-Germain-des-Prés.
———. 1982. *La Mise à Jour*. Paris: St-Germain-des-Prés.
Ghousoub, Maï. "Feminism—or the Eternal Masculine—in the Arab World." *New Left Review*, no. 161.
Jabbra, N. W. 1980. "Sex Roles and Language in Lebanon." *Ethnology* 19, no. 4:459–74.
Joseph, Suad. 1978. "Women and the Neighborhood Street in Borj Hammoud, Lebanon." In Lois Beck and Nikki Reddie, eds., *Women in the Muslim World*. London: Harvard.
"Jouir." 1983. *Les Cahiers du Grif*, no. 26 (dir., ed. Francoise Collin). Trimestriel-Mars.
Khair-Badawi. 1986. *Le Désir Amputé* (vécu sexuel des femmes libanaises). Paris: L'Harmattan.
Khaled, Leila. 1973. *Mon Peuple Vivra* (L'autobiographie d'une révolutionnaire rédigée par George Hajjar). Paris: Gallimard.
Khayat-Bennaï El, Ghita. 1985. *Le Monde Arabe au Féminin*. Paris: L'Harmattan.

Laborit, Henri. 1970. *L'agressivité Detournée*. Paris: U.G.E.

Lapierre, Jean-William, and Anne-Marie de Vilaine. 1981. "Femmes: Une Oppression Millénaire." *Alternatives Non-Violentes: Femmes et Violences*, no. 40, Printemps.

Lemsine, Aïcha. 1983. *Ordalie des Viox: Les Femmes Arabes Parlent*. Paris: Encre.

"Liban, Remises en Cause." 1982. *Peuples Méditerranéens*, no. 20. Paris, Juillet-Sept. (Direct. de Publ. Paul Vieille.)

"L'Indépendance Amoureuse." 1985. *Les Cahiers du Grif*, no. 32 (dir., ed. Francoise Collin). Editions Tierce, Hiver.

Macciocchi, Maria-Antonietta. 1974–75. *Eléments Pour une Analyse du Fascisme*. Paris VIII: Vincennes, Tome 1, no. 1026.

———. 1978. *Les Femmes et Leurs Maîtres*. Paris: Bourgeois.

Makarem, May. 1988. "Avec la Non-Violence Laure Moghaïzel, L'autre Visage du Liban." *L'Orient-Le Jour* (Beirut), 16 March.

Makhlouf, Issa. 1988. *Beyrouth ou la Fascination de la Mort*. Paris: La Passion.

Mernissi, Fatima. 1983. *Sexe, Idéologie, Islam*. Paris: Tierce.

Mikdadi, Lina. 1983. *Surviving the Siege of Beirut: A Personal Account*. London: Onyx.

Mokhtar, Khaoula. 1983. "Se Libérer à Beyrouth." *Peuples Méditerranéens*, nos. 22–23, Paris, Janv.-Juin.

Moraga, Cherríe. 1983. *Loving in the War Years*. Boston: South End Press.

Patton, Paul, and Ross Poole, eds. 1985. *War/Masculinity*. Sydney: Intervention.

Peristiany, J. G. 1976. *Mediterranean Family Structures*. Cambridge: University Press. (Three articles on Lebanon.)

Peters, Emrys. 1978. "The Status of Women in Four Middle East Communities." In Lois Beck and Nikki Keddie, eds., *Women in the Muslim World*. London: Harvard.

Pierce, Judith. 1983. "Outside the Tribe." *The Middle East* (London, September).

Polity-Charara, Yolla. 1980. "Women in Politics in Lebanon." In *Femme et Politique*. Paris: L'Harmattan.

———. 1983. "Women and Politics in Lebanon." In Miranda Davies, ed., *Third World—Second Sex*. London: Zed Press.

Reardon, Betty A. 1985. *Sexism and the War System*. New York/London: Teachers College Press, Columbia University.

Reich, Wilhelm. 1981. *L'irruption de la Morale Sexuelle*. Paris: Payot (first published in German in 1932).

Samman, Ghada. 1975. *Bayrut 75* (novel). Beirut: Ghada Samman.

Saoudi, Fathia. 1986. *L'oubli Rebelle* (Beyrouth 82). Paris: L'Harmattan.

Sayegh, Rosemary. 1979. *Palestinians, from Peasants to Revolutionaries: A People's History*. London: Zed Press.

Scarry, Elaine. 1985. *The Body in Pain: The Making and Unmaking of the World*. New York: Oxford University Press.

Souriau, Christiane, ed. 1980. *Femmes et Politique autour de la Méditerranée*. Paris: L'Harmattan.

Stephen, Wafa. 1984. "Women and War in Lebanon." *Al-Raïda*, no. 30. Beirut: I.W.S.A.W.

Tabbara, Lina Mikdadi. 1979. *Survival in Beirut: A Diary of Civil War*. London: Onyx Press.

Timerman, Jacobo. 1982. *The Longest War*. New York: Vintage.

Tueni, Nadia. 1979. *Liban, Vingt Poèmes Pour un Amour*. Beirut: Zakka.

———. 1982. *Archives Sentimentales d'une Guerre au Liban*. Paris: Pauvert.

———. 1984. *La Terre Arrêtée*. Paris: Belfond.

Vial-Mannessier, Thérèse. 1981. "Fascisme et Mystification Misogyne." *Alternatives Non-Violentes: Femmes et Violences*, no. 40, Printemps.

Vilaine, Anne-Marie de. 1981. "La Maternité Detournée." *Alternatives Non-Violentes: Femmes et Violences*, no. 40, Printemps.

Waring, Marilyn. 1985. *Women, Politics and Power*. Foreword by Robin Morgan. Wellington, London: Unwin.

Woolf, Virginia. 1966. *Three Guineas*. London/New York/San Diego: Harvest/HBJ.

GENDER AND ISLAMIC FUNDAMENTALISM

Feminist Politics in Iran

Nayereh Tohidi

Millions of Iranian women boldly stepped out from behind the four walls of their homes into the public arena in the Revolution of 1979. Their involvement in the revolution took many forms: some collected and disseminated news or distributed leaflets; others gave shelter to the wounded or to political activists under attack. Many actively marched and demonstrated in the streets, some went so far as to help erect barricades against the police, and a few even took up arms and went underground as members of a guerrilla movement.

During the early months of 1979, some women activists, particularly the university-educated and middle-class women, while opposing the Shah as the symbol of tyranny, gradually grew suspicious of the movement as they noted that many of the women participating in the demonstrations wore veils. Their anxiety increased as Khomeini took over the leadership of the revolution and as the streets filled with repetitive cries of "Islamic Rule!" and "God's Party Is the Only Party!" Nevertheless, like many of their male friends, these women dismissed their anxiety by assuming that Khomeini was simply playing a spiritual role, and that clerical rule would be incompatible with Iran's developing capitalist system. They felt that the dynamic process so inherent in the revolution would eventually expose and eliminate the retrogressive and reactionary factions from the leadership. Or so they thought.

Many Iranian activists at the time, both women and men, considered the veil a part of the superstructure or a secondary phenomenon which bothered only Western feminists or a few Iranian women intellectuals.

The immediate concern was to rid the country of the Shah's regime and his imperialist supporters. Thus, as contradictory as it might seem to Western feminists, many women, even nonreligious, nontraditional, and highly educated women, took up the veil as a symbol of solidarity and opposition to the Shah (AZ 1981). At rallies and demonstrations, chadors (veils) and roosaries (large scarves) were extended to the unveiled women, who felt obliged to show their solidarity with the majority. Many university-educated, middle-class and leftist women, who may not have worn the veil before or usually would have seen it as nonprogressive, considered it a minor concession for the sake of unity against the common enemy.

During the early months of 1979, amid the exhilaration at the Shah's defeat, the active organization of several women's groups provided an encouraging sign for women's emancipation. For the first time in many women's lives, after years of repression, women were organizing for women. As March 8, 1979, approached—International Women's Day (IWD)—women's groups worked hard to mobilize thousands of Iranian women to commemorate the event. The days of optimism and euphoria did not last long, however. Two days before the event was to take place, Khomeini began to announce restrictive measures against women. His ultimatums enraged the women. Instead of causing them to abandon their plans to rally, they resulted in an outburst of spontaneous militant demonstrations. Women were outraged that the veil was once again becoming compulsory and that the government would dare to try to eliminate women from serving as judges in the courts. Women refused to accept the repeal of the Family Protection Law of 1975 which restricted polygyny and men's unilateral right to divorce and to child custody. Instead of the planned one-day rally, the storm raged for nearly a week. It was the first and most open confrontation that Iranian women were able to mount against the fundamentalist rulers.

Although the government cautiously restrained itself from immediately imposing these new measures, the forward march of the popular movement was, for all practical purposes, brought to a grinding halt. The quest for social justice, democracy, and independence had to be unwillingly abandoned as the revolution was coercively aborted. Women, members of national ethnic minorities, popular and progressive organizations, workers and newly formed labor councils, intellectuals journalists, publishers—one by one, all became victims of the waves of terror imposed by a theocracy that showed itself to be more and more regressive. Of all these groups that actively participated in the revolution, the Iranian women played perhaps the least understood and most enigmatic role.

How regrettable that most of those who identified with the left and other democratic movements and those who were progressive in their thinking could not have perceived the hateful misogynist character of the newly imposed religious law and the fundamentalist and reactionary regime. In this essay, I would like to suggest the results of such a misperception and the possible reasons for it.

Present Situation of Women in Iran

Today, in spite of the massive participation of Iranian women in the revolution, women's position has worsened rather than improved. Women experience the same subjugations as before—except in most cases, they have increased in scope. The official rights and duties of women along with the expected behavior patterns and sex roles that accompany them have progressed no further than during the oppressive Pahlavi rule. In many cases, the situation more closely mirrors Iran's precapitalist days. Some of the most blatant violations of women's rights by the Islamic regime are as follows:

Under the civil code currently practiced in Iran, all women, including non-Muslims and foreigners, are required to wear the veil and observe Islamic *Hejab* (complete covering of a woman). As Khomeini commanded, "no part of a woman's body may be seen except her face and the part of her hand between the wrist to the tip of her fingers." Appearing without *Hejab* is considered a crime punishable by seventy-five lashes or up to a year's imprisonment. Bands of club-wielders, employed by the "Center to Fight the Undesired," impose *Hejab* upon women. Slogans such as "Death to Those without *Hejab*" cover the walls in cities, inciting action against unveiled women.[1]

Many public areas are now sex-segregated, including schools and universities. A number of girls' schools have had to close because of the shortage of women teachers. The illiteracy rate among women, particularly in the rural areas, has been increasing. In higher education, women are banned from entering certain fields of study, such as law, agriculture, geology, archaeology, and mining engineering. Married women are prohibited from attending public school altogether.

The legal age for marriage has also changed, a further reflection of the regressive attitude toward women and young girls. When Khomeini first came to power, he lowered the minimum legal age for girls to marry from eighteen to thirteen years, and now it has been lowered to nine. Polygyny, previously restricted by the Family Protection Law, has been reinstated: a man may have up to four wives officially, as well as others on a temporary basis (*sigh'a* or *Mut'a*). Under the *Shari'a* (Islamic Code of Ethics), as interpreted by Iranian *Shi'a* clergy, temporary marriage can be contracted for a fixed period of time—ranging from a few minutes to ninety-nine years—after a nominal fee is paid to the woman and a verse is repeated. This type of marriage takes place for the sole purpose of men's sexual pleasure (Haeri 1983). By relegitimizing and officially encouraging *Mut'a*, the Islamic regime has, in reality, endorsed a form of prostitution.

Except in extremely unusual circumstances, women cannot seek a divorce. If a woman is divorced, she loses the custody rights of her children automatically to the father (after the age of seven for girl children, and after the age of two for boy children). A woman does not have the right of guardianship over her children during marriage, after divorce, or even after the death of her husband.

In terms of control over their bodies, sexually and reproductively, women have few rights. Abortion is illegal. Women convicted of adultery are stoned to death; and acts of homosexuality are punishable by death if the "offense" is repeated. Thousands of women imprisoned for their political beliefs have been tortured and executed.

With regard to mobility and occupational choices, women's lives are very restricted. For instance, a woman is legally not allowed to leave the house without her husband's permission, and she must get written permission before traveling abroad. Besides having to get her husband's written permission before taking a job, a woman is officially discouraged from gaining employment outside the home. Of those who are employed, many are fired under the pretense of failure to observe Islamic *Hejab*, are laid off, or are made to retire early. According to a bill passed by the Islamic parliament, full-time women employees are restricted to part-time employment. The government announced that "in order to promote motherhood and family life, the salary of any male employee will be raised 40 percent if his wife quits her job." Formerly existing child-care centers have been closed down.

In keeping with the above measures, the Law of Retribution (*Quasas*) was passed in 1982 which states that the value of a woman's life is only half that of a man's. The testimony of two women equals that of one man; and in the case of major crimes, such as murder, a woman's testimony is not considered at all. To study this important part of Iran's penal system, see the text of the Bill of Retribution (Appendix).

Finally, the eight-year-long genocidal war between Iran and Iraq has further compounded the effects of economic deterioration, high unemployment, high rate of inflation, brain drain, and the exodus of professionals from the country. There are a vastly increasing number of widowed, displaced, and refugee women who are all undergoing unbearable economic hardship and emotional suffering.

It is important to note that, on the other hand, the Islamic government has not been totally successful in implementing all of its ideological objectives. Some of the patriarchal demands of the clergy are, inevitably, in contradiction with the structural imperatives of the Iranian capitalist economy. Contemporary Iranian women's social role, their literacy level (35 percent), the participation rate of urban women in the labor force (12 percent), and, particularly, their recent massive political participation in the revolution have made it difficult for the present ruling clergy to radically transform women's socioeconomic roles and return all women back to the domestic sphere. Economic necessities, for example, force many women into low-paid jobs in the formal and informal sector and domestic wage labor. Some educated women with prior work experience are self-employed. Thus, the mere participation of women in public economic activities and the violations of the Islamic code of *Hejab* on their part have undermined the fundamentalist notion of women's role and have worked in resistance to total subjection.

Why Did Women Rally behind Khomeini?

Considering the extent to which so many Iranian women wholeheartedly endorsed and involved themselves in the revolution, one must seek to explain the present tragic fate of women in Iran. A major question is, Why haven't women continued to vehemently protest against the Islamic government's imposition of the veil and other oppressive measures? Do women of all social strata perceive their present situation as devastating and deteriorating? And finally, why do some groups of women still support the Islamic Republic of Khomeini?

The postrevolutionary changes that have affected women negatively can be overemphasized if they are not seen in the context of past and present laws and if class differences and social context are ignored (Higgins 1985, 483). The historical, socioeconomic, political, cultural, and psychological factors behind the revolution all must be considered in the analysis of women's situation. In Iran, as in most other "Third World" countries, women's issues and organizations have been related to the national anticolonial and antiimperialist movements. Consequently, the fate of the women's movement and women's social status have been closely intertwined with the general course of national and class struggles.

The historical precedent and social tradition for massive participation of women in the Iranian Revolution of 1977–79 go back to the 1905–1911 constitutional movement. This movement never managed to overthrow feudalism and neocolonial domination, and did not succeed in implementing its bourgeois-democratic goals for women. However, the seeds were planted for future struggle and consciousness raising.[2]

Iran, under the Pahlavi reign (1922–1979) and through neocolonialist imposition, was changing rapidly from a semifeudal Asiatic society to a centralized capitalist state dependent mainly upon the United States.

However, the uneven process of capitalist development and the restricted character of industrialization, along with an absolutist and corrupt monarchy, tended to reinforce the persistence of precapitalist modes of production to a considerable extent (Jazani 1980). This in turn continued to reproduce traditional social relationships, values, attitudes, and behavior patterns, including gender roles and family arrangements.

While the process of modernization, i.e., capitalist development and Westernization, was advantageous to an important sector of the upper class and the emerging middle class, it was often harmful to the traditional segment of the middle class (the merchant [bazaar] bourgeoisie and petite bourgeoisie), as well as their historical ally the clergy. Bazaar merchants and artisans often suffered ruinous competition from Western goods, and later on from larger commercial and industrial enterprises of their own Westernized upper class. Therefore, conflict and friction were set in motion between the growing "modernized" social strata, who imitated and aspired to a Western lifestyle, and the powerful clergy and traditional bazaaries, who perceived the cultural and economic changes as jeopardizing their very existence.

It was the women who belonged to these latter strata, of traders, merchants, shopkeepers, and artisans, whose lifestyle, religious beliefs, and cultural identity were being challenged, negated, ridiculed, and sometimes coercively taken away by the Westernization process of the Shah's state.[3] In the 1970s, the younger generation of women from this strata were caught up in two conflicting and competing value systems—the traditional one reinforcing their families and the religious standards of public morality, and the more modern one aligning them with a Westernized imported culture reinforced by the state. To resolve this dilemma, many fell back on their "traditional roots," intrigued by the Islamic model of womanhood presented by ideologues such as Ali Shariati or even the more conservative fundamentalists opposing the Shah. And it was they who, later on, made up the core of veiled militant contingents who demonstrated in the streets.

One reason for the appeal of the more traditional image is that the rapid changes imposed by the Shah did not serve the needs of the majority of women. The emergence of a new market which attracted cheap female labor was just one inevitable process of capitalist development, industrialization, and land reform in Iran. As a consequence of the restricted character of industrialization and proletarianization, however, women were, for the most part, absorbed by the growing sector of services and state employment. While the number of literate, highly educated, and wage-earning women in urban centers increased, no genuine change or fundamental process took place in the status, social relations, and/or conditions of everyday life for the majority of Iranian women. A few reforms pertaining to the legal rights of women, e.g., the Family Protection Law (1975), while positive and progressive on paper, did not affect the majority of women. Similarly, peasant women did not noticeably benefit from the Shah's land reform (Tabari and Yeganeh 1982). As in many "Third World" countries, development was directed and manipulated by multinational corporations and resulted in a sharp deterioration in the conditions of women's daily lives, intensifying their exploitation and degraded status.

On the other hand, the very act of leaving behind the old traditions and of participating in social production in the public sphere was a step forward for urban working women in terms of gaining autonomy. Yet the lack of corresponding supportive social provisions, and effective legal reforms, made working outside the home a perpetual struggle. Women were subject to continual exploitation. Besides receiving low wages, they were exposed to constant sexual harassment on the workplace, and were discouraged by resentful negative attitudes from relatives and family members at home.

The model for the "new woman" proposed by the Shah's regime did not appeal to many Iranians. According to traditional norms, a woman was to hide her body in public and submit herself like an obedient servant or piece of property, first to her father, and later to her husband. The "new women," on the other hand, was expected to ornament and show herself in order to please both the public and her husband, while at the same time serve as a cheap commodity in the labor force (AZ 1981).

The constant exposure of women to the modernized version of "woman" and the corresponding values of Western culture, and the deliberate efforts made to cultivate a mass-consumption consciousness— slavish imitation of European fashions, preoccupation with self-presentation, and, in short, commercialization of women—created a confused and, in part, "alien" model of womanhood, thus hardly preferable to the traditional one. The resultant dual value system, with its constant dilemmas and the alienation it caused many women, manifested itself in the formation of two distinct groups: one group, made up of the highly educated and professional women, modified their traditional attitudes and adapted to the new environment; and the other group, often under great pressure from their families, resisted the "imposed, alien, corrupt, and non-Islamic" standards and embraced the traditional forms. The latter group, made up of members of the bazaar merchants and traditional petite bourgeoisie, felt excluded, isolated, and put down by the Western dominant culture. This, in turn, resulted in resentment, distrust, and hidden hostility toward unveiled "modern" women.[4]

Traditional models of womanhood were reintroduced by the leaders and ideologues of the Islamic opposition, such as Ali Shariati, Taleghani, and Motahari.[5] Fatimeh, the daughter of the Prophet Mohammad and the wife of Ali, the first Imam, became the personification of virtue and obedience; and Zeinab, sister of Hossein, the Third Imam, who was martyred by the corrupt rulers of the day, became the symbol of outspoken, aggressive, and militant women. These role models, while they were reintroduced in deliberately modified political portraits, provided women with an identity and a much-needed defense mechanism. In such a situation, and given the factors enumerated above, the clergy found a climate ripe for channeling the genuine grievances of women into a puritanical Islamic movement.

Other sociopolitical factors also contributed to the acceptance of fundamental Islam as an alternative to the Shah. Specifically, a history of failure of nationalist and communist forces in Iran and the subsequent distrust and disillusionment with the left, combined with the Shah's systematic and ruthless repression of newly forming democratic and leftist organizations, created a vacuum of progressive alternatives for the anti-Shah movement. Unlike Islamic groups, the left lacked a national network to communicate effectively with the majority of people in Iran, and they were unable to offer a vocabulary more familiar to the populace. As a result, progressive ideas did not find their appropriate place in society. The leftist forces were under constant suppression and, thus, could only offer the image of an underground guerrilla woman (such as that of Ashraf Dehghani and Marzieh Oskooei, two well-known Fedaee), and such a model could not be adopted by the majority of women.

Furthermore, the left relied mostly on an economic deterministic analysis of Iranian society, and this limited its perspective on the situation of women. Analysis of the oppression of women and a more general democratic and cultural evaluation of Iranian society required a more thorough analysis which the left failed to initiate and develop (Azari 1983). Moreover, illiteracy (65 percent) and political inexperience prevailed, especially among women. Historically, women had no outside public associations except with the mosques. There were no popular women's groups that were solely and truly organized to raise feminist consciousness. It was in such a social and political context that Islam became the expected and familiar vent for protest. Fundamentalists in countries such as Iran, Lebanon, Morocco, and Pakistan gain control by channeling people's frustration and anger into a familiar language, ideology, and value system.

It is clear that the changes and policies implemented by the Islamic Republic of Iran (IRI) have generally had a negative and retrogressive impact on the economic and cultural conditions of the majority of the population, both women and men. But while the IRI has restricted the rights and opportunities of women in most aspects, there is still a group of women (supportive of the Islamic regime) who, because of their social class and cultural background, have gained certain privileges, as well as a positive self-concept and a sense of power, dignity, and pride (Higgins 1985). Although their role in community politics has remained indirect, protected, and secondary to that of men, they have managed to retain their subsequently gained activism in the public sphere (Hegland 1986). However, as far as the women's movement and feminism are concerned, the activism, ideology, and point of view of this group of Iranian women resemble those of Phyllis Schlafly in the United States, except that she does not wear a veil!

At the same time, Islam should not be conceptualized as an autonomous, monolithic, and static structure that has shaped the socioeconomic process and all social relationships, including women's status (Moghadam 1983). Iran's present predicament, and that of Iranian women in particular, cannot be explained by focusing exclusively on the compulsory veil, the *Shari'a*-based restrictive legal rights, or the Islamic fundamentalism of the present regime. The prevailing conditions of women in Iran are not the overnight result of Khomeini's regime with its Islamic rules. Nor is it Islam that subjugates women any more than fundamentalist Catholicism does in Latin America. As el Saadawi (1980) writes, "the great religions of the world uphold similar principles in so far as the submission of women to men is concerned."

Like many other Middle Eastern countries, Iranian society is characterized by the uneven development of capitalism and industrialization. Therefore, the persistence of the traditional orthodox school of Islam and its formidable laws and regulations in terms of sex roles correspond to the persistence of precapitalistic modes of production. The direct and indirect consequences of years of patriarchy, repression, dictatorial monarchy, and cultural and economic penetration of imperialist forces have all contributed to the present backlash in Iran.

Yet it is very important to realize the place and function of Islamic ideology in the struggle for social change. To view the Islamic fundamentalist revival in the Middle East as an ostensibly "antiimperialist," radical, and militant trend has the potential for great deception, as it continues to influence both women and men and their approach to politics in the Middle East. It obscures and distorts the objectives and direction of the national liberation movements. Furthermore, local and international reactionary forces have been indirectly and covertly reinforcing the pan-Islamic and fundamentalist revival in the Middle East; for instance, by redirecting the aims of the movement and by dividing people into religious factions, they have been building a strong and subtle "barrier against communism."[6] Consider, for instance, the role of fundamentalist forces such as *Amal, Aldaawa, Ekhwan al Muslemin,* and *Hezbollah* in Lebanon,

Iraq, Egypt, and Iran. These forces must be more adequately dealt with rather than passively accepted as part of the revolution which will go away later.

With regard to women's movements, especially in Iran, Egypt, Pakistan, Lebanon, and Palestine, there is an urgent need to fight back and reverse the fundamentalist trend, in terms of both educating and organizing people. The ideological significance of Islam as a political alternative to which the masses have turned must be understood, and appropriate measures must be drawn up in response to it (Tabari and Yeganeh 1982). A call for separation of the state from religion as a democratic principle should be included in any progressive platform of political groups faced with the threat of fundamentalism. Women must insist on holding out for this principle more than ever.

"Third World" women's movements and their people's national democratic and antiimperialist struggles are closely interrelated theoretically and empirically (Chinchilla 1977; Sen and Grown 1987). Alone, a women's movement can never transform the foundations of sexism and sexual oppression. Neither can a revolution which seeks to transform class relationships meet its goals if it does not incorporate the question of women's oppression. Specific demands of women must be incorporated into the national antiimperialist movement and class struggle right from the beginning. *The women's question should not be relegated to the days after the revolution*—as has been, unfortunately, the tendency of many left and revolutionary movements. Cases such as the Algerian and Iranian revolutions have proven that the success of a nationalist or even a socialist revolution does not automatically lead to liberation for women.

In the case of Middle Eastern women, in particular because of the recent spread of religious fundamentalism, it is more important than ever to raise women's issues and integrate the women's question into the national and class struggle. Therefore, mobilization of women in democratic and autonomous organizations through the process of revolution must utilize women's political power inside the revolution. Otherwise, "women may be used by the revolution as tools, as cheap labor, cheap fighters—to die first and be liberated last!" (el Saadawi 1980).

APPENDIX

The Bill of Retribution

The following is a selection of the articles from the Bill of Retribution (Qisas) which affect women.* This bill was developed and passed by the Parliament of the Islamic Republic of Iran.

Article 5: If a Muslim man willfully murders a Muslim woman, he will be sentenced to *qisas* (retaliation), but the woman's guardian must pay the murderer one-half of a man's blood-money before he receives *qisas*.

Article 6: If a Muslim woman willfully murders a Muslim man, she will be sentenced only to *qisas* and will not have to pay anything to the guardian of the blood.

Article 23: Murder requires *qisas* provided the victim does not religiously deserve to be killed—e.g., someone who swears at the Great Prophet (may praise be upon Him), the Chaste Imams (may peace be upon them), or Saint Zahra (may peace be upon her); or someone who violates one's *harim* (bounds) and could not be repulsed but by murder; or that the husband should see someone committing adultery with his wife, in which case it is only permissible for the husband to kill both of them. In all of the above cases it is not admissible to carry out *qisas* on the murderer.

Article 33: Testimony: (a) A case of willful murder is proved only on the basis of two righteous men's testimony; (b) A case of semiwillful or unintentional murder is proved on the basis of the testimony of two righteous men, or of one righteous man and two righteous women, or the testimony of one righteous man and the plaintiff's oath.

Article 46: If a man murders a woman, the guardian of the blood has the choice of carrying out the *qisas* and paying the murderer one-half of the full amount of the blood-money, or demanding the woman's blood-money from the murderer.

Article 50: A pregnant woman who is sentenced to *qisas* must not receive the *qisas* before she has given birth. After the delivery, if *qisas* could lead to the child's death, then it must be postponed until the danger of death is over.

Article 60: Men and women are equal in *qisas* pertaining to limbs, and the criminal man inflicting a woman with the loss of a limb will be sentenced to *qisas* on a similar limb. So long as the blood-money for the damaged limb does not exceed one-third of the full blood-money, nothing shall be paid to the man. If the blood-money for the damaged limb exceeds one-third of the full blood-money, e.g., the

---

*From *Women and Struggle in Iran*, no. 3 (1984).

blood-money for a hand, the criminal man shall receive *qisas* on the similar limb provided he is paid one-half of the blood-money for that limb.

The *Hadd* for Adultery

Article 81: Should a man copulate with a woman not lawful to him, whether in the front or in the back, and whether he ejaculates or does not ejaculate, adultery will have taken place, and the man and the woman are both considered adulterers.

Article 82: Adultery leads to *hadd* if the adulterer (the man) meets the following qualifications: maturity, sanity, free will, consciousness of the facts. Therefore the adultery committed by an immature or insane person, or by someone under duress, or by someone who commits adultery with a woman as a result of a mistake, or by someone who, being unaware of the religious verdict, marries and copulates with a woman where the marriage is not sanctioned by religion, does not lead to *hadd*.

Note 1: If a man does not know of the lawfulness of a marriage to a woman, and does not consider its lawfulness to be probable, and marries her without inquiring about the religious verdict, and enters her, then he will be sentenced to *hadd*.

Note 2: If a woman is permissible for him and he enters her, then only the woman and not the man will be sentenced to the *hadd* for adultery, and if the man is aware and the woman is not, then only the man and not the woman will be sentenced to the *hadd* for adultery.

Article 83: If the man or the woman who copulate with each other claim to have been unaware, provided it is considered probable that the claim is correct, then that claim will be accepted without any witnesses or oath taking and the *hadd* will be dropped.

Article 84: If a woman claims to have been unwillingly pushed into committing adultery, her claim, provided there is no positive knowledge against it, will be accepted.

Article 90: If a woman who does not have a husband becomes pregnant, she shall not be subjected to *hadd* because of the mere fact of pregnancy, unless her having committed adultery is proved by one of the methods stipulated in this law.

Article 91: B. Testimony: Adultery is proved on the basis of testimonies by four righteous men, or three righteous men and two righteous women, whether it leads to *jald* (flogging) or *rajm* (stoning).

Article 92: In cases where adultery would lead to a *jald*, it could also be proved on the basis of testimonies by two righteous men or four righteous women.

Note: Women's testimonies alone or accompanied by one righteous man's testimony do not prove adultery, but those witnesses will receive *hadd* for the libel.

Types of *Hadd* for Adultery: Killing

Article 100: Adultery leads to killing in the following cases: (1) Adultery with consanguineous kin with whom marriage is not permitted leads to killing; (2) Adultery with a step-mother leads to killing; (3) Adultery between a non-Muslim (man) and a Muslim woman leads to the killing of the adulterer; (4) Rape and adultery by pushing someone into unwillingly committing it would lead to the killing of the adulterer who does the forcing.

Stoning

Adultery leads to stoning in the following cases: (1) Adultery by a *mohsan* man— i.e., a young man who has a permanent spouse, with whom he copulates and can do so whenever he desires—leads to stoning, whether he commits adultery with an adult or an underage person; (2) Adultery by a *mohsaneh* woman—i.e., a young woman who has a permanent husband with whom copulation has been achieved, and whose husband regularly sleeps with her—with an adult man would lead to stoning. A *mohsaneh* woman's adultery with an underage person would lead to the *hadd* of lashing, not to stoning.

Note 1: Adultery by a man or a woman who does have a permanent spouse, but who does not have access to his (her) spouse because of traveling, imprisonment, or other valid excuses, would not lead to stoning.

Note 2: A revocable divorce does not free the man or the woman from wedlock before the days of *eddah* (waiting) are over, but an irrevocable divorce does free them from wedlock.

The Lash and the Lash Accompanied by the Shaving of the Head and Banishment

Adultery by a man who does not have a wife, and also adultery by an old woman not meeting the conditions of marriage, requires that before they are stoned, the *hadd* of the lash is enforced on them.

Adultery by a man who is married but has not entered (his wife yet) would lead to the *hadd* of the lash, the shaving of the head, and banishment for one year to a place determined by the religious judge.

Note: In the above verdicts there is no difference between committing adultery with a live or a dead woman.

Article 103: The *hadd* of killing or of stoning shall not be enforced on a woman during pregnancy or labor, nor shall it be enforced after the delivery if the infant has no guardian and there is fear of his (perishing). However, if a guardian is found, then the *hadd* shall be enforced on her.

Article 104: If the enforcing of the *hadd* of the lash on a pregnant or nursing woman could cause damage to the fetus or to the suckling, then the enforcing of the *hadd* shall be delayed.

Article 105: If a sick woman or a woman with excessive menstruation is sentenced to killing or to stoning, the *hadd* shall be enforced on her, but if she is sentenced to the lash, one must wait for the illness to go away or for the woman with excessive menstruation to become cleansed.

Note: It is permissible to enforce the *hadd* during menstruation.

Article 112: A man is lashed standing up without any clothes except something covering his private parts, and all his body except for the head, the face, and his private parts shall be lashed, whereas a woman is lashed while sitting down with her clothes tied around her.

Article 114: When *rajm* (stoning) is being administered on a man, he must be placed in a pit almost down to his waist, and when administered on a woman, she must be placed in a pit almost down to her chest.

Article 128: Women's testimony by itself or accompanied by a man's testimony does not prove the *hadd* for the alcoholic drink.

Article 157: *Mosaheqah* is lesbianism with the woman's sexual organs.

Article 158: Methods for proving *mosaheqah* in the court are the same as those for proving men's homosexual activity.

Article 159: The *hadd* for *mosaheqah* (lesbianism) is 100 lashes.

Article 160: The *hadd* for *mosaheqah* shall be decreed against a person who meets the following conditions: maturity, sanity, free will, intention.

Note: In the *hadd* for *mosaheqah*, there shall be no difference between the active and the passive party, or between Muslims and non-Muslims.

Article 161: Should *mosaheqah* be repeated three times, with *hadd* being administered on each occasion, they shall be killed on the fourth occasion.

Article 162: Should the person indulging in *mosaheqah* repent before the witnesses testify, then the *hadd* shall be dropped, and if she repents after the testimonies have been offered, the *hadd* shall not be dropped.

Article 163: Should *mosaheqah* be proved on the basis of the person's confession, and should she repent, then the religious judge can pardon her.

Article 164: Should two naked women be under one cover, they shall receive less than 100 lashes. Should this act be repeated, then 100 lashes shall be administered on the second occasion.

Article 168: The *hadd* for *qiyadat* (pandering) is 75 lashes and banishment from place of residence, the duration of which shall be determined by the religious judge.

Note: The *hadd* for *qiyadat* in the case of women shall be 75 lashes only.

Article 169: *Qadf* (calumny) is someone's attributing adultery or *levat* (pederasty) to a person.

Article 176: Any insult which irritates the person hearing it, but which does not entail *qadf*—e.g., a person telling his wife that she had not been a virgin, or calling someone a lewd person, a drinker of wine, etc.—shall lead to punishment provided the person addressed did not deserve to be insulted.

Article 181: Should a man calumniate his wife who is dead, if that woman has no inheritors except the offspring of the same man, then *hadd* shall be proved;

but should that woman have an inheritor other than the same man's offspring—such as a child from another husband—then *hadd* shall be proved.

Article 183: Should a mother calumniate her child, then she shall be sentenced to *hadd*.

Committee for Women's Democratic Rights in Iran

ISA-WC
P.O. BOX 5542
Glendale, CA. 91201
U.S.A.

NOTES

1. One of the methods of reprisal against unveiled women was formulated by Hashemi Rafsanjani, one of the most influential clergy, who serves as speaker of the Islamic parliament and the commander in chief. In one of his Friday sermons (May 4, 1986) broadcast by radio, TV, and print media, Mr. Rafsanjani announced that those women who are still not in perfect compliance with the Islamic *Hejab* (categorized in Farsi as *Bad Hejab*), meaning those who are not covered properly, e.g., revealing some hair beneath their headscarves and wearing bright colors, will be arrested and put in a concentration camp to undergo reindoctrination and do forced labor. Unlike regular or political prisoners, these women must have their daily expenses paid by husbands or male kinsmen.

It should be noted, however, that recently, following the end of the Iran-Iraq war (August 1988), there has appeared a shift toward moderation in the regime's policy with respect to women's dress code. Ironically, Rafsanjani himself is one of those who have started speaking in favor of a less rigid policy and attitude toward women and men's clothing, as well as other restrictions against arts and music. The seriousness and consistency of the Islamic regime's recent move toward openness remain to be seen. But despite the present uncertainty, one needs to explore the reasons behind such a shift and its subsequent implications, particularly since it has coincided with a renewed wave of persecution and execution of political opponents.

2. For a comprehensive historical account of the Iranian women's movement, see Sanasarian (1982) and *Women and Struggle in Iran*, no. 4 (1985):5–15.

3. For example, women were forced to remove their veils in 1935 under Reza Shah (the late deposed Shah's father). This measure was designed to help "modernize" Iran. To enforce the idea, police were ordered to physically remove the veil from any woman wearing it in public. Undoubtedly, this would have been a progressive step if women had chosen to do it themselves. Instead, it humiliated and alienated many Iranian women, who resorted to staying behind closed doors and not venturing into the streets in order to avoid this embarrassing confrontation.

Consequently, the veil became politicized. Not to wear it became associated with identifying with the West, and the abusive and brutal policies of the Pahlavi regime. This partially explains why the adoption of the veil became a symbolic protest against the Shah. For further discussion on politicization of the veil in Iran, see Sanasarian (1982, 137–39).

4. It is interesting and revealing to note that the present harsh and aggressive punishment and surveillance of women who fail to observe Islamic *Hejab* are usually carried out by women from the very same traditional groups who call themselves "*Hezbollahee* women," i.e., "Partisans of God" or "Zeinab's Sisters." Their deeply rooted hostility toward unveiled women can be explained in part by their previous sociopsychological experiences under the Shah.

5. For further elaboration, see Azari (1983, 66).

6. Note the issue of Reagan's secret deals and support of the Iranian fundamentalist government, as well as overt support of Afghanistan's Islamic fundamentalists fighting the Afghan government. In both cases, Reagan's justification is that these forces—no matter how repressive, backward, and reactionary they are—should be supported and deserve to be called "moderate" or "freedom fighters as long as they are anti-communist."

REFERENCES

AZ. 1981. "The Women's Struggle in Iran." *Monthly Review* (March):22–30.
Azari, F. 1983. *Women of Iran: The Conflict with Fundamentalist Islam*. London: Ithaca Press.
Chinchilla, Norma S. 1977. "Mobilizing Women: Revolution in the Revolution." *Latin American Perspectives* 4, no. 4 (Issue 15):83–101.
el Saadawi, Nawal. 1980. *The Hidden Face of Eve: Women in the Arab World*. London: Zed Press.
Haeri, S. 1983. "The Institution of *Mut'a* Marriage in Iran: A Formal and Historical Perspective." In G. Nashat, ed., *Women and Revolution in Iran*. Boulder, Colo.: Westview Press.
Hegland, Mary E. 1986. "Political Roles of Iranian Village Women." *Middle East Report (MERIP)*, no. 138, pp. 14–19.
Higgins, Patricia J. 1985. "Women in the Islamic Republic of Iran: Legal, Social, and Ideological Changes." *Signs: Journal of Women in Culture and Society* 10, no. 3:477–94.
Jazani, B. 1980. *Capitalism and Revolution in Iran*. London: Zed Press.
Moghadam, V. 1983. "Peripheral Capitalism and Feminism." *Women and Struggle in Iran*, no. 3, pp. 20–25.
———. 1988. "Women, Work, and Ideology in the Islamic Republic." *International Journal of Middle East Studies* 20:221–43.
Sanasarian, E. 1982. *The Women's Rights Movement in Iran: Mutiny, Appeasement, and Repression from 1900 to Khomeini*. New York: Praeger.
Sen, G., and C. Grown. 1987. *Development, Crisis, and Alternative Visions: Third World Women's Perspectives*. New York: Monthly Review Press.
Tabari, A., and N. Yeganeh. 1982. *In the Shadow of Islam: The Women's Movement in Iran*. London: Zed Press.

4 Race, Identity, and Feminist Struggles

THE CONSTRUCTION OF THE SELF IN U.S. LATINA AUTOBIOGRAPHIES

Lourdes Torres

In the 1980s we have witnessed a proliferation in the publication of literary works by U.S. Latina[1] writers. This growth, however, only begins to address the virtual absence of this literature on the marketplace and in the pages of literary journals. The sexism that predominates in both the Anglo and Latino presses has been a significant factor in its suppression. Since Anglo publishers rarely publish work by Latinas (or Latinos), the only recourse available has been Latino publishing concerns, which are male-run and until recently have shown little interest in the publication of Latina works (see Sánchez 1985 for a discussion of this situation). In the recent past, however, Latino publishers such as Arte Público Press and Bilingual Review Press have "discovered" Latina writers; in addition, since 1981 the Latina-run journal (and press) *Third Woman* has been dedicated exclusively to the writings of Latinas, both in the United States and internationally. Also, small feminist presses such as Kitchen Table: Women of Color Press and white feminist presses have begun to publish U.S. Latina titles.

In terms of what has been published thus far, poetry collections predominate, followed by short-story collections and, to a lesser extent, novels. Recently, a new genre has begun to be explored by U.S. Latina writers—the autobiography. To date three such collections exist: *Loving in the War Years: Lo Que Nunca Pasó Por Sus Labios,* by Cherríe Moraga

(South End Press, 1983), *Getting Home Alive,* by Aurora Levins Morales
and Rosario Morales (Firebrand Books, 1986), and *Borderlands/La Frontera,* by Gloria Anzaldúa (Spinsters/Aunt Lute Book Co., 1987).[2]

Seizing the Podium: Creating Latina Autobiography

These collections are both revolutionary and subversive at many levels. They challenge traditional notions about the genre of "autobiography" through their form and their content. They subvert both Anglo and
Latino patriarchal definitions of culture. They undermine linguistic norms
by using a mixture of English, Spanish, and Spanglish. All address the
question of the politics of multiple identities from a position which seeks
to integrate ethnicity, class, gender, sexuality, and language. The three
texts appropriate a new space for Latinas where they too partake in the
interpretation of symbols and the creation of meaning, and most important, they theorize a politics from which to forge the survival of Latinas
and other women of color.

Both the form and the content of the three works being considered
subvert conventions of canonized autobiographies. Estelle Jelinek (1980)
in "Women's Autobiography and the Male Tradition" highlights differences of content and style in the autobiographies of men and women.
One difference she notes is the degree of orderliness in the self-portraits;
men's works generally are presented as chronologically linear wholes,
while women's stories tend to consist of fragmented, disjunctive units.
Recent autobiographies written by women of color, in addition to possessing these characteristics, tend to mix genres in a manner we have not
seen in mainstream autobiographies. For example, *Zami* (1982) by Audre
Lorde and *The Woman Warrior* (1979) by Maxine Hong Kingston combine
biographical details with fictional tales, myths, and fantasies to tell their
stories. Similarly, the three Latina autobiographies we are considering are
composed of essays, sketches, short stories, poems, and journal entries.
In all three, to a greater or lesser extent, there is no attempt to privilege
any of the various genres. History—public and private—myth, fiction, and
fantasy are all juxtaposed. As such, these collections are a fundamental
subversion of mainstream autobiographies' traditions and conventions.

Getting Home Alive by Aurora Levins Morales and Rosario Morales
encompasses yet another departure from typical autobiographies by
bringing together the experiences and points of view of a mother and
daughter. In this collection the two authors' words, stories, and poems
are not separated into sections according to authors, but rather are all
woven together. Occasionally a piece written by the mother is responded
to by the daughter in the following piece, but this is not always the case.
While conventional criticism might dismiss this ordering as fragmentary

and confusing, the series of fragments and their apparent orderlessness can also be interpreted as a daring experiment with structure.

Moraga's text is likewise characterized by a mixture of genres. In her introduction, she states that her pieces are not arranged chronologically according to when they were written, but rather in terms of her political development. Anzaldúa, on the other hand, presents her personal history and the history of her people in narrative sequences in the first half, and in the second half continues to explore these aspects in poetry. These autobiographies are a blending of the imagined and real; that is, myths and fantasies coexist with historical realities. The project of presenting the personal and collective selves takes precedence over conventional stylistics or established structures. In a sense the structure is parallel to the content, in that the main thematic concern of the texts, as in all autobiographies, is the question of identity and the presentation of the self, but in these texts is complicated by the problematic of the fragmented, multiple identity.

The use of fiction does not lessen the need of readers and critics to consider the extratextual conditions which produce the text—that is, the social and political forces that shaped the "self" who produced the text—although this reading practice is not fashionable in present-day literary criticism. In this context it is important to note that as people of color have begun to define and construct their subjectivity, the construction of a "subject" suddenly has become antitheoretical and problematic according to the dictates of current critical theory. However, as Elizabeth Fox-Genovese (1988) points out in an essay examining black women's autobiographies,

> Feminist critics, like critics of Afro-American and third world literature, are beginning to refuse the implied blackmail of Western, white male criticism. The death of the subject and of the author may accurately reflect the perceived crisis of Western culture and the bottomless anxieties of its most privileged subjects—the white male authors who presumed to define it. Those subjects and those authors may, as it were, be dying. But it remains to be demonstrated that their deaths constitute the collective or generic deaths of the subject and author. There remain plenty of subjects and authors who, never having had much opportunity to write in their own names or the names of their kind, much less in the name of the culture as a whole, are eager to seize the abandoned podium. The white male cultural elite has not in fact abandoned the podium; it has merely insisted that the podium cannot be claimed in the name of any particular experience. And it has been busily trying to convince the world that intellectual excellence requires depersonalization and abstraction. The virtuosity, born of centuries of privilege, with which these ghosts of authors make their case, demands that others, who have something else to say, meet the ghosts' standards of pyrotechnics. (P. 67)

Through their subversion of the autobiography, the Latina authors are seizing the podium, telling their own stories, creating new images, and contesting the often negative and degrading images which others have used to construct the Latina.

In a recent wave of feminist writings about women's autobiographies, male criteria for the construction of the autobiography are also being challenged. Susan Stanford Friedman (1988), for instance, argues that the traditional approach to autobiography which emphasizes the individual as a supreme and unique being is inappropriate to explain the creation of the female or "minority" self. Such an approach does not consider the externally imposed cultural identities of women and other oppressed groups and the particular socialization processes that women and people of color undergo in a racist and sexist culture. Women can never assume an individual identity because they are at every turn reminded of their gender (and color if they are not white). Meanwhile, since they personify the cultural categories privileged in Western culture as human, those who are white, male, and heterosexual can think of themselves as individuals. Friedman states, "The emphasis on individualism as the necessary pre-condition for autobiography is thus a reflection of privilege, one that excludes from the canons of autobiography those who have been denied by history the illusion of individualism" (p. 35).

Like black autobiographers (Butterfield 1974), Latina autobiographers do not create a monolithic self, but rather present the construction of the self as a member of multiple oppressed groups, whose political identity can never be divorced from her conditions. The subject created is at once individual and collective. For people who have been maligned or who have not had the power to name their own experience, the autobiography, as Sheila Rowbotham (1973, 27) points out, is a means by which to "project its own image on to history." This is, of course, far removed from the dominant and traditional autobiographical construction of the "superior" individual who seeks to separate himself from his community and perhaps, in part, accounts for why the works of women of color have been marginalized by the white male, heterosexual literary world.

Women's autobiographies generally challenge the male-imposed construction of their identity. As Simon (1987) states, "women approach autobiography from the position of speakers at the margins of discourse" (p. 44). If this is true for white, heterosexual, middle-class women, what does it mean for the construction of self in the autobiographies of working-class, lesbian women of color? It is not enough to speak of double or triple oppression; rather, women of color are themselves theorizing their experience in radical and innovative terms. Their condition as women, as people of color, as working-class members, and in some cases as lesbians, has led them to reject partial, social, and political theories such as middle-class, white, mainstream feminism and Marxist socialism which have failed to develop an integrated analysis sensitive to the simultaneous oppression that women of color experience. Rather, third world women are making connections between the forces of domination which affect their lives daily and are actively participating in the creation of a movement committed to radical social and political transformation at all levels.

Forging an Identity

In *Getting Home Alive, Loving in the War Years*, and *Borderlands/La Frontera*, the Latina authors engage in the process of claiming, as Michelle Cliff (1980) puts it, an identity they have been taught to despise. In order to do this, they must work through all the cultural and gender socialization and misinformation which has left them in a maze of contradictions. This results in the fragmentation of identity, and the inability to speak from a unified, noncontradictory subject position. No existing discourse is satisfactory because each necessitates the repression of different aspects of the self. Moraga, Anzaldúa, Levins Morales and Morales create a new discourse which seeks to incorporate the often contradictory aspects of their gender, ethnicity, class, sexuality, and feminist politics. The radicalness of the project lies in the authors' refusal to accept any one position; rather, they work to acknowledge the contradictions in their lives and to transform difference into a source of power. They find that being marginalized by multiple discourses, and existing in a borderland, compels them to reject prescriptive positions and instead leads them to create radical personal and collective identities.

At this point, given that identity politics has become a popular target for criticism by feminists of all varieties (cf. Bourne 1987, Kappeler 1989, Adams 1989), it is important to stress what identity politics means to these authors. All recognize that the most radical, activist politics develop when one comes to understand the dynamics of how one is oppressed and how one oppresses others in her daily life. It is from this place that connections with other oppressed people are possible; when one comes to understand the basis of one's own pain and how it is connected to the pain of others, the possibility of forming coalitions with others emerges. As Moraga states, "Without an emotional, heartfelt grappling with the source of our own oppression, without naming the enemy within ourselves and outside of us, no authentic, non-hierarchical connection among oppressed groups can take place" (p. 53). Identity politics, as conceived of by radical women of color (Moraga and Anzaldúa 1983, Smith 1983), has never meant bemoaning one's individual circumstances, or ranking oppressions, or a politics of defensiveness around one's issues. Rather, identity politics means a politics of activism, a politics which seeks to recognize, name, and destroy the system of domination which subjugates people of color.

In *Getting Home Alive*, Rosario Morales and her daughter Aurora explore the creation of their identities from an internationalist perspective. Rosario, daughter of Puerto Rican immigrants, was born and raised first in New York City, in the El Barrio community among Puerto Ricans, and then in a Bronx Jewish Community. As an adult she became involved in the communist movement. Early in her marriage to a white Jew, they decided to migrate to Puerto Rico to escape political difficulties. They remained there for thirteen years and raised two children. Aurora, coauthor of the autobiography, is thus the daughter of a Puerto Rican mother and a white, Jewish father. Interestingly, mother and daughter both identify with the Puerto Rican and Jewish struggle. Throughout the book the two women discuss the pull they feel to identify with one or the other identity. They refuse the pressure to choose, and in the last piece in their book, entitled "Ending Poem," the two authors fuse their voices and their histories and speak in a single voice. The first stanza reads:

> I am what I am.
> A child of the Americas.
> A light-skinned mestiza of the Caribbean.
> A child of many diaspora, born into this continent at a crossroads.
> I am Puerto Rican. I am U.S. American.
> I am New York Manhattan and the Bronx.
> A mountain-born, country-bred, homegrown jibara child,
> up from the shtetl, a California Puerto Rican Jew.
> A product of New York ghettos I have never known.
> I am an immigrant
> and the daughter and granddaughter of immigrants.
> We didn't know our forbears' names with a certainty.
> They aren't written anywhere.
> First names only, or hija, negra, ne, honey, sugar, dear.
> (P. 212)

Through the joining of their different identities, the authors recognize that they are creating something new, something that is more than the sum of the parts of the identities they bring together.

In the texts by Moraga and Anzaldúa we again experience the intense pressure many people of color feel to choose between cultures. The most apparent options, assimilation to white culture or affirmation of native cultures, are paved with contradictions. For the Latina lesbian woman in the U.S. context, the discourses which claim her identity are multiple and the contradictions greater than those encountered by other, less marginalized groups. The two Latina lesbian writers, Moraga and Anzaldúa, attest to the "craziness" they felt growing up in a borderland situation where they were being pulled in many directions. They experienced conflicting expectations as women from white, Chicana, and Indian cultures, as well as from heterosexual and lesbian cultures. They describe feeling great self-hatred, feeling marginalized, and without a center to grasp onto because each center asks them to or makes them feel that they must choose. The pressure to choose between possible identities is experienced by both as maddening.

In *Loving in the War Years,* for example, Moraga explores the impact that being the child of a Mexican mother and a white Anglo father had on her development. As a light-skinned Chicana she was able to, and for a period of time did, pass as white. She explains that she moved away from Chicano culture and became anglicized in order to gain autonomy and be free of the sexual and gender restrictions placed upon her within her community. While she found Anglo society also to be sexist, she remarks that she still had less to risk in an Anglo context which did not hold personal power over her in the way that Chicano culture did.

The question of her sexuality increases the confusion felt by Moraga. Despite early attempts to repress her lesbianism, she seems always to have experienced the heterosexual identity she sought to live out as immensely contradictory. Although eventually she found the space to express her sexuality in an Anglo context, she was constantly forced to confront racism within the white, lesbian feminist community. Moraga felt that white women failed to acknowledge the privilege their skin color accorded them. The white feminist agenda ignored the concerns of Chicana and third world women such that Chicanas were invited to participate in the movement as followers but no space was provided to incorporate the culturally specific concerns or analyses of women of color. These contradictions within the white women's movement led her back to her mother and therefore to her Chicana roots, where she again feels the contradiction of being connected to, but simultaneously rejected by, her people. She writes:

> When I finally lifted the lid to my lesbianism, a profound connection with my mother reawakened in me. It wasn't until I acknowledged and confronted my own lesbianism in the flesh, that my heartfelt identification with and empathy for my mother's oppression—due to being poor, uneducated, and Chicana—was realized. My lesbianism is the avenue through which I have learned the most about silence and oppression, and it continues to be a tactile reminder to me that we are not free human beings. (P. 52)

Similarly, Anzaldúa, failing to identify exclusively with either Mexican or Anglo-American culture, experiences a sense of being pulled by both identities. The tug of war is so strong as to make her feel totally annihilated: "I have so internalized the borderland conflict that sometimes I feel like one cancels out the other and we are zero, nothing, no one. A veces no soy nada, ni nadie. Pero hasta cuando no lo soy, lo soy" (p. 63).

Discussing her sexuality, Anzaldúa declares that despite being brought up as a Catholic and socialized as straight, she made a conscious choice to be lesbian. Reflecting on this decision, she states,

> It is an interesting path, and one that continually slips in and out of the white, the catholic, the Mexican, the indigenous, the instincts. In and out of my head. It makes for loquería, the crazies. It is a path of knowledge—one of knowing (and of learning) the history of oppression of our raza. It is a way of balancing, of mitigating duality. (P. 19)

Both Moraga and Anzaldúa view their coming out as lesbians as a path that led them to become more politicized; it led them to explore how they are oppressed based on their sexuality and, crucially, how this particular type of oppression is related to other forms of oppression. The discussion of sexuality in Moraga and Anzaldúa is concerned with challenging the construction of female sexuality by the family, the state, and the church. Moraga's analysis of sexuality specifically considers how this construction affects the relationships between Chicano men and women, as well as between Chicana women; she explores how women are denied a right to their bodies through the repression of their sexuality, the lifelong threat of sexual violence, and the denial of reproductive rights.

The insistence on naming the specific oppression they experience as lesbians has earned writers such as Moraga and Anzaldúa the wrath of Marxists and Marxist feminists who argue that issues of sexuality, and particularly of lesbianism, are not central to the lives of third world women and should therefore not be discussed alongside the "real" issues such as hunger, poverty, imperialism, and liberation struggles (cf. Gilliam, this volume). One variation of this tired argument suggests that only U.S. women of color who are in a position of privilege relative to their third world sisters have the luxury of taking up these concerns, since third world women are more concerned with issues of basic survival and liberation struggles. These critiques often come from U.S.-based third world feminists who, despite their own location in the West, feel that they are somehow in a better position to articulate the "real" political agendas of women of color internationally. To suggest that third world women aren't grappling with issues of sexuality (yes, even of lesbianism), to suggest that these are merely the trivial concerns of indulgent bourgeois, middle-class white women and privileged Westernized third world women, is to condescendingly silence an essential part of the lives and struggles of third world women. As is clear from the work of Accad (this volume), Barroso and Bruschini (this volume), and Ramos (1987), and from reports that have emerged from the various Latin American encuentros (cf., for example, Yarbro-Bejarano 1989), women internationally are recognizing the centrality of gender and sexuality to their lives and the importance of incorporating these issues into their politics.

The Politics of Language

The problem of identity again emerges in the three texts in discussions of language and how to give voice to a multiple heritage. The obvious and yet revolutionary answer is through the use of the mixing of the codes that have shaped their experience. Although all four authors engage in this process to a greater or lesser extent, the issue of language is played out differently for each writer. Moraga, for example, like many U.S. Latinos, lost her ability to use Spanish, one of the languages she grew up with, because she internalized the racism of the society around her and rejected her mother tongue. One of her most important concerns as she became politicized was to reclaim Spanish as an important part of her culture. Moraga's journal entry of September 1, 1981, reads:

> I called up Berlitz today. The Latino who answered refused to quote me prices over the phone. "Come down and talk to Mr. Bictner," he says. I want to know how much it's going to cost before I do any train riding into Manhattan. "Send me a brochure," I say, regretting the call.
>
> Paying for culture. When I was born between the legs of the best teacher I could have had. (P. 141)

Moraga feels that she has been brainwashed and separated from her language; she feels that English does not speak the truth of her experience and that while she is fluent in it, English somehow restricts her expression. Therefore, she struggles to regain her mother tongue, which she expects will allow her to express emotions and ideas which seem difficult for her to convey in English.

In contrast to Moraga's ambivalence about the use of the English language, both Aurora Levins Morales and Rosario Morales are comfortable with the fact that they are English-dominant. Unlike the Moraga and Anzaldúa collections, Getting Home Alive has few pieces that are written entirely in Spanish, although the work is sprinkled with Spanish words and phrases. The theme of Spanish as a lost tongue to be reclaimed does not permeate this text as it does the other two, yet the authors' uneasiness around their lack of fluency in Spanish emerges. Rosario Morales, who as an adult moved with her family to Puerto Rico for eleven years, remembers how difficult it was to reactivate her childhood Spanish, and she states that she will always be "clumsy with the language" (p. 79). Most of her life has been more linked to English, as she was born in New York and associated primarily with English-speakers. She states, "I am Boricua as Boricuas come from the isle of Manhattan" (p. 138), and in her case this means living in a predominantly English-speaking environment.

Her daughter, Aurora, born and raised in Puerto Rico, identifies more strongly with that island and claims that her first language is "Spanglish," although she, too, feels more comfortable with English. She refuses to apologize for this fact, which, as she acknowledges, is a product of her middle-class upbringing. In her "Class Poem" she proclaims that she will not feel guilty about the advantages that she has had:

> This is a poem to say:
> my choosing to suffer gives nothing
> to Tita and Norma and Angelina
> and that not to use the tongue, the self confidence,
> the training
> my privilege brought me
> is to die again for people who are already dead
> and who wanted to live. (P. 47)

Aurora Levins Morales correctly anticipates that criticism will be leveled at her for not being fluent in Spanish and preferring English by those who argue that Latino/as who do not maintain their Spanish language are assimilating, and are forgetting their culture. Her class poem responds to this criticism by suggesting that she is using her middle-class advantage in the service of her people because denying her privilege and the skills that it implies would be an insult to those who came before her and struggled so that she would have the advantages that they have been denied.

Anzaldúa, in contrast to Levins Morales, Morales and Moraga, does not prioritize either Spanish or English; rather, she affirms the use of "Chicano Spanish," or "Tex-Mex." She speaks of "linguistic terrorism" as coming from all sides. Anzaldúa points out that Chicano Spanish is found to be deficient by Mexicans and Latin Americans, while Chicano English is scorned by Anglos, and she refers in this context to Chicanos as "linguistic orphans." Anzaldúa's concern is to highlight the damage that such criticism effects on the identity of the person. She writes,

> Until I can take pride in my language, I cannot take pride in myself. Until I can accept as legitimate Chicano Texas Spanish, Tex-Mex and all the other languages I speak, I cannot accept the legitimacy of myself. Until I am free to write bilingually and to switch codes without having always to translate, while I still have to speak English or Spanish when I would rather speak Spanglish, and as long as I have to accommodate the English speakers rather than having them accommodate me, my tongue will be illegitimate.

I will no longer be made to feel ashamed of existing. I will have my voice: Indian, Spanish, white. I will have my serpent's tongue—my woman's voice, my sexual voice, my poet's voice. I will overcome the tradition of silence. (P. 59)

Despite their differences, then, all four writers reject the dominant culture's attempts to silence them; and they insist on their right to use the language that best speaks to their experience, without having to translate for those who cannot or will not understand. Readers, then, especially English monolingual readers, are shaken from their linguistic complacency, particularly when they read Moraga and Anzaldúa.

Cultural Genealogy

In addition to addressing language issues, all four authors explore issues related to their cultural origins. While both Moraga and Anzaldúa affirm their Chicana and Indian roots, they acknowledge that as women the positions afforded to them in these cultures are limited. In *Getting Home Alive*, Rosario Morales and Aurora Levins Morales also affirm their Puerto Rican heritage, but Aurora tends to idealize her homeland, producing a romanticized and idyllic vision of Puerto Rico.[3] In addition, the authors seem somewhat reluctant to critique patriarchal domination in their own Latino culture. While they (especially Rosario) respond to the sexism they have experienced, they only superficially develop this analysis in their writings.

Anzaldúa and Moraga are more critical of their cultures. They both affirm what they value most about their culture, for example the closeness of the women and the stories and myths with which they grew up. Yet they do not idealize these aspects; they acknowledge their limitations and work to transform them. Anzaldúa devotes much of the text to recovering the female myths and symbols that are the basis of Chicano mythology and spirituality. She argues that the three dominating figures in Chicana history—the Virgin Guadalupe, La Malinche, and La Llorona—are all ambiguous symbols that have been subverted and used to oppress women. She reinterprets the myths concerning these female deities and reclaims a woman-centered mythology. This strategy is not an alternative to radical structural change but a means to challenge the misogynist mythology which plays an important part in the cultural history of the Chicano people.

Moraga, while discovering a profound connection to the women in her family, realizes that the allegiances of women ultimately belong to the men no matter how often they hurt and betray women. While she refuses to give up this connection, she recognizes its potential to hurt her. She writes,

> Todavía soy la hija de mi mamá. Keep thinking, it's the daughters. It's the daughters who remain loyal to the mother. She is the only woman we stand by. It is not always reciprocated. To be free means on some level to cut that painful loyalty when it begins to punish us. Stop the chain of events. La procesión de mujeres, sufriendo. . . . Free the daughter to love her own daughter. It is the daughters who are my audience. (P. 34)

Moraga explores how this strong deference to Chicano men and traditional family structures seems a necessity given the history of oppression and the threat of genocide Chicanos have experienced in the U.S. She argues that only an honest examination and transformation of the rigid sex roles in Chicano families will create the strength and unity necessary to resist the dominant culture, but acknowledges that this self-criticism of Chicano culture is strongly resisted in the community.

New Modes of Consciousness: The Mestiza

The realization that a noncontradictory, unified self is impossible within the discourses they traverse opens up the possibility of radical change for these Latina writers. All four women reject the frustration, the madness, that comes from embracing a stifling subject position offered in one of the many discourses they are produced by and invited to take up. Instead they defy prescriptions and expectations and forge new possibilities. Anzaldúa, after experiencing the illness brought about by trying to repress contradictions, arrives at a state she describes as the new mestizaje. She states,

> The new mestiza copes by developing a tolerance for contradictions, a tolerance for ambiguity. She learns to be an Indian in Mexican culture, to be a Mexican from an anglo point of view. She learns to juggle cultures. She has a plural personality, she operates in a pluralistic mode—nothing is thrust out, the good the bad the ugly, nothing rejected nothing abandoned. Not only does she sustain contradictions, she turns the ambivalence into something else. (P. 79)

Moraga attempts to bring together the lesbian and "Chicana" elements of her experience through the creation and participation in a third world women's feminist movement. Such a movement would strive for the liberation of all oppressed peoples. Moraga envisions a women's movement that does not insist that participants deny essential aspects of their identity in order to make "revolution" more acceptable to others. In this she concurs with the thinking of the Combahee River Collective (1983), a group of black feminists who in 1977 wrote,

> We are actively committed to struggling against racial, sexual, heterosexual, and class oppression and see as our particular goal the development of in-

tegrated analysis and practice based upon the fact that the major systems of oppression are interlocking. The synthesis of oppressions creates the conditions of our lives. (P. 210)

The building of a women-of-color movement presents a new series of contradictions. The traditions, cultures, and priorities of third world women differ and make connections difficult. Rosario Morales, in a piece entitled "Double Oppression," discusses the difficulty of forging connections with other women. She reports that during a workshop to heal differences between women of color, participants argued about whose particular pain was the most damaging. She leaves the workshop devastated by this attempt to rank oppressions and determined to "sew" herself together with the "thread" spun from so many places. The Moraleses, similarly to Moraga and Anzaldúa, end up accepting and embracing difference as a positive factor which if confronted and analyzed could empower a third world women's movement.

Like Audre Lorde (1984), all four authors find that it is not the differences between women that separate them, but the fear of recognizing difference, naming it, and understanding that we have been programmed to respond to difference with fear and loathing. Lorde suggests that radical change is possible only when we analyze difference and incorporate it into our lives and politics. She states,

Advocating the mere tolerance of difference between women is the grossest reformism. It is a total denial of the creative function of difference in our lives. Difference must not be merely tolerated, but seen as a fund of necessary polarities between which our creativity can spark like a dialectic. Only then does the necessity for interdependency become unthreatening. Only within that interdependency of different strengths, acknowledged and equal can the power to seek new ways of being in the world generate, as well as the courage and sustenance to act where there are no charters. (P. 111)

While Lorde is speaking of acknowledging and transforming differences between women, Moraga and Anzaldúa suggest that a similar process must first occur at a personal, individual level. Latinas must come to terms with the contradictions inherent in their own beings as mestizas before connections with others become possible. This entails overcoming the learned self-hatred that renders them immobile and incapable of acting to transform the interrelated forces which oppress all women and people of color. The new being and the new movement these authors are theorizing will analyze differences and use them to enrich their analysis and develop strategies for change.

The contradictions and barriers experienced by all four Latinas bring them to similar positions. Levins Morales and Morales in the course of the text attempt to integrate all differences in their identity. In the following stanza they trace their history and then declare themselves to be "new." They refuse to ignore who they are for anyone's convenience; their project is to integrate the various parts of their individual experiences and collective histories to create a new self. They announce,

> I am not African.
> African waters the roots of my tree, but I can not return.
>
> I am not Taína . . .
> Taíno is in me, but there is no way back.
>
> I am not European, though I have dreamt of those cities . . .
> Europe lives in me but I have no home there . . .
>
> We are new.
> They gave us life, kept us going,
> brought us to where we are.
> Born at a crossroads.
> Come, lay that dishcloth down. Eat, dear, eat.
> History made us.
> We will not eat ourselves up inside any more.
>
> And we are whole.
> (Pp. 212-13)

Similarly, Anzaldúa's new mestizaje and Moraga's third world women's movement are not stable, prescriptive positions but rather are radical because they are about producing a consciousness and a movement which does not insist on their fragmentation. The autobiographies produced by Levins Morales, Morales, Anzaldúa, and Moraga, through their form, language, and content, engage the reader in this radical, continual process. The reader also is prevented from fixing the authors in any stable position and must begin to question her desire to do so. The authors embrace a shifting and multiple identity which is in a state of perpetual transition. Anzaldúa best expresses the implications of such a politics when she predicts,

> En unas pocas centurias, the future will belong to the mestiza. Because the future depends on the breaking down of paradigms, it depends on the straddling of two or more cultures. By creating a new mythos—that is, a change in the way we perceive reality, the way we see ourselves, the way we behave—la mestiza creates a new consciousness. (P. 80)

In the work of all four authors, the power of this new consciousness is located in the continual creative motion that keeps breaking down the unitary aspect of all prescriptive paradigms offered to those who are marginalized. A narrow politics based exclusively on any of the forces that shape their experience (national origin, class, ethnicity, gender, or sexuality) is rejected, and a new "politics of the flesh" (Moraga and Anzaldúa 1983) confronting all the conditions which shape the lives of U.S. Latinas is articulated.

The importance of such a contribution for U.S. Latinas is conveyed beautifully in the following quote from a letter by nineteen-year-old Alma Ayala to Gloria Anzaldúa, written to express appreciation for the book *This Bridge Called My Back: Writings by Radical Women of Color*:

> The women writers seemed to be speaking to me, and they actually understood what I was going through. Many of you put into words feelings I have had that I had no way of expressing. . . . The writings justified some of my thoughts telling me I had a right to feel as I did. (Preface to 2nd ed., p. xvii)

Like *This Bridge Called My Back*, the autobiographies are particularly empowering to the U.S. Latinas who rarely have the opportunity to encounter texts which speak to their lives and which seek to analyze the realities and complexities of living on the borderlands. The writers resist both silence and the lies and distortions that are offered to Latinas in dominant discourses. Instead, Anzaldúa, Moraga, Levins Morales, and Morales construct a politics of personal and collective transformation which is built on the strength of difference and a disentangling of the contradictions inherent in their multiple identities.

NOTES

1. *U.S. Latina* refers to women of Latin American descent born in the United States, or those who have immigrated to the U.S. This paper considers work of two Chicanas: Cherríe Moraga and Gloria Anzaldúa, and two Puerto Ricans: Rosario Morales and Aurora Levins Morales.

Chicanas/os and Puerto Ricans are the largest Latina/o populations in the United States. Both peoples have a history of being colonized by the U.S. *Chicana/o* is a term of self-identification taken on by persons of Mexican ancestry in the U.S. context. The term may refer both to persons who were born in the U.S. but trace their background to Mexico, and to those whose families have lived for generations in what is today known as the Southwest, in the states (California, Texas, Arizona, New Mexico, Utah, and parts of Colorado) that were annexed by the U.S. from Mexico in 1848.

Puerto Rico has been a colony of the United States since 1898, when the U.S. took possession of the Caribbean island following the Spanish-American War. While the island has a population of over three million people, approximately two million Puerto Ricans reside in the continental United States. As citizenship was conferred on the Puerto Rican people in 1917, entry into the U.S. was facilitated.

The history of the Puerto Rican people is characterized by periods of mass migration to the U.S. (especially following the two world wars) and cycles of back-and-forth migration primarily determined by economic factors. The following sources provide historical and sociocultural information on Chicana/os and Puerto Ricans: Acuña (1972), Mirandé and Enríquez (1979), Lewis (1963), and Morales (1986).

2. Given the revolutionary nature of these three texts, it is interesting to note which of the publishing houses have been prepared to take the risk of publishing feminist, bilingual, and, in the case of Moraga and Anzaldúa, lesbian works. While Latino presses have in the past published bilingual editions as works that have included code-mixing, this has generally not been the case for non-Latino publishing houses. Yet these three texts, all of which to a greater or lesser extent alternate English and Spanish, were published by Anglo presses. Latino presses, which as stated before have only recently begun to publish the work of U.S. Latina women, were probably not excited by the prospect of publishing books such as Moraga's and Anzaldúa's which challenge not only the dictates of "Latino culture" but also the institution of heterosexuality. This is not to imply, however, that mainstream publishers are anxious to publish such texts either. All three texts were published by small presses. Two of the books were published by feminist concerns—Spinsters/Aunt Lute Company and Firebrand—which are relatively new women's presses, and Moraga's book was published by South End, a press that publishes leftist works.

3. The idealization of life in Puerto Rico is a tendency that is prevalent in much of the literature of U.S. Puerto Rican writing, cf. Barradas and Rodríguez 1980.

REFERENCES

Acuña, Rodolfo. 1972. *Occupied America: The Chicano's Struggle toward Liberation.* San Francisco: Canfield Press.
Adams, Mary Louise. 1989. "There Is No Place like Home: On the Place of Identity in Feminist Politics." *Feminist Review,* no. 31 (Spring).
Anzaldúa, Gloria. 1987. *Borderlands/La Frontera.* San Francisco: Spinsters/Aunt Lute.
Barradas, Efraín, and Rafael Rodríguez, eds. 1980. *Herejes y Mitificadores: Muestra de Poesía Puertorriqueña en los Estados Unidos.* Rio Piedras, P.R.: Ediciones Huracán.
Benstock, Shari, ed. 1988. *The Private Self.* Chapel Hill: University of North Carolina Press.
Bourne, Jenny. 1987. "Homelands of the Mind: Jewish Feminism and Identity Politics." *Race and Class* (Summer).
Butterfield, Stephen. 1974. *Black Autobiography in America.* Amherst: University of Massachusetts Press.
Cliff, Michelle. 1980. *Claiming an Identity They Taught Me to Despise.* Watertown, Mass.: Persephone Press.
Combahee River Collective. 1983. "A Black Feminist Statement." In Cherríe Moraga and Gloria Anzaldúa, eds., *This Bridge Called My Back.* New York: Kitchen Table: Women of Color Press.
Fox-Genovese, Elizabeth. 1988. "My Statue, My Self: Autobiographical Writings of Afro-American Women." In Shari Benstock, ed.

Jelinek, Estelle C. 1980. "Introduction: Women's Autobiography and the Male Tradition." In Estelle C. Jelinek, ed., *Women's Autobiography: Essays in Criticism.* Bloomington: Indiana University Press.

Kappeler, Susanne. 1989. "Putting the Politics Back into Sex." *Trouble and Strife,* no. 15 (Spring).

Kingston, Maxine Hong. 1979. *The Woman Warrior: Memoirs of a Girlhood among Ghosts.* New York: Vintage Books.

Lewis, Gordon K. 1963. *Puerto Rico: Freedom and Power in the Caribbean.* New York: Monthly Review Press.

Lorde, Audre. 1982. *Zami: A New Spelling of My Name.* Watertown, Mass.: Persephone Press.

———. 1984. *Sister Outsider.* New York: Crossing Press.

Mirandé, Alfredo, and Evangelina Enríquez. 1979. *La Chicana.* Chicago: University of Chicago Press.

Moraga, Cherríe. 1983. *Loving in the War Years: Lo Que Nunca Por Sus Labios.* Boston: South End Press.

Moraga, Cherríe, and Gloria Anzaldúa, eds. 1983. *This Bridge Called My Back.* New York: Kitchen Table: Women of Color Press.

Morales, Aurora Levins, and Rosario Morales. 1986. *Getting Home Alive.* New York: Firebrand Books.

Morales, Julio. 1986. *Puerto Rican Poverty and Migration.* New York: Praeger Publishers.

Ramos, Juanita, ed. 1987. *Compañeras: Latina Lesbians.* New York: Latina Lesbian History Project.

Rowbotham, Sheila. 1973. *Women's Consciousness, Man's World.* London: Penguin.

Sánchez, Rosaura. 1985. "Chicana Prose Writers: The Case of Gina Valdés and Silvia Lizárraga." In Maria Herrera-Sobek, ed., *Beyond Stereotypes: The Critical Analysis of Chicana Literature.* Binghamton: Bilingual Press/Editorial Bilingue.

Simon, Sidonie. 1987. *A Poetics of Women's Autobiography.* Bloomington: Indiana University Press.

Smith, Barbara. 1983. *Home Girls.* New York: Kitchen Table: Women of Color Press.

Stanford Friedman, Susan. 1988. "Women's Autobiographical Self: Theory and Practice." In Shari Benstock, ed.

Yarbro-Bejarano, Yvonne. 1989. "Primer Encuentro de Lesbianas Feministas Latinoamericanas y Caribeñas." *Third Woman,* vol. 4.

SOCIALIST FEMINISM

Our Bridge to Freedom

Nellie Wong

We work for enough to live each day,
    Without a day off, like the labor laws say.
The price of noodles, 12 hours' work don't pay,
    So, change our working conditions. Hey!

(Refrain)
Fellow workers, get it together,
    For prosperity in our land
Fellow workers, rise up together,
    To right things by our hand.

When we get our monthly paychecks,
    Our monthly worries merely grow,
Most of it goes for some rice and the rent—
    Our private debts we still owe.

Lifeless, as if they were poisoned,
    Are those fine young men,
Who once promised to work hard for us—
    Oh, revive your lost bravery again.

    Song of factory women, February 1973
    ("Change Our Working Conditions" 1982, 13)

This song illustrates only one of many working-class struggles being waged by women throughout the world. It shows that Korean women workers recognize their multi-issue oppression; their low wages won't pay for the price of noodles, their monthly paychecks do not alleviate their ongoing private debts, and they must take action into their own hands, independent from the men in their lives who act as if they were "poisoned" by their government's antilabor stance. South Korea's leading exports are textiles, shoes, and electronic goods—industries with a mostly female work force ("Change" 1982, 13). A primarily female work force has helped maintain Korea's economic growth. However, women workers are the lowest-paid and work under the bleakest conditions. Sister workers in the Philippines, Singapore, Japan, Hong Kong, and Taiwan also suffer long hours, unpaid overtime, and sexual harassment. The conditions of Korea's women workers are typical of the majority of Asia's industrial workers.

Women continue to be a part of the ongoing liberation movements throughout the world. In 1982, during International Women's Day, I spoke at a public forum sponsored by the Anti-Family Protection Act Coalition in Los Angeles, California, where I paid tribute to international working women:

> Women workers started the Russian Revolution.
> Women workers sparked the shipyard strikes in Poland.
> Women workers and housewives marched by the thousands to protest the inhumane, antiwoman repression in Iran.
> Women workers protested the sexist antiworker conditions in textile factories in Korea.
> Women militants fought the Kisaeng tourism/prostitution in Korea.
> Women workers formed a 100-year marriage resistance in Kwangtung, China.
> Women fighters, young and old, fought in liberation struggles in Vietnam, Nicaragua, Cuba, El Salvador, South Africa, Lebanon.
> Women workers are fighting to end nuclear testing in the Marshall Islands.

And in the United States, women continue to participate on all political fronts, from reproductive rights to union organizing, for social, economic, political, racial, and sexual equality.

Dine and Hopi women, mostly grandmothers and mothers, in 1986 were leading the resistance to the U.S. government's forced "relocation" from Big Mountain, Arizona, of people from ancestral homelands in an area jointly held by the Navajo and Hopi nations. Giant energy corporations such as Peabody Coal, Kerr McGee, and Exxon want unhampered access to the estimated 44 billion tons of high-grade coal and deposits of oil, natural gas, and uranium found on and around Big Mountain (O'Gara and Hodderson, 1986).

The resistance of women is nothing new; however, it must be seen in the context of political, social, and economic conditions in which the total emancipation of women, as a sex, is hampered. The liberation of women cannot be relegated to simply overthrowing the patriarchy because male chauvinism is not eternal, any more than racism, anti-Semitism, or anti-gay bigotry is eternal. They are all products of the historical development of private property, where a few had everything, and most had virtually nothing (Hill 1984, 19). Resistance to the patriarchal institutions of private property has always existed. Opposition to the current epoch's patriarchal institution—capitalism—is, by definition, socialist. Without overthrowing the economic system of capitalism, as socialists and communists organize to do, we cannot liberate women *and* everybody else who is also oppressed.

Socialist feminism is our bridge to freedom. By feminism, I mean the political analysis and practice to free *all* women. No woman, because of her race, class, sexuality, age, or disability, is left out. Feminism, the struggle for women's equal rights, is inseparable from socialism—but is not identical to socialism. Socialism is an economic system which reorganizes production, redistributes wealth, and redefines state power so that the exploiters are expropriated and workers gain hegemony. Feminism, like all struggles for liberation from a specific type of bondage, is a reason for socialism, a catalyst to organize for socialism, and a benefit of socialism. At the same time, feminism is decisive to socialism. Where male supremacy functions, socialism cannot, because true socialism, by definition, connotes a higher form of human relations that can't possibly exist under capitalism. Revolutionary Trotskyist feminism sees the most oppressed sections of the working class as decisive to revolution—working women and particularly working women of color. This is the theory which integrates socialism and feminism.

Socialist feminism is a radical, disciplined, and all-encompassing solution to the problems of race, sex, sexuality, and class struggle. Socialist feminism lives in the battles of all people of color, in the lesbian and gay movement, and in the class struggle. Revolutionary feminism also happens to be an integral part, a cornerstone, of every movement. It objectively answers the ideological search of black women and men. It is the political foundation of the new revolutionary vanguard: socialist feminist people of color (Hill 1984, 19).

As a Chinese American working woman, I had been searching for many years to arrive at the heart and soul of my own liberation struggle. As a long-time office worker, I was laid off after eighteen and one-half years' service with Bethlehem Steel Corporation, the second-largest steelmaker in the United States. As a Chinese American, one of seven children of Cantonese immigrants, I questioned over and over why our lives were shaped by racism and sexism and our oppression as workers in this country. Historically, our lives as Chinese Americans are linked to those of other Asians, all people of color—of blacks who have been enslaved, and who are still fighting for their civil rights; of Japanese Americans who were incarcerated during World War II; and of other groups of workers who were brought in to build America.

I did not have the opportunity to attend college immediately after I graduated from high school. Economics, and the Confucianist and feudal ideology pervasive in the Chinese American community, dictated my taking a secretarial job at the age of seventeen. As a young office worker, I learned that my secretarial career was supposed to be temporary—that if I met the "right" man, got married, and had children, I would become a "real" woman fulfilling what society ordained; and that in itself, life as a woman worker had no value, particularly when that woman worker took shorthand, typed, and filed for a living.

My feminist consciousness began to take hold when I got married and when I began college in my mid-thirties while still working full time. Silenced most of my life, I began to articulate my experiences through creative writing courses. My seemingly personal and private deprivation and angst as a Chinese American working woman began to express itself in a social milieu—with other women, other Asian Americans, other people of color, other feminists, and other workers. What I had thought was personal and private was truly political, social, and public. What a jolt it was to realize what I had learned from a capitalist bourgeois society— through the public school system and the workplace—that as a woman-of-color worker, I was simply an individual left to my own capacities and wiles! What a revelation, as long in coming as it was, to learn that workers everywhere were connected to one another—that it was our labor that provided wealth for a few, and that a class analysis of our lives was essential to find the root causes of our multifaceted oppression.

My development to integrate all parts of me—my gender, my ethnicity, my class, and my worker status—grew by leaps and bounds when I joined Radical Women and the Freedom Socialist party, two socialist feminist organizations which integrated the study of class, race, sex, and sexuality as interlocking roots of the capitalist system. Not only did we study, but we were consistently active in the democratic movements for radical social change.

To speak seriously as one who is committed to building a socialist feminist society at home and abroad takes real change; it takes examining one's attitudes which have been shaped by a powerful capitalist system through the institutions of the state, the schools, the media, the church, and monogamous marriage. I had absorbed "my place." I had kept silent because I was Asian and a woman, and I had been determined not to appear too smart because I wouldn't be able to attract and hold a man.

Attending college at night as an adult, being married, working full-time, and organizing and socializing with feminists and radicals brought me to socialist feminism: the belief that unless every woman, every lesbian and gay man, every worker, and every child is free, none of us is free. Such is the beauty and triumph of radical, social knowledge. Such is the basis upon which I have committed myself to working for a socialist feminist society. Such is the foundation upon which the leadership of all the oppressed is being built.

Socialist feminism is the viable alternative to capitalism and world imperialism, which use sexism, racism, colonialism, heterosexism, homophobia, and class oppression to keep us down. Although revolutions waged in Soviet Russia, Cuba, Vietnam, Nicaragua, and China have brought about changes, oppression against women, sexual minorities, and workers still exists. While we can learn from the gains made by women in countries where revolutions have taken place, many inequalities still exist, and nowhere have women achieved total liberation. Gay oppression and racism still exist in these countries, and there are far too few democratic freedoms. For example, abortion rights are denied in Nicaragua, as the influence of the Catholic church dominates in Latin America. In China, feminism—at least officially—is deemed to be a product of decadent, bourgeois capitalist society.

While true socialism is to be strived for in each context, socialism cannot exist within a single country but must be a worldwide system, supplanting world capitalism. The nations of the world are wholly interdependent, and without an international system of socialism, countries can share only their poverty, rather than the world's wealth. Worldwide socialism will break the stranglehold of worldwide imperialism. It will end the exploitation of one country for the profit of another country's capitalist class. And that is why the U.S., as the most powerful capitalist country in the world, dominates the global market, and why there is a need for a socialist feminist revolution in the U.S. Socialism alone is not the answer. Feminism alone is not the answer. There won't be a socialist revolution in this country without socialist feminists in the lead, and there won't be true emancipation of women without a socialist overthrow of capitalism. Socialism without feminism is a contradiction in terms (Hill 1984, 21).

Our oppression as workers is rooted in the capitalist system. As women workers of color, we get the message, loud and clear, that if we only pull ourselves up by our own bootstraps, we will "succeed" as members of a capitalist society, and miraculously, our multi-issue oppressions as women and people of color will disappear. Within the women's movement, bourgeois feminist ideology teaches us that if we take the path of *partial* resistance, we might just make it to the executive boardroom. And if we do, we can become one of the bosses to stifle worker militance, and to uphold the profit-seeking status quo. Or radical feminist ideology teaches us that if we just overthrow the patriarchy, women will truly be free. Radical feminism does not take into account the oppression of gay men and men of color.

Multi-issue feminism is necessary to fight back and win against all forms of oppression. As my Asian American comrade Emily Woo Yamasaki says, "I cannot be an Asian American on Monday, a woman on Tuesday, a lesbian on Wednesday, a worker/student on Thursday, and a political radical on Friday. I am all these things every day." We are discriminated against as *workers* on the economic plane, as racial *minorities* on the economic and social planes, and as women on all three planes—economic, social, and domestic/family. We must cope with the world and with men as a unique category of people—women-of-color workers. We have been subjected to humiliations and brutalities unknown to most whites or even to men of color.

Feminism, in general, and socialist feminism, in particular, do have a vibrant history of militant struggle in this country. Today, increasing numbers of women of color and their allies are calling for an end to racism, sexism, and homophobia. Black women, Chicanas and Latinas, Native American women, and Asian/Pacific women have already demonstrated to the world their capacity for taking upon their shoulders the responsibility for social leadership. This talent and drive stem directly from the triple oppression unique to our position.

Women leaders have emerged from the radical movements of the 1950s, 1960s, and 1970s. In 1959, a black woman, Rosa Parks, refused to move to the back of the bus, inspiring the Montgomery Bus Boycott. In 1974, a Jewish woman, Clara Fraser, walked out on strike at Seattle City Light to protest unfair working conditions. Clara won a seven-year fight against the public utility based on a historic suit of political ideology and sex discrimination. Her fight and victory inspired a class-action suit against the utility by many more women workers who were fed up with sexism and racism on the job!

In 1982, a Chinese-Korean American lesbian, Merle Woo, was fired from her job as a lecturer in Asian American Studies at the University of California, Berkeley, for openly criticizing the right-wing moves of the Ethnic Studies Department. Merle was fired unfairly, though she received outstanding student evaluations and had been promised Security of Employment when she was first hired. Her firing, based on the pretext of an arbitrary rule limiting lecturers' employment to four years, was imposed upon two thousand lecturers throughout the university system. Although the Public Employment Relations Board (PERB) had ruled that Merle and other affected lecturers were to be rehired with back pay, the university appealed the decision. Merle then filed a federal complaint charging discrimination based on race, sex, sexuality, and political ideology and abridgment of her First Amendment free-speech rights, which were the real reasons she was fired. In 1984, she was reinstated at the university. Merle fought back by organizing with the Merle Woo Defense

Committee, composed of people of various communities who believed in the necessity of unifying around all of the issues.[1]

Henry Noble, a Jewish socialist feminist man, also fought an employment-rights case in Seattle. After several years with the Hutchinson Cancer Research Center, Henry's hours were reduced to 75 percent time. Why? Because he actively and successfully organized a union with his primarily female coworkers.

The workplace, where workers—people of color and white—often work side by side, offers a social arena in which the struggle against multi-issue oppressions can take place. Clearly, class analysis and action strike at the heart of capitalist exploitation of workers, whose rights are denied as workers, as women, and as people of color. The economy of capitalism could not have survived as long as it has if it did not depend on sexism and racism to split workers apart, and on the immense profits from paying people of color and women low, low wages. After all, combined, we represent the majority of workers, and that adds up to a lot of profits (Hill 1984, 19)!

Our politics and strategies must be forged through political action independent of the twin parties of capitalism, the Republicans and the Democrats. It was two Democratic presidents—Roosevelt and Truman—who signed Executive Order 9066 and dropped the first atomic bombs on the Japanese cities of Hiroshima and Nagasaki during World War II. Militarism engenders profits. Defense contracts and the manufacture of guns, airplanes, and bombs perpetuate the warmongering drive of the capitalists, both Republicans and Democrats. A labor party could further our multi-issue political struggle, and that labor party must be led by women of color, lesbians, and feminist men. Its program would express the interests and needs of workers and their allies. It would provide an effective alternative and challenge to the boss-party politics dominating the electoral arena. It would be democratic. Anyone could join who agreed with the program, and it would be ruled by the will of the majority, not the labor bureaucrats.

But whether the road taken is via a labor party or some other organization or a combination of strategies for struggle, solidarity and victory will be realized only through the understanding that in unity there is strength. There must be solidarity and mutual aid between all the oppressed for the genuine liberation of any one group. But that unity can come about only if it is based solidly on the demands of the most oppressed strata. We need the unity of blacks, Native Americans, Jews, Chicanos, Latinos, Asian Americans, Puerto Ricans, the working class, the elderly, youth, women, sexual minorities, the disabled—all of the oppressed groups—to win our liberation.

And it is women, especially women of color, who are equipped by our bottommost socioeconomic position to serve as the vanguard on the way to solidarity. We must because nobody needs revolutionary social change as much as we—working women of all races and orientations—need it to survive. We can honor and support the revolutionary and working-class struggles throughout the world by building a socialist feminist revolution here on the soil of the United States. The American revolution will be decisive to international socialism because when U.S. capitalism is dismantled, world capitalism will be dismantled, along with its tyrannical and oppressive forms of institutionalized racism, sexism, and homophobia, and its global greed for profits. While we fight for a socialist feminist society, however, we must, at the same time, fight for reforms under capitalism. Reforms alone, though, are not enough, for they provide only a band-aid solution to the tremendous political, social, and economic problems that we face.

Radical labor history and women's history have taught us that women workers/leaders of all races will lead the way for our total emancipation, as shown in this poem titled "A Woman":

I am a woman
and if I live
I fight and
if I fight
I contribute to
the liberation
of all Women
and so victory
is born even in the darkest hours. ("Good News" 1980, 19)

A new song of factory women, under a vibrant socialist feminist society, might go like this:

We work for enough to live each day.
    With three days off, like the labor laws say.
The price of noodles, 15 minutes' work will pay.
    So, our working conditions are better. Hey!

(Refrain)
Fellow workers, get it together,
    For prosperity in our land
Fellow workers, rise up together,
    We've made things right with our hand.

When we get our monthly paychecks,
    Our monthly worries do not grow,
Some it goes for some rice and the rent—

Our private debts are part of the old.

Spirited as they smile and work with us
    Are those fine young men,
Who promise to work and keep fighting back
    Oh, our bravery is revived again.

Sisters, brothers, we now have time
    To write and paint and dance together
Our backs no longer ache from working all day
    We love our children, with them we learn and play.

Notes

This essay was first presented as a speech at the conference "Common Differences: Third World Women and Feminist Perspectives," held at the University of Illinois, Urbana-Champaign, April 11–13, 1983. This version contains changes and updates since that presentation.

1. In June 1986, Merle Woo was terminated with no consideration for reappointment from her position as a visiting lecturer in the Graduate School of Education, University of California, Berkeley. Woo has filed a grievance with the American Federation of Teachers (AFT) based on UC's violation of her settlement agreement and the Academic Personnel Manual.

References

"Change Our Working Conditions." 1982. *Connexions: An International Women's Quarterly,* no. 6 (Fall).
"Good News for Women." 1980. *Asian Women's Liberation,* no. 2 (April).
Hill, Monica. 1984. "Patriarchy, Class and the Left." (Speech) *Discussion Bulletin* (of Freedom Socialist party, Los Angeles, California) 1, no. 1 (February):19–21.
O'Gara, Debra, and Guerry Hoddersen. 1986. "Dine Elders Resist Eviction from Big Mountain." *The Freedom Socialist* 9, no. 3:2.
Radical Women. *Radical Women Manifesto.* Seattle, Wash.: Radical Women Publications.

"WE CANNOT LIVE WITHOUT OUR LIVES"*

White Women, Antiracism, and Feminism

Ann Russo

> Our racism divides us from our allies, aligns
> us with the enemy, and prevents us from
> participating in the realization of any
> version of a new, just culture.
> —Moore and Wolverton (1981)

> What threatens our movement . . . is our
> refusal to acknowledge that to change the
> world we have to change ourselves—even
> sometimes our most cherished, block-hard
> convictions. . . . I must confess I hate the
> thought of this. Change don't come easy.
> For anyone. But this state of war we live in,
> this world on fire provides us with no other
> choice.
> —Moraga (1983)

For many years as an active feminist I thought issues of race and class were important to deal with in the women's movement, yet until I began to work and hang out with women of color,[1] I did not fully understand the enormous ramifications of multiracial groups of women developing feminist theory and working together for social change. For seven years, while I was in graduate school and living in Champaign-Urbana, as a result of my involvement with the "Common Differences"

*Barbara Deming, *We Cannot Live without Our Lives* (1974).

conference,[2] I worked and hung out with a wonderful group of women, black, Latina, third world,[3] Jewish, and white, lesbian and heterosexual, coming from poor, working-class, and middle-class backgrounds. We talked about our lives, discussed and argued politics, ate, sang, and danced, as well as organized events, encouraged each other in our work, and formed groups working against racism in the context of local feminist organizing. It was from my experiences that I eventually understood, at a basic level, Cherríe Moraga's statement that "so often the women seem to feel no loss, no lack, no absence when women of color are not involved; therefore there is little desire to change the situation. This has hurt me deeply" (Moraga 1981, 33). When I read this in 1981, I understood what she was saying intellectually, and I felt guilty about the limitations of much feminist theory and the exclusionary practices of many parts of the women's movement in which I had been previously active, but I didn't realize the enormity of what I had lost because of these limitations until I began to work actively with women of color. This loss feels even greater now since I moved away from this community to Boston, where I have encountered few multiracial groups of feminists working together for social change. However, because of my experiences in Champaign-Urbana, I know the importance of integrating race, class, sexual, ethnic, and other identifications into my daily life and politics, and the possibility and necessity of working with women different from myself on issues which affect all of us, particularly, for me, the sexual violence women face in our public and private lives.

The women's movement and feminist perspectives in the United States have been associated primarily with white women, though this is not because many women of color have not identified with the basic issues or even stated goals of parts of the movement, but rather because many of the more visible organizations and leaders identified as feminist have been white (see Joseph 1981, 20–42). Many women of color have not been integrally involved in the more visible self-identified feminist organizations for reasons alluded to and elaborated upon by the authors in this book (also see Moraga and Anzaldúa 1981, Davis 1981, hooks 1981). Yet in the past ten years, we have seen in this country (and around the world) a pronounced development and growth of specifically feminist theory, activism, and organizations by, for, and about women of color. Some of this work has been in response to the limitations (due to racism, classism, homophobia, etc.) of previous feminist theorists, activists, and organizations, and much of it also grows from women's home communities and historical traditions. At any rate, women of color have challenged white feminists to deal with racism and classism, arguing that if feminism is about the empowerment of *all* women and change in the conditions of *all* women's lives, change is needed within the women's movement itself. Given these challenges, many white feminists have had to respond and make changes in our analyses and politics. This essay is in part an explication and analysis of some of the responses of white feminists that I have seen and participated in, their results, and some suggestions for the directions white feminists might take both individually and collectively in our work, both separately and together with women of color, to build a stronger women's movement.

What Does Race Have to Do with White Women?

Central to developing feminist theory and organizing around specific issues, I feel white women must analyze our relationship to race, ethnicity, class, and sexuality. Denying or ignoring our privilege as white and/or middle-class women will not build a strong women's movement, nor will minimizing the specifics of sexual oppression. If we want to be involved in a movement which speaks from and to the commonality as well as diversity among women, it is necessary for us to acknowledge our privilege, understand how the conditions of our lives are connected to and made possible by the conditions of other women's lives, and use what we have gained from that privilege in the service of social change. In addressing racism, bell hooks (1989) has suggested, and I agree, that it might be helpful to speak of white supremacy, rather than just racism. White supremacy correctly places the responsibility on white women and men, rather than focusing on people of color simply as victims of an amorphous racism. "White supremacy" as a concept forces us to look power directly in the face, and when we do that there is less room for denial, guilt, and paternalism in trying to change it, since it shifts the focus from people of color to white people (see Katz 1978). It seems that we (white women) may be moved to action, then, because nonaction would necessarily imply acceptance of the status quo. To move away from responses of denial and guilt, which promote immobilization and passivity, toward responsibility, action, and mutual exchange with women of color is key to disestablishing white supremacy within the context of the women's movement.

Part of the problem is that many of us white feminists still do not see racism as our issue, as significantly affecting our lives and survival. Typically when we (white women) raise the issue of racism, we tend to focus solely on the lives and experiences of women of color—black, Puerto Rican, Mexican American, Asian, and American Indian. As a result, working on the problem of racism becomes a matter of "helping" *these* women out, as if the problem of racism were "their" problem. Focusing on white supremacy means that we look at racism as a white problem and issue. While it is true that racism bears its impact on "minority women" in the

United States (or third world women around the world), racism originates
with and is perpetuated by white people. Moreover, race intricately shapes
our identities, experience, and choices in our lives, both in giving us
privileged status with respect to women of color, and also in shaping the
specifics of the oppression we face as women. Not seeing race as a white
issue is part of the privilege of being white (see Frye 1983). Understanding
the impact of race on our lives—what we gain and what we lose—would
encourage us to see the issue of racism as our issue. As Barbara Smith
(1982, 49) suggests, "You have to comprehend how racism distorts and
lessens your own lives as white women—that racism affects your chances
for survival, too, and that it is very definitely your issue."

Just as women of color insist on the specificity of their experience in
developing theory, I think white women also need to insist on the specificities of our experiences with respect to race. As a radical feminist who
believes that the "personal is political" and that the best theory and
politics come from an understanding of the materiality of our lives—
economically, physically and bodily, racially, sexually, emotionally, psy-
chologically—I believe that theory and politics addressing the interconnections of race, sex, sexuality, class, and ethnicity must also come from
a close analysis of our own daily lives as well as the lives of others. Some
white feminists have begun to describe and develop such theory and
politics. For instance, Minnie Bruce Pratt (1984), in *Yours in Struggle*, offers
a very insightful analysis of how race has affected her life experiences
and political perspective as a white woman who grew up in the South.
She offers invaluable commentary on the ways in which her understandings of race, class, and anti-Semitism have grown through the challenges
of women of color—personally, socially, and politically; and she demonstrates how her identity influences her understanding of history (individual and collective) and her day-to-day life experiences. Pratt and
Adrienne Rich (1986), among others, offer important suggestions for a
feminism and politics which take seriously racism and other power divisions among women (see also Lillian Smith 1949). White feminists
around the country have also formed antiracism consciousness-raising
groups, recognizing, as Terry Wolverton suggests, "how much more empowered we would be if we would admit and study our racism, actively
pursue solutions to it, and will ourselves to change" (Moore and Wolverton 1981, 44). She further suggests that "it was only by examining
race and racism in my own life, my relationships with people of color,
my identity and function as a white lesbian, that I was able to translate
my analysis into action" (Moore and Wolverton 1981, 45). These efforts
are essential in our work toward social justice, equality, and mutual respect, both within and outside the women's movement, and much more
needs to be done.

Some Responses of White Feminists to Challenges of Racism

White feminist responses to challenges of racism and classism have not generally led to substantial change in the overall women's movement. Women of color have been forced to continue arguing for the same basic issues in feminist political organizing, women's studies courses, and conferences. Issues of representation, accountability, responsibility, and equal sharing of power and control continue to be major problems in feminist organizing. This has been due in part to white feminists' not seeing racism as fundamentally a white issue, a feminist issue, and one which affects all women, not just women of color.

There are a number of paths which white feminists can take in dealing with the reality of racism, both in the general society and within the context of the women's movement. First, of course, we could, and some do, completely avoid the issue and just continue working in the same ways with the same analyses and with the same women as if there weren't a large group of women left out of our politics and vision. We could also, and some do, acknowledge that racism exists, and see that our organization or women's studies course or event doesn't appeal to or include women of color, and in response add race and class to our list of issues, or a book or two to our reading list, or a woman of color to our panel, though this clearly leads to tokenism and little change in our overall understanding of the issues. In response to this problem, we could, and again some do, retreat from the problem and continue to leave out women of color—thinking this is better than tokenism. And some of us retreat altogether from feminism, thinking that it has been doomed from the start in addressing issues of racism, and so we should use our energy in other areas. Basically I don't believe any of these are effective responses to challenges of racism because they do not contribute to transforming our existing frameworks for addressing sexism and misogyny in the face of differences and divisions among women, nor do they honestly involve women of color as central to the theory and practice of feminism.

Simply adding women of color to a list of women's issues, I would argue, actually leads to guilt and condescension, as well as to a partial and limiting politics and vision. An illustrative example of the inadequacies of an "add-on" approach to race and racism can be drawn from my own experience as a participant in a training session at a community rape crisis center which was primarily white. In addressing the issue of racism, both within the organization and in preparing us for women-of-color rape victims/survivors, one evening of the training was devoted to discussing racism and women of color, while the rest of the sessions assumed "generic" women (which translates into white). With this marginalization, women of color became "special cases" and were defined solely as victims—given race, sex, and class, and racism itself was seen as separate from the overall context of rape, and important only when dealing with women of color. The result was that potential women-of-color callers were made doubly other and considered "problems" in terms of how we, as white women, would approach them. Moreover, racism was discussed primarily as stereotypes and misperceptions due to growing up in a racist culture, while little attention was given to the context of power in the relationships among and between white and black women and men, or to the importance of white responsibility (personally, socially, institutionally) in addressing the interconnections of sexual violence and racism (historically, institutionally, culturally). The group climate in the room during this training session tended to be one of guilt for being white and for being part of a racist culture, and many of the women noted their resulting discomfort with people of color (with no analysis of the guilt or possible resolutions to the discomfort). Also, since women of color were mostly described as doubly and triply oppressed, and very much "other" from us in the room, some women expressed condescension toward potential women-of-color callers on the crisis line. At the same time, these same women expressed fear at the prospect of angry women of color who might not want to talk with white women. These dynamics were at least in part a result of how race was addressed in our training and of the place of women of color in the overall agenda, and I think are responsible for making respect and the possibility of mutual exchange between white women and women of color next to impossible.

In contrast, I would suggest that we approach race as integral to sexism and misogyny, not simply as an example of it, and recognize in our analysis and politics that race affects all women, including white women (by virtue of the fact that we are defined racially as are all people of color). Analyzing the intersections of race, sex, class, and sexuality in the incidence of rape, the impact of rape on women and the communities we live in, and social and institutional responses to rape is essential to understanding the intricacies and complexities of violence against women. I try to do this, for instance, in my course "Violence against Women" at MIT. Currently, my method is to raise the general societal and institutional frameworks of racism, classism, homophobia, and anti-Semitism, particularly, though not exclusively, as they are intertwined with sexism and misogyny, at the beginning of the course (see, for instance, Davis 1987; "Violence against Women and Race," special issue of *Aegis: Magazine on Ending Violence against Women* [March/April 1979]; Burns 1986; Pharr 1986; Beck 1988). Throughout the rest of the course we discuss the centrality of these to understanding in part the incidence of rape but also, and even more important, the sources of violence. We discuss how these frameworks are drawn upon as rationales and explanations of rape, sometimes by family, friends, and community, and most certainly by lawyers, doctors, judges, journalists, etc., in attempts to downplay the sexual violence and/or blame it on the women themselves. When race and racism become integral to our discussions from the beginning, then the "otherness" implied and magnified when we deal specifically with women of color does not as readily emerge, while at the same time, differences and divisions among women are acknowledged and analyzed.

When we cease to make women of color fundamentally different and opposed, then I think we can work more effectively *with* women, not *for* women of color. A special focus on racism and homophobia is still necessary within organizations and in women's studies courses, but unless we address race (and class, sexuality, ethnicity, looks) as integral to sexism and misogyny, our work remains fragmented, white women remain at the center of analysis and activism, and work against violence against women (or whatever issues) will at best be fragmentary and diluted. Evelyn Nakano Glenn (1985), suggesting the ramifications for addressing the experience of diverse women in our teaching, writes "we will attain a clearer sense of ourselves and our connection to others. We will find that our histories and experiences are not just diverse, they are intertwined and interdependent."

Another response to challenges of racism, mostly, I would argue, encouraged by those identified with the left, has been to abandon or dismiss feminist politics altogether, arguing that they are essentially white and middle-class. Such abandonment fails to address the issues raised by women of color, and ignores the fact that we ourselves continue to be white and middle-class. Moreover, it obscures the fact that Marxism and socialism (theory and practice) operate under similar limitations and biases. From my experience in many left groups, and evident in the writings of leftists about feminism, white leftist men and some white women seem to take great pleasure in attacking white middle-class women and feminism (see Delphy 1984 for an excellent discussion of this phenomenon). From their perspective, white middle-class women, by virtue of race and class, are not oppressed, and/or if so are unworthy of work for social change. And, white feminists certainly take a lot of shit—as do any women of color who hang out with white feminists—because at some level there is a fundamental denial of women's oppression *as women* (that is, on the basis of gender). In this case, it seems that some white feminists have decided that to deal with racism (and/or classism, imperialism, etc.), they must deny their own oppression as women and/or abandon feminist analyses of the conditions of women's lives (particularly radical feminist analyses which analyze male power and domination), and instead focus on issues which seemingly affect women and men equally (working-class, poor, people of color). This is not to say that there is no racism or classism on the part of white feminists, nor that some feminist theories/analyses do not have significant race and class limitations; rather, I am questioning the response of simply abandoning feminism. I would suggest instead that white feminists take the challenges of racism seriously, work to transform ourselves and our politics, and work with women of color to build a stronger feminist movement.

In the last several years, I think there has been a movement of feminists out of specifically feminist and lesbian organizations into male political organizations structured around international issues, particularly Central America and South Africa. I am *not* saying that these issues are not important feminist concerns, but I am questioning the movement *out of* feminist and lesbian organizations, many times away from issues we are facing in our home communities (which are equally embedded in race, class, and sex), and away from strong feminist analysis which critiques the world from the perspective of women, under the guise of being antiracist and not wanting to be associated with white middle-class feminism. It seems questionable to me that many activist women are ignoring women's experience of rape, child sexual assault, sexual harassment, and wife battering, as well as the serious setbacks in reproductive rights and child custody, and embracing perspectives which deny or minimize the integral relationship of sexism and misogyny to national and international issues.

In other words, I am questioning the gender-neutral analysis and politics that I see being espoused by many feminists active in groups struggling around international issues. I do not accept the view that feminism is relevant only for white middle-class women. In contrast, I think we should not retreat from feminism, but work toward making the movement larger, not smaller, and develop analyses and politics which at their base are feminist, and which address the interconnections and intricacies of racism, classism, and imperialism within the context of sexism and misogyny. There are some feminist activists and theorists now doing this kind of work, and we should work to build these politics so they become the norm within the women's movement.

Another related response to challenges of race or class has been for white middle-class feminists to deny who we are in order to work for the betterment of less-privileged women. When I first started focusing on racism and classism within the women's movement, I accepted the viewpoint that white middle-class women and white lesbians were simply less oppressed and had not suffered, and that we should be more concerned with the "real" struggles of women of color, poor women, working-class women, third world women. And within this context it was understood that raising the issue of lesbianism (or sexism, misogyny) would necessarily alienate women of color (of course, here assuming that lesbians of color didn't exist, or if they did, would not feel lesbianism is a significant part of their life, and/or that radical feminists of color don't exist). In the initiation and organization of the "Common Differences: Third World Women and Feminist Perspectives" conference (1983), for instance, I accepted the view that for the conference to succeed, lesbianism and radical feminism would have to take a back seat, especially for me in that I was one of the co-coordinators of the conference. The homophobia exhibited during the meetings, from choice of speakers to some women's decision to work with us as a group, reinforced our fears, but no direct challenges were made to the homophobia for fear of alienating women of color and third world women. Latina lesbians were the only invited lesbian speakers from outside the community (and the only out lesbians of color who were in the formal program), and this was because the main Latina involved in the organizing agreed to their participation (she too being a closeted lesbian at the time).

As a result, lesbians, particularly the Latina lesbians because of their visibility as major speakers, were singled out and attacked for speaking to lesbian issues, and lesbianism became a much-contested topic at the conference, despite the fact that in reality lesbians were underrepresented. In retrospect I deeply regret not insisting on lesbian representation, and not directly dealing with the homophobia. Instead we allowed homophobic women and politics to intimidate us into silence, in the name of not alienating women of color and imposing our own biases.

After the conference, seeing the results of our inability and unwillingness to deal directly with homophobia, I came out as a lesbian to the organizing committee. I found much more openness, curiosity, and interest than I had anticipated. The homophobia did not disappear, but at least it was out on the table for discussion. As a result, we were able to discuss more candidly and honestly our commonalities as well as our differences, both in life and in our political perspectives, and our future work together recognized and even used these differences as positive and enriching, rather than as destructive. As Audre Lorde (1981, 99) has suggested, and I have now learned from experience, "difference must be not merely tolerated, but seen as a fund of necessary polarities between which our creativity can spark like a dialectic. Only then does the necessity for interdependency become unthreatening. Only within that interdependency of different strengths, acknowledged and equal, can the power to seek new ways to actively 'be' in the world generate, as well as the courage and sustenance to act where there are not charters." I learned from this experience that in working with women of color with mutuality and respect, I must not deny who I am—the lesbian part of me, the white part of me, the middle-class part of me, the woman part of me; and moreover,

I need not presume what others can and cannot deal with based on national, racial, or economic grouping.

Racism and Power in the Women's Movement

White supremacy, in the context of the women's movement as in the society generally, is not simply a matter of ideology, ideas, stereotypes, images, and/or misguided perceptions. It is about power and control, be it in terms of money, construction of ideology, or control over organizational agenda. When I began to take seriously the problems of racism and classism within the movement, I really thought that once they were pointed out, white women would make a commitment to change—and would not strive to always retain control. Of course, in retrospect, I cannot believe how naive I was (and sometimes continue to be). Since I have become more aware of how racism operates within the movement, primarily through my work and social relationships with women of color, I am more attuned to the resistance and even hostility women of color face when issues of power and control are raised.

For instance, in the planning of a women's studies conference, a group of friends formed a multiracial group of women committed to making sure that underrepresented women's issues would be central in programming and that women of color would be actively engaged as participants in the conference. We started out as a cooperative group working with the larger committee organizing the conference. Yet from the start we were viewed as hostile. Interestingly, the group was characterized and talked about as if it consisted only of women of color (and in fact mostly black), even though it was made up of black and Latina as well as white (Christian-raised and Jewish) women, and a mixture of lesbian and heterosexual students and community women. Our eagerness to participate was almost consistently analyzed as antagonistic and threatening; for example, at a meeting of a cultural arts committee, when we challenged the lack of representation of women of color and questioned the criteria being used for "good art," the group of white women were very defensive and resistant to our involvement. They kept saying, "Just give us names," or "We're doing outreach and we'll take care of it." While it was acceptable (although barely) to have some input, so as to diversify the arts component of the conference, they wanted to be in control of who was asked and how the women were approached. They refused to work cooperatively and share the power of decisionmaking with women of color, and interpreted the meeting as a failure because of black women's hostility and anger, not white women's racism and control. Their behavior reminded me of the many meetings in leftist organizations where feminists have been characterized as manhaters for criticizing a group for its male dominance. Rather than being similarly alarmed and upset that women of color had been left out, the women were defensive and guilt-ridden, and so no change took place.

Change must occur, as in any other arena, at the level of leadership and access to resources. And for this to happen, white women must let go of control in more than a token way. In doing so, I think we'll find out (as I already have from my own experience) that we have so much to gain, individually and as a movement, from such changes. Bettina Aptheker (1982, 15), addressing race and class issues within the context of women's studies, suggests,

> If we were, however, to assent to a relational equality with women of color; accept leadership from women of color; respect the diverse cultures, heritages, and racial pride of women of color; steep ourselves in the literature, the history, and the lives of women of color—we would begin to understand that their collective knowledge and experience form a serious, vital center from which to view the world, and the place of women within it. This, in combination with our own experiences, heritages, struggles, and intimate knowledge of the oppressor, would make a formidable alliance indeed.

This kind of challenge, however, is quite difficult to institute given already existing hierarchies in many organizations. White feminists within these organizations must break the patterns and power dynamics which keep us in control. This means that white women must not automatically assume positions of power (in theory or in practice), or participate in policies and practices which facilitate race and class hierarchies in groups. We must confront and challenge other white women on racist and sexist practices, not in self-righteousness but as a practice toward building equality among all of us. Basically, white middle-class women must give up sole control of jobs and resources, of organizational purpose and structure, of political agenda, of style and tradition. In truth, white women will have to give up power, and while the changes will be difficult for some of us, if not many, they are necessary if we are committed to equality within the movement and in society.

From Guilt to Outrage

Before we can truthfully and authentically work against racism and simultaneously make alliances with women of color, I believe we must acknowledge our own pain and suffering, so that our connection with women of color is one of mutual desire and need, not pity or arrogance. I do my best work in confronting racism within myself, within the white lesbian and feminist community, and in society generally when I do not lose sight of sexism, misogyny, and homophobia, particularly that which has borne itself out on my mind, heart, and body. As Cherríe Moraga (1981, 53) has so eloquently suggested, "Without an emotional, heartfelt grappling with the source of our own oppression, without naming the enemy within ourselves and outside of us, no authentic, non-hierarchical connection among oppressed groups can take place." By facing the ways in which I have been oppressed—through sexual abuse and violence, male domination, and homophobia—in my family, in the educational community, and in the larger society, I am more able to empathize with the oppression of women of color, in both its similarities and differences. When I have denied the abuse I have suffered, primarily through men's sexual violence in my family and interpersonal relationships, and when I've seen myself as only privileged, I have been less able to connect with women of color because I see myself as too different, and as only an oppressor. The more I have come face to face with the reality of my life and of how skin and class privilege have not always "protected" me (though clearly I have reaped many benefits as well), the more I have come to understand how my survival is intricately linked with the survival of women of color and that real freedom can be a reality only when all of us are free. Moreover, I have found that when I am not in denial, and when I am in touch with my own enormous grief and anger at the conditions of our lives, I am best able to connect with the grief and anger of women of color, in terms of sexual violence and oppression as well as of the complexities of race and class in determining each of our experiences. I am also, then, best able to hear, feel, and take seriously the anger women of color feel toward white feminists about our racism, exclusionary practices, and limited politics, because I can empathize with that anger, and I can see that the resolution is active change, not defensiveness and guilt.

We, white feminists, must learn to listen to the anger of women of color and be similarly outraged about racism, rather than guilty, and to recognize that we are not powerless in outrage, particularly as white women. It is very difficult not to feel guilty as white women in the face of the oppression of women of color, and I think that many white feminists may feel genuinely bad about racism, but do not know what to do—our guilt and feelings of hopeless responsibility lead many of us to passivity and/or defensiveness, both of which maintain our position of power.

The movement of consciousness from guilt and defensiveness to outrage has been the most difficult and challenging for white feminists. I think this has to do in part with the reality of our identity and thus the loyalty (conscious or unconscious) we feel as white people. While white feminists have directed our anger at white men for their sexual (and other) atrocities, there remains a common historical and cultural heritage which carries with it a certain familiarity and even subconscious loyalty to our skin and class privilege. This familiarity may seem very appealing, particularly in the face of the anger of women of color, given the lack of a known and well-established historical and cultural tradition between women of color and white women. We (white women) may find it easier to retreat from women of color, or defend ourselves as whites, or feel immobilized by guilt, rather than actively engage with women of color on our historical, political, and social mistrust and antagonism.

In dealing with the challenges of racism, I think we must accept that we *are* privileged as white people, and through our actions and inactions we have purposefully (or not) participated in and benefited from race and class (if middle-class) privilege in this society. This does not mean, however, that we are incapable of action and change, or that we are always/ already oppressors. As Barbara Smith (1984, 77) suggests,

> Being honest about our differences is painful and requires large doses of integrity. As I've said in discussions of racism with white women who are sometimes overwhelmed at the implications of their whiteness, no one on earth had any say whatsoever about who or what they were born to be. You can't run the tape backward and start from scratch, so the question is, what are you going to do with what you've got? How are you going to deal responsibly with the unalterable facts of who and what you are, of having or not having privilege and power? I don't think anyone's case is inherently hopeless. It depends on what you decide to do once you're here, where you decide to place yourself in relationship to the ongoing struggle for freedom.

Thus while we cannot change who we are racially, ethnically, or nationally, we can change to whom and what we remain loyal. When we respond to challenges of racism solely at the level of defensiveness and/ or guilt, we are still limiting ourselves to our position and identity as oppressors.

Audre Lorde's writing has much to offer us as we work to develop social and political alliances with women different from ourselves, particularly when those differences have to do with power and historical mistrust. In speaking of the anger between women of color and white women who come together to define and build a feminist politics not limited by race and class bias, Lorde (1984, 129) writes: "Anger is a grief of distortions between peers, and its object is change. . . . We have been raised to view any difference other than sex as a reason for destruction, and for Black women and white women to face each other's angers without denial or immobility or silence or guilt is in itself a heretical and generative idea. It implies peers meeting upon a common basis to examine difference, and to alter those distortions which history has created around our difference. For it is those distortions which separate us."

Building Common Ground

It is clear within the women's movement that because of racism and classism, white women and women of color do not automatically feel an alliance with one another, particularly since there has been little historical tradition upon which to build. Familiarity, of which social and political alliances are made, is not "natural" for women; we do not automatically have a mutually developed heritage, though because we are women, we share some commonality in terms of the kinds of abuse we face—sexual violence within and outside the family, social, economic, and legal inequality. Just as women of color are not "just" women, white women are also not "just" women. As Bernice Johnson Reagon (1983) points out, "It does not matter at all that biologically we have being women in common. We have been organized to have our primary cultural signals come from some other factors than that we are women. We are not from our base acculturated to be women people, capable of crossing our first people boundaries—Black, White, Indian, etc." Creating this familiarity, recognizing and acting on our commonalities, learning to use our differences in the service of change, and building social and political alliances across race and class boundaries are all a part of the work we must do to build a strong multiracial women's movement. This work is not only difficult, but many times painful and unsuccessful. But it is possible.

In summary, I do not believe that working with women of color means that white women must erase or deny our own identities, nor must we retreat from feminist analysis and vision, but we must be more open to the experiences, histories, cultures, and alliances of women different from ourselves, recognizing how these differences have many times been to our advantage. And most important, we must be willing to work with women of color as peers, which means we must give up sole power and control of feminist organizations, political agendas, and theoretical perspectives. We need to build common grounds, which may not have the same centers, e.g., universality, sameness, but do have shared commitments to the survival of all of us. As Audre Lorde (1981, 99) challenges us: "*survival is not an academic skill.* It is learning how to stand alone, unpopular and sometimes reviled, and how to make common cause with those others identified as outside the structures, in order to define and seek a world in which we can all flourish."

NOTES

The political context of this paper is primarily feminism within the United States, although many of the issues I raise may apply to relationships between first world and third world women and the international women's movement. I would like to especially thank Lourdes Torres, Cindy Jenefsky, and Barbara Schulman for providing commentary and encouragement in developing the ideas and analysis present in this essay. And I'd like to thank my group of friends, "the regulars," who were an integral part of my life and politics in Champaign, Illinois, who initially included Cheryl West, Linda Clark, Pat Cramer, Vic Christensen, Gin Goines, Carla Peyton, Elaine Shelley, Lourdes Torres, Sandy Tutwiler, and Ann Walker—and all those who have followed since in the tradition.

1. For the purposes of this paper I am referring to women of color and to white women as whole groups, although clearly there are many differences among us, and these differences as well must be addressed; for instance, other major issues of division among feminists and lesbians are national identity, anti-Semitism, age, looks, class and ethnic identity, education, color, etc., each of which needs to be (and is at some level) being addressed in the women's movement.

2. Chandra Talpade Mohanty and I were the co-coordinators of the "Common Differences: Third World Women and Feminist Perspectives" conference, held April 9–13, 1983, at the University of Illinois, Urbana-Champaign.

3. *Third world* refers to women from so-called third world countries.

REFERENCES

Aptheker, Bettina. 1982. "Race and Class: Patriarchal Politics and Women's Experience." *Women's Studies Quarterly* 10, no. 4 (Summer):10–15.
Beck, Evelyn Torton. 1988. "From 'Kike' to 'JAP.' " *Sojourner* (September):18–19.
Bourne, Jenny. 1983. "Towards an Anti-racist Feminism." *Race and Class* 25, no. 1:1–22.
Bulkin, Elly. 1980. "Racism and Writing: Some Implications for White Lesbian Critics." *Sinister Wisdom* 13 (Spring):3–22.
Bulkin, Elly, Minnie Bruce Pratt, and Barbara Smith. 1984. *Yours in Struggle: Three Feminist Perspectives on Anti-Semitism and Racism.* Brooklyn, N.Y.: Long Haul Press.
Burns, Maryviolet, ed. 1986. *The Speaking Profits Us: Violence in the Lives of Women of Color.* Seattle, Wash.: Center for the Prevention of Sexual and Domestic Violence.
Cross, Tia, Freada Klein, Barbara Smith, and Beverly Smith. 1982. "Face-to-Face, Day-to-Day—Racism CR." In Gloria T. Hull et al., *But Some of Us Are Brave.* Old Westbury, N.Y.: Feminist Press.
Culbreth, Pamela. 1982. "A Personal Reading of *This Bridge Called My Back.*" *Sinister Wisdom* (Fall):18–28.
Davis, Angela. 1981. *Women, Race and Class.* New York: Random House.
———. 1987. *Violence against Women and the Ongoing Challenge to Racism.* Latham, N.Y.: Kitchen Table: Women of Color Press.
Delphy, Christine. 1984. "Our Friends and Ourselves: The Hidden Foundations of Various Pseudo-feminist Accounts." In *Close to Home: A Materialist Analysis of Women's Oppression.* Amherst: University of Massachusetts Press. 106–37.
Deming, Barbara. 1974. *We Cannot Live without Our Lives.* New York: Grossman/ Viking.
Frye, Marilyn. 1983. "On Being White: Toward a Feminist Understanding of Race and Race Supremacy." In *Politics of Reality.* Trumansburg, N.Y.: Crossing Press.

Gibbs, Joan, and Sara Bennett, comps. 1980. *Top Ranking: A Collection of Articles on Racism and Classism in the Lesbian Community*. New York: February 3 Press.

Glenn, Evelyn Nakano. 1985. "Incorporating Racial Ethnic Women into the Curriculum." *Women's Studies Newsletter* [University Center at Binghamton, New York] (March):2–6.

hooks, bell. 1981. *Ain't I a Woman?* Boston: South End Press.

———. 1989. "Overcoming White Supremacy: A Comment." In *Talking Back*. Boston: South End Press. 112–19.

Hull, Gloria T.; Patricia Bell Scott; and Barbara Smith, eds. 1982. *All the Women are White, All the Blacks Are Men, but Some of Us Are Brave*. Old Westbury, N.Y.: Feminist Press.

Joseph, Gloria. 1981. "White Promotion, Black Survival." In Gloria Joseph and Jill Lewis, *Common Differences: Conflicts in Black and White Feminist Perspectives*. New York: Doubleday. 19–42.

Katz, Judy H. 1978. *White Awareness: A Handbook for Anti-Racism Training*. Norman: University of Oklahoma Press.

Lorde, Audre. 1981. "The Master's Tools Will Never Dismantle the Master's House." In Cherríe Moraga and Gloria Anzaldúa, eds., *This Bridge Called My Back*. Watertown, Mass.: Persephone Press.

———. 1984. "The Uses of Anger: Women Responding to Racism." In *Sister Outsider*. Trumansburg, N.Y.: Crossing Press.

McIntosh, Peggy. 1988. "White Privilege and Male Privilege: A Personal Account of Coming to See Correspondences through Work in Women's Studies." Working Paper No. 189. Wellesley College Center for Research on Women, Wellesley, Massachusetts.

———. 1989. "White Privilege: Unpacking the Invisible Knapsack." *Peace and Freedom* (July-August):10–12.

Moore, Tracy, and Terry Wolverton. 1981. "Including Ourselves in the Future: White Lesbian Anti-racism." *Common Lives, Lesbian Lives* (Fall):42–50.

Moraga, Cherríe. 1981. "La Guera." In Cherríe Moraga and Gloria Anzaldúa, eds., *This Bridge Called My Back*. Watertown, Mass.: Persephone Press.

———. 1983. "Refugees of a World on Fire." Foreword to the 2nd ed. of *This Bridge Called My Back*. New York: Kitchen Table: Women of Color Press.

Moraga, Cherríe, and Gloria Anzaldúa, eds. 1981. *This Bridge Called My Back*. Watertown, Mass.: Persephone Press.

Murphy, Lindsay, and Jonathan Livingstone. 1985. "Racism and the Limits of Radical Feminism." *Race and Class* 26, no. 4:61–70.

Pence, Ellen. 1982. "Racism: A White Issue." In Hull et al., *But Some of Us are Brave: Black Women's Studies*. Old Westbury, N.Y.: Feminist Press. 45–47.

Pharr, Suzanne. 1986. "The Connection between Homophobia and Heterosexism." *Aegis* 41:35–37.

Pratt, Minnie Bruce. 1984. "Identity: Skin Blood Heart." In Elly Bulkin et al., *Yours in Struggle*. Brooklyn, N.Y.: Long Haul Press.

Reagon, Bernice Johnson. 1983. "Coalition Politics: Turning the Century." In Barbara Smith, ed., *Home Girls: A Black Feminist Anthology*. New York: Kitchen Table: Women of Color Press.

Rich, Adrienne. 1986. *Blood, Bread and Poetry: Selected Essays, 1979-1985*. New York: W. W. Norton. (See "Resisting Amnesia: History and Personal Life" [1983]; "North American Tunnel Vision" [1983]; and "Notes towards a Politics of Location" [1984]).

Smith, Barbara. 1982. "Racism and Women's Studies." In Gloria T. Hull et al., *All the Women Are White, All the Blacks Are Men, but Some of Us Are Brave*. Old Westbury, N.Y.: Feminist Press.

————. 1984. "Between a Rock and a Hard Place: Relationships between Black and Jewish Women." In Bulkin et al., *Yours in Struggle*. Brooklyn, N.Y.: Long Haul Press. 65–88.
Smith, Lillian E. 1949. *Killers of the Dream*. New York: W. W. Norton.

COMMON THEMES, DIFFERENT CONTEXTS

Third World Women and Feminism

Cheryl Johnson-Odim

This essay seeks more to explicate issues than to present empirical research or to synthesize theory. However, the basic issues which it raises and endeavors to explain regarding conceptual and practical differences between Third World and Euro-American First World women in relation to feminism will, it is hoped, inform both the generation of research questions and the construction of theory. While it is true that the oppression of impoverished and marginalized Euro-American women is linked to gender *and* class relations, that of Third World women is linked also to race relations and often imperialism. These added dimensions produce a different context in which Third World women's struggles must be understood. Still, while this essay looks at women in these two contexts, it does so primarily to highlight certain historical and contemporary differences that have produced tensions between them, in order to be able to identify underlying misunderstandings and contribute to resolving them.

The term *Third World* is frequently applied in two ways: to refer to "underdeveloped"/overexploited geopolitical entities, i.e., countries, regions, and even continents; and to refer to oppressed nationalities from these world areas who are now resident in "developed" First World countries. I will be using the term with this dual definition throughout this essay, for despite their great diversity, Third World women seem to have much in common in their relationship to an international women's movement.

While it may be legitimately argued that there is more than one school of thought on feminism among First World feminists—who are not, after all, monolithic—there is still, among Third World women, a widely accepted perception that the feminism emerging from white, middle-class Western women narrowly confines itself to a struggle against gender discrimination. It is also widely felt that this is the "mainstream" feminism of the West and that it holds the most sway and has the most adherents. Joseph (1981), hooks (1981), Moraga and Anzaldúa (1981), Okeyo (1981), Savane (1982), and others have all attested to this perception, and many have defined it as a liberal, bourgeois, or reformist feminism, and criticize it because of its narrow conception of feminist terrain as an almost singularly antisexist struggle.

While it is clear that sexual egalitarianism is a major goal on which all feminists can agree, gender discrimination is neither the sole nor perhaps the primary locus of the oppression of Third World women. Thus, a narrowly defined feminism, taking the eradication of gender discrimination as the route to ending women's oppression, is insufficient to redress the oppression of Third World women, for reasons which I hope this essay will make clear. A number of Third World feminists, including hooks (1981, 1984), Moraga and Anzaldúa (1981), Joseph and Lewis (1981), Okeyo (1981), Hull, Scott, and Smith (1982), Savane (1982), Smith (1983), and many others, have tackled this problem of broadening the definition of feminism and making it relevant (in both philosophy and agenda articulation) to the struggles of Third World women. Still, it remains a challenge at both the national and international levels to construct definitions of feminism that allow for autonomy and that are of immediate relevance in feminist struggles in various places, and yet have the breadth needed for the widest consensus and cooperation.

In reaction to a narrowly defined feminism, some Third World women have elected not to use the term *feminist* at all. Alice Walker, an Afro-American woman writer, has chosen to use the term *womanist* rather than *feminist*. Walker (1983) partially describes a womanist as "a Black feminist or feminist of color" and says "womanist is to feminist as purple to lavender" (xi). She further states that a womanist is "committed to survival and wholeness of entire people, male and female" (xi). Walker's comments underscore the feelings among Third World women that their struggle as feminists is connected to the struggles of their communities against racism, economic exploitation, etc. Her desire to coin a new term has nothing to do with a lack of commitment to women's equality and everything to do with her vision of the interconnectedness of her life as a black

316 Race, Identity, and Feminist Struggles

woman and her perception that "mainstream" (i.e., liberal gender-specific) feminism has been too narrow to encompass it.

Let me take a moment here to say that it is clear that there have always been some radical white feminists who have understood the connections between race, class, and gender in the lives of Third World women. There are even many more who know that, in the United States at least, the greatest periods of feminist struggle have emerged out of the African-American movement against racism. The early radical feminism of the 1960s was, in fact, often broadly defined as being antiracist and antiimperialist, but much of that movement has been displaced by the far more popular liberal feminism which has not sufficiently defined racism and imperialism as major feminist issues. I would agree with Smith (1983), hooks (1984), and others that it is in fact the involvement of Third World women, both within and outside the United States, that has accounted for the broadening definitions of feminism to incorporate race and class analysis.

In any case, I have chosen for the purpose of this essay to remain with the term *feminism* for two reasons: (1) I am more concerned with the participation of Third World women in defining feminism and setting its agenda than with changing the terminology; and (2) the term *feminism* sets this essay in a political context to which women are integral. Since "modern-day" feminism is still in a process of incarnation, especially at the international level, I question whether the coining of a new term simply retreats from the debate, running the risk of losing sight of the fair amount of universality in women's oppression.

In the decade of the 1970s, when attempts at constructing an international feminist movement began to take shape, many women in the Third World were fairly recently emerging from colonialism, and many Third World women in the West were emerging from the most important civil rights movement of the twentieth century. Neither the advent of independence in the former colonies nor the legislation passed as a result of the civil rights movement was to prove immediately victorious in improving the quality of life for the overwhelming majority of Third World women. Undoubtedly, these were factors in shaping Third World women's visions of feminism as a philosophy and a movement for social justice that was inclusive of their entire communities, in which they were equal participants, and which addressed the racism, economic exploitation, and imperialism against which they continued to struggle. Evans (1979), Giddings (1984), and a host of others have argued that the feminism of the 1960s and 1970s in the U.S. emerged from the civil rights movement. They also point out, however, that while many of the women had been involved in antiracist work, this in no way guaranteed a lack of racism in the women's movement or enough attention to the role of racism in the oppression of all women.

At three major international conferences of women held between 1970 and 1980 (Mexico City, 1975; Wellesley, 1976; Copenhagen, 1980), the battle lines were often drawn between First and Third World feminists over what constituted a feminist issue, and therefore what were legitimate feminist foci and goals. Okeyo (1981), Barrow (1985), Cagatay, Grown, and Santiago (1986), and others remark on the tensions between First and Third World women that surfaced at the first two United Nations Decade conferences for women (Mexico City, 1975, and Copenhagen, 1980). The formation of Third World caucuses frequently included women of color who were residents of the First World (though according to Cagatay, Grown, and Santiago, Nairobi was the first at which a significant proportion of attendees from places such as the United States were women of color). These caucuses sought to broaden the agenda and treat feminism as a fundamentally political movement connected as much to the struggle of their communities for liberation and autonomy as to the work against gender discrimination.

Awe (1977) remarked on the same phenomenon at the Women and Development Conference hosted by the Center for Research on Women in Higher Education at Wellesley College in 1976. I was in Nigeria when a number of friends returned from Wellesley. They returned angry, convinced that, in Okeyo's words (1981), "women of the developed world seek to define for themselves a leading role both in academia and through development assistance programs" in defining the needs, aims, and priorities of Third World women. These schisms developed at least partially because Third World women felt First World women were attempting to depoliticize the conferences and implicitly construct a women's movement and a feminism which confined itself to issues of gender discrimination. It was part of the mission, in fact, of the official U.S. delegation to Nairobi to keep "politics" out of the conference, and to instead concentrate on "women's issues" (Okeyo, 1981, 9).

While Cagatay, Grown, and Santiago (1986) maintain that far more of a spirit of coming together among Third and First World women obtained at the NGO [nongovernmental forum] than at the official sessions, and while it is unlikely that the official U.S. delegation (especially of 1985) was representative of even "mainstream" (i.e., liberal gender-specific) U.S. feminists, this tension over "politicization" of the conferences had also arisen at Mexico City and Copenhagen. Okeyo (1981) speaks to this point when she says, "Another assumption that is often voiced by Western feminists in international fora is that women's issues should not be politicized . . . [but] for African women the subject of women's advancement is highly political because it is an integral part of our quest for justice not only at the household level but all the way within the local, national and world economic order." Okeyo is describing African women's struggle as taking place equally at the "household level," i.e., within the family including between men and women, and at the international level, where many of the same things which oppress women (i.e., racism, imperialism, economic exploitation) also oppress men, though not, sometimes, without differences. But these differences are usually in the manifestation of the oppression, not in the source.

Third World women resident in the First World also must deal with these issues. Any cursory observation of feminist organizations in the United States, for instance, will reveal that Third World women often prefer to organize separately from Euro-American women. These Third World women's organizations take a critical stance regarding the feminist movement, constantly seeking to inject issues which they see this movement as neglecting. Historically separate organization was often the result of racism in the feminist movement which caused it to exclude women of color, and often poor working-class and white women as well. The discrimination suffered by African-American women in the woman suffrage movement and the Club Women's movement has been well documented by Harley and Terbourg-Penn (1978), Davis (1981), Aptheker (1982), Giddings (1984), and many others, as has the exploitation of Native American, Chicana, Puerto Rican, Asian-American, and other non-European American women.

In the current context, however, separate organization is often the choice of Third World women who know that a gender-based analysis alone, without the factoring in of issues of race and class, can never describe their oppression. And since racism in the current women's movement is one of the issues Third World women seek to raise among feminists, racism also plays its part in contemporary separate organization. Moraga and Anzaldúa (1981), hooks (1981, 1984), Hull, Scott, and Smith (1982), and Smith (1983), among others, have delineated the need for Third World women to organize separately, and to construct a feminist theory relevant to their needs. Joseph (1981) pointedly states that black women have as much in common, in terms of their oppression, with black men as they do with white women. Understanding African-American women's history for black women in the United States is critical to understanding Joseph's assertion. In her study of black women in slavery, White (1985) documents ways in which the slaveocracy juxtaposed the images of black and white women. Black women were cast as nonwomen, as "unfeminine," as a necessary precondition for exploiting both their productive and reproductive labor to the fullest. But the definition of "femininity" foisted upon white women was that of totally dependent beings. Consequently, for every "Aunt Jemima" who was maligned as a nonwoman, there was a "Miss Ann" imprisoned by the definition of her femininity. Still, it is hard to accept the argument that white women suffered as much from this antagonism as black women. But there is a more important and contemporary question which emerges from the era of slavery which is an analogy of sorts.

Poor whites, it is true, suffered greatly because of slavery. The exploitation and appropriation of black labor (along with the land on which it produced wealth) made paid white labor, even when cheap, nearly superfluous except to help police the black labor force. However, most poor southern whites did not embrace the antislavery struggle; rather, they aspired to be "masters." Thus, their definition of the problem was not that the system of slavery oppressed both them and black people and therefore should be ended, but that they themselves needed the opportunity to be able to benefit from slavery. Black American women sometimes suspect that the movement which purports to represent the interests of "women" is, similarly, the desire of a few white women to enter the corporate boardroom. The metamorphosis which this feat in itself would require in a patriarchal society might slightly better the lives of some women, but would only basically change the sex of the "master."

Thus the fundamental issue for Third World women is not generally whether there is a need for feminism, i.e., a general movement which seeks to redress women's oppression, but rather what the definition and agenda of that feminism will be. The need for feminism arises from the desire to create a world in which women are not oppressed. If there is no term or focus, no movement which incorporates the struggle against sexism, women run the risk of becoming invisible. We do not have to look far to understand why women fear this invisibility. The revolutions in Algeria and Iran raise serious questions about the degree to which women benefited from their participation. Even in socialist revolutions where women's position has been greatly improved and continues solidly toward a goal of equality, such as in Cuba, Nicaragua, Angola, and Mozambique, the changes have required not only the commitment of men but also the constant vigilance and organization of women. The need for feminist theory and organization is clear.

It is also true that Third World women outside the United States find that the source of their oppression cannot be limited or perhaps even primarily attributed to gender alone. Marie Angelique Savane (1982), president of the Association of African Women Organized for Research and Development (AAWORD), has written:

> For although the oppression of women is universal in nature. . . . It is time to move beyond simple truisms about the situation of women to a more profound analysis of the mechanisms perpetuating the subordination of

women in society. . . . In the Third World, women's demands have been explicitly political, with work, education and health as major issues *per se* and not so linked to their specific impact on women. In addition, women of the Third World perceive imperialism as the main enemy on their continents and especially of women. . . . (5)

Steady (1985) writes that "in the developing world, equality of women is often viewed as linked to national and economic development" (6). At an October 1984 meeting in Tanzania, in preparation for the U.N. Conference in Nairobi, representatives of twenty-five nongovernmental organizations of women from seventeen African countries affirmed that they recognized that the overriding obstacles to women's progress "lay first in the dual factors of the increasing poverty throughout the African continent and in its unhealthy relation to the inequities of the current world economic order" (Barrow 1985, 10).

In "underdeveloped" societies it is not just a question of internal redistribution of resources, but of their generation and control; not just equal opportunity between men and women, but the creation of opportunity itself; not only the position of women in society, but the position of the societies in which Third World women find themselves. Leacock (1977) comments that the urgency of the need for economic development applies as much to "underdeveloped" national groups in the heart of the "developed" industrialized world as to the so-called developing countries. Thus, Third World women cannot afford to embrace the notion that feminism seeks only to achieve equal treatment of men and women and equal access and opportunity for *women*, which often amounts to a formula for sharing poverty both in the Third World and in Third World communities in the West.

Therefore, gender oppression cannot be the single leg on which feminism rests. It should not be limited to merely achieving equal treatment of women vis-à-vis men. This is where feminism as a philosophy must differ from the shallow notion of "women's rights." Although on a theoretical level, women in the industrialized societies of the West can achieve a semblance of parity with men through legal and moral challenges to patriarchal systems, issues of race and class undermine the potential success of such a movement for all women. In addition, the economic surplus in the West is often directly related to oppression in the Third World. Savane (1982) discusses the "free trade zones" established by transnationals in Third World countries. These zones render special privileges (everything from tax breaks to making labor organization illegal) to corporations in exchange for locating there. The entire August 1983 issue of *Multinational Monitor* is devoted to a series of articles detailing the particular ways that multinationals and the existence of free trade zones operate to oppress Third World women. Seidman (1981) examines the ways in which colonialism marginalized women in Africa and chronicles how generally the independence process barely altered inherited colonial institutions which both excluded women and perpetuated externally dependent political economies and philosophies. These policies, she contends, reinforced an inequitable sexual division of labor in the process of creating a "hospitable investment climate" for multinational corporations. Steady (1985) proposes that the operation of race and class is important in preventing false polarizations between men and women. She states:

> Rather than seeing men as the universal oppressor, women will also be seen as partners in oppression and as having the potential of becoming primary oppressors themselves. Above all, by studying the Black woman we can avoid isolating sexism from the larger political and economic forces operating in many societies to produce internal colonialism and economic dependency— all of which affect both men and women in Africa, the Caribbean, South America and impoverished sections of the United States. (3)

Although certainly the circumstances and status of women differed at various times and places throughout the Third World, it is a totally ahistorical assumption often nourished by contemporary images that women in the Third World have somehow been more oppressed by an indigenous patriarchy than women in the West. Etienne and Leacock (1980) helpfully remind us that "it is critical to clarify the fact that egalitarian relations between women and men are not an imported Western value and that, instead, the reverse is true. Egalitarian relations or at least mutually respectful relations were a living reality in much of the world in precolonial times, which was far from the case in Western culture" (v-vi). The argument is neither that there was no precolonial patriarchy in non-Western societies nor that an analysis of the *degree* of different women's oppression is useful. The point is that factors other than gender figure integrally in the oppression of Third World women and that, even regarding patriarchy, many Third World women labor under indigenous inequitable gender relationships exacerbated by Western patriarchy, racism, and exploitation. For Third World women resident in the West, race and class, along with gender, have been indivisible elements in their oppression.

Third World women can embrace the concept of gender identity, but must reject an ideology based solely on gender. Feminism, therefore, must be a comprehensive and inclusive ideology and movement that incorporates yet transcends gender-specificity. We must create a feminist movement which struggles against those things which can clearly be shown to oppress women, whether based on race, sex, or class or resulting from imperialism. Such a definition of feminism will allow us to isolate the

gender-specific element in women's oppression while simultaneously relating it to broader issues, to the totality of what oppresses us as women.
If the feminist movement does not address itself also to issues of race,
class, and imperialism, it cannot be relevant to alleviating the oppression
of most of the women of the world.

In addition to broadening the parameters of feminism, there is the
problem of setting a common agenda. One example of this difficulty is
the issue of female circumcision, especially in Africa. Cagatay, Grown,
and Santiago (1986) discuss the condemnations of female circumcision
by First World women at the U.N. Conference in Copenhagen and the
ensuing tensions between First and Third World women over how this
topic was raised.

Certainly, there are a number of African women who are leading the
battle against female circumcision, but many resent what they feel to be
the sensationalistic nature of the campaign by many First World feminists.
More important, however, is the fact that female circumcision is one issue
which can be raised in a manner which is disconnected from the broader
struggle. That is, it is tied to an indigenous cultural context which frequently posits an opposition between women and men. In Africa, problems of nutrition, infant mortality, illiteracy, health-care delivery, skill
training, etc., are of central importance in women's lives, and many African women have expressed that they wish these issues had the same
kind of exposure within the feminist movement in the West as does female
circumcision. But to raise these other problems requires feminism to take
an antiimperialist position; it necessitates identifying and fighting against
the structural elements in many developed countries which participate in
the oppression of Third World women. Many Third World women feel
that their self-defined needs are not addressed as priority items in the
international feminist agenda, which does not address imperialism. Internationally orchestrated exploitation bears on the oppression of women
in the Third World as much as patriarchy does in their societies.

Third World women resident in Euro-America also feel neglected in
the agenda-setting process. Black American women, for instance, know
they must articulate a feminism which has a clear relationship to the
general movement of the black community against oppression. Black
women recognize that, historically, white women have been no less racist
than have white men. They are aware that in the late nineteenth and
early twentieth centuries, racism was pervasive in the women's movement
(see Davis 1981; hooks 1981; Hull, Scott, and Smith 1982). They wonder,
therefore, if white feminists will embrace the struggle against racism as
vehemently as they exhort black women to join in the fight against sexism.

Moreover, certain feminist issues, such as rape and contraception, are
perceived as double-edged swords in the black American community.

While no black feminist would argue anything other than that rape is a violent, inexcusable crime for which the victim is still too often blamed, we know only too well how often racism has excused the rape of black women. We also remember that rape, or even the perceived or concocted threat of rape, has historically posed nearly as great a danger to the safety of black men as to that of black women. For centuries, besides fearing for their own security, black women have feared the maiming, lynching, or jailing of their husbands, brothers, and sons on charges that they were rapists, no matter how unsubstantiated. We are not so far removed from the fraudulent and racist rape or attempted rape charges against the Scottsboro Nine, Emmett Till, Delbert Tibbs, and many others. Every feminist, black and white, should read Davis's (1981) brilliant chapter on "Rape, Racism and the Myth of the Black Rapist," which connects rape not only to racism but to sexism against black *and* white women. This chapter painstakingly documents and makes clear that if we are to combat the treatment rape has received in American society, it must be connected not only to misogyny but to racism as well.

The creeping alliance, in the early twentieth century, between the movement for birth control and eugenics holds lessons (and latent fears) not lost upon the black American community (Davis 1981, 213-16). The fact that surgical sterilization remains free and that federal funding for abortions has been disallowed means that it is poor women to whom the *choice* to abort is denied, and their ranks are disproportionately populated by women of color. The vehement advocacy of contraception and sterilization in the Third World as a method of population control leads to the conclusion that overpopulation is the primary cause of poverty in "underdeveloped" nations. This is a dangerous, false, and simplistic analysis. The testing of contraceptives in the Third World, often before they are approved for distribution in the United States and Europe, is a crime against women. Beneria and Sen (1981) remark on the similarities in the responses of poor Third World women (both in the West and in the Third World) to issues of reproductive freedom. Often they are suspicious about the safety of contraceptive devices and drugs and about the motives of researchers and distributors, even though many feel desperate for safe, effective, affordable, and voluntary birth control. It is not that black or other Third World feminists take a position against contraception, but that they seek to frame the discussion in a context which incorporates the impact of race and class on reproductive issues. The primary responsibility for addressing these questions in this broader context is incumbent on the Third World feminist community, but it is also incumbent on the feminist community as a whole.

The participation of Third World women in defining feminism and setting a feminist agenda is often primarily a question of power. Smith

(1983) has discussed the difficulties which black feminists in the West face in being heard, published, and paid attention to. Because Third World women are members of relatively powerless communities, they do not have the same potential for access to resources that First World women have. This calls not only for separate organization to clarify the issues within Third World communities, but also for the development of a working and equal relationship with First World women. We must ensure that the issues that Third World feminists raise become a part of serious discussions of feminist theory and that they are not relegated and ghettoized to a subculture of feminism.

Third World women must articulate needs through the crucial process of constructing a body of relevant feminist theory, which goes beyond mere criticism of First World women. This is, in fact, happening. Moraga and Anzaldúa (1981), hooks (1981, 1984), Hull, Scott, and Smith (1982), Joseph and Lewis (1981), Smith (1983), and others have all been actively engaged in attempts to define a feminism which is acceptable and relevant to communities of women who suffer as a consequence of racism, sexism, structural poverty, and economic exploitation. In so doing, women of color often labor against suspicions of feminism within their communities, where it is generally perceived as having a white, middle-class agenda— that is, an agenda that creates opportunities for people who are already the most advantageously placed to take advantage of them, and which views gender discrimination as the only fundamental inequality in all women's lives. If this perception describes only bourgeois reformist elements of the feminist community, then it is even more urgent that those among us who have a broader vision articulate it and organize around it.

First World women must constantly challenge the racism of their communities, and acknowledge and struggle against the complicity of their communities in the oppression of Third World women. According to Cagatay, Grown, and Santiago (1986), in analyzing the events at Nairobi, there were several reasons for a greater hopefulness about cooperation between First and Third World women. Conferences during the U.N. International Decade for women, despite tensions within them, have exposed women from around the world to one another. Third World women have been able to have a voice at those conferences normally unavailable to them because of lack of access to financial and media resources. At Nairobi, there were more Third World women from Western nations than at any of the previous conferences. Cagatay, Grown, and Santiago maintain that more First World women were exposed to what it means to be a woman in a Third World setting and that, with that experience, more had moved to a broader definition of feminism:

> Feminism . . . constitutes the political expression of the concerns and interests of women from different regions, classes, nationalities, and ethnic backgrounds. There is and must be a diversity of feminisms, responsive to the different needs and concerns of different women, and defined by them for themselves. This diversity builds on common opposition to gender oppression and hierarchy which, however, is only the first step in articulating and acting upon a political agenda. (Cagatay, Grown, and Santiago 1986, 411)

Four years earlier, Marie Angelique Savane, first president of AAWORD, had a similar analysis:

> Feminism is international in defining as its aim the liberation of women from all types of oppression and in providing solidarity among women of all countries; it is national in stating its priorities and strategies in accordance with particular cultural and socioeconomic conditions.
>
> We consider that national and ethnic traditions must be respected and maintained so as to create a genuine sense of nationhood. However, aspects of our culture which discriminate, restrict and devalue women's physical, psychological and political development must be eliminated. To achieve this, women must be mobilized politically for action.
>
> In order to create an alternative culture, responsive to national needs and open to international solidarity, we women defend our right to speak from a woman's perspective and to express this in writings and through action. We demand that society give and maintain value and respect for women's contributions in their roles within the labour force, in the family and culturally. At the same time, as individuals, as citizens, as mothers, and as wives, we women deplore the loss of resources and of lives in the present senseless resistance to change towards a more equal and just society. Equally, we condemn discrimination and injustice based on race or ethnicity just as much as that based on gender. We believe our hope lies in joining with those progressive forces which will achieve a future human society in harmony with the environment and free of discrimination and inequality between men and women, black and white, believer and unbeliever. (Savane 1982, 15)

But there is a broad base on which First and Third World feminists must agree if feminism is truly to be concerned about redressing the oppression of women. This broad base must at least recognize that racism and economic exploitation are primary forces in the oppression of most women in the world. It must acknowledge that while gender is a potential bond, women participate in the oppression of other women all over the world. It must respect different cultures, and it must agree that women in various places are perfectly capable of having their own voice. This can be a beginning. It must also strive to see the world through noncolonial eyes. For example, I remember a few years ago being asked to give a paper (during Women's History Week) on African women in Africa.

This was at a major university in the Midwest. I arrived to discover that the paper had been assigned to a panel on minority women. Since African women are not a minority in Africa, I felt the assignment of the paper to that panel (rather than the creation of an international panel) reflected an ahistorical Eurocentric mindset in which all non-Europeans are somehow viewed as minorities. We must stop reproducing pictures of the world only from the inside out, and try to look from the outside in. If we view the world in raw numbers rather than power relationships, most people are non-European.

We must discontinue reproducing our own oppression in the ways we treat one another, in the ways we raise our children, in our misdiagnosis or half-definition of the problem. Based on the things we have in common as women, which are greater in number through space and time when we make the right connections between them, we must view women's oppression in the context of all oppression. We must challenge a feminist perspective to envisage a human-centered world, in which the satisfaction of human needs, justly met, is a primary goal.

REFERENCES

Aptheker, Bettina. 1982. *Woman's Legacy*. Amherst, Mass.: University of Massachusetts Press.
Awe, Bolanle. 1977. "Reflections on the Conference on Women in Development: 1." *Signs* 3, no. 1:314–16.
Barrow, Nita. 1985. "The Decade NGO Forum." *Africa Report* (March/April):9–12.
Beneria, Lourdes, and Gita Sen. 1981. "Accumulation, Reproduction, and Women's Role in Economic Development: Boserup Revisited." *Signs* 7, no. 2:279–98.
Cagatay, Nilufer, Caren Grown, and Aida Santiago. 1986. "Nairobi Women's Conference: Toward a Global Feminism?" *Feminist Studies* 12, no. 2 (Summer):401–12.
Davis, Angela. 1981. *Women, Race and Class*. New York: Random House.
Etienne, Mona, and Eleanor Leacock, eds. 1980. *Women and Colonization: Anthropological Perspectives*. New York: Praeger.
Evans, Sara. 1979. *Personal Politics: The Roots of Women's Liberation in the Civil Rights Movement and the New Left*. New York: Vintage.
Giddings, Paula. 1984. *When and Where I Enter: The Impact of Black Women on Race and Sex in America*. New York: William Morrow.
Harley, Sharon, and Rosalyn Terborg-Penn, eds. 1978. *The Afro-American Woman*. Port Washington, N.Y.: Kennikat Press.
hooks, bell. 1981. *Ain't I a Woman?* Boston: South End Press.
———. 1984. *Feminist Theory: From Margin to Center*. Boston: South End Press.
Hull, G., P. Scott, and B. Smith, eds. 1982. *But Some of Us Are Brave*. Old Westbury, N.Y.: The Feminist Press.

Joseph, Gloria. 1981. "The Incompatible Ménage à Trois: Marxism, Feminism and Racism." In Lydia Sargent, ed., *Women and Revolution*. Boston: South End Press. 91–107.

Joseph, Gloria, and Jill Lewis. 1981. *Common Differences: Conflicts in Black and White Feminist Perspectives*. New York: Anchor Books.

Leacock, Eleanor. 1977. "Reflections on the Conference on Women and Development: III." *Signs* 3, no. 1:320–22.

Moraga, C., and G. Anzaldúa, eds. 1981. *This Bridge Called My Back: Writings by Radical Women of Color*. Watertown, Mass.: Persephone Press.

Okeyo, Achola Pala. 1981. "Reflection on Development Myths." *Africa Report* (March/April):7–10.

Savane, Marie Angelique. 1982. "Another Development with Women." *Development Dialogue* 1, no. 2:8–16.

Seidman, Ann. 1981. "Women and the Development of Underdevelopment." In R. Dauber and M. Cain, eds., *Women and Technological Change in Developing Countries*. Boulder, Colo.: Westview Press.

Smith, Barbara, ed. 1983. *Home Girls: A Black Feminist Anthology*. New York: Kitchen Table: Women of Color Press.

Steady, Filomina Chioma. 1985. "African Women at the End of the Decade." *Africa Report* (March/April):4–8.

Walker, Alice. 1983. *In Search of Our Mother's Gardens*. New York: Harcourt, Brace, Jovanovich.

White, Deborah. 1985. *Ar'n't I a Woman: Female Slaves in the Plantation South*. New York: W. W. Norton.

BIOGRAPHICAL NOTES

EVELYNE ACCAD was born and raised in Beirut, Lebanon. She is the author of *Veil of Shame: The Role of Women in the Contemporary Fiction of North Africa and the Middle East* (Sherbrooke, Quebec: Naaman, 1978); *Contemporary Arab Women Writers and Poets*, with Rose Ghyroyyeb (Beirut: Institute for Women's Studies in the Arab World, 1986); and two novels, *L'Excisée: The Mutilated Woman* (Paris: L'Harmattan, 1989) and *Coquelicot du massacre* (Paris: L'Harmattan, 1988). Her most recent work is *Women Unmask War Unveils Men: Sexuality, War and Literature in the Middle East* (New York: New York University Press, 1989).

M. JACQUI ALEXANDER is Assistant Professor of Sociology at Brandeis University. She teaches courses on race and ethnic relations, development theory, and feminist politics, and is coeditor of the collection *The Third Wave: Feminist Perspectives on Racism*, forthcoming from Kitchen Table: Women of Color Press.

CARMEN BARROSO, Professor in the Sociology Department of the University of São Paulo and researcher at the Carlos Chagas Foundation in Brazil, has co-authored two books on sex education with Cristina Bruschini. She is currently working on the recent history of contraceptive research. She is active in the Third World women's movement, and has written extensively on health and reproductive rights.

CRISTINA BRUSCHINI, sociologist and researcher at the Carlos Chagas Foundation, São Paulo, is coauthor of two books on the subject of sex education, *Sex Education: An Open Forum* (Petropolis: Vozes, 1982) and *Sex and Youth* (2nd ed., São Paulo: Brasiliense, 1983). She is currently working on themes such as women and work, family relations, and daily life. She is author of the book *Women and Work: An Assessment of the Decade, 1975-1985* (Novem/CECF, 1985) and of a Ph.D. dissertation on the structure of the São Paulo family and the daily life of middle-class urban families.

REY CHOW is Assistant Professor of Comparative Literature at the University of Minnesota, where she is also affiliated with the Departments of East Asian Studies and Women's Studies. She has contributed articles to *Cultural Critique; Modern Chinese Literature;* and *New German Critique.* Her book *Woman and Chinese Modernity: The Politics of Reading between West and East* is forthcoming from the University of Minnesota Press.

JUANITA DIAZ-COTTO is an adjunct lecturer at Hunter College. She is currently working on a doctoral dissertation for Columbia University on Latino men and women imprisoned in New York State.

ANGELA GILLIAM teaches at Evergreen State College and has taught in Portugal and Papua, New Guinea. She has been active in women's issues and has investigated the relationship between cultural contact and power in Brazil, Mexico, and Papua, New Guinea.

FAYE V. HARRISON, Associate Professor of Anthropology at the University of Tennessee-Knoxville, is the editor of "Black Folk in Cities Here and There: Changing Patterns of Domination and Response," a special issue of *Urban Anthropology and Studies in Cultural Systems and World Economic Development.* Her studies of grassroots activism, crime and outlawry, and the African Diaspora have been published both in journals and in edited collections. She is currently collaborating on an anthology, *Decolonizing Anthropology,* and writing a book-length manuscript on forms of accommodation and resistance in a Jamaican slum.

CHERYL JOHNSON-ODIM is Assistant Professor of History at Loyola University of Chicago. She was formerly Assistant Director of the Program of African Studies at Northwestern University. She has written a chapter in the book *Women and Class in Africa* and a number of articles on African women that have appeared in journals such as the *African Studies Review* and *Tarikh.* She recently edited (with Margaret Strobel) a 500-page collection of essays on the histories of women in Africa, Asia, Latin America, the Caribbean, and the Middle East.

CHANDRA TALPADE MOHANTY is Assistant Professor of Women's Studies and the Sociology of Education at Oberlin College. Her intellectual and political interests and commitments include racial and transnational dimensions of feminist theory, the intersections of gender, race, and education, international development and postcolonial studies, and feminist and antiracist pedagogy in the U.S. academy. She is currently working on a book entitled *Gender, Race, and Cross-Cultural Analysis: Revising Feminist Theory.*

ANN RUSSO teaches the course "Violence against Women in Contemporary U.S. Society" at the Massachusetts Institute of Technology, where she also works with other women on issues of sexual harassment, abuse, and assault on campus and in the community. She assisted Cheris Kramarae in compiling and editing *A Feminist Dictionary* (1985), and is coeditor of *The Radical Women's Press of the 1850s* (forthcoming). She is currently working on a book which is an analysis and critique of the feminist debates over the antipornography civil-rights ordinance (drafted by Andrea Dworkin and Catharine MacKinnon).

BARBARA SMITH has been active in the black feminist movement since 1973. She is the coeditor of *All the Women Are White, All the Blacks Are Men, but Some of Us Are Brave: Black Women's Studies* with Gloria T. Hull and Patricia Bell Scott (New York: The Feminist Press). She is the editor of *Home Girls: A Black Feminist Anthology* (New York: Kitchen Table: Women of Color Press), and contributor to *Yours in Struggle: Three Feminist Perspectives on Anti-Semitism and Racism* (New York: Long Haul Press). She is the cofounder and publisher of Kitchen Table: Women of Color Press.

NAYEREH TOHIDI, Assistant Professor of Psychology and Women's Studies at UCLA, was a leading activist in the Iranian women's movement during the 1978–

79 revolution. She is the editor of *Women and Struggle in Iran*. Since her exile, she has taught in several areas, including cross-cultural study of women, women and development, and psychology of gender. Her articles have appeared in numerous journals. Currently, she is teaching at UCLA and conducting research on gender-role changes among Iranian immigrants in Southern California.

LOURDES TORRES is Assistant Professor of Spanish Linguistics at the State University of New York, Stony Brook. Her teaching and research interests include sociolinguistics, language change, women and language issues, Spanish varieties in the United States, and U.S. Latina/o literature. She is currently engaged in researching language change and social networks in a New York Spanish-speaking community.

CHERYL L. WEST, a Chicago native and a resident of Champaign for the past nine years, has written and directed plays on the subject of AIDS and the black community, intergenerational relations among women, illiteracy, interracial relationships, and parent/teen communication. She was recently published in *Essence Magazine* and has been the recipient of a National Institute on Drug Abuse Fellowship and an International Rotary Foundation Fellowship, which supported her one-year study (1986–87) at the Jamaica School of Drama and with Sistren, a Jamaican women's theater collective in Kingston. To support herself and her writing, Ms. West has been a caseworker, teacher, and counselor. She holds an undergraduate degree in Administration of Justice and a master's in Rehabilitation Administration from Southern Illinois University and a second master's in Journalism from the University of Illinois at Urbana-Champaign.

NELLIE WONG, author of two collections of poetry, *The Death of Long Steam Lady* (Albuquerque: West End Press, 1986) and *Dreams in Harrison Railroad Park* (Berkeley: Kelsey St. Press, 1977), is a social feminist activist with the Freedom Socialist party and Radical Women. Her poems and essays have appeared in many anthologies and journals, including *This Bridge Called My Back: Writings by Radical Women of Color*; the *Iowa Review*; *Breaking Silence: An Anthology of Asian American Poets*; *Berkeley Fiction Review*; *Heresies*; *Condition*; *The Forbidden Stitch*; and *Making Waves*. She is featured with poet Mitsuye Yamada in the documentary film *Mitsuye and Nellie, Asian American Poets*, produced by Allie Light and Irving Saraf.

INDEX